ORIGINS
OF THE MODERN WEST

Essays and Sources in Renaissance & Early Modern European History

ORIGINS
OF THE MODERN WEST
Essays and Sources in Renaissance & Early Modern European History

THEODORE K. RABB
Princeton University

Sources Edited and Introduced by
SHERRIN MARSHALL
U.S. Department of Education

McGraw-Hill, Inc.
New York St. Louis San Francisco Auckland Bogotá
Caracas Lisbon London Madrid Mexico City Milan
Montreal New Delhi San Juan Singapore
Sydney Tokyo Toronto

ORIGINS OF THE MODERN WEST
Essays and Sources in Renaissance & Early Modern European History

Permissions Acknowledgments appear on pages 305–311, and on this page by reference.

3 4 5 6 7 8 9 0   DOC/DOC   9 9 8

ISBN 0-07-041231-6

This book was set in Caledonia by Better Graphics, Inc.
The editor was Niels Aaboe;
the designer was Joan E. O'Connor;
the production supervisor was Al Rihner.
The project was supervised by Editorial Services of New England, Inc.
R. R. Donnelley & Sons Company was printer and binder.

Cover painting: S. Buonsignori, Pianta Detta "Della Catena." Firenze. Museo di Firenze
Com'era. Scala/Art Resource, NY.

This book is printed on acid-free paper.

Library of Congress Cataloging-in-Publication Data

Rabb, Theodore K.
    Origins of the modern West: essays and sources in renaissance & early modern
    european history
    / Theodore K. Rabb; sources edited and introduced by Sherrin Marshall.
        p.   cm.
    Includes bibliographical references.
    ISBN 0-07-041231-6
    1. Europe—History—476–1492.   2. Europe—History—1492–1648.
    3. Renaissance.   I. Renaissance (Television program)   II. Title.
D228.R13   1993
940.1—dc20   92-43374

*For the students of Humanities 202
and Humanities 204*

About the Authors

Theodore K. Rabb is Professor of History at Princeton University. He received his Ph.D. from Princeton and subsequently taught at Stanford, Northwestern, Harvard, and Johns Hopkins Universities. He is the author of numerous articles and reviews, and he has been editor of *The Journal of Interdisciplinary History* since its foundation. Among the books he has written or edited are *The Struggle for Stability in Early Modern Europe, Renaissance Lives,* and *The New History.* He is coauthor of *The Western Experience.* Professor Rabb has held offices in various national organizations, including the American Historical Association and the Social Science History Association. Most recently he has been involved in preparing the PBS multipart television series on the Renaissance.

Sherrin Marshall received her Ph.D. from Tufts University and taught history at several Boston area colleges and universities before becoming an academic administrator. She is now Associate Director for Program Planning and Evaluation, Fund for the Improvement and Reform of Schools and Teaching, in the U.S. Department of Education's Office of Educational Research and Improvement. Marshall's scholarly work has been supported by the American Council of Learned Societies (ACLS), National Endowment for the Humanities (NEH), and the Folger Shakespeare Library, as well as other funding sources, and includes *The Dutch Gentry* (1987) and *Women in Reformation and Counter-Reformation Europe: Public and Private Worlds* (1989), which she edited.

Contents

List of Maps and Illustrations

Preface

Although this book is intended to stand on its own as an introductory text and collection of primary documents, it was originally written for college students as a companion to the instructional films based on the television series entitled "Renaissance." Naturally, therefore, the five one-hour films in the original television series determined much of the book's content and thus its application to college courses. In particular, since a basic purpose of the films was to examine some of the political, social, and cultural transformations of a distant era that helped shape the modern world, the telecourse of which this book is a part should be regarded not merely as an account of some central aspects of a historical period, but also as an introduction to the origins of the corresponding features of the modern West. A brief explanation of the structure of "Renaissance" should serve to clarify further the aims of the pages that follow.

What will soon be apparent is that neither the films nor the book provide a comprehensive narrative account of the era of European history that, in traditional descriptions, covers both the Renaissance and the early modern era. The coverage is topical rather than chronological, and the subject matter extends, very broadly, from the middle of the fourteenth century to the last decades of the seventeenth. Within this time span, moreover, no attempt has been made to ensure that every major landmark receives due attention. Indeed, some of the most famous and influential figures of the age—Boccaccio, Columbus, Ferdinand of Aragon, Erasmus, Rabelais, Palestrina, Jakob Fugger, and Shakespeare, to name but a few—receive barely a mention or none at all. By contrast, others of less fame or moment, such as Paracelsus, are examined at length. And the same discrimination is apparent in the treatment of individual periods and specific topics—less on the late fourteenth century than on the late sixteenth, for example, and less on the papacy or the Black Death than on magic or Mannerism.*

* For an account that attempts to be inclusive, students and teachers should turn to S. H. Thomson's *Europe in Renaissance and Reformation* (New York: Harcourt, Brace, & World, Inc., 1963), an 850-page survey which, though thirty years old, still offers reliable guidance on almost all significant topics from 1300 to 1650.

Why is there such selectivity, and what are its implications for the classroom uses of the book and the films? The reasons for the structure, it should be emphasized at the outset, were both practical and pedagogic. In the course of five one-hour films, only some 20,000 words can be spoken (around 60 printed pages). Within these limitations it is far more effective to make a few highlights as vivid as possible than to try to cover all bases. It was clear that a focus on five central topics, emblematic of the transformations associated with the Renaissance and early modern times, was more likely to evoke the period as a whole than an attempt to give every significant milestone or era its due. The five films and their subjects—chosen because they seemed especially suitable for making connections with modern times—are:

"The Prince," on the growth of centralized government

"The Warrior," on military developments and their effects on society

"The Dissenter," on changes in religious belief and their results

"The Artist," on the creation of a new aesthetic and new roles for art

"The Scientist," on the revolution in views of the natural world

But there is also a pedagogic purpose to the concentration on a limited number of well-defined themes. It is now widely appreciated by teachers of history that comprehensive coverage of an era is an illusion and that the very effort to achieve it can leave students overwhelmed by information and convinced that there is no shape to the past. By limiting the breadth of the subject matter and the number of discrete details that have to be absorbed, one can try not only to offer deeper insights into an age but also to fashion coherent stories whose very clarity can help bring an age to life. Such focused explorations, moreover, can illuminate an unfamiliar world with a richness that is immediately appealing, and the student, presented with comprehensible and self-contained accounts, can gain a sense of the period from just a few of its features.

Whether these goals have been achieved here, only readers and viewers can judge. It should now be plain, however, both why many traditional topics of Renaissance and early modern history have been omitted and why their absence may promote rather than hinder the attainment of historical understanding by beginners in this field. It should be clear, too, that the readings from original sources have been chosen with a similar intent: to suggest the flavor of the age rather than to survey its written records. In only one area—economic change and the rise of capitalism—did the constraints imposed by the film series cause an omission that seemed unacceptable for the purposes of the telecourse. Had there been a sixth film, it would have been "The Merchant." Even without such a program, however, it was deemed essential to include the equivalent chapter on "The Merchant" in the book and to prepare, in addition, appropriate classroom films on economic change for the telecourse.

The opening and closing chapters of this book, for which there are also no equivalents in the five-part television series (though there are in the telecourse), are similar to the chapter on "The Merchant" in that they provide students with the background they will need to put the films in context. The first chapter offers a narrative overview of the entire period, geared to the subjects of the chapters that follow so that they can be fitted into an overall chronological framework. And the final chapter outlines some of the modern connections that the entire book is designed to suggest. In this regard, it echoes one of the recurrent themes of the films—the interviews with contemporary equivalents of Renaissance figures, such as modern artists and scientists, who convey the continuing influence in our own world of the concerns that animated their Renaissance and early modern predecessors. A number of crucial respects in which our society and culture have been shaped by the past should emerge from a recognition of the persistence, to this day, of the questions and problems that absorbed our ancestors.

To make sure that we have before us the full story of how those questions were first posed and elaborated, the word "Renaissance" has been defined in the broadest terms. What this requires is a rejection of the strict boundaries established by the first great student of this period in modern times, Jacob Burckhardt, who limited the word to Italy between approximately 1300 and the 1520s. Although most historians would extend the term to include much of the rest of western Europe, a number of them might agree that it should not be used after the 1520s—a position that would win the support of art historians who perceive a new style, Mannerism, coming into vogue in that decade. For general historians, too, it often seems convenient to use the label "Reformation" to identify a new era beginning around that time and to call the years from the mid-sixteenth to the late-seventeenth century "early modern." Moreover, there are medievalists who would object to the opening date of 1300, claiming that there was no significant break in historical development before 1500: What then deserves to be called a Renaissance?

None of these objections can be dismissed, but this is true of most arguments for particular periodizations or labels. For our purposes, however, it was essential to find a single term that could be used broadly to define the entire period under consideration. The beginning and end seemed clear. Unless the accounts of our five subjects could begin in the mid-1300s, it would be impossible to explain how the era's basic ambition—to revive and imitate the achievements of antiquity—arose in the generation of Petrarch. And unless we could finish in the second half of the seventeenth century, we could not bring to a proper conclusion the stories of the rise of science (with Newton), the acceptance of dissent (with Milton), or the triumph of central government (with Hobbes and Locke).

No single term can characterize these centuries as accurately as "Renaissance," because all the issues under consideration here began their course through European history in that era (even narrowly defined) and can rightly be seen as Renaissance initiatives. Moreover, as will be argued in the first chapter, the new ambitions that were first defined in the fourteenth century—the revival of antiquity demanded by Petrarch and the quest for individual faith launched by Wycliffe—did not lose their force as engines of change until the late-seventeenth century. To the extent that Milton was still driven by some of the same aspirations as Petrarch—and is regularly described as a poet of the Renaissance—it is entirely appropriate to see the years that link them as a coherent period. Nor did the struggles over religious belief die down until the last years of Milton's life. Indeed, many areas of scholarship make use of the term "Renaissance" well beyond 1650. Not until the Battle of the Books in the late-seventeenth century, when it was argued that contemporaries had at last outstripped the achievements of the ancient world, did it become clear that those who were forming European culture had moved beyond

Petrarch's ideals. And the same deferral, until after 1660, of a final resolution for the struggles that had been set in motion in the fifteenth and early sixteenth centuries colors political and military history (the acceptance of central power and the control of gunpowder warfare), the story of the rise to prominence of the artist, and the history of science.* Accordingly, "Renaissance" seemed the most appropriate summary title for the television series and hence for the telecourse, though the title of this volume acknowledges the attention given to the early modern period and periods beyond.

The latter bears emphasizing: Just as it is appropriate not to regard the book or the films as comprehensive accounts of an era, so too is it important that their implications not be limited to this one age, however expansively defined. The subjects they pursue—the roles of government, warfare, unorthodoxy, capitalism, art, and science in Western civilization—have been highlighted precisely for their relevance long after 1700. Indeed, the testimony of the modern counterparts of Renaissance figures, interviewed in the films, is intended to demonstrate the pertinence to this day of the long-standing issues they embody. And these connections—these suggestions of origins—enable the telecourse to address themes that transcend its chronology. The political, social, economic, religious, artistic, and intellectual conflicts that are its subject have been essential to the creation of the modern West and are therefore crucial to the study of history and the humanities throughout the last 600 years. A central purpose of this book is to add the detail and background that will enable students to examine these themes within the larger context of Western civilization. One can only hope that they will then come to understand how vital to the development of the modern world was the age we have called Renaissance.

McGraw-Hill and the authors would like to thank the following reviewers for their many helpful comments and suggestions: Joseph Berrigan, University of Georgia; Lawrence Bryant, California State University at Chico; Edward Muir, Louisiana State University; Frederick I. Murphy, Western Kentucky University; John Weakland, Ball State University; and Ronald Witt, Duke University.

---

* I have examined the issues which dominated European history from around 1500 to the late-seventeenth century, and the general "crisis" which resolved them, in greater detail in *The Struggle for Stability in Early Modern Europe* (New York: Oxford University Press, 1975). The present book takes some of *The Struggle for Stability*'s themes back to their Renaissance origins before 1500.

ONE

Four Centuries:
A Brief Overview

The transformations that began in Europe in the 1300s were not called a Renaissance until long after they had run their course. Even the major changes that are the subject of this book, which in some cases continued into the late 1600s, were only occasionally given that name while they were under way. Some contemporaries did refer to a *rinascita*, or "rebirth," of the arts and letters after a period of darkness that had started with the fall of ancient Rome. Only in the 1800s, however, did historians looking at these years begin to speak of a comprehensive transformation of Europe; before then, people might have spoken of a revival of antiquity in some areas, but never of an entire period shaped by an attempt to revive the values of ancient Greece and Rome.

Yet this is what we have in mind when we think of the Renaissance today. Starting with a movement in philosophy and education, this was an age that deliberately rejected its immediate past and was inspired by what it found in the world of antiquity to move in new directions in almost every sphere of life. There was much else that contributed to this refashioning of society and ideas—political, economic, and demographic change; advances in technology and warfare; overseas discoveries; and struggles over religious and scientific beliefs—but nothing had so profound or pervasive an impact as the turn to the distant past. In the words of Jacob Burckhardt, the historian of Italian civilization who formed our understanding of this period, it was a time "colored in a thousand ways by the influence of the ancient world." This coloration is what has given the era its image as a time of rebirth—of renaissance. Our overview of its history and main features, and of the early modern period in general, must therefore begin with the origins of that fascination with Greece and Rome.

1

HUMANISM

If so broad a movement as the revival of antiquity can be said to have begun with one person, it was Francesco Petrarca, known as Petrarch. Born in 1304, trained as a lawyer, and ordained as a cleric, Petrarch in fact lived the life of a man of letters. What drove him to write was his deep concern that nowhere in the world around him could he find a model of virtuous behavior that he could respect. The Church was certainly no help. This is how he described the papal court:

You can see with your own eyes what this new Babylon really is: seething, obscene, terrible. Whatever perfidy and fraud, whatever cruelty and arrogance, whatever shame-lessness and unbridled lust you have heard of, whatever impiety and immorality—all this you may see heaped up there.

Petrarch concluded that no guide from his own times or the immediate past would serve, especially by comparison with the examples of the moral life he found in his readings about ancient Rome.

How, then, could one be a good person? By imitating such figures from antiquity as Cicero and Augustine, who knew what proper values were and pursued them in their own lives, despite temptations and the distractions of public affairs. The period between their time and his own—what Petrarch came to regard as a "middle" age of darkness—he considered contemptible. His own world, he felt, would improve only if it tried to emulate the ancients, and in fact, a central purpose of education ought to be to teach what the ancients did and said. In particular, Petrarch believed that only a restoration of the mastery of the written and spoken word that had distinguished the great Romans—an imitation of their style, of the way they had conveyed their ideas—would enable his contemporaries to learn to behave like them.

The program Petrarch laid out soon attracted attention in Florence (Figure 1), the city from which his family had come and where he found influential friends and disciples. They argued that, by advocating Petrarch's ideas, the Florentines would be identified with a distinctive and powerful vision that would become the envy of their rivals among the cities and states of Italy. And this was indeed what happened. Known as "humanists," these campaigners for the revival of antiquity started a revolution in education that soon began to take hold in Italy. The writing and speaking skills they emphasized came to be in demand at princely courts (including that of the papacy), and their crusade to study and imitate the ancients transformed art, literature, and even political and social values.

It was as a direct consequence of the humanists' activities, in other words, that a number of changes took place that we think of as the heart of the achievements of the Renaissance. Perhaps the most famous was the creation of a radically new style in painting, sculpture, and architecture. For all the many influences that shaped Italian art in the 1400s (and thus, eventually, all of European art), none had anything like the impact of the effort to rediscover, and bring back to life, the techniques and aesthetics of ancient Greeks and Romans. Beginning in Florence in the 1420s, this movement inspired generations of artists, who deliberately turned their backs on the style of their immediate predecessors. Indeed, we owe the word "Gothic" as a way of describing medieval art to those who later wanted to discredit it by

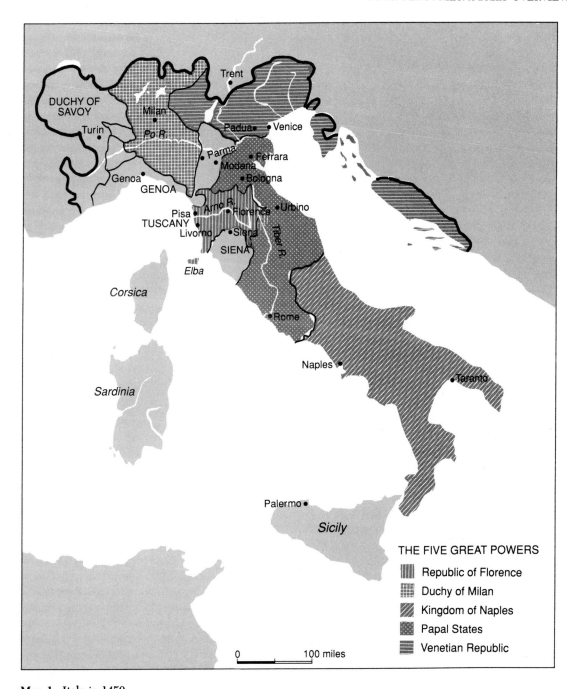

THE FIVE GREAT POWERS

Republic of Florence
Duchy of Milan
Kingdom of Naples
Papal States
Venetian Republic

0   100 miles

Map 1. Italy in 1450

associating it with the barbarian invaders (the Goths) who had destroyed Rome's empire.

The influence of antiquity also helped reshape the form and content of literature. In both poetry and drama there was a new interest in classical models, from the epic to the bawdy comedy. Purely secular themes, without religious purpose, became more common. And works of history grew increasingly analytic, openly acknowledging such ancients as Thucydides, Livy, and Tacitus as their inspiration. Moreover, new school and university curricula based on Latin writings, a new attention in philosophy to Plato and to the ideas of the Stoics and sceptics of antiquity, and a close scrutiny of classical writers that led to major changes in scientific and political thought—all these shifts not only demonstrated the influence of the humanists but also helped send European thought in new directions.

Yet the reverence for the distant past had an impact not only on intellectual life but also on public affairs. One of the issues the humanists struggled with, as they tried to absorb the lessons of antiquity, was the difficulty of deciding which of two routes offered the best means of attaining true virtue. Should individuals try to cut themselves off from the larger world, with its corruptions and compromises, and focus only on what they called (using its Latin name) the *vita contemplativa*—the contemplative life—or should they try to improve that world through the *vita activa*—the active life? Petrarch was not sure. Cicero taught him that both lives were necessary; Augustine was fearful of outside temptations.

In the generations following Petrarch, however, the doubts declined, and it became a commonplace of humanism that only by participating in public life, seeking higher ends for one's society as well as for oneself, could an individual be truly virtuous. By the early 1500s, for instance, the Florentine Niccolo Machiavelli was arguing that the reason for the decline of his native land was that its citizens (unlike those of the Roman Republic) did not enlist in its army or engage in its politics. His contemporary, the Englishman Thomas More, made the case for both approaches in his book, *Utopia* (1516), but he, too, preferred public service, and he, like Machiavelli, became involved in government. Ironically, both men suffered for choosing the active life: Machiavelli was tortured and exiled, and More eventually sacrificed his life for his principles.

Apart from inspiring new goals for politics, humanism also gave the elite a new way of measuring social distinction. It soon became apparent that the ability to quote Vergil or some other ancient writer was not so much a sign of moral seriousness as a badge of superiority. What differentiated people was whether they could use or recognize the quotations, and this was why the new curriculum was so popular—even though it seemed to consist, more and more, of endless memorizations and repetitions of Latin texts.

At the same time, however, the admiration for the humanists and their teachings gave an important boost to the patronage of arts and letters. In the age of gunpowder, which began to affect warfare in the 1400s and which made armored knights on horseback obsolete, it was no longer so easy to make physical bravery the chief quality of the noble. Instead, aristocrats began to turn to the ideas of the humanists, who argued that fame could also be attained through the *vita contemplativa* and by patronizing artists and writers whose praise would make their benefactors famous. Princely courts thus became centers of art and learning. A new

Figure 1. *Depiction of Florence Around 1490.* Florence in 1490, in the age of Lorenzo de Medici, was a walled city about one square mile in area, with about 60,000 inhabitants. It was dominated by Brunelleschi's famous dome on the cathedral.

image of gentlemanly behavior, which included refinement, taste, and elegance, as well as courage, became widely accepted, especially as laid out in the book *The Courtier* (1528), by the Italian Baldassare Castiglione. One duke, Federigo Montefeltro of Urbino, even had his portrait painted sitting in his study dressed in armor but reading a book.

Humanism, then, has to be seen as the first and most persistent of the new movements that shaped Renaissance culture and society. By the mid-1400s it was a dominant intellectual force throughout Italy, and by the end of the century it was sweeping all of Europe, transmitted not only by its devoted adherents but also by a recent invention, printing, which made the texts of both humanists and ancients far more easily available. Dozens of new schools and universities were being founded, and no court of any significance was without its roster of artists and writers familiar with the latest ideas. Even legal systems were being affected, as the principles of Roman law (which tended to endorse the power of the ruler) were adopted in many countries. By the early 1500s, however, other movements were under way which were to accelerate the transformation of Renaissance Europe.

A CENTURY OF UPHEAVAL

Between the late 1400s and the late 1500s a series of dramatic events and struggles caused such radical changes in the structure and outlook of European society that at least one part of the humanists' program—to reject what the Middle Ages had taken for granted—seemed to have been accomplished. In politics, the economy, religion, even the very understanding of the shape of the world, few of the landmarks remained standing. For a while it appeared that all generally accepted norms would vanish and that hardly any traditional assumptions could survive.

The first set of changes, which started in the last third of the fifteenth century, was demographic and economic. After well over a hundred years of stagnation and decline, Europe's population began to rise. Why this should have happened we do not fully know. The Black Death, which had first erupted in 1348 and had been largely responsible for a drop of some thirty-five percent in Europe's population between 1300 and 1400, had been succeeded by regular bouts of plague, but it is possible that these became less severe. In any case, by 1500 most of the losses had been made up, and Europe again approached its 1300 population of about 70 million (which was to reach nearly 80 million by 1550). And, as there came to be more people, other changes followed.

On the positive side, the market for goods grew. The increased demand for food, clothing, and housing opened up new economic opportunities. This, in turn, enabled the suppliers of the goods—farmers with surpluses, brickmakers, and so forth—to charge higher prices. But there were losers, too. With more mouths to feed, a village might no longer be able to support all its inhabitants—especially if, as often happened, wages began to level off because there was now more competition for jobs, while at the same time landlords, faced with an inflation of prices, tried to raise rents. The result was the appearance, in the 1500s, of sizable bands of vagrants roaming the countryside. Some ended up in the expanding armies of the day. Most, however, drifted toward cities, which, especially after 1550 or so, experienced enormous growth throughout Europe. And cities also had contradictory effects on their societies: On the one hand, they created new jobs; on the other, they were conspicuous centers of crime, poverty, disease, and high death rates.

Accelerating all these effects was the Europeans' development of empires overseas. Starting with the voyage of Columbus in 1492 and the discovery of a sea route to India by the Portuguese in 1498, this effort not only created vast markets, an abundant source of goods, and opportunities for both geographic and social mobility—over a million Europeans were living in other continents by 1700—but also (because it led to huge imports of silver, which was used in coins) promoted the inflation of prices. Inflation, too, had both positive and negative effects, enlarging profits and reducing debts for some, while raising the cost of living for others. And even the opening up of new territories, with their boundless resources, had its less admirable side in the exploitation and decimation of the natives and the wars that were caused by the competition for empire. The very discovery of unknown lands and peoples, however, helped undermine traditional ideas about the world and about the easy acceptance of received truths.

In general, therefore, the demographic and economic developments of the 1500s served to challenge old assumptions and unsettle those who lived through them. The same was true of the military and political changes of the period. It was around 1500 that people first became fully aware of the dramatic difference gunpowder was making in warfare. Spanish troops were coming to be recognized as the finest in Europe—a dominance they were to maintain for nearly 150 years—and the source of their reputation was their disciplined effectiveness in using the guns and cannon that were transforming the battlefield. Ever larger numbers of men were recruited for gunpowder armies, and the noise, smoke, and heavy casualties they now encountered were unlike anything that had been known previously in war.

It was also partly because of the soaring costs of the military that governments were taking on new responsibilities and demanding higher and higher taxes during

Map 2. Major territorial states of Europe around 1415

this period. The huge increase in their bureaucracies during the 1500s and their growing presence—through tax collectors, army recruiters, and other officials—in the lives of their citizens, although still minimal by modern standards, were yet other signs that the world was changing. Especially in Spain, France, and England, monarchs were claiming an authority and assuming a prominence that was unprecedented, and over the next century and a half they were to tame both the Church and the nobility that had long been their rivals for control over the people.

The subjects of these kings and queens could have been forgiven, therefore, if they felt that in this sphere, too, traditional assumptions about political and social relations could no longer be taken for granted. Machiavelli's *Prince* (1513) certainly suggested that long-standing commitments to the moral, and even religious, underpinnings of politics no longer carried any weight. All that seemed to matter was the accumulation and preservation of power itself, both within states and in international affairs, where such grandiose ideals as uniting for a Christian crusade had given way to discussions of the balance of power among territorial rivals.

It was into this already bewildering situation of demographic, social, economic, geographic, military, and political change that the Reformation burst forth, shattering one of Europe's most fundamental and enduring traditions: the unity of faith. The great irony of this era is that so much was transformed even as the culture proclaimed its reverence for the past. To the humanists, after all, "innovation" was a pejorative term. Everything good had already happened; what was needed was to bring an ideal past back to life. Some of them worried that this meant giving too much respect to pagans like Plato and Cicero, who had, of course, lived before Christ. What this prompted, around 1500, was a movement known as "Christian humanism," in which the same principle of imitation was applied not to the Greeks and Romans, but to the heroes of the New Testament. Moral guidance now came from Christ himself and from the apostles, St. Paul, and the early saints (including Petrarch's favorite, St. Augustine), whose message had lost its force in the intervening centuries. The leading Christian humanist, the Dutchman Erasmus, loved all of antiquity, but the morality he urged had a distinctly religious purpose.

This reverence for the past, which was an essential quality of Renaissance thought that had already inspired the study of Greece and Rome, was inherently conservative. The aim was to revive and conserve, not to innovate. Nevertheless, despite the best of intentions, the backward look in this case led to revolution. Luther and the other Protestants were not content, like Erasmus, merely to emphasize that individual Christians ought to conduct their lives according to Christ's original teachings. They felt that the Church, by increasingly distorting those teachings over the centuries, *prevented* the believer from finding true faith. Consequently, there was no point in maintaining even outward allegiance to the papacy and the institution it led. In order to go back to a perfect past, a separate Church would have to be created. The result was a clash that not only inspired a multitude of new definitions of true Christianity and a splintering of the faithful into dozens of competing groups but also promoted a vicious fanaticism that tore European society apart.

Armed conflict of various kinds was endemic in this period. There were wars between France and Spain for the control of Italy from 1494 to 1559. There were bitter revolts by peasants and townspeople who felt crushed by the growing demands of governments in both the Holy Roman Empire (today's Germany) and Spain in the 1520s. And there were fights between Christians and Turks along the Mediterranean and in the Balkans, between neighbors around the Baltic, between Spain and much of the rest of Europe, and within many countries as well. None of these confrontations, however, generated as much violence and inhumanity as the wars over religion. Starting in the Holy Roman Empire in the 1530s, spreading to France in the 1560s, and inspiring ghastly persecutions everywhere, these attempts to crush heresy by force brought out the worst in the society of the time. The horrors that every one of the faiths perpetrated on the others—Catholics on Protestants, Protestants on Catholics, and, when they could not find a convenient enemy, all of them on Jews, witches, and other easy victims—are among the grimmest spectacles in Western history. The mayhem continued for over a century, killing tens of thousands of people, despite occasional pleas for sanity, calls for Christian charity, and attempts to restore some degree of order and calm.

The consequences of these destructive outbursts were predictable. The last shred of cohesion seemed to be removed from European society, and the sense that all solid or familiar landmarks were disappearing only intensified with each passing year. Some responded by adopting unswerving beliefs, dismissing all doubts; others sank into despair at the loss of clear guidance amid so many conflicting claims. What was unmistakable by the late 1500s was that no comforting answers were available to counteract the bewildering effects of rapid change.

Even those who were putting forward new ideas about the structure of nature— the pioneers of what we call the "scientific revolution," such as the Polish mathematician and astronomer Nicholas Copernicus, who published startling conclusions about the heavens in 1543—were at this point offering more questions than answers. The work they had done by around 1600, although often citing the inspiration of the ancients, had cast doubt on the received wisdom about astronomy, about the physics of motion, and about the workings of anatomy, but it had provided no new assurance in place of the old truths. In other words, the students of nature were only adding to the uncertainties of the age. The reaction of one writer, the Frenchman Michel de Montaigne, exemplified the skepticism and mistrust that arose in the late 1500s as it became increasingly difficult to choose among rival and conflicting authorities:

> It was the stars and the heavens that were in motion for three thousand years. Or so everyone believed until [an ancient astronomer] decided that it was not the stars but the earth that moved. Now, in our time, Copernicus has so firmly established this doctrine that it supports everything we can observe. What shall we conclude from this, except that it is hardly worth heating ourselves up over one or the other? Who knows but that in a thousand years from now a third opinion may supplant them both?

Not surprisingly, the community of artists, after bringing the revival of ancient forms that had started in the 1420s to new heights in the early 1500s—in the period that is called "High Renaissance" by art historians—also moved on to very different aims when they began to reflect the anxieties and disruptions that surrounded them later in the century. The dominant style of the years following the 1520s has been called "Mannerism," and its distortions and unsettling effects contrasted sharply with the serenity of much that had gone before. Art, too, was caught up in the upheavals, the crumbling of familiar landmarks, that characterized this troubled century.

CRISIS AND RESOLUTION

The promise of the early days of the Renaissance, with its high hopes of moral improvement based on a revival of the ideals of antiquity, seemed by the early 1600s to have dissolved into a bad dream. Although looking to the past, Europeans had created a series of revolutions that had undermined familiar landmarks without putting anything very dependable in their place. It seemed that as much misery as good had been caused by the increase in population, by the expansion of trade and overseas empires, by the new powers of the military and of governments, by the Reformation, and by the challenges to old assumptions in intellectual and artistic endeavors. Every one of these fundamental transformations had begun in optimism; by 1600, however, it was far from clear that the optimism had been justified.

What happened over the next fifty or sixty years was that a massive effort was launched, in every region of Europe and in all areas of life, to come to terms with the changes of the 1500s. Some tried to turn the clock back, not to antiquity, but to a time when, so they believed, central governments did *not* undermine the traditional authority of the local region. Others tried to overcome the uncertainties by promoting ever more urgently the solutions they themselves found appealing, whether a particular set of religious doctrines, a belief in science, or a powerful artistic or political vision. For a while, however, it seemed that the only way to bring under control the mounting costs and casualties of the endless wars that the upheavals of the 1500s had caused or to resolve the questioning of all authority that those same upheavals had inspired was to intensify those very clashes. Not until a final spasm of conflict in the mid-1600s (of which one observer wrote, echoing a widespread view, "These days are days of shaking, and this shaking is universal") did Europeans finally cease to struggle over the changes that had engulfed them. It was only when this crisis of authority passed that, at last, a sense of resolution could be reached, and the heritage of the Renaissance could become central to the further development of Western society and thought.

Although religious disputes were undoubtedly the source of the worst violence of the 1500s, the most destructive of these upheavals took place in the next century. The Thirty Years' War, beginning in 1618, was unparalleled in its viciousness and its loss of life until the World Wars of the twentieth century. It was as if the Catholics and Protestants needed one final bloodletting, the most murderous of all, before they could agree to live with each other in peace. As the horrors intensified, the combatants gradually lost their religious zeal—significantly, alliances began to be made across confessional lines, and everyone ignored the Pope when he denounced the treaties that ended the fighting—and major efforts were now made to reestablish order both within countries and on the international scene.

The result was the creation of a comprehensive diplomatic system unlike any that had existed before. At the Peace of Westphalia, which ended the Thirty Years' War in 1648 after seven years of negotiation, nearly every major dispute was resolved, and the map of Europe was drawn along lines that were not basically challenged for over 150 years. Starting in Italy in the mid-1400s, the elaborate system of resident ambassadors and protocol that is at the heart of modern diplomacy had gradually been developed, and it now became an essential part of European politics. The first efforts to devise a body of laws governing the relations between states were made during the war, and in general, after 1648, there was the realization that one of the chief causes of instability of the previous century—the anarchy of international affairs—had been removed.

This sense of settlement also emerged from the series of events that was the most obvious manifestation of the crisis of the mid-1600s. In just about every country in

Europe in the 1640s and 1650s there was a rebellion or at least some movement of resistance against the central government. The seriousness of the outbreaks ranged from a major revolution in England to a brief period of tension in Sweden. Everywhere, however, these disturbances were indications of long-standing resentments that traditional rights and the independence of local areas were being destroyed by the increasingly powerful rulers and bureaucrats of the age. Again and again, the demands were for an end to outside interference in a region, for lower taxes, and for the removal of intrusive officials—a rolling back, in other words, of the very means by which central governments were expanding their control over their states.

The irony of this wave of revolts was that even though a number of them brought about changes in the structure of a regime, none of them led to a decline in the powers of central authorities. In England, for example, the king had to pay far more attention after the revolution than before to the representatives of the country who sat in Parliament, but the dominance of London over national affairs only increased in the years that followed. The same was true of Paris, Madrid, Vienna, Berlin, St. Petersburg, and the other great capitals which increasingly became the heart of European life. People had learned to accept centralization and the dwindling autonomy of the locality. Even the great blaze of revolutions that burst forth a hundred years later, starting in 1789, did not reverse this trend. The political changes of the Renaissance thus turned out to have a permanent effect on Western society.

Remarkably enough, the renewed orderliness and stability also extended to military affairs. Largely in reaction to the anarchy and devastations of the Thirty Years' War, governments made a major effort to strengthen their control over the destructiveness of warfare. Although armies continued to grow, their discipline became noticeably tighter, and casualties on the battlefield were far fewer. It helped, too, that religious passions were no longer a significant cause of conflict.

At the same time, both demographic and economic trends reflected not only the deterioration of the first two-thirds of the seventeenth century but also the recovery thereafter. Around 1620, the rise in population, the growth of trade, and the inflation of prices that had shaped European society over the preceding 150 years came to an end. The stagnation that followed partly caused and partly intensified the disruptions of the mid-1600s. There can be little doubt that the experience of crisis was made worse by economic and demographic difficulties. Moreover, the fact that the Netherlands and England suffered fewer of these dislocations than other areas enabled the Dutch and the English not only to win new prominence in, and soon to dominate, European commerce but also to challenge successfully the monopoly Spain and Portugal had long enjoyed in overseas empires. By the late 1600s, this shift in the economic balance of power was unmistakable, as was the resumption of growth in both population and trade. People also had come to accept—as was clear in both Amsterdam and London—that central governments would exert their powers in close cooperation with their merchant communities in order to strengthen the economies of their states.

The progression from ever more strenuous efforts to conquer doubt to an atmosphere of calm reassurance, which indicated that the crisis had passed, can be traced in the worlds of the arts and thought as well. In sharp contrast to the unsettling vision of the Mannerists, the aesthetic of Baroque painting, sculpture, and architecture, which conquered Europe after 1600, emphasized exuberance, power, and grandiosity. Uncertainties were to be swept aside by sheer magnificence, by vast aesthetic schemes, and by a theatricality that relied on emotion to overcome doubt and resistance. It was entirely appropriate that the new sensation of the age, opera, should have claimed, with an audacity that was typical of the times, that it could overwhelm its audience by combining every conceivable art form—architecture, sculpture, and painting (in the sets), music, singing, dance, and literature.

This is not to say that the imitation of antiquity had come to an end. Indeed, one of the justifications used by the creators of the first operas was that they believed Greek dramas had been sung and danced in magnificent settings. Accordingly, their works, which often presented classical stories, such as those of Orpheus—appropriately, since he had had the power to enchant even the trees with his music—and Ulysses, were said to be authentic recreations of an ancient form. Practitioners of the visual arts, too, used their mastery of dramatic and powerful effects to bring to life themes that had been favorites of Greece and Rome, from the myths of the gods of Olympus to the events of Roman history. But the aim, at all times, was to dazzle the senses.

In the last years of the seventeenth century, these aesthetic purposes began to change. Vast strivings began to give way to more delicate and decorative creations. By 1700, a new style, "Rococo," which emphasized lightness, elegance, and ornamentation, had come to the fore. In the organization of cultural activity, too—especially in France, which increasingly set the pace for Europe, as the largest country and strongest military power of the late 1600s—an insistence on order and regulation was replacing the extravagance of the Baroque. French academies, supported by the government, laid down rules for what was acceptable in the arts and helped promote a reaction against passion and enthusiasm. And the leading patrons of the day, aristocratic women who organized cultural gatherings in their salons (or "drawing-rooms"), encouraged the same qualities of restraint and refinement. The shift in the tone and purpose of the arts reflected the more relaxed atmosphere after the crisis years of the mid-1600s.

In literature the change was even commented on by contemporaries. The scintillating variety of William Shakespeare and Miguel Cervantes in the early 1600s (both died in 1616) had resisted constraint. They roamed across all human experience in lavish outpourings of language. Their younger contemporaries, John Milton and Pierre Corneille, had created vast structures of epic poetry and classic drama that echoed the grandiose aims of Baroque art. By the late 1600s, however, these ambitions had faded, and both poetry and drama had lowered their sights to focus, once again, on elegance, lightness, and grace. The feeling that, with Milton gone, nobody could even try to equal his power and range was summed up by a younger English poet, Andrew Marvell in 1674:

Pardon me, Mighty Poet, nor despise
My causeless, yet not impious surmise.
But I am now convinced, and none will dare
Within thy labors to pretend a share.

Thou hast not missed one thought that could be fit,
And all that was improper dost omit:
So that no room is here for writers left,
But to detect their ignorance or theft.

And it is significant that in France the last of the great imitators of the passion and intensity of Greek theater, Jean Racine, said in 1684 that the supreme accomplishment of his most famous predecessor was that "Corneille brought reason upon the stage."

The reason Racine's comment is significant is its emphasis on reason. This was the heart of the new aesthetic that arose in the late 1600s, taking its inspiration from the movement that had come to be regarded as the embodiment of reason and thus as a savior in an age of crisis, namely, the rise of science. For the study of nature, which until around 1600 had been a highly specialized subject, of interest only to a handful of scholars and experimenters, suddenly became quite popular in midcentury. Moreover, instead of serving mainly to undermine old truths without establishing solid new ones in their place, as had been true in the 1500s, the theories and investigations of these "natural philosophers" (as they were called at the time) now began to suggest that new answers could indeed be found.

The single figure most closely associated with these two changes was the Italian mathematician, physicist, and astronomer Galileo Galilei, born in 1564. His discoveries with a new instrument, the telescope, became the sensation of the intellectual circles of the day when they were first described in 1610. And then, in 1632, Galileo published a major study of astronomy in Italian so that it could be read not only by scholars (for whom works were always written in Latin) but also by a general audience. The condemnation of this book, *Dialogue on the Two Chief World Systems*, by the Roman Inquisition only made Galileo's work all the more famous. The result was a broad awareness of the importance of studies of the physical world that had not existed before and a feeling that science, alone among the conflicting theories and systems of thought of the time, could achieve clear and irrefutable solutions to venerable problems.

Galileo was not alone, of course, in helping to create these perceptions. There were many extraordinary discoveries in the 1600s and a number of eloquent propagandizers of science who argued that it offered the best model for all forms of thinking. They suggested, too, that its practitioners deserved an honored place in society, including the patronage of kings. What was remarkable, however, was not that such arguments were made, but that they were so widely accepted. Europe in an age of crisis, mired in turmoil, was looking for a redeemer. For over 150 years, familiar landmarks had been overturned, to be replaced by doubt and unease. Now, at last, there was a group of people who seemed to promise certainty and assurance. It was only natural, therefore, for the culture at large to embrace them with delight. Here was a model of order, rationality, and decorum that everyone could accept as a cure for the upheaval and scepticism of a difficult time. No wonder the highest compliment Racine could offer was to say that Corneille had brought reason onto the stage.

The triumph of science became the touchstone of the new confidence, the sense of settlement, of the late 1600s. And it was in these years that Europeans began to overcome the reverence for antiquity that had been the driving force of the Renaissance since the humanists had first looked back, three centuries before. Around 1700 a major dispute broke out over the relative merits of the ancients and the moderns. Some continued to argue that nobody in their time had achieved the wisdom or brilliance of the great figures of Greece or Rome. But their opponents were able to make a case for the superiority of the moderns and to win increasing acceptance for this view, largely because they were able to claim that the discoveries of the scientists had gone far beyond anything known in antiquity. As one of them put it, they might have been pygmies standing on the shoulders of giants, yet those pygmies could see further than the giants.

The willingness to modify the reverence for the past, as well as to assert the value of the achievements of contemporaries, can be seen as marking the end of a stage in the development of European culture and society that had begun over three hundred years before—that is, the end of what we have called Renaissance and early modern times. The changes identified with that period had been absorbed, after a long struggle, and relative stability had been restored. That new demands for change were soon to arise was going to be a matter that a very different society, the Europe of the 1700s, would have to address.

If, then, it is a relatively coherent progression over nearly four centuries that has been described in outline in this chapter, we can now take a look in more detail at some of the more specific developments that are associated with the Renaissance and the early modern world. In particular, we will examine six aspects of the age—its politics, its warfare, its religion, its commerce, its art, and its science—to see how six pursuits that were central to this society were transformed during these centuries and how they, in turn, helped shape the world in which we now live.

Original Sources

The Renaissance era witnessed transformations in virtually every sphere of life throughout Europe. As the chapter text points out, these broad changes were not called by that name until the 1800s, although some contemporaries recognized that they were living in an era of change and wrote of that change from a number of different perspectives.

However, it was not until the work of the Swiss historian Jacob Burckhardt in the nineteenth century that the Renaissance came to be identified as an age of progress, epitomized by its love for the classical period—the time of the Greeks and Romans. In his work, *The Civilization of the Renaissance*, Burckhardt emphasized the integration of numerous elements that are highlighted throughout this book: The Renaissance was to be known as a time of artistic and literary genius, intimately connected with political and social developments.

As is always the case, the historians who followed Burckhardt revised his ideas. Some historians noted that other revivals of ancient thought had occurred and that other periods of economic change and renewal had been recognized. Others have questioned whether this "Renaissance" included women. Still others have concluded that ideas in and of themselves do not have the power to bring about change. Nevertheless, the period that has been labeled the "age of the Renaissance" did incorporate a great many elements that we recognize today as "modern" and exemplified them in ways that we recognize as unique.

Selection 1
Preface, *Lives of the Artists*

Giorgio Vasari

In his text, Vasari (1511–1574) included an historical introduction written for the benefit of the artists and craftsmen he hoped would find meaning in his work. He clearly recognized that in the arts, at least, a rebirth had taken place that had restored the ancients to their place in history. His hope was that his writing would help the same to happen for the artists of his own age. This wish was fulfilled, since Vasari's work was a best-seller when it was first published in 1550 and has remained a best-seller since.

. . . So far I have been talking about the origins of sculpture and painting, perhaps at greater length than was called for at this stage. However, the reason for my doing so has been not so much my great love of the arts as the hope that I would say something useful and helpful to our own artists. For from the smallest beginnings art attained the greatest heights, only to decline from its noble position to the most degraded status. Seeing this,

artists can also realize the nature of the arts we have been discussing: these, like the other arts and like human beings themselves, are born, grow up, become old, and die. And they will be able to understand more readily the process by which art has been reborn and reached perfection in our own times. And if, which God forbid, because of indifference or evil circumstances or the ruling of Providence (which always seems to dislike the things of this world proceeding undisturbed) it ever happens at any time that the arts once again fall into the same disastrous decline, then I hope

Source: Giorgio Vasari, *Lives of the Artists*, vol. 1, trans. by George Bull (London: Penguin Classics, 1987), pp. 46–47.

that this work of mine, such as it is, if it proves worthy of a happier fate may, because of what I have already said and what I am going to write, keep the arts alive, or at least may inspire some of the more able among us to give them every possible encouragement. In this way, my good intentions and the work of outstanding men will, I hope, provide the arts with support and adornment of a kind which, if I may be allowed to say this outright, they have been lacking hitherto. . . .

Selection 2
Gargantua and Pantagruel
François Rabelais

In his giant work, *Gargantua and Pantagruel*, first published in 1532, Rabelais puts the following discourse on the Renaissance into Gargantua's mouth:

. . . Thanks to divine goodness, learning has been restored to its former brightness and dignity. . . . Now all the branches of instruction have been established, and the study of languages has been revived: Greek, without which a man may be ashamed to call himself a scholar, and Hebrew, Chaldean, and Latin. Printing, used so elegantly and so perfectly, was invented in my time, by divine inspiration; as, by contrast, artillery was inspired by diabolical suggestion. The whole world is full of knowledgeable persons, of most learned schoolmasters and of vast libraries, and it appears to me as a truth that neither in Plato's time, nor Cicero's nor Papinian's was there ever such opportunity for study as we see at present. Nor must anyone hereafter appear or present himself in company that has not been well-polished in Minerva's shop. I consider robbers, hangmen, adventurers, and grooms more learned now than the doctors and preachers were in my time. . . .

Source: François Rabelais, *La Vie de Gargantua et de Pantagruel: Livre Second*, vol. 3 (Paris: Dalibon, 1823), pp. 259–261. Trans. by A. Borchert.

Selection 3
Jacob Burckhardt Characterizes the "Renaissance Man"

In this selection, Burckhardt suggests that at the time of the Renaissance, a transformation occurred in the ways individuals perceived and identified themselves. Ever since, the characteristics Burckhardt identified have been termed those of the "Renaissance man."

. . . When this impulse to the highest individual development was combined with a powerful and varied nature, which had mastered all the elements of the culture of the age, then arose the "all-sided man"—*l'uomo universale*—who belonged to Italy alone. Men there were of encyclopaedic knowledge in many countries during the Middle Ages, for this knowledge was confined within narrow limits. Even in the twelfth century there were universal artists, but the problems of architecture were comparatively simple and uniform, and in sculpture and painting the matter was of more importance than the form. But in Italy at the time of the Renaissance, we find artists who in every branch created new and perfect works, and who also made the greatest impression as men. Others, outside the arts they practiced, were masters of a vast circle of spiritual interests. . . .

Source: Jacob Burckhardt, *The Civilisation of the Renaissance in Italy*, trans. by S. G. C. Middlemore (New York: Macmillan & Co., 1890), pp. 134–135.

The fifteenth century is, above all, that of the many-sided men. . . .The Florentine merchant and statesman was often learned in both the classical languages; the most famous humanists read the ethics and politics of Aristotle to him and to his sons; even the daughters of the house were highly educated. It is in these circles that private education was first treated seriously. The humanist, on his side, was compelled to the most varied attainments, since his philological learning was not limited, as it is now, to the theoretical knowledge of classical antiquity, but had to serve the practical needs of daily life. . . .

Selection 4
Burckhardt's View of Society at the Time of the Italian Renaissance

Here Burckhardt explains how the interactions of social groups at the time of the Renaissance in Italy differed from their interactions during the Middle Ages. Within the walls of the Italian cities, nobles and middle-class citizens, or burghers, not only lived together but also were bound by their shared devotion to the cities in which they lived.

THE EQUALIZATION OF CLASSES

Every period of civilisation, which forms a complete and consistent whole, manifests itself not only in political life, in religion, art, and science, but also sets its characteristic stamp on social life. Thus the Middle Ages had their courtly and aristocratic manners and etiquette, differing but little in the various countries of Europe, as well as their peculiar forms of middle-class life.

Italian customs at the time of the Renaissance offer in these respects the sharpest contrast to mediaevalism. The foundation on which they rest is wholly different. Social intercourse in its highest and most perfect form now ignored all distinctions of caste, and was based simply on the existence of an educated class as we now understand the word. Birth and origin were without influence, unless combined with leisure and inherited wealth. Yet this assertion must not be taken in an absolute and unqualified sense, since medieval distinctions still sometimes made themselves felt to a greater or less degree, if only as a means of maintaining equality with the aristocratic pretensions of the less advanced countries of Europe. But the main

Source: Jacob Burckhardt, *The Civilisation of the Renaissance in Italy,* trans. by S. G. C. Middlemore (New York: Macmillan & Co., 1890), pp. 359–365.

current of the time went steadily towards the fusion of classes in the modern sense of the phrase.

The fact was of vital importance that, from certainly the twelfth century onwards, the nobles and the burghers dwelt together within the walls of the cities. The interests and pleasures of both classes were thus identified, and the feudal lord learned to look at society from another point of view than that of his mountain-castle. The Church, too, in Italy never suffered itself, as in northern countries, to be used as a means of providing for the younger sons of noble families. Bishoprics, abbacies, and canonries were often given from the most unworthy motives, but still not according to the pedigrees of the applicants; and if the bishops in Italy were more numerous, poorer, and, as a rule, destitute of all sovereign rights, they still lived in the cities where their cathedrals stood, and formed, together with their chapters, an important element in the cultivated society of the place. In the age of despots and absolute princes which followed, the nobility in most of the cities had the motives and the leisure to give themselves up to a private life free from political danger and adorned with all that was elegant and enjoyable, but at the same time hardly distinguishable from that of the wealthy burgher. And after the time of Dante, when the new poetry and literature were in the hands of all Italy, when to this was added the revival of ancient culture and the new interest in man as such, when the successful Condottiere became a prince, and not only good birth, but legitimate birth, ceased to be indispensable for a throne, it might well seem that the age of equality had dawned, and the belief in nobility vanished for ever.

From a theoretical point of view, when the appeal was made to antiquity, the conception of nobility could be both justified and condemned from Aristotle alone. Dante, for example, adapts from the Aristotelian definition, 'Nobility rests on excellence and inherited wealth,' his own saying, 'Nobility rests on personal excellence or on that of predecessors.' But elsewhere he is not satisfied with this conclusion. He blames himself, because even in Paradise, while talking with his ancestor Cacciaguida, he made mention of his noble origin, which is but as a mantle from which time is ever cutting something away, unless we ourselves add daily fresh worth to it. And in the 'Convito' he disconnects 'nobile' and 'nobiltà' from every condition of birth, and identifies the idea with the capacity for moral and intellectual eminence, laying a special stress on high culture by calling 'nobiltà' the sister of 'filosofia.'

And as time went on, the greater the influence of humanism on the Italian mind, the firmer and more widespread became the conviction that birth decides nothing as to the goodness or badness of a man. In the fifteenth century this was the prevailing opinion. Poggio, in his dialogue 'On nobility,' agrees with his interlocutors—Niccolò Niccoli, and Lorenzo Medici, brother of the great Cosimo—that there is no other nobility than that of personal merit. The keenest shafts of his ridicule are directed against much of what vulgar prejudice thinks indispensable to an aristocratic life. 'A man is all the farther removed from true nobility, the longer his forefathers have plied the trade of brigands. The taste for hawking and hunting savours no more of nobility than the nests and lairs of the hunted creatures of spikenard. The cultivation of the soil, as practised by the ancients, would be much nobler than this senseless wandering through the hills and woods, by which men make

themselves liker to the brutes than to the reasonable creatures. It may serve well enough as a recreation, but not as the business of a lifetime.' The life of the English and French chivalry in the country or in the woody fastnesses seems to him thoroughly ignoble, and worst of all the doings of the robber-knights of Germany. Lorenzo here begins to take the part of the nobility, but not—which is characteristic—appealing to any natural sentiment in its favour, but because Aristotle in the fifth book of the 'Politics' recognises the nobility as existent, and defines it as resting on excellence and inherited wealth. To this Niccoli retorts that Aristotle gives this not as his own conviction, but as the popular impression; in his 'Ethics,' where he speaks as he thinks, he calls him noble who strives after that which is truly good. Lorenzo urges upon him vainly that the Greek word for nobility means good birth; Niccoli thinks the Roman word 'nobilis' (i.e. remarkable) a better one, since it makes nobility depend on a man's deeds. Together with these discussions, we find a sketch of the condition of the nobles in various parts of Italy. In Naples they will not work, and busy themselves neither with their own estates nor with trade and commerce, which they hold to be discreditable; they either loiter at home or ride about on horseback. The Roman nobility also despise trade, but farm their own property; the cultivation of the land even opens the way to a title; 'it is a respectable but boorish nobility.' In Lombardy the nobles live upon the rent of their inherited estates; descent and the abstinence from any regular calling constitute nobility. In Venice, the 'nobili,' the ruling caste, were all merchants. Similarly in Genoa the nobles and non-nobles were alike merchants and sailors, and only separated by their birth; some few of the former, it is true, still lurked as brigands in their mountain-castles. In Florence a part of the old nobility had devoted themselves to trade; another, and certainly by far the smaller part, enjoyed the satisfaction of their titles, and spent their time, either in nothing at all, or else in hunting and hawking.

The decisive fact was, that nearly everywhere in Italy, even those who might be disposed to pride themselves on their birth could not make good the claims against the power of culture and of wealth, and that their privileges in politics and at court were not sufficient to encourage any strong feeling of caste. Venice offers only an apparent exception to this rule, for there the 'nobili' led the same life as their fellow-citizens, and were distinguished by few honorary privileges. The case was certainly different at Naples, which the strict isolation and the ostentatious vanity of its nobility excluded, above all other causes, from the spiritual movement of the Renaissance. The traditions of medieval Lombardy and Normandy, and the French aristocratic influences which followed, all tended in this direction; and the Aragonese government, which was established by the middle of the fifteenth century, completed the work, and accomplished in Naples what followed a hundred years later in the rest of Italy—a social transformation in obedience to Spanish ideas, of which the chief features were the contempt for work and the passion for titles. The effect of this new influence was evident, even in the smaller towns, before the year 1500. We hear complaints from La Cava that the place had been proverbially rich, as long as it was filled with masons and weavers; whilst now, since instead of looms and trowels nothing but spurs, stirrups and gilded belts was to be seen, since everybody was trying to become Doctor of Laws or of Medicine, Notary, Officer or Knight, the most intolerable poverty prevailed. In Florence an analogous change appears to have taken place by the time of Cosimo, the first Grand Duke; he is thanked for adopting the young people, who now despise trade and commerce, as knights of his order of St. Stephen. This goes straight in the teeth of the good old Florentine custom, by which fathers left property to their children on the condi-

tion that they should have some occupation. But a mania for title of a curious and ludicrous sort sometimes crossed and thwarted, especially among the Florentines, the levelling influence of art and culture. This was the passion for knighthood, which became one of the most striking follies of the day, at a time when the dignity itself had lost every shadow of significance.

'A few years ago,' writes Franco Sacchetti, towards the end of the fourteenth century, 'everybody saw how all the work-people down to the bakers, how all the wool-carders, usurers, money-changers and blackguards of all descriptions, became knights. Why should an official need knighthood when he goes to preside over some little provincial town? What has this title to do with any ordinary bread-winning pursuit? How art thou sunken, unhappy dignity! Of all the long list of knightly duties, what single one do these knights of ours discharge? I wished to speak of these things that the reader might see that knighthood is dead. And as we have gone so far as to confer the honour upon dead men, why not upon figures of wood and stone, and why not upon an ox?' The stories which Sacchetti tells by way of illustration speak plainly enough. There we read how Bernabo Visconti knighted the victor in a drunken brawl, and then did the same derisively to the vanquished; how German knights with their decorated helmets and devices were ridiculed—and more of the same kind. At a later period Poggio makes merry over the many knights of his day without a horse and without military training. Those who wished to assert the privilege of the order, and ride out with lance and colours, found in Florence that they might have to face the government as well as the jokers. . . .

TWO

The Prince

The most notable feature of political power in Europe in the fourteenth century, on the eve of the Renaissance, was its fragmentation. Hundreds of individual nobles, princes, and city councils exercised authority over areas that ranged from a few acres to broad regions. Although monarchs claimed dominion over empires and kingdoms with substantial populations, such as England, they could exercise little effective control across large territories. It was essentially the locality that determined its own affairs, took whatever taxes were raised, and employed the few public officials who functioned in this period. Except for the Church, which was Europe's largest (though also locally run) institution, the chief consumer of funds was war, but even this activity was small scale and could be sustained only by soldiers whom local leaders drew from their dependents.

Between the mid-fifteenth and the late-seventeenth centuries, this situation changed in almost every respect. Rulers took control of ever-larger domains, accumulated vast hordes of officials, drove taxes relentlessly higher, and assembled massive armies. A new phenomenon, the territorial state, which previously had existed largely in name, became a reality for most of Europe's inhabitants. Few villages could live in isolation any longer or ignore the army recruiters and tax collectors of a distant government. And the new relationships were quickly justified by lawyers and theorists who treated the states and their rulers as divinely or naturally ordained. It was a breathtaking change, and at its heart lay the remarkable transformation in the ambitions, image, and capabilities of the prince.

THE ACCUMULATION OF POWER

In order to be able to exercise effective control over increasingly wider areas, a government had to subdue alternative sources of authority. The way this was done varied dramatically, as did the results. Indeed, the consequences of success or failure in this regard during the Renaissance and early modern period were to shape

Map 3. Europe in the reign of Charles V

the fate of different countries for centuries to come. Two rivals, above all, had to be swept aside, and this process was the engine of the princes' drive to dominate their realms.

The first and most conspicuous of these rivals was the Church. The Pope was an international figure who received the direct loyalty of tens of thousands of clerics. The clergy had their own hierarchy, their own taxes, and their own legal system.

What this independence created was a separate enclave in every society. The Church did not need the secular power for either its income or its law, because it raised money directly from its parishioners and had its own law courts. There was little, therefore, to encourage its members to feel any allegiance to the particular territory in which they lived or to accept the demands of its rulers. Quite the contrary, the clergy represented a distinct (and, in their view, higher) set of loyalties, which sometimes clashed directly with the interests of the prince. Popes had excommunicated kings, and kings, in turn, had had churchmen killed. No government could claim full control as long as so major an alternative to its authority had the adherence of its subjects.

In the course of the 1500s and 1600s, this problem was tackled, and essentially resolved, throughout Europe. In the North—in England, Scandinavia, much of Germany, Switzerland, and the Netherlands—the acceptance of the Protestant Reformation removed the Roman Church and put in its place religious institutions that were usually willing to abide by, and even endorse, the wishes of central governments. In regions that remained Catholic, the threat of conversion and the growing power of monarchs achieved much the same effect by around 1650. The Catholic kingdoms of France and Spain gained control over Church appointments and taxation, rejected papal interference in their affairs, and created a model of secular control that smaller territories copied. When, in 1648, the Pope condemned as contrary to Catholic interests the Treaties of Westphalia, which brought to an end thirty years of devastating warfare, his views had no effect. From then on, beliefs might shape individuals' attitudes and even inspire them to challenge their governments (see the chapter "The Dissenter"), but institutional churches were no longer serious rivals to secular authorities.

The second competitor, particularly for the rulers of large areas, was the locality, which inspired an allegiance and solidarity among its people that exceeded even what the Church aroused. This feeling was usually embodied by a lord and was much more difficult to subdue, especially since it was encouraged and protected by local leaders—often a great aristocratic family, though it could also be a city or even an institution, such as a regional assembly. What all these entities had in common, however, was a strong sense of their autonomy and of the inviolability of their customs, which they combined with a deep distrust of outsiders. Again, localities often had their own taxes and legal systems, and to their inhabitants, a king in some distant capital was no more real than a figure in a fairy tale.

The single most important political struggle of the period from around 1500 to around 1650 was the assault by ambitious governments on the traditional independence of the local region. Their basic goal—the power to impose their will throughout the territories they ruled—was finally achieved after bitter conflict and a remarkable series of revolts in the mid-1600s, but even then, not in all areas of Europe. Since the process was so distinct in each major area, it can best be understood if we examine the main examples of the different patterns it followed.

The first region where conscious consolidation took place and people recognized that independent states with strong central direction had emerged was in Italy, the source of so many of the changes of the Renaissance. By 1450, five regimes, each built around an important city, had come to dominate the peninsula. In the South, Naples was the capital of the one kingdom in Italy, and since the king of Aragon became its ruler in 1443, he had considerable resources—notably an army—for imposing his will on his subjects. Further north, the Popes, with their European-wide wealth, were able to build a tightly organized territory around Rome. And three major city-states, Venice, Florence, and Milan, carved up the rest of the country. Venice, an immensely wealthy republic, with possessions throughout the eastern Mediterranean, was run by a small set of patrician families who occupied all government and military positions. Florence, a wealthy banking and manufacturing city that controlled much of central Italy, was ostensibly a republic but was, in fact, dominated by a single family, the Medici. And Milan, a duchy, was openly ruled by a succession of dictatorial families. As these five states established themselves and pursued aggressive policies toward their neighbors, they were driven to create a more orderly way of dealing with each other. The result was a new structure of interstate communications—with permanent ambassadors, standardized diplomatic procedures and protocol, and formal means of resolving disputes—that was to spread throughout Europe and was to be the origin of the modern system of international relations. Its very appearance at this time, moreover, even among states as small as those in Italy, indicated how determinedly governments were organizing their territories into distinct and independent domains.

Of the large kingdoms of the late Middle Ages, England was the one that achieved this cohesiveness the earliest and was least troubled by regional autonomies. The reason went back to the reign of William the Conqueror. When he captured the entire country in the year 1066, he made sure that he kept significant amounts of land—the source of power—in all areas so that he could meet on equal terms any local lords who might seek to become what were called "overmighty subjects." To administer the realm, his successors created a system of cooperative government: In return for their support of the king's wishes, local leaders were given authority over the localities. What gradually emerged was an assembly, Parliament, that represented all these local interests. It had to approve major taxes and policies and thus served as a restraint on royal power, but on the other hand, it did give the central government the ability to enforce decisions throughout the country.

This ability was not enjoyed by the Spanish and French monarchs, rulers of Europe's two other major kingdoms. Spain was a confederation of separate territories, each of which defended its own traditions of independence. Local pride, upheld by powerful aristocrats, ensured that the royal government would have to keep up a constant struggle to impose its will on all areas of the country. In France, too, the conflict between center and regions was relentless. Here the king controlled directly only a small region around Paris and throughout the 1400s and 1500s fought with aristocrats and city leaders (and after 1550 with Protestants) to ensure that his authority was accepted throughout the kingdom.

Apart from the subjection of the Church, these kings had four prime means of extending their power. First, they had a monopoly on force. As a result of the revolution wrought by gunpowder, only central governments could afford the cannon, handguns, and ever-increasing numbers of troops that were essential to sixteenth- and seventeenth-century armies. Few rivals at home could compete with such power, and war against foreign enemies bolstered the princes yet further. Moreover, to pay the rapidly mounting costs of the military, governments raised taxes unrelentingly—thus providing themselves with the resources that were a

Map 4. States of Europe in 1660

Legend:
- Brandenburg-Prussia
- Spanish Habsburgs
- Austrian Habsburgs
- Boundary of the Holy Roman Empire

second source of their strength. These two, in fact, fed one another: War required more taxes, and a strong military helped ensure that taxes could be raised. Only in England—where Parliament restrained royal budgets and standing armies were never permitted except during the revolutionary years 1642 to 1660—was this vicious circle broken.

The third instrument of aggrandizement, however, was common to all Europe: the proliferation of officials. Governments in 1500 were relatively tiny, with rarely more than a few hundred servants. By 1700, every self-respecting state had thousands of bureaucrats, and in the larger kingdoms the numbers went into the tens of thousands. Bureaucrats were the means by which control was exercised and power was imposed. Finally, there was everywhere an imposition of standardized legal practices. Each country had its own system, but all were administered by professionals, whose implicit aim was to remove every hint of exceptionalism or local custom. Again, the center was asserting its uniform authority.

Since each of these shifts in the relationship between rulers and ruled threatened the authority of nobles and regional traditions, it was not surprising that the princes should have encountered growing resistance to their policies. Their wars overrode all other needs—even for manpower, goods, or food if an army marched through an area; their taxes ate away at what people could contribute to their lords or to the Church; their officials undermined familiar local authorities; and their laws replaced ancient customs. Eventually, the response turned violent, though it took different forms in different countries. In Spain revolts broke out in 1640 as the regions tried to topple the dominance of the central region, Castile. In France the nobility rebelled in 1648 and, drawing on local loyalties and religious passions, sought to hold back the central government. And in England a major revolution erupted in 1642 over the issues of religious tolerance and individual rights. The upheavals reached a climax in almost all parts of Europe during the 1640s and 1650s, causing civil wars and revolts from Portugal to Poland, from Naples to Scotland. This "general crisis" was resolved by the 1660s, when central governments emerged largely victorious. Although other challenges lay ahead, the notion of consolidated political power at the center was not seriously challenged by the localities again.

Yet it was only those states which had managed to create well-organized structures—in western Europe and in Sweden and the Netherlands—that emerged with new strength after 1660. In much of Germany, Italy, and eastern Europe, fragmentation continued, with political control remaining in the hands of local rulers. No central regime emerged—although Prussia was eventually to play that role in Germany—and the result was that these areas were often at the mercy of their formidable neighbors. Regardless of individual successes or failures, however, what was unmistakable by 1700 was that Europe was dominated by its monarchs. Their splendid courts and capitals dazzled all who saw them, and their armies and bureaucrats ensured that everyone felt, quite directly, the power of the prince. Even a few examples from these 300 years will indicate how, in practice, this massive transformation in the relations between ordinary people and their rulers came about.

SOME PRINCES

A prince who inherited authority might have all kinds of problems enforcing his wishes, but it was even more difficult to win such authority in the first place. This was something a number of rulers accomplished during the Renaissance, and we will see examples of the process at different periods. Already in the 1400s, however, the Medici family of Florence provided a famous example of such an ascent, accomplished not through military force—which was the only way of winning a principality that was familiar—but by more subtle means.

Figure 2. Benozzo Gozzoli, *Procession of the Three Kings to Bethlehem* (detail), Palazzo Medici–Riccardi, Florence. This enormous fresco in the Medici palace in Florence, completed in 1459, gives place of honor in the biblical scene of the procession of the Magi to the future ruler of Florence, the ten-year-old Lorenzo de Medici, riding a white horse, and to his grandfather Cosimo de Medici, the founder of the dynasty's power, who is behind Lorenzo, also on a white horse.

Cosimo and Lorenzo de Medici (1434–1492)

The founder of the dynasty's power was Cosimo de Medici, a rich banker who emerged in the 1430s out of a group of powerful families to become the real ruler of Florence, the chief city of Tuscany (Figure 2). He gained his ascendancy by careful use of his wealth and by threats of force, but also by keeping a low profile. As Vespasiano da Bisticci, a protegé of Cosimo's, put it:

> He knew the difficulty of ruling a state like Florence in the face of the opposition of influential citizens who had rated themselves his equals in former times. He acted privately with the greatest discretion in order to safeguard himself. Whenever he sought some end, he contrived to let it appear that it had been set in motion by someone else, so that he escaped envy and unpopularity. He never spoke ill of anyone; he always performed what he promised, and then let the petitioner know his wishes had been

granted. His replies were brief and sometimes obscure, so that they might bear a double meaning.

The shrewdness and determination were unmistakable; Cosimo was reputed to have said, "One cannot rule a city with prayers." Even his extensive art patronage and his building program were intended to be ways of winning gratitude and stamping the Medici name throughout Florence. When he died in 1464, the citizens, who appreciated his public works and the peace he brought, referred to him as "father of the fatherland."

Cosimo's grandson Lorenzo took control of the city in 1469. He was much more ostentatious not only in promoting great artistic programs but also in displaying his power. Consequently, Lorenzo did not avoid major plots against his rule, and shortly after his death in 1492, the family was expelled from Florence. In 1512 they returned, however, and soon, as Grand Dukes of Tuscany, they became princes of European stature, numbering among their descendants queens and kings of some of the greatest thrones of the age. It was a remarkable demonstration of the power that could be won by political shrewdness, artful patronage, and the clever manipulation of resources and popular feelings.

Henry VIII (1509–1547)

A very different path was followed by the man who became king of England just seventeen years after Lorenzo died, Henry VIII (Figure 3). He did not have to win his authority: It came to him by birth. But he felt a constant obligation to maintain it and, given the ambitions of the day, to expand it as well. Henry regularly assumed that he could master any problem; when a particularly difficult one arose, there-fore—the absence of a male heir who would ensure the continuation of the family on the throne—he accepted no restraint in pursuing his goal.

The result was an enormous increase in royal power. When the Pope would not allow him to divorce a wife who failed to produce a son, Henry removed England from the Roman Church. At the same time, he streamlined his government and used the vast profits from confiscations of Church lands to enlarge the body of officials who served him. To ensure that he had the country behind him, he summoned Parliament, gave it broad new responsibilities (which eventually would come to challenge the monarch's own authority), and had it pass legislation in 1534 to establish himself as head of an English national church:

> The King's majesty justly and rightly is the supreme head of the Church of England; yet nevertheless, for confirmation thereof, for increase of virtue in religion within this realm of England, and to repress all errors, heresies, and other abuses, be it enacted by the authority of Parliament that the King our sovereign lord shall be taken and reputed the only supreme head in earth of the Church of England.

This was precisely the kind of leap in power, the assertion of new jurisdiction, that was characteristic of the princes of the age. And even seemingly unrelated developments—in this case, the new religious ideas and structures created by the Reformation—could help the process of aggrandizement along.

· ANNO · ÆTATIS ·   · SVÆ · XLIX ·

Figure 3. Hans Holbein the Younger, *Henry VIII* (1540). This portrait of Henry VIII in 1540, toward the end of his reign, emphasizes the richness and massive presence of one of the increasingly powerful and assertive kings of the sixteenth century.

Charles V (1519–1556)

Henry VIII's contemporary, the Emperor Charles V, experienced the effects of the Reformation very differently. Ostensibly, he was the most powerful ruler in Europe. As Holy Roman Emperor, he was supposedly as supreme in the secular realm as the Pope was in the religious. In fact, however, the Emperor's political control had for centuries extended little beyond the German-speaking areas of central Europe. With Charles this changed, because he had already inherited the throne of Spain, its overseas empire, and territories in Italy and the Netherlands. Even a partial listing of his titles suggests that he was making real the position he held in theory:

> Holy Roman Emperor, King of the Romans, King of Spain, Sicily, Jerusalem, the Canary Islands, the Indies, and the mainland on the far side of the Atlantic, Archduke of Austria, Duke of Burgundy, Brabant, Styria, Luxemburg, Athens, and Patras, Count of Habsburg, Flanders, and Tyrol, Landgrave of Alsace, Count of Swabia, Lord of Asia and Africa.

The truth was that his effective rule extended to parts of central Europe and the possessions of Spain, but even in these areas he had a constant struggle to sustain his position.

Charles was almost perpetually on the move, traveling from domain to domain in order to assert his authority (Figure 4), but he simply did not have the communication network, the officials, the taxes, or the army to enforce his policies. He was often at war with his neighbors, notably the king of France and the Turkish sultan, and in his own territories he had to face the revolt of Protestant princes who were trying to break away from the Roman Church he felt obliged to defend. Religious conflict was the final straw for the overburdened Emperor, who at the end of his reign had to grant toleration to Germany's Lutherans and a large measure of independence to their princes. He abdicated in 1556 and divided his realm: The title of Emperor and the central European lands went to his brother; the rest went to his son Philip. The day of the cohesive territorial state was emerging, and after Charles's reign, the notion of a single government ruling such a multitude of diverse peoples no longer made sense.

Elizabeth I (1558–1603)

The new sense of distinct political boundaries was perfectly embodied by the ruler of England in the next generation, Elizabeth I. She did not begin her reign with anything like the legitimacy of other monarchs. Her mother had been the new queen after Henry VIII had divorced his first wife, and, therefore, she was considered a bastard by those who regarded the divorce as invalid without papal approval. Moreover, the monarch she succeeded, Mary I (the daughter of that first wife), was a fervent Catholic who tried to overturn the religious reform Henry had started. With many of her subjects thus doubting her right to govern and confused by the changes in religion, Elizabeth set about identifying herself with the interests of England by stirring up patriotic feelings, committing the country irrevocably to Protestantism, and conducting a masterful propaganda campaign to win affection and respect.

Elizabeth was one of the great wizards of public relations in history. She carefully regulated all portraits of herself (Figure 5), she was highly effective at gauging the attitude of a Parliament and then sweet-talking the members into agreement, and she took long trips through the countryside, known as "progresses," so that ordinary people could see her and even hear her whenever she stopped—as she often did— to receive a welcome from a small town or village. For all its danger, even the attempted invasion of the country by the Spanish Armada in 1588 was turned to advantage, for the victory made Elizabeth a heroine, and the speech she gave her troops became famous:

Figure 4. Titian, *Charles V at the Battle of Mühlberg* (1548). Because a statue of an ancient Roman emperor showed him in this pose, it was thought in the Renaissance that a ruler appeared at his most magnificent on a horse, and in full armor. Equestrian sculptures appeared in the fifteenth century, but this 1548 portrait is the first such painting. Titian created a heroic Charles V, even though the emperor had not been present at the military victory of the previous year which the picture celebrates.

Figure 5. *The "Ermine" Portrait of Elizabeth I,* artist unknown. So conscious was Elizabeth I of her image that it was forbidden to produce a picture of the queen unless it met certain requirements of accuracy and magnificence. This picture, in dazzling clothes and jewels, and with the sword of authority at her side, easily met the requirements.

My loving people, we have been persuaded by some to take heed for fear of treachery. But I assure you I do not desire to live to distrust my faithful and loving people. Let tyrants fear. I have placed my chiefest strength in the loyal hearts of my subjects. Therefore I am come to live or die amongst you all. I know I have the body of a weak and feeble woman, but I have the heart and stomach of a king, and a king of England too, and think foul scorn that Spain should dare to invade the borders of my realm. To which I myself will take up arms, I myself will be your general, judge, and rewarder.

Better than any of her contemporaries, Elizabeth understood how essential public perceptions could be in bolstering the power of a prince. Because she cultivated her image so brilliantly, she became a legend to her people for centuries to come.

Figure 6. Alonso Sanchez Coello, *Portrait of Philip II*. In contrast to Henry VIII or Elizabeth I, Philip II liked to emphasize his simplicity and austerity. He is holding a rosary, symbol of his devout adherence to the Catholic faith.

Philip II (1556–1598)

Elizabeth's chief nemesis, the monarch who sent the Armada against her, was Charles V's son, Philip (Figure 6). He inherited the wealthiest and most powerful collection of territories of his age, for he was ruler of Spain, much of Italy, the Netherlands, and rich lands in America and Asia. But the very extent of his possessions was his chief problem. At a time when it could take over a year to get a message to Peru and a reply back to Spain, the question of the prince's control over his subjects was often academic. Even within the Iberian peninsula there were distinct regions with proud traditions of independence. Somehow, the central government had to circumvent these local allegiances and find a way to enforce its views throughout its far-flung domains.

Philip's solution was to hire as many officials as possible and place the administration of his many realms in their hands. In essence, he bureaucratized Spain. For all the difficulties of such an approach—above all, the endless delays caused by elaborate procedures and the need to obtain Philip's approval whenever a major decision was made—it did at least ensure that the monarch had the means to impose his wishes on all his subjects. That he isolated himself in a huge palace near Madrid and often made terrible mistakes (including the Armada) did not detract from the enormous power he wielded and the fear he aroused in all of Europe. He had the best army of the day and more money and officials than any other ruler. His bureaucratic system, in particular, became a much-imitated model for princes who sought to control a large territory.

Catherine de Medici (1547–1589)

The daughter of the Medici family who became queen of France in 1547, and to all intents and purposes the ruler of her adopted land as queen mother after she became a widow in 1559, had few of the successes of her contemporary princes (Figure 7). Her experiences demonstrated how tenuous the growing power of central governments still was in the late-sixteenth century. The brave hopes she expressed to her daughter about dealing with factions that resisted royal rule were in fact little more than hopes:

> Although the Admiral [a great noble] remains at Court, he will be here as if he were dead, because I shall not let myself be governed either by one party or the other, having learned only too well that they all love God, the King, and your mother less than their own profit, their own greatness, and the satisfaction of their own ambitions. Since they know I will not let them ruin the King and the kingdom, they love me only in words, knowing that my only aim is to preserve the King, the kingdom, and his brothers. Therefore I trust no one.

Unfortunately for Catherine, most of the last thirty years of her life were a time of terrible civil war, which pitted the greatest noble families of France against each other and Protestants against Catholics. Because the country was in such chaos, Catherine never had the resources or the soldiers to confront the warring parties, and she therefore had no choice but to trust one or another of them at various times if she was to have any say at all. Even her constant efforts to bring about a reconciliation, which might have helped restore royal authority, were in vain. The situation she endured was a classic example of the centrifugal forces, the threat of fragmentation, that every prince feared. Only weariness, and the victory of one of the factions, enabled order and the power of the central government to be restored in France in the 1590s.

Oliver Cromwell (1649–1658)

It may seem strange to include the greatest revolutionary of the age in this roster of princes, and yet a prince is what he was. Until the 1640s, Cromwell seemed to be no

Figure 7. Jean Clouet, *Portrait of Catherine de Medici*. Throughout her thirty years as Queen Mother of France, Catherine remained a widow, and in all her portraits she was dressed in black. The gravity and dignity she conveyed did not conceal the effects of her troubled life.

more than a prominent landowner from the east of England, educated at Cambridge, and a devout Puritan, that is, an extreme Protestant who believed that the Church of England had kept too much of the ceremony and hierarchy of the Catholics. As he watched the power of England's kings grow in the 1620s and

Figure 8. *The Execution of Charles I* (engraving). This Dutch engraving, which appeared soon after the event, is a remarkably accurate record of Charles I's execution in 1649. A scaffold was built in front of the Banqueting House in London (which is there to this day), Charles came through one of the windows, and he was decapitated as a huge crowd watched. The dripping head was then raised for all to see (on the right of the platform).

1630s—especially their neglect of Parliament and the traditional individual rights (such as freedom from arbitrary arrest) that it represented and their attempts to enforce loyalty to the Church of England—he, like many of his countrymen, grew increasingly dismayed. Eventually, in 1642, a civil war erupted between Parliament and king, the most violent and prolonged of the many efforts around Europe in the 1640s and 1650s to roll back the powers princes had accumulated over the previous 150 years. Revolts in Portugal, Spain, Italy, France, Germany, and Poland and confrontations in the Netherlands, Denmark, and Sweden reflected the widespread unhappiness at the rise in taxation, the growth of armies, and the crushing of long-standing local customs.

Nowhere, however, was the struggle so bitter as in England. Thousands died, and in 1649 the victorious parliamentarians executed the king (Figure 8). Cromwell, the commander of their army, now became the ruler of the land and remained so until his death in 1658. A man of high principle, he hoped that all the causes he had fought for—the liberty of the individual, religious toleration, the supremacy of Parliament as the representative of the people, the return of political decision making to the localities, and the shrinking of the central government—would now be victorious. His tragedy was that under constant pressure from royalists at home and abroad who hoped to overturn the revolution and a multitude of rivals and critics among the parliamentarians, he was forced to keep tight control over the country through his army. As his grip tightened, Parliament assumed he ought to become king himself, but his hopes for his regime had been very different:

I am ready to serve, not as a King, but as a Constable. I have thought often that I could not tell what my business was, save by comparing myself to a good Constable, keeping the peace of the parish. God has so dealt with Kings that he blasted the title. I will not set up what Providence has destroyed and laid in the dust. I will not build Jericho again.

Ironically, the great enemy of central government found himself adopting its methods, and even taking them to excess, once he had to defend his own policies. Cromwell's revolution did, in the long run, secure important individual rights and place restraints on the English monarchy when it returned in 1660. Yet his failure to slow the growth of the powers that had been accumulating for over a century indicated how irreversible the process had become and how fruitless it was to try to return to an older, more diffuse political system.

Louis XIV (1643–1715)

The climax of this process was reached in the reign of Louis XIV of France, especially after he took control of his government in 1661 following a regency and the death of the minister who was his chief mentor. His administration of the realm brought to new heights all the techniques that had been developed since the days of Cosimo de Medici. Louis had higher taxes, more bureaucrats, and a larger army than had ever been seen. His propaganda was a triumph of the art: He filled his palace at Versailles with a constant round of ceremonies glorifying himself, and he made sure that his image, as Apollo god of the sun, was inescapable, whether on buildings or on coins (Figure 9). For Louis it was no fiction to say that *"L'Etat, c'est moi"*—"I am the state"—because he could see no distinction between the kingdom and himself or accept any limitation on his authority. Law emanated from him, as did the regulation of all aspects of French life, from culture to the economy. As he told his son:

> The interests of the Prince and those of the people are one. The tranquility of subjects depends only on their obedience: less harm results to the public if it bears rule with submission than if it finds fault with even bad government by Kings, whom God alone can judge. What they seem to be doing in opposition to law is more often based on reasons of State, which form the first of all laws, but are the least understood by all who do not govern.

In other words, Louis always knew best. It was no wonder that when he defined his role, he resorted to the most grandiose terms:

> This thought should govern you, as you govern others: this is how God would act. This thought should awaken you each morning: today I have to play the part of God. This question should end your day: today, have I been God or Man?

Unfortunately for Louis, reality did not always cooperate. He often had his way, both at home and when he intimidated his neighbors during the 1660s and 1670s, the early years of his direct rule. But foreign affairs turned sour in the 1680s, and soon resistance, unrest, and economic difficulties revealed the limits of his dominance at home. Regardless of the image of absolute power that he cultivated, he needed the cooperation of nobles and local areas to make his government work, and he had to treat his bureaucrats with great care. However far central governments

Figure 9. Hyacinthe Rigaud, *Portrait of Louis XIV*. By 1701, when this portrait was painted, the glorification of a monarch was achieved by creating a scene of almost unbelievable magnificence. The rich hangings and the cloak covered in the symbol of France (the *fleur de lys*) are so extraordinary that they almost distract us from the person of the king himself.

had come since 1400 and however futile efforts to roll back their powers were, they still had a long way to go before it was possible to create the fearsome regimes that have become familiar in the twentieth century. Yet the changes in theories about the nature of power that appeared in this period suggest how profound had been the transformation in politics that the princes had brought about.

POLITICAL THEORY

Of the many observers who tried to understand the new power of governments, four theorists in particular can be taken to embody the revolution in the way people conceived of politics and the role of the prince: Machiavelli, Bodin, Hobbes, and Locke.

Niccolo Machiavelli lived through Lorenzo de Medici's last years and then served as a diplomat for the republican government that replaced the Medici in 1494. When the Medici family returned to power with foreign help in 1512, Machiavelli was arrested, tortured, and sent into exile. Bitter and unhappy, especially about the collapse of Italian states in the face of French and Spanish armies, he wrote in a few weeks a short work, *The Prince*, which shattered traditional illusions about the way power works. Casting aside the morality and religious concerns that had justified rulers in the past, he argued that ruthlessness, cunning, and determination were the keys to winning and retaining political power.

In a famous passage, he analyzed in a new way how the relationship between prince and subjects should be manipulated:

> It has been asked, whether it is better to be loved than feared. If it is necessary to choose, then it is safer to be feared than loved. Mankind in general is ungrateful, fickle, timid, untrustworthy, and self-interested. If you can serve them, they are devoted to you; but in the day of need they turn their back on you. Men are more inclined to submit to someone who is dreaded than to one who tries to be loved. But a prince ought at least to avoid the hatred of his subjects, which he can do by respecting their property and the honor of their wives. Men sooner forget the death of their relations than the loss of their inheritance.

This was a chilling look at the sources of success in politics, and although it was denounced by most critics, *The Prince* became one of the most influential books in history—a remarkable testimony to the growing aggressiveness of the princes of the age.

Over fifty years later, the Frenchman Jean Bodin looked at the issues in a broader context. He had lived through more than a decade of the civil wars that Catherine de Medici had been unable to suppress, and he had witnessed massacres and chaos. What he tried to do, in a work entitled *Six Books of the Commonwealth* that he published in 1576, was to step back and figure out how, in theory, the territorial states of Europe operated. Even if a particular government, such as France's, failed to keep order, there had to be an underlying structure that explained why authority had grown as it had and why it was accepted. His hope, clearly, was that if he could explain the principles by which a prince ruled, it might be possible to see how stability could be restored to his troubled realm.

The heart of the political system, said Bodin, was a quality called "sovereignty," which he defined fully for the first time. Sovereign power was absolute and perpetual, and although it had to observe divine commands and the sanctity of property, it seemed essentially unrestrained. And yet there were limits:

> The prince is not subject even to his own laws, or to those of his predecessors. But he is bound by the just and reasonable obligations which concern the interests of his subjects individually or collectively.

Thus, although a tyrant could be a true sovereign, government had a moral basis:

> If justice is the end of law, law the work of the prince, and the prince the image of God, it follows that the law of the prince should be modelled on the law of God.

The trouble was that once such issues of principles were raised, they could cut both ways. Against order one could cite freedom; against authority there arose ethical considerations. Bodin's own preference, given the situation of France, was to come down on the side of the sovereign, but his searching analysis of the theoretical basis for the power of Europe's newly aggressive governments raised issues that were to be argued for centuries.

As the conflict between obedience and liberty intensified during the English civil war, one theorist, Thomas Hobbes, came up with a new understanding of the roots of political power. His purpose was to solve the major problem raised by the execution of the king—What is the source of the legitimacy of a political regime? Hobbes published his book, *Leviathan,* in 1651, just two years after Charles I was executed, and he laid out perhaps the most comprehensive justification for the unlimited power of government ever written (Figure 10). The Leviathan was a

Figure 10. Thomas Hobbes, *Leviathan* (1651), frontispiece. The title page of Hobbes's book, published in 1651, foretells its contents. The huge Leviathan, the sovereign's body, dominating the land, is made up of the tiny people who are his subjects. On the left are the symbols of war and power, and on the right the church and mitre indicate his control over spiritual life.

gigantic and irresistible mythical beast, and this was essentially how Hobbes regarded political authority. It was completely free of restrictions, and its subjects' alternatives were to obey or to leave—the only right the individual retained was the protection of life.

The reason for this stern assessment was that Hobbes viewed human beings as innately competitive and aggressive. Left alone in a natural state—before government was established—they fought constantly, and as a result, the state of nature, according to Hobbes, was a state of war:

> Every man is enemy to every man. In such condition, there is no place for industry, because the fruit thereof is uncertain, and consequently no culture of the earth, no navigation, no building, no knowledge of the earth, no account of time, no arts, no letters, no society; worst of all, continual fear and danger of death, and the life of man, solitary, poor, nasty, brutish and short.

Anything was better than this. Hence there was a need to give government total and absolute power and to insist that all citizens were obliged (by an implicit agreement that united all of them) to submit themselves to the sovereign for their own self-preservation. For Hobbes, this was the only solution in a world filled with revolt, upheaval, and the dangers of chaos, but in his quest for order he laid out a vision of complete dominance that not only reflected the rise of the Renaissance prince but also has given food for thought ever since.

Yet this was not the only possible reaction to the growing power and assertiveness of political leaders. A Louis XIV might seem, at times, to embody Hobbes's Leviathan, but across the Channel, in England, Cromwell's revolution had established important individual rights and had put significant restraints on the monarch. This seemed to be the other side—the stress on freedom—of Bodin's equation, and in the generation after Hobbes, an Oxford professor, John Locke, used this perspective to fashion a new way of understanding the role of government in society.

Locke began with Hobbes's state of nature, but in his view, human beings created political structures not just out of fear, but because of their ability to reason. Accordingly, they retained important individual rights—not only life, but also liberty and property—that the ruler could not arbitrarily remove. Government had to maintain order, but it had to do so justly and reasonably. As he put it in his principal work, *The Second Treatise of Civil Government*, published in 1690:

> Though men, when they enter into society, give up the equality, liberty, and power they had in the state of nature, into the hands of society; yet it being only with an intention in every one to preserve himself, his liberty and property, the power of society can never extend farther than the common good, but is obliged to secure every one's property. So whoever has the supreme power is bound to govern by establishing laws, and not by decrees; by upright judges; and to employ force only in the execution of such laws. And all this to be directed to no other end, but the peace, safety, and public good of the people.

What Locke laid out was a liberal vision that has inspired political reformers down to our own time. Looking back at the spectacular results of the rise of the prince, he acknowledged that strong centralized regimes were probably here to stay, but this did not mean, in his view, that individuals had to abandon all rights to them. Instead, he put forward an ideal of good government that remains one of the goals of every society and is one of our most important inheritances from Renaissance and early modern times.

Original Sources

The Renaissance witnessed vast changes in political structure and the exercise of power, as well as in the prerogatives of individual rulers—queens and kings, princesses and princes, duchesses and dukes—and their ministers. During the early Italian Renaissance, around 1400, the political fragmentation of the Middle Ages still prevailed. Nonetheless, Italian rulers gradually consolidated their power over principalities and tiny kingdoms in a much more personal and widesweeping fashion than had medieval monarchs.

By the end of the seventeenth century, rulers north of the Alps had built increasingly large kingdoms, often with a small army of bureaucrats to support them and maintain their authority. Those over whom they ruled did, however, have some say in the matter. In fact, the delicate balance between the rights of ruler and ruled was a constant issue in Renaissance and early modern politics. Indeed, the changes in political philosophy—the rationale for political authority—that had occurred by 1700 remain influential to this day.

I. THE MEDIEVAL POLITICAL LEGACY

The key difference between the Middle Ages and the Renaissance in political terms—apart from the fragmentation that has already been mentioned—was the relative importance of religion. The political and religious structure operated side by side, and religious beliefs buttressed the political system. Although a few crises in the Middle Ages threatened this ideal, for the most part it was accepted and institutionalized in many aspects of the medieval political framework.

Selection 1
The Coronation of Charles the Bald

This selection describes the coronation of Charles the Bald in 869 in what would be France today. It clearly reveals the early medieval merger of secular and spiritual elements that gave the king his real authority.

THE CORONATION OF CHARLES II IN THE REIGN OF HLOTHAR II

Blessings said over King Charles before Mass and at the altar of Saint Stephen

Adventius, Bishop of Metz: O God, You Who care for Your people with indulgence and rule them with love, grant to this man, Your servant, the spirit of knowledge, to whom You have given the rule of discipline so that so that he, devoted with his whole heart to You, in governing the kingdom may remain always suitable and persevering in good works, may with Your guidance, attain the eternal kingdom. Through the Lord, etc.

Hatto of Verdun: We ask, Lord, that you grant to this Your servant Your generosity, so that in following Your commandments with Your help he may attain the consolation of the present and future life. Through the Lord, etc.

Arnulf of Toul: We seek, Lord, that you be favorable to our times under the rule of Your

Source: "The Coronation of Charles the Bald," from the "Ordo Coronationis Karoli II" in "Regno Hlotharii II Factae," *Capitularia Regum Francorum*, ed. by A. Boretius (Monumenta Germaniae Historica, Legum Sectio II, Vol. II, Hanover, 1890), pp. 456–458. Trans. by A. Keaney.

servant, so that with Your help both our security and Christian devotion will be administered. Through the Lord, etc.

Franco of Tongern: Lord, grant, we beseech You, to this Your servant health of mind and body so that by adhering to good works he will always deserve to be defended by Your power. Through the Lord, etc.

Hincmar of Lardun: May this Your servant, Lord, accept Your blessing, saved by which in body and mind he would display grace and grateful servitude to You always and may be always find the benefits of Your favor. Through the Lord, etc.

Odo of Beauvais: Save, we beseech You, Lord, this Your servant and purify him mercifully with the abundance of Your blessings, so that he will always grow with Your teachings and gifts. Through the Lord, etc.

The blessing of Archbishop Hincmar: May the all-powerful Lord stretch out the right hand of His blessing and pour out over you the gift of His mercy and surround you with a happy wall in the custody of His protection, through the intercession of the merits of holy Mary and all the saints. Amen.

May He forgive you all the bad which you have committed, and give you grace and mercy, which you humbly ask from him; and may he free you from all adversities and from all plots of enemies, seen and unseen. Amen.

May He position His good angels, always and everywhere to precede, accompany and follow you; may He by His power free you from sin or the sword or the risk of all dangers. Amen.

May he convert your enemies to the kindness of peace and charity, and toward those who hated you may He make you gracious and loving. Also, may He cover those eager for revolt and hate against you with a healing confusion. Moreover, may eternal sanctification flower over you. Amen.

At the words: "May the Lord crown you," Hincmar the archbishop anointed him with chrism on the right earlobe and on the forehead and up to the left earlobe and on the head.

May the Lord crown you with the crown of glory in mercy and His acts of compassion and anoint you in the ruling of the kingdom with the oil of the grace of His Holy Spirit, with which he had

anointed priests, kings, prophets and martyrs, who through faith have defeated kingdoms and worked justice and gained the promises; may you by the grace of God be made worthy of the same promises until you deserve to enjoy the assembly of those in the heavenly kingdom. Amen.

May He make you forever victorious and triumphant over enemies, seen and unseen; and may He pour equally the fear and love of His Holy Name continuously in your heart; and in correct Faith and good works may He make you persevere; and giving you peace in your day, may he lead you to the heavenly kingdom. Amen.

And He who has wished to set you as ruler over His people, may he grant that you be happy in the present age and the partaker of eternal happiness. Amen.

May he allow you to govern happily the clergy and the people, whom he wished to be under your word, that with His dispensation to be under your authority; for a long time; so that, obeying divine warnings parents, lacking all adversities, being joyful in all good circumstances, be obedient to your office in faithful love, both benefitting quietly in this age of peace and with you deserve to achieve the inheritance of the eternal citizens. Amen. May he deign to grant them.

At the words "May The Lord crown you," the bishops place the crown on his head.

May the lord crown you with the crown of glory and justice, so that with right faith and the multiple fruit of good works you attain the crown of the eternal kingdom through his generosity, whose is the kingdom and power forever.

At the words "May the Lord give you the will," they gave him the palm and scepter.

May the Lord give you the will and the power to do as He commands, so that in ruling the kingdom following His will, going ahead with the palm of persistent victory until you attain the palm of eternal glory, with the grace of Our Lord Jesus Christ, Who lives . . .

Prayers in the Mass: Grant to us, all-powerful God, that the venerable solemnity of Your martyr, blessed Gorgonius, may increase both devotion and salvation in us. Through the Lord . . .

We beseech, Almighty God, that your servant who with your mercy has taken the rule of the kingdom, that he may attain from You further increments of virtues, adorned with which he may avoid the monsters of vice and may he in grace come to You, Who are "The Way, the truth and life," Who lives and rules with God.

Offertory: Behold, Lord, the gifts of Your people with the votive festivity of Your saints, and may the profession of your truth lead to our salvation. Through the Lord . . .

We seek, Lord, the gift of holy offerings that the body and blood of Your only-begotten Son exist for us and help Charles our king to obtain the salvation of soul and body through Your generosity. Through the same One . . .

After Communion: May the communion received of your sacraments save and strengthen us in the light of Your truth. Through the Lord . . .

May this communion of salvation, Lord, save Your servant from all difficulties that he may obtain the tranquility of ecclesiastical peace and after the span of this time may he achieve his eternal inheritance. Through the Lord . . .

Selection 2
Frederick Barbarossa's Constitution Concerning Fiefs

Centuries after Charles the Bald's coronation, the German Emperor Frederick I (Barbarossa) sought to strengthen his power somewhat differently. He interpreted the obligations owed him by his subjects in terms of an older Roman conception of imperial rule and a medieval, feudal notion of kingship. Although religion is not as explicit as it was in the earlier selection, vassals held their lands as a result of an act of homage that was founded on religious obedience and faith. Thus much of the underpinning of the political system continued to be implicitly religious.

Frederick, by the grace of God, Roman Emperor and eternal Augustus, to the subjects of the Empire:

1. It befits the wisdom of the Emperor so to concern himself with the care of the State and the good of his subjects that the effectiveness of the kingdom remain uncorrupted and the status of individuals remain unharmed. Wherefore, while sitting in judgment at Roncaglia according to the custom of our predecessors, we have received from Italian princes—rectors of churches as well as other faithful subjects—not a few complaints, to the effect that the benefices and fiefs which their vassals held from them have been, without permission of their masters, mortgaged, sold and by some legal trickery otherwise disposed of: as a result, they were losing services due them, and the honor of the empire and the full effect of our military expedition was being lessened.

2. Therefore, having held a council of bishops, dukes, margarves and counts, as well as Palatine judges and other nobles, God favoring, by this edict we make it a matter of law, of permanent validity, that no one may sell, in whole or in part, his fief, or mortgage or on any way alienate same or endow it for charity without permission of the superior lord to whom the fief is known to pertain. This is why the emperor Lothar, concerned only with the future, promulgated a law against these practices.

3. We, however, looking to the larger effectiveness of the kingdom not only in the future but with reference to illegal alienations of this kind perpetrated before up to this time, we declare them null and void by this binding law: without

Source: "Frederick Barbarossa's Constitution Concerning Fiefs," from "Constitutio de Iure Feudorum," *Constitutiones et Acta Publica imperatorum et regum,* ed. L. Weiland (Monumenta Germaniae Historica, Legum Sectio IV, Hanover, 1893), pp. 247–249. Trans. by Anna Keaney.

consideration of the period of time involved, a person who bought in good faith may bring suit against the seller for the price. To prevent the clever machinations of certain men, who, acting under the guise of an investiture which they claim is legal for them, sell fiefs or transfer them to others, lest such a fictitious practice or anything else be thought up to defraud this enactment, we totally forbid it: with the complete authority that is ours [we enact] that buyer and seller alike, who are discovered to have made such illegal deals, are to lose the fief and that this is to return to the lord without payment. Further, the scribe who knowingly writes up an instrument for this kind of dealing, after the loss of his office with danger of infamy, is to have his hand cut off.

4. Further, if anyone over fourteen years of age without a fief, through carelessness or neglect, goes for a year and a day without seeking an investiture of the fief from his own lord, he should lose the fief after this time has passed and it should return to the lord.

5. We firmly declare that, when a military expedition has been publicly declared in Italy as well as in Germany, whoever summoned to this expedition by his lord rashly neglects to come or fails to send a substitute suitable to his lord or who does not supply half the annual income from his fief to his lord, he is to lose the fief he has from a bishop or from another lord, and the lord of the fief is to have the power to manage it for his own purposes in every way.

6. Further, a duchy, march or country is not be divided from now on. However, if those who share it want, another fief may be divided, so that all who have part of the fief, now divided or about to be divided, swear fealty to the lord. This, however, in such a way that a vassal may not be compelled to have a number of lord for one fief, nor may a lord transfer the fief to another against the will of his vassals.

7. Further, if the son of a vassal should offend against a lord, his father, when required by the lord, should bring the son to give satisfaction to the lord, or separate himself from the son: otherwise, he is to be deorived of his fief. But if the father is willing to bring to son for satisfaction and the son refuses, on the death of the father the son is not to succeed to the fief, unless he has previously made satisfaction to the lord. And let a vassal do likewise for all in his household.

8. This also we instruct that, if a vassal should have another vassal from his fief and that vassal offends against his lord's lord, unless he did so in the service of another lord whom he legally had previously, he is to be deprived of his fief, and it is to go to the lord from whom he had it, unless, being summoned, he is prepared to make satisfaction to the superior lord whom he offended, and unless the vassal and the same lord, summoned by his lord, requires him who offended the superior lord to make satisfaction, he is to lose his fief.

9. Further, if there is a quarrel about a fief between two vassals, let the decision be the lord's and let the quarrel be concluded through him. If a dispute should arise between a lord and a vassal, let it be concluded by the peers of the court who have duly sworn an oath of fealty.

10. This also we declare binding, that in every oath of fealty, the name of the emperor be included.

II. RENAISSANCE RULERS: IMAGE AND REALITY

There are no easy generalizations about Renaissance rulers, since their power was in many instances the result of an accident of birth. However, rulers could make much or little of what they had, and the differences were often due to talent, regional or national circumstances, and the specific events that might support or undermine their policies. Throughout, the balance between ruler and ruled was crucial.

Selection 3
A Contemporary View of Federigo, Duke of Urbino

Federigo, Duke of Urbino (1422–1482), was one of the best-loved rulers of Renaissance Italy. Not only was he considered by his contemporaries to be a wise and just ruler, but he embodied many of the personal virtues that they held dear. The Duke was a patron of the arts and letters, for example, and an extremely learned man in his own right. This excerpt from the *Memoirs* of a prominent citizen of Florence, Vespasiano da Bisticci, reveals how those traits were exemplified by Federigo's actions.

. . . Up to this point, I have spoken of [the duke's] deeds of arms, then of his literary works in conjunction with them, since to wish to produce a man excelling in military matters without letters, one cannot possess that skill which his lordship had, without having joined one with the other. Coming now to the third contingency joined to these two— this is to know how to govern states and principalities—rarely found are men with all these qualities which were in him. His era witnessed no equal in governing one's subjects and one's house. First, in order that his rule be joined to religion, he was most religious and most observant of the divine precepts, since his rule could not endure without religion and without offering good examples from his own life. There was never a morning in which he did not hear mass on his knees. He fasted on all the holy days commanded by the Church and all the days of Lent. The year before he died, Signor Ottaviano, loving him as he did, thinking that Lent would be burdensome, gained a dispensation from the papal court so as for him [the Duke] not to observe Lent. One morning during Lent, while he was at table, this dispensation was presented to him. He turned to Signor Ottaviano and began to laugh and said that he thanked him: again he turned to him and said: "If I can do it and I can fast, what's the reason you don't want me to? What kind of example would I give to my people, if I don't fast?" And he proceeded to observe fasting, as he had done up to that day. And every morning, with all his household and those

people of the town who wanted to come, he listened to the preaching; afterwards, he attended mass. Every morning, while fasting, he had read to him some sacred book, or the sermons of Pope Leo, or other sacred works. Always, when there came a noteworthy passage, he made the reader stop, wishing to understand it properly, and every day he made Master Lazzaro read a passage from Holy Scripture.

Having spoken of the way he governed his household, let us speak of his subjects. He treated them with such humanity that they seemed not subjects, but his children. He did not want anyone to speak to his Lordship [himself] for any one of his subjects, because at any hour of the day they could speak to him themselves. He would listen to all with the greatest humanity, to all he responded alike and he was in no way bored. If there were matters he could facilitate for them, he did it without anyone having to come back to him, and there not many whose business he could not look to the day they came, so that they wouldn't lose time. And when he saw someone who wished to speak with him but was reluctant, he had him called forward and gave him the confidence to say what he needed. He was so humane toward his subjects that they so loved him that, when he passed through Urbino, they knelt on the ground, men and women, and said: "God preserve you, milord." He went often through the town on foot. Coming upon a shop of one or another artisan, he asked how they were doing and if they needed anything, with such kindness that all loved him, no differently from the way his sons love their father. It was unbelievable to see the way he ruled his domain. All his subjects were well-off and enjoyed

Source: Da Vespasiano da Bisticci, *Vite di Uomini Illustri del Secolo XV,* ed. by Da Ludovico Frati (Bologna: Romagnoli-Dall'Acqua, 1893), pp. 302–304, 307–315, 317–320. Trans. by A. Keaney.

good profits in the works he had created for them. In that part of his territory no one was obliged to beg. If it happened that through some unpleasantness, or through not observing the statutes or the laws someone was condemned, he would go to the magistrate for clemency. The Duke was merciful toward all offences save one: this was blasphemy toward God or the Virgin Mary or the saints. For a blasphemer he wished neither clemency nor mercy.

His unparalleled humanity was displayed not only to his townspeople but to all. Once I saw him on market-day go to the square and ask the men and women what they wanted for the things which they had to sell: then he turned and said, jokingly: "I am the Signore and I don't carry money: I know that you won't believe me and fear that I won't pay you." And thus his humanity pleased everybody, old and young. Peasants went away so happy and satisfied at having conversed with the lord that he could have treated them however he wanted. When he was riding, he found no one on the road who did not greet him and ask how he was. He travelled sometimes with few, sometimes with many: none of his group carried weapons. In summer, he rode at dawn, when he was in Urbino, with four or six horses, and no more, and one or two servants at stirrup, unarmed, and he went three or four miles outside of town and returned and then went into a garden with all its entrances open. When mass was concluded, he gave an audience to anyone who wished it until it was time for breakfast. At table, all the doors were open and anyone could approach him: he never ate unless the room was full. Depending on the time of year, there were readings, as was said: in Lent, spiritual matters; at other times, the *Histories* of Livy: everything was in Latin. His food was plain: he didn't eat sweets, and abstained from wines, except those made from pomegranates or fruit, like cherries or apples. Whoever wanted to speak with him, after or while eating, could. When he finished eating, he had an appeal-judge, a most excellent man, who brought before him, in Latin, the cases he had, case by case. The duke decreed, and spoke in Latin. The judge told me that the decisions of the duke in those cases were such that

neither Bartolo nor Baldo would have decided them differently. There were letters of recommendations brought to him and he went along with what was in them. One day I saw a letter for a doctor who wanted a letter of recommendation to the people of Ancona. He said: "Put in this clause: if they need a doctor, let them take him: and if they don't need one, let them do whatever seems good: I don't want them to do what they don't want to do, because I was willing to write for him."

One day he mentioned to me what kind of a person the man who governed a kingdom or a lordship or a republic or a popular state should be. Any man, however large or small in stature should be humane, because, he said, that was the most important thing which was needed in a leader, and he reproached those who thought the opposite. Although someone might excuse himself for his lack of humanity, saying that was his nature, he [the Duke] replied that this was no excuse, because nothing could be more common to great men than a humanity which was strong enough to make friends out of enemies. Conversely, when a person was not humane, and someone came to speak with him and he was unwilling to listen, or he listened in a way which showed that he had no esteem for the person, this made an enemy out of a friend, as many have observed. This inhumanity damaged many, as well it should. There might be someone who pretends to be kind in listening to someone he doesn't want to, and the replies which he makes are such that the other goes away discontented and sees himself badly served and little esteemed by the person he was asking.

It is a long time since Italy had a man so worthy of imitation in everything as the duke of Urbino. One day it happened that, while he was having dealings with a merchant involving a large sum of money, one of his household told him that the merchant was making a lot of money out of him and that the merchandise he gave him was not worth what he was paying for it. He began to laugh, and said that he was quite happy that the merchant was making money from him, and that he could not have made that profit, if he didn't deserve it: that he was more obliged to the merchant than the latter knew: for he had trusted him to the tune of five or six thousand florins, when he was new to the State [of Urbino] and poor and could find no one who would lend him a single florin. For this reason, he was happy that he provided the profit which the other deserved. In this way he silenced his servant, and made him ashamed.

One day while discussing some matters at Milan with duke Galeazzo, the duke [of Urbino] said: "I would like always to be in arms and to have your lordship with me, and I would never be defeated: but we will proceed softly." The duke continued: "All these things I learned from his excellency, your father, duke Francesco." Galeazzo remained silent and did not reply, apparently being unable to make a response to what had been said.

He had another admirable quality, to speak badly of none: He praised and did not blame, and took it badly when someone in his presence spoke evilly of another, thinking that to be very wicked. Moreover, it was alien to his nature to hear those who praised what they had done and to shower him with compliments. In this he was very modest, and preferred that another speak, rather than that he should speak of himself. By nature he was choleric, but he knew how to control himself very well and softened this natural impulse with a measured prudence. He gave total attention to his State, to keep all most content; and especially—among his other praiseworthy virtues—when he learned of a quarrel, he sent for the parties and did not rest until his clever skill produced peace between them. In a notable legal dispute he acted to get rid of any scandal: it happened that one of his subjects of very upright family took to wife a young woman of the same social background as her husband, and she had many relatives. There arose a terrible quarrel between her husband and her relatives, so great a quarrel that he no longer wanted her as wife. The quarrel grew into such a dispute of honor that the husband was likely to be cut into pieces by one set of relatives or the other. The duke, aware of the scandal which was sure to follow, set a day by which he instructed the parties to settle the dispute. When they came, he began with those who were with the girl, using most humane language—he knew how, since his natu-

ral eloquence was paramount—and showed them many reasons for taking the proper course of action. As is the case with the naturally ignorant, the more he spoke to them, the more resistant they became. Seeing this, and turning to the husband, the duke said: "If I wanted you to become a relative of mine, wouldn't you do it, when you saw my status? Wouldn't that be an advantageous relationship?" The man, who was a peasant, hesitated while the duke quizzed him whether it would be advantageous and the duke forced him to reply: "It would not be very advantageous, considering the status of his lordship and the great difference between the two." The duke turned to him and said: "Don't you have respect for what contents me?" The peasant, persuaded, said that he was satisfied. The duke: "I esteem this young woman, for her virtue and her goodness, as if she were my own daughter. Therefore you become a relative of mine and not of theirs: thus, I want you for a relative." The duke so constrained him that he could not reply and was forced to consent: and so he took the girl and all wished them well. The duke took them by the hand, saying that he wished them well, that from now on they were his relatives, and he wanted them to respect him and in time of need to count on him. And he gave them a wonderful marriage-banquet. Both sides then departed, successfully, and both husband and wife got along beautifully. These are the duties required of every prince: to bring peace to his subjects. . . .

Since the air at Ferrara was not good and not suited to him, his health began to get somewhat worse: he had a slight fever like those that develop often in swampy areas. Becoming increasingly ill, he began to attend to the care of his soul, and to arrange all the affairs of State. To this end he arranged matters spiritual as well as temporal, including every small detail, in his will. In reference to divine worship, he ordered that a monastery, of the order of St. Francis of the Observance, about a mile outside Urbino, called St. Donatus, be made a church again, and the monastery be fully fitted out so that it lacked nothing, as afterwards was done. Because of his piety, he wanted to be buried in that church alongside Count Guido.

He left no instructions in his will, for anything

to be done respecting divine worship or the governance of his house. Everything was to be left in a good state so that no one could complain about what his Lordship had done. As experience afterward showed: there was nothing to give the slightest offence in what he had done for his household or his subjects: such was his unparalleled prudence. When he had arranged for what pertained to his sons, he began to attend to the good state of his soul, and confessed several times like a good and faithful Christian, and made all the arrangements for the salvation of his soul, receiving all the sacraments of the Church at the proper time. God gave him grace to do all these things with mature judgment, and he examined properly all he had to do, not omitting anything which befit a good Christian. Having had virtuous habits, and persevering in these to the end of his life, God gave him great grace. Beyond everything else were his [the Duke's] laudable works of piety, to love God and to fear Him, and, as noted, to observe all the requirements of divine worship, and to omit nothing. He was most pious and most merciful in everything, so that he could deservedly be called father and protector of the miserable and afflicted.

When he passed away and was buried with the most lavish possible funeral, he was brought to St. Donatus as he had ordered in his will. The greater part of what he had left remained for the judgment of his close relative, Ottaviano, toward whom he had complete loyalty because of the love which they had for each other. The great part of State affairs pertinent to his sons he left to the judgment of Ottaviano, because of the confidence he had in him. So much did he love him that he wanted him to be his heir in the State if Count Guido should be without sons, demonstrating in every detail his singular love for him. There are many things worth memorializing which could be written about his Lordship, but individual details will be set down in the history of his life. I have written only a brief commentary for the use of ordinary people as well as those who read Latin. Most of the things I have written I have witnessed, since I belonged to his court: what I did not witness I learned from excellent gentlemen who were attached to his Lordship.

Selection 4
Charles V Affirms the "Joyous Entry," 1515

Dating from the mid-fourteenth century, the "Joyous Entry" was an oath sworn by rulers of Brabant, one of the most important provinces of the Low Countries. When Charles came of age, he, too, affirmed its rights and principles. There is a clear emphasis in this oath on the balance between ruler and ruled—in this instance, all *groups* of subjects are meant, that is, the clergy, the nobility, and the commoners. When the Revolt of the Netherlands began in 1566, it was small wonder that the people used the "Joyous Entry" as part of the rationale for their own seizure of power.

Charles, by God's grace Prince of Spain, the Sicilies, etc., Archduke of Austria, duke of Burgundy, Lorraine, Brabant, Styria, Carinthia, Carniola, Limburg, Luxemburg, and Gelderland, count of Flanders, Habsburg, Tyrol, Artois, Bur-

Source: "Charles V affirms the Joyous Entry, 1515," from Jeanne Mennes, "De Staten van Brabant en de Blijde Inkomst van Kroonprins Filips in 1549," *Anciens Pays et Assemblees d'Etats/Standen en Landen*, vol. 18 (Louvain: Edition E. Nauwelaerts, 1959) pp. 56–58, 64–68, 72–78, 156–164. Trans. by S. Marshall.

gundy, the Palatinate of Hainaut, landgrave of Alsace, Margrave of Burgau and of the Holy Empire, count of Holland, Zeeland, . . . lord of Friesland . . .and Malines.

To all present, now and future, salutations. For as it is proper and fitting for the prince and sovereign of a land to bestow the gift and grace of right and privileges to his good subjects and people, and since we are mindful of the great and numerous services, affection, and loyalty which our good people and subjects of our lands of Brabant, Limburg, and our other lands beyond the Maas often gave to our ancestors of blessed memory, such as good people owe to their rightful rulers, and confident that they will continue to give the same to us, we have granted, given, and affirmed in this Entry and reception in these said lands, and do hereby grant, give, and affirm those privileges, points, and affirmations of rights as follow below, promising and taking an oath for ourselves, our heirs, and descendants, to maintain them and to have them maintained firmly and without interruption forever.

Item, that we will be good judges and true lords over them and permit no violence or arbitrary action to be done to them in any way, and that we will not do or permit anything to be done to them outside the law, but will treat all our houses of God, barons, nobles, good people and subjects of our cities . . . through the courts which have authority over them, and that these judges in our said lands must hold their sessions without any delay on any pretext of commission or omission, provided that these said judges may put off trials in lordships one time but no more. . . .

Item, we further have confirmed and ratified and do confirm and ratify all other prelates, cloisters, houses of God, barons, knights, cities, fran-

chises, and all our other subjects and good people of our lands of Brabant and beyond the Maas in all their rights, liberties, privileges, charters, customs, and practices, which they now possess and were given and granted under seal by our forefathers, the dukes and duchesses, and also those which they have followed, practices and continue. . . . And should it happen that we, our heirs or successors, should by our own action or that of others violate them in whole or in part, in any manner, we consent and concede to our said prelates, barons, knights, cities, and to all our other said subjects, that they need not do us, our heirs or successors any services, nor obey us in any other things we might need or which we might request of them, until such time as we shall have corrected the mistaken course previously pursued toward them, and have completely abandoned and reversed it, and for this purpose we will decree and declare that all officers installed in their offices in a way contrary to the Entry of our aforementioned great-great-grandfather Duke Philip shall be dismissed immediately; and further that for the future as well any innovation contrary to established custom which might be initiated shall be null and void, nor shall it be upheld in the future. . . .

Selections 5 and 6
Elizabeth I as Renaissance Monarch

These two documents indicate Elizabeth I of England's ability to personify the same characteristics as the male rulers of the time. In the first passage, her former tutor Roger Ascham discusses her as a student. The second is a more complete version of the 1588 speech quoted in the chapter text.

Selection 5

. . . The lady Elizabeth has accomplished her sixteenth year; and so much solidity of understanding, such courtesy united with dignity, have never been observed at so early an age. She has the most ardent love of true religion and of the best kind of literature. The constitution of her mind is exempt

Source: Lucy Aikin, *Memoirs of the Court of Queen Elizabeth*, vol. 1 (London: Longman, Hurst, Rees, Orme and Brown, 1819), pp. 94–95.

from female weakness, and she is endued with a masculine power of application. No apprehension can be quicker than her's, no memory more retentive. French and Italian she speaks like English; Latin, with fluency, propriety and judgment; she also spoke Greek with me, frequently, willingly, and moderately well. Nothing can be more elegant than her handwriting, whether in the Greek or Roman character. In music she is very skilful, but does not greatly delight. With respect to personal decoration, she greatly prefers a simple elegance to show and splendor, so despising 'the outward adorning of plaiting the hair and of wearing of gold,' that in the whole manner of her life she rather resembles Hippolyta than Phaedra.

She read with me almost the whole of Cicero and a great part of Livy; from these two authors, indeed, her knowledge of the Latin language has been almost exclusively derived. The beginning of the day was always devoted by her to the New Testament in Greek, after which she read select orations of Isocrates and the tragedies of Sophocles, which I judged best adapted to supply her tongue with the purest diction, her mind with the most excellent precepts, and her exalted station with a defence against the utmost power of fortune. For her religious instruction, she drew first from the fountains of Scripture; and afterwards from St. Cyprian, the 'Common places' of Melancthon and similar works which convey pure doctrine in elegant language. In every kind of writing she easily detected any ill-adapted or far-fetched expression. She could not bear those feeble imitators of Erasmus who bind the Latin language in the fetters of miserable proverbs; on the other hand, she approved a style chaste in its propriety and beautiful by perspicuity: and she greatly admired metaphors when not too violent, and antitheses when just and happily opposed. By a diligent attention to these particulars, her ears became so practised and so nice, that there was nothing in Greek, Latin, or English, prose or verse, which, according to its merits or defects, she did not either reject with disgust, or receive with the highest delight. . . .

Selection 6

My loving People, We have been persuaded by some that are careful of our safety, to take heed how we commit ourselves to armed multitudes, for fear of treachery; but I assure you, I do not desier to live to distrust my faithful and loving people.

Let tyrants fear; I have always so behaved myself, that, under God, I have placed my chiefest strength and safeguard in the loyal hearts and good will of my subjects, and therefore I am come amongst you, as you see, at this time, not for my recreation and disport, but being resolved in the midst and heat of the battle, to live or die amongst you all, to lay down for my God, and for my kingdoms, and for my people, my honour and my blood, even in the dust.

I know I have the body but of a weak and feeble woman; but I have the heart and stomach of a king, and of a king of England too; and think foul scorn that Parma or Spain, or any prince of Europe should dare to invade the borders of my realm; to which rather than any dishonour shall grow by me, I myself will take up arms, I myself will be your general, judge, and rewarder of every one of your virtues in the field.

I know already, for your forwardness you have deserved rewards and crowns; and we do assure you in the word of a prince, they shall be duly paid you. In the mean time my lieutenant-general shall be in my stead, than whom never prince commanded a more noble or worthy subject; not doubting but by your obedience to my general, by your concord in the camp, and your valour in the field, we shall shortly have a famous victory over those enemies of my God, of my kingdoms, and of my people.

Source: Walter Scott (ed.), *A Collection of Scarce and Valuable Tracts, on the most interesting and entertaining Subjects: but chiefly such as relate to the History and Constitution of these Kingdoms,* vol. 1 (London: T. Cadell and W. Davies, 1809), pp. 429–430.

Selection 7
James I Articulates the Divine Right of Monarchy

Elizabeth I's successor was James VI of Scotland (1567–1625), who reigned as James I of England after her death (1603–1625). James, a scholar as well as a monarch, published anonymously a widely read book, *True Law of Free Monarchies*, in 1598. This selection from that work points up the ways in which he saw Parliament's power as inimical to his own. That position was further elaborated in the excerpt from a speech he gave to Parliament in 1610. James laid the foundation for further expressions of the divine right of monarchs, best seen in the writings of Louis XIV of France.

TRUE LAW OF FREE MONARCHIES

According to these fundamental laws already alleged, we daily see that in the parliament (which is nothing else but the head court of the king and his vassals) the laws are but craved by his subjects, and only made by him at their rogation and with their advice: for albeit the king make daily statutes and ordinances, enjoining such pains thereto as he thinks meet, without any advice of parliament or estates, yet it lies in the power of no parliament to make any kind of law or statute, without his sceptre be to it, for giving it the force of a law. . . . And as ye see it manifest that the king is over-lord of the whole land, so is he master over every person that inhabiteth the same, having power over the life and death of every one of them: for although a just prince will not take the life of any of his subjects without a clear law, yet the same laws whereby he taketh them are made by himself or his predecessors; and so the power flows always from himself; as by daily experience we see good and just princes will from time to time make new laws and statutes, adjoining the penalties to the breakers thereof, which before the law was made had been no crime to the subject to have committed. . . . And where he sees the law doubtsome or rigorous, he may interpret or mitigate the same, lest otherwise *summum jus* be *summa injuria:* and therefore general laws made publicly in parliament may upon known respects to the king by his authority be mitigated and suspended upon causes only known to him.

Source: G. W. Prothero (ed.), *Select Statutes and Other Constitutional Documents Illustrative of the Reigns of Elizabeth and James I* (Oxford: Clarendon Press, 1913), pp. 293–294, 400–401.

As likewise, although I have said a good king will frame all his actions to be according to the law, yet is he not bound thereto but of his good will, and for good example-giving to his subjects. . . . So as I have already said, a good king, though he be above the law, will subject and frame his actions thereto, for example's sake to his subjects, and of his own free will, but not as subject or bound thereto. . . .

SPEECH OF JAMES I BEFORE PARLIAMENT, 21 MARCH, 1610

. . . The state of monarchy is the supremest thing upon earth: for kings are not only God's lieutenants upon earth and sit upon God's throne, but even by God himself they are called gods. There be three principal similitudes that illustrate the state of monarchy: one taken out of the word of God, and the two other out of the grounds of policy and philosophy. In the Scriptures kings are called gods, and so their power after a certain relation compared to the Divine power. Kings are also compared to fathers of families: for a king is truly *parens patriae*, the politic father of his people. And lastly, kings are compared to the head of this microcosm of the body of man. . . .

I conclude then this point touching the power of kings with this axiom of divinity, That as to dispute what God may do is blasphemy, . . . so is it sedition in subjects to dispute what a king may do in the height of his power. But just kings will ever be willing to declare what they will do, if they will not incur the curse of God. I will not be content that my power be disputed upon; but I shall ever be willing to make the reason appear of all my doings, and rule my actions according to my laws. . . .

Now the second general ground whereof I am to speak concerns the matter of grievances. . . . First then, I am not to find fault that you inform yourselves of the particular just grievances of the people; nay I must tell you, ye can neither be just nor faithful to me or to your countries that trust and employ you, if you do it not. . . . But I would wish you to be careful to avoid three things in the matter of grievances.

First, that you do not meddle with the main points of government: that is my craft: *tractent fabrilia fabri;* to meddle with that, were to lesson me. I am now an old king . . . ; therefore there should not be too many Phorimos to teach Hannibal: I must not be taught my office.

Secondly, I would not have you meddle with such ancient rights of mine as I have received from my predecessors, possessing them *more majorum:* such things I would be sorry should be accounted for grievances. All novelties are dangerous as well in a politic as in a natural body: and therefore I would be loath to be quarrelled in my ancient rights and possessions: for that were to judge me

unworthy of that which my predecessors had and left me.

And lastly I pray you, beware to exhibit for grievance anything that is established by a settled law, and whereunto (as you have already had a proof) you know I will never give a plausible answer: for it is an undutiful part in subjects to press their king, wherein they know beforehand he will refuse them. Now if any law or statute be not convenient, let it be amended by Parliament, but in the meantime term it not a grievance; for to be grieved with the law is to be grieved with the king, who is sworn to be the patron and maintainer thereof. But as all men are flesh and may err in the execution of laws, so may ye justly make a grievance of any abuse of the law, distinguishing wisely between the faults of the person and the thing itself. As for example, complaints may be made unto you of the High Commissioners: if so be, try the abuse and spare not to complain upon it, but say not there shall be no Commission, for that were to abridge the power that is in me. . . .

Selection 8
Louis XIV's System of Rule

Louis XIV ruled France from 1643 to 1715. His longevity gave him opportunities to develop and maintain his political philosophy and political system that were virtually unparalleled. These selections from his *Memoirs* contain advice that he prepared for his son, in addition to his own reflections and musings, and illustrate the manner in which he identified himself with the state—which is what posterity has done as well.

THE KING'S MEMOIR, 9 MARCH, 1661

My Lord Cardinal, sensing the approach of death and wishing to unburden himself of all earthly matters and devote his thoughts to eternity, gave the last moments of his temporal life to the love which he always had for the welfare of my state, and my own glory. With this in mind, he left me several very important counsels, among them being those which follow and which I have assembled as well as I could. . . .

That I should have at my side servants of great capacity and absolute loyalty. That it was my affair to detect the qualities which each had, and to employ him according to his talents.

That I should take the greatest care to let everyone know that I am the master; that favours should be looked for from me alone; and above all that I should distribute them only to those who deserve them by their services, their capacity and their attachment to my own person.

That I should take care that all the members of my Council should live in a good understanding with one another, lest their division should be to the prejudice of my service; that I should listen to

Source: H. G. Judge, *Louis XIV* (London: Longman's, 1965), pp. 3–4, 6–12.

their advice on matters in hand and seek always the best solution among their differing opinions; that I should take the decision myself and then maintain it loftily without permitting the least questioning of my authority. . . . Two things without doubt were absolutely necessary: very hard work on my part, and a wise choice of persons capable of seconding it.

As for work, it may be, my son, that you will begin to read these Memoirs at an age when one is far more in the habit of dreading than loving it, only too happy to have escaped subjection to tutors and to have your hours regulated no longer, nor lengthy and prescribed study laid down for you.

On this heading I will not warn you solely that it is none the less toil *by which* one reigns, and *for which* one reigns, and that the conditions of royalty, which may seem to you sometimes hard and vexatious in so lofty a position, would appear pleasant and easy if there was any doubt of your reaching it.

There is something more, my son, and I hope that your own experience will never teach it to you: nothing could be more laborious to you than a great amount of idleness if you were to have the misfortune to fall into it through beginning by being disgusted with public affairs, then with pleasure, then with idleness itself, seeking everywhere fruitlessly for what can never be found, that is to say, the sweetness of repose and leisure without having the preceding fatigue and occupation.

I laid a rule on myself to work regularly twice every day, and for two or three hours each time with different persons, without counting the hours which I passed privately and alone, nor the time which I was able to give on particular occasions to any special affairs that might arise. There was no moment when I did not permit people to talk to me about them, provided that they were urgent; with the exception of foreign ministers who sometimes find too favourable moments in the familiarity allowed to them, either to obtain or to discover something, and whom one should not hear without being previously prepared.

I cannot tell you what fruit I gathered immediately I had taken this resolution. I felt myself, as it were, uplifted in thought and courage; I found myself quite another man, and with joy reproached myself for having been too long unaware of it. This first timidity, which a little self-judgment always produces and which at the beginning gave me pain, especially on occasions when I had to speak in public, disappeared in less than no time. The only thing I felt then was that I was King, and born to be one. I experienced next a delicious feeling, hard to express, and which you will not know yourself except by tasting it as I have done. For you must not imagine, my son, that the affairs of State are like some obscure and thorny path of learning which may possibly have already wearied you, wherein the mind strives to raise itself with effort above its purview, more often to arrive at no conclusion, and whole utility or apparent utility is repugnant to us as much as its difficulty. The function of Kings consists principally in allowing good sense to act, which always acts naturally and without effort. What we apply ourselves to is sometimes less difficult than what we do only for our amusement. Its usefulness always follows. A King, however skilful and enlightened be his ministers, cannot put his own hand to the work without its effect being seen. Success, which is agreeable in everything, even in the smallest matters, gratifies us in these as well as in the greatest, and there is no satisfaction to equal that of noting every day some progress in glorious and lofty enterprises, and in the happiness of the people which has been planned and thought out by oneself. All that is most necessary to this work is at the same time agreeable; for, in a word, my son, it is to have one's eyes open to the whole earth; to learn each hour the news concerning every province and every nation, the secrets of every court, the mood and the weaknesses of each Prince and of every foreign minister; to be well-informed on an infinite number of matters about which we are supposed to know nothing; to elicit from our subjects what they hide from us with the greatest care; to discover the most remote opinions of our own courtiers and the most hidden interests of those who come to us with quite contrary professions. I do not know of any other pleasure we would not renounce for that, even if curiosity alone gave us the opportunity.

I have dwelt on this important subject longer than I had intended, and far more for your sake than for my own; for while I am disclosing to you these methods and these alleviations attending the greatest cares of royalty I am not unaware that I am likewise depreciating almost the sole merit which I can hope for in the eyes of the world. But in this matter, my son, your honour is dearer to me than my own; and it if should happen that God call you to govern before you have yet taken to this spirit of application and to public affairs of which I am speaking, the least deference you can pay to the advice of a father, to whom I make bold to say you owe much in every kind of way, is to begin to do and to continue to do for some time, even under constraint and dislike, for love of me who beg it of you, what you will do all your life from love of yourself, if once you have made a beginning.

I gave orders to the four Secretaries of State no longer to sign anything whatsoever without speaking to me; likewise to the Controller, and that he should authorise nothing as regards finance without its being noted down in a very abridged abstract form in which at any moment, and at a glance, I could see the state of the funds, and past and future expenditure.

The Chancellor received a like order, that is to say, to sign nothing with the seal except by my command, with the exception only of letters of justice, so called because it would be an injustice to refuse them, a procedure required more as a matter of form than of principle; and I allowed to remain the administering and remissions of cases manifestly pardonable, although I have since changed my opinion on this subject, as I will tell you in its proper place. I let it be understood that whatever the nature of the matter might be, direct application must be made to me when it was not a question that depended only on my favour; and to all my subjects without distinction I gave liberty to present their case to me at all hours, either verbally or by petitions.

At first petitions came in very great numbers, which nevertheless did not discourage me. The disorder in which my affairs had been placed was productive of many; the novelty and expectation, whether vain or unjust, attracted not less. A large number were presented connected with law-suits, which I could not and ought not to take out of the ordinary tribunals in order to have them adjudicated before me. But even in these things, apparently so unprofitable, I found great usefulness. By this means I informed myself in detail as to the state of my people; they saw that I was mindful of them, and nothing won their heart so much. Oppression on the part of the ordinary tribunals might be represented to me in such a way as to make me feel it desirable to gain further information in order to take special measures when they were required. One or two examples of this kind prevented a thousand similar ills; the complaints, even when they were false and unjust, hindered my officers from giving a hearing to those which were more genuine and reasonable.

Regarding the persons whose duty it was to second my labours, I resolved at all costs to have no prime minister; and if you will believe me, my son, and all your successors after you, the name shall be banished for ever from France, for there is nothing more undignified than to see all the administration on one side, and on the other, the mere title of King.

To effect this, it was necessary to divide my confidence and the execution of my orders without giving it entirely to one single person, applying these different people to different spheres according to their diverse talents, which is perhaps the first and greatest gift that Princes can possess.

I also made a resolution on a further matter. With a view the better to unite in myself alone all the authority of a master, although there must be in all affairs a certain amount of detail to which our occupations and also our dignity do not permit us to descend as a rule, I conceived the plan, after I should have made choice of my ministers, of entering sometimes into matters with each one of them, and when they least expected it, in order that they might understand that I could do the same upon other subjects and at any moment. Besides, a knowledge of some small detail acquired only occasionally, and for amusement rather than as a regular rule, is instructive little by little and without fatigue, on a thousand things which are not without their use in general resolutions, and which we ought to know and do ourselves were it possible that a single man could know and do everything.

It is not so easy for me to tell you, my son, what ought to be done in the choice of different ministers. In this matter fortune plays always, in spite of us, as large or a greater part than sagacity; and in the part that sagacity is able to play, intuition can do far more than taking thought.

Neither you nor I, my son, will seek out men for those kinds of employment whom distance or their own obscurity hides from our view, whatever be the capability they may possess. Of necessity, one must decide from a small number whom chance presents, that is to say, from among those who are already occupying some post, or men whom birth or inclination have placed nearest to us.

And for this art of knowing men, which will be so important to you, not only in this matter, but in all the occasions of your life, I will tell you, my son, that it is one that may be learnt, but cannot be taught.

I could, doubtless, have discovered men of higher consideration, but not of greater capacity than these three [Lionne, le Tellier, Fouquet]; and a small number, as I have already said, appeared to me to be better than a larger.

To lay bare to you all that was in my mind, it was not to my interest to choose subjects of a more eminent quality. Before all else it was needful to establish my own reputation, and to let the public know from the very rank from which I chose them, that it was my intention not to share my authority with them. It was important that they should not conceive hopes of higher things than what it pleased me to give them—a matter which is difficult in the case of people of high birth. And these precautions were so necessary that even on that question the world was a fairly long time in getting to know me thoroughly.

Several were able to persuade themselves that within a short time some one of those who approached me would take possession of my mind and my affairs. The greater number regarded the assiduity of my labours as a fervour which would relax, and those willing to judge it more favourably were waiting to form their opinion by results.

Time has shown what to believe, and I have now been pursuing for ten years fairly consistently, as it seems to me, the same course, without relaxing my application; kept well informed of everything; listening to the least of my subjects; at any hour knowing the number and quality of my troops, and the state of my fortified towns; unremitting in issuing my orders for all their requirements; dealing at once with foreign ministers; receiving and reading despatches; doing myself a portion of the replies and giving to my secretaries the substance of the others; regulating the State receipts and expenditure; requiring those whom I placed in important posts to account directly to me; keeping my affairs to myself as much as any one before me had ever done; distributing my favours as I myself chose, and retaining, if I mistake not, those who served me in a modest position which was far removed from the elevation and power of prime ministers, although loading them with benefits for themselves and their dependants.

But I know, my son, and can sincerely protest to you, that I had no aversion or rancour in my mind as regards my officers of justice. On the contrary, if old age in men is venerable, it appeared still more so to me in this so ancient a body [Parlement]. I am persuaded that possibly in no other branch of my State is the work so great, nor the rewards smaller. I have for all of them the affection and consideration that is their due; and you, my son, who, according to all appearances will find them still further removed from these former vain pretensions, should practise with all the more diligence what I myself do every day. I mean you should give them evidence on occasion of your esteem, you should know the chief representatives and those who possess the greatest merit, and let them see that you know them (for it is a gracious thing in a Prince to show that he is well informed on everything and that duties performed far away from him are not lost); you should consider them and their families in the distribution of appointments and emoluments, and favour their plans when they wish to attach themselves more particularly to you, and in a word, accustom them to seeing you now and again by treating them well and giving them a friendly word instead of encouraging the practice of the past century when it was one of their understood rules not to go near the Louvre. And this was from no bad intention, but from the false idea of some imaginary opposition between the interests of the Prince and those of the people whose defenders they constituted themselves, not considering that these two interests are only one, that the tranquillity of subjects rests only on their obedience, that less harm results to the public by bearing with submission than by finding fault with even bad government by Kings, of whom God alone is the Judge, and that what they seem to be doing in opposition to the common law is more often based on reasons of State, which by universal consent form the first of all laws, but the least understood and the most obscure to all who do not govern.

III. THE THEORY OF RENAISSANCE POLITICS

No discussion of politics and princes in this period would be complete without some mention of the new developments in Renaissance and early modern political theory, for some of the greatest political theorists who ever lived wrote in this age. Their thinking has influenced the development and expression of political theory and its application ever since.

Selection 9
"Of the Things for Which Men, and Especially Princes, Are Praised or Blamed"
Niccolo Machiavelli

Niccolo Machiavelli (1469–1527), perhaps more than any political thinker of his time, exemplified the break with the medieval past. Although *The Prince* is a short book, its influence has far surpassed its length. Machiavelli regarded politics in strongly secular terms. He considered that the state was a human creation and that rulers were, themselves, only human. Thus he concluded that rulers must disregard questions of good and evil and govern according to the practical considerations of real life.

CHAPTER XV

Of the things for which men, and especially princes, are praised or blamed

It now remains to be seen what are the methods and rules for a prince as regards his subjects and friends. And as I know that many have written of

Source: Niccolo Machiavelli, *The Prince and the Discourses*, intro. by Max Lerner, trans. by Luigi Ricci, rev. by E. R. P. Vincent (New York: Random House, Inc., 1950), pp. 56–57, 63–66.

this, I fear that my writing about it may be deemed presumptuous, differing as I do, especially in this matter, from the opinions of others. But my intention being to write something of use to those who understand, it appears to me more proper to go to the real truth of the matter than to its imagination; and many have imagined republics and principalities which have never been seen or known to exist in reality; for how we live is so far removed from how we ought to live, that he who abandons what is done for what ought to be done, will rather learn to bring about his own ruin than his preservation. A man who wishes to make a profession of goodness in everything must necessarily come to grief among so many who are not good. Therefore it is necessary for a prince, who wishes to maintain himself, to learn how not to be good, and to use this knowledge and not use it, according to the necessity of the case.

Leaving on one side, then, those things which concern only an imaginary prince, and speaking of those that are real, I state that all men, and especially princes, who are placed at a greater height, are reputed for certain qualities which bring them either praise or blame. Thus one is considered liberal, another *misero* or miserly (using a Tuscan term, seeing that *avaro* with us still means one who is rapaciously acquisitive and *misero* one who makes grudging use of his own); one a free giver, another rapacious; one cruel, another merciful, one a breaker of his word, another trustworthy, one effeminate and pusillanimous, another fierce and high-spirited; one humane, another haughty; one lascivious, another chaste; one frank, another astute; one hard, another easy; one serious, another frivolous; one religious, another an unbeliever, and so on. I know that every one will admit that it would be highly praiseworthy in a prince to possess all the above-named qualities that are reputed good, but as they cannot all be possessed or observed, human conditions not permitting of it, it is necessary that he should be prudent enough to avoid the scandal of those vices which would lose him the state, and guard himself if possible against those which will not lose it him, but if not able to, he can indulge them with less scruple. And yet he must not mind incurring the scandal of those vices, without which it would be difficult to save the state, for if one considers well, it will be found that some things which seem virtues would, if followed, lead to one's ruin, and some others which appear vices result in one's greater security and wellbeing. . . .

CHAPTER XVIII

In what way princes must keep faith

How laudable it is for a prince to keep good faith and live with integrity, and not with astuteness, every one knows. Still the experience of our times shows those princes to have done great things who have had little regard for good faith, and have been able by astuteness to confuse men's brains, and who have ultimately overcome those who have made loyalty their foundation.

You must know, then, that there are two methods of fighting, the one by law, the other by force: the first method is that of men, the second of beasts; but as the first method is often insufficient, one must have recourse to the second. It is therefore necessary for a prince to know well how to use both the beast and the man. This was covertly taught to rulers by ancient writers, who relate how Achilles and many others of those ancient princes were given to Chiron the centaur to be brought up and educated under his discipline. The parable of this semi-annual, semi-human teacher is meant to indicate that a prince must know how to use both natures, and that the one without the other is not durable.

A prince being thus obliged to know well how to act as a beast must imitate the fox and the lion, for the lion cannot protect himself from traps, and the fox cannot defend himself from wolves. One must therefore be a fox to recognise traps, and a lion to frighten wolves. Those that wish to be only lions do not understand this. Therefore, a prudent ruler ought not to keep faith when by so doing it would be against his interest, and when the reasons which made him bind himself no longer exist. If men were all good, this precept would not be a good one; but as they are bad, and would not observe their faith with you, so you are not bound to keep faith with them. Nor have legitimate grounds ever failed a prince who wished to show colourable excuse for the non-fulfilment of his promise. Of this one could furnish an infinite number of modern examples, and show how many times peace has been broken, and how many promises rendered worthless, by the faithlessness of princes, and those that have been best able to imitate the fox have succeeded best. But it is necessary to be able to disguise this character well, and to be a great feigner and dissembler; and men are so simple and so ready to obey present necessities, that one who deceives will always find those who allow themselves to be deceived.

I will only mention one modern instance. Alexander VI did nothing else but deceive men, he thought of nothing else, and found the occasion for it; no man was ever more able to give assurances, or affirmed things with stronger oaths, and no man observed them less; however, he always succeeded in his deceptions, as he well knew his aspect of things.

It is not, therefore, necessary for a prince to have all the above-named qualities, but it is very necessary to seem to have them. I would even be bold to say that to possess them and always to observe them is dangerous, but to appear to possess them is useful. Thus it is well to seem merciful, faithful, humane, sincere, religious, and also to be so; but you must have the mind so disposed that when it is needful to be otherwise you may be able to change to the opposite qualities. And it must be understood that a prince, and especially a new prince, cannot observe all those things which are considered good in men, being often obliged, in order to maintain the state, to act against faith, against charity, against humanity, and against religion. And, therefore, he must have a mind disposed to adapt itself according to the wind, and as the variations of fortune dictate, and, as I said before, not deviate from what is good, if possible, but be able to do evil if constrained.

A prince must take great care that nothing goes out of his mouth which is not full of the above-named five qualities, and, to see and hear him, he should seem to be all mercy, faith, integrity, humanity, and religion. And nothing is more necessary than to seem to have this last quality, for men in general judge more by the eyes than by the hands, for every one can see, but very few have to feel. Everybody sees what you appear to be, few feel what you are, and those few will not dare to oppose themselves to the many, who have the majesty of the state to defend them; and in the actions of men, and especially of princes, from which there is no appeal, the end justifies the means. Let a prince therefore aim at conquering and maintaining the state, and the means will always be judged honourable and praised by every one, for the vulgar is always taken by appearances and the issue of the event; and the world consists only of the vulgar, and the few who are not vulgar are isolated when the many have a rallying point in the prince. A certain prince of the present time, whom it is well not to name, never does anything but preach peace and good faith, but he is really a great enemy to both, and either of them, had he observed them, would have lost him state or reputation on many occasions.

Selection 10
A Defense of Liberty Against Tyrants
Philippe Mornay

This excerpt, from a work first published in 1579, has been attributed with near certainty to the political philosopher Philippe Mornay. It reflects the realities of the Wars of Religion in mid-sixteenth-century France. As a follower of the Protestant reformer Calvin, Mornay feared that an absolute ruler would impose Catholicism on the French people. Thus political circumstances led him to oppose the idea of absolute rule. His ideas later influenced those who spoke and wrote in support of representative government.

THE THIRD QUESTION

Whether it be lawful to resist a prince who doth oppress or ruin a public state, and how far such

Source: Philippe Mornay and Hubert Languet, *Vindiciae contra tyrannos: A Defense of Liberty Against Tyrants or the Lawful Power of the Prince over the People, and of the People over the Prince* (London: Richard Baldwin, 1689), pp. 57–73.

resistance may be extended: by whom, how, and by what right or law it is permitted

For so much as we must here dispute of the lawful authority of a lawful prince, I am confident that this question will be the less acceptable to tyrants and wicked princes; for it is no marvel if those who receive no law, but what their own will and fancy dictate unto them, be deaf unto the voice of that law which is grounded upon reason. But I persuade myself that good princes will willingly entertain this discourse, insomuch as they sufficiently know that all magistrates, be they of never so high a rank, are but an inanimated and speaking law. Neither though anything be pressed home against the bad, can it fall within any inference against the good kings or princes, as also good and bad princes are in a direct diameter opposite and contrary: therefore, that which shall be urged against tyrants, is so far from detracting anything from kings, as on the contrary, the more tyrants are laid open in their proper colors, the more glorious does the true worth and dignity of kings appear; neither can the vicious imperfections of the one be laid open, but it gives addition of perfections and respect to the honor of the other.

But for tyrants let them say and think what they please, that shall be the least of my care; for it is not to them, but against them that I write; for kings I believe that they will readily consent to that which is propounded, for by true proportion of reason they ought as much to hate tyrants and wicked governors, as shepherds hate wolves, physicians, poisoners, true prophets, false doctors; for it must necessarily occur that reason infused into good kings as much hatred against tyrants, as nature imprints in dogs against wolves, for as the one lives by rapine and spoil, so the other is born or bred to redress and prevent all such outrages. It may be the flatterers of tyrants will cast a supercilious aspect on these lines; but if they were not past all grace they would rather blush for shame. I very well know that the friends and faithful servants of kings will not only approve and lovingly entertain this discourse, but also, with their best abilities, defend the contents thereof. Accordingly as the reader shall find himself moved either with content or dislike in the reading hereof, let him know that by that he shall plainly discover either the affection or hatred that he bears to tyrants. Let us now enter into the matter.

Kings are made by the people

We have showed before that it is God that does appoint kings, who chooses them, who gives the kingdom to them: now we say that the people establish kings, put the scepter into their hands, and who with their suffrages, approves the election. God would have it done in this manner, to the end that the kings should acknowledge, that after God they hold their power and sovereignty from the people, and that it might the rather induce them, to apply and address the utmost of their care and thoughts for the profit of the people, without being puffed with any vain imagination, that they were formed of any matter more excellent than other men, for which they were raised so high above others; as if they were to command our flocks of sheep, or herds of cattle. But let them remember and know, that they are of the same mold and condition as others, raised from the earth by the voice and acclamations, now as it were upon the shoulders of the people unto their thrones, that they might afterwards bear on their own shoulders the greatest burdens of the commonwealth. Divers ages before that, the people of Israel demanded a king. God gave and appointed the law of royal government contained in the seventeenth chapter, verse fourteen of Deuteronomy, when, says Moses, "thou art come unto the land which the Lord thy God giveth thee, and shalt possess it, and shalt dwell therein, and shalt say, I will set a king over me like as all the nations that are about me, thou shalt in any wise set him whom the Lord thy God shall choose from amongst thy brethren, etc." You see here, that the election of the king is attributed to God, the establishment to the people: now when the practice of this law came in use, see in what manner they proceeded.

The elders of Israel, who presented the whole body of the people (under this name of elders are comprehended the captains, the centurions, commanders over fifties and tens, judges, provosts, but principally the chiefest of tribes) came to meet Samuel in Ramah, and not being willing longer to endure the government of the sons of Samuel, whose ill carriage had justly drawn on them the people's dislike, and withal persuading themselves that they had found the means to make their wars hereafter with more advantage, they demanded a king of Samuel, who asking counsel of the Lord, he made known that He had chosen Saul for the governor of His people. . . .

And for David, by the commandment of God, and in a manner more evident than the former, after the rejection of Saul, Samuel anointed for king over Israel, David, chosen by the Lord, which being done, the Spirit of the Lord presently left Saul, and wrought in a special manner in David. But David, notwithstanding, reigns not, but was compelled to save himself in deserts and rocks, oftentimes falling upon the very brim of destruction, and never reigned as king until after the death of Saul: for then by the suffrages of all the people of Judah he was first chosen king of Judah, and seven years after by the consent of all Israel, he was inaugurated king of Israel in Hebron. So, then, he is anointed first by the prophet at the commandment of God, as a token he was chosen. Secondly, by the commandment of the people when he was established king. And that to the end that kings may always remember that it is from God, but by the people, and for the people's sake that they do reign, and that in their glory they say not (as is their custom) they hold their kingdom only of God and their sword, but withal add that it was the people who first girt them with that sword. The same order offered in Solomon. Although he was the king's son, God had chosen Solomon to sit upon the throne of his kingdom, and by express words had promised David to be with him and assist him as a father his son. David had with his own mouth designed Solomon to be successor to his crown in the presence of some of the principal of his court.

But this was not enough, and therefore David assembled at Jerusalem the princes of Israel, the heads of the tribes, the captains of the soldiers, and ordinance officers of the kings, the centurions and other magistrates of town, together with his sons, the noblemen and worthiest personages of the kingdom, to consult and resolve upon the election. In this assembly, after they had called upon the name of God, Solomon, by the consent of the whole congregation, was proclaimed and anointed for king, and sat (so says the text) upon the throne of Israel; then, and not before, the princes, the noblemen, his brothers themselves do him homage, and take the oath of allegiance. And to the end, that it may not be said that that was only done to avoid occasion of difference, which

might arise amongst the brothers and sons of David about the succession, we read that the other following kings have, in the same manner, been established in their places. It is said, that after the death of Solomon, the people assembled to create his son Rehoboam king. After that Amaziah was killed, Ozias, his only son, was chosen king by all the people, Ochosias after Joram, Joachim, the son of Josias, after the decease of his father, whose piety might well seem to require that without any other solemnity, notwithstanding, both he and the other were chosen and invested into the royal throne, by the suffrages of the people. . . .

It may be collected from this, that the kingdom of Israel was not hereditary, if we consider David and the promise made to him, and that it was wholly elective, if we regard the particular persons. But to what purpose is this, but to make it apparent that the election is only mentioned, that the kings might have always in their remembrance that they were raised to their dignities by the people, and therefore they should never forget during life in what a strict bound of observance they are tied to those from whom they have received all their greatness. We read that the kings of the heathen have been established also by the people; for as when they had either troubles at home, or wars abroad, someone, in whose ready valor and discreet integrity the people did principally rely and repose their greatest confidence, him they presently, with a universal consent, constituted king.

Cicero says, that among the Medes, Diocles, from a judge of private controversies, was, for his uprightness, by the whole people elected king, and in the same manner were the first kings chosen among the Romans. . . .

Briefly, for so much as none were ever born with crowns on their heads, and scepters in their hands, and that no man can be a king by himself, nor reign without people, whereas on the contrary, the people may subsist of themselves, and were, long before they had any kings, it must of necessity follow, that kings were at the first constituted by the people; and although the sons and dependents of such kings, inheriting their fathers' virtues, may in a sort seem to have rendered their kingdoms hereditary to their offsprings, and that in some kingdoms and countries, the right of free election seems in a sort buried; yet, notwithstanding, in all well-ordered kingdoms, this custom is yet remaining. The sons do not succeed the fathers, before the people have first, as it were, anew established them by their new approbation: neither were they acknowledged in quality, as inheriting it from the dead; but approved and accounted kings then only, when they were invested with the kingdom, by receiving the scepter and diadem from the hands of those who represent the majesty of the people. One may see most evident marks of this in Christian kingdoms, which are at this day esteemed hereditary; for the French king, he of Spain and England, and others, are commonly sacred, and as it were, put into possession of their authority by the peers, lords of the kingdom, and officers of the crown, who represent the body of the people, no more nor less than the emperors of Germany are chosen by the electors, and the kings of Polonia, by the yawodes and palatines of the kingdom, where the right of election is yet in force. . . .

But not to wander from France, the long continuance and power of which kingdom may in some sort plead for a ruling authority, and where succession seems to have obtained most reputation. We read that Pharamond was chosen in the year 419, Pepin in the year 751, Charles the Great, and Charlemain, the son of Pepin, in the year 768, without having any respect to their fathers' former estate. Charlemain dying in the year 772, his portion fell not presently into the possession of his brother Charles the Great, as it ordinarily happens in the succession of inheritances, but by the ordinance of the people and the states of the kingdom he is invested with it; the same author witnesses, that in the year 812, Louis the Courteous, although he was the son of Charles the Great, was also elected; and in the testament of Charlemain, inserted into the history written by Nauclere, Charlemain does entreat the people to choose, by a general assembly of the estates of the kingdom, which of his grandchildren or nephews the people pleased, and commanding the uncles to observe and obey the ordinance of the people by means whereof, Charles the Bold, nephew to Louis the Courteous and Judith, declares himself to be-

chosen king, as Aimonius the French historian recites.

To conclude in a word, all kings at the first were altogether elected, and those who at this day seem to have their crowns and royal authority by inheritance, have or should have, first and principally their confirmation from the people. Briefly, although the people of some countries have been accustomed to choose their kings of such a lineage, which for some notable merits have worthily deserved it, yet we must believe that they choose the stock itself, and not every branch that proceeds from it; neither are they so tied to that election, as if the successor degenerate, they may not choose another more worthy, neither those who come and are the next of that stock, are born kings, but created such, nor called kings, but princes of the blood royal.

The whole body of the people is above the king

Now, seeing that the people choose and establish their kings, it follows that the whole body of the people is above the king; for it is a thing most evident, that he who is established by another, is accounted under him who has established him, and he who receives his authority from another, is less than he from whom he derives his power. Potiphar the Egyptian sets Joseph over all his house; Nebuchadnezzar, Daniel over the province of Babylon; Darius the six score governors over the kingdom. It is commonly said that masters establish their servants, kings their officers. In like manner, also, the people establish the king as administrator of the commonwealth. Good kings have not disdained this title; yea, the bad ones themselves have affected it; insomuch, as for the space of divers ages, no Roman emperor (if it were not some absolute tyrant, as Nero, Domitian, Caligula) would suffer himself to be called lord. Furthermore, it must necessarily be, that kings were instituted for the people's sake, neither can it be, that for the pleasure of some hundreds of men, and without doubt more foolish and worse than many of the other, all the rest were made, but much rather that these hundred were made for the use and service of all the other, and reason requires that he be preferred above the other, who was made only to and for this occasion: so it is, that for the ship's sail, the owner appoints a pilot over her, who sits at the helm, and looks that she keep her course, nor run not upon any dangerous shelf; the pilot doing his duty, is obeyed by the mariners; yea, and of himself who is owner of the vessel, notwithstanding, the pilot is a servant as well as the least in the ship, from whom he only differs in this, that he serves in a better place than they do.

In a commonwealth, commonly compared to a ship, the king holds the place of pilot, the people in general are owners of the vessel, obeying the pilot, while he is careful of the public good; as though this pilot neither is nor ought to be esteemed other than servant to the public; as a judge or general in war differs little from other officers, but that he is bound to bear greater burdens, and expose himself to more dangers. By the same reason also which the king gains by acquist of arms, be it that he possesses himself of frontier places in warring on the enemy, or that which he gets by escheats or confiscations, he gets it to the kingdom, and not to himself, to wit, to the people, of whom the kingdom is composed, nor more nor less than the servant does for his master; neither may one contract or oblige themselves to him, but by and with reference to the authority derived from the people. Furthermore, there is an infinite sort of people who live without a king, but we cannot imagine a king without people. And those who have been raised to the royal dignity were not advanced because they excelled other men in beauty and comeliness, nor in some excellency of nature to govern them as shepherds do their flocks, but rather being made out of the same mass with the rest of the people, they should acknowledge that for them, they, as it were, borrow their power and authority.

The ancient custom of the French represents that exceeding well, for they used to lift up on a buckler, and salute him king whom they had chosen. And wherefore is it said, I pray you, that kings have an infinite number of eyes, a million of ears, with extreme long hands, and feet exceeding swift? Is it because they are like to Argos, Gerien, Midas, and divers others so celebrated by the poets? No, truly, but it is said in regard of all the people, whom the business principally concerns, who lend to the king for the good of the commonwealth, their eyes, their ears, their means, their faculties. Let the people forsake the king, he presently falls to the ground, although before, his hearing and sight seemed most excellent, and that he was strong and in the best disposition that might be; yea, that he seemed to triumph in all magnificence, yet in an instant he will become most vile and contemptible: to be brief, instead of those divine honors wherewith all men adore him, he shall be compelled to become a pedant, and whip children in the school at Corinth. Take away but the basis to this giant, and like the Rhodian Colossus, he presently tumbles on the ground and falls into pieces. Seeing then that the king is established in this degree by the people, and for their sake, and that he cannot subsist without them, who can think it strange, then, for us to conclude that the people are above the king?

Now that which we speak of all the people universally, ought also to be understood, as has been delivered in the second question, of those who in every kingdom or town do lawfully represent the body of the people, and who ordinarily (or at least should be) called the officers of the kingdom, or of the crown, and not of the king; for the officers of the king, it is he who places and displaces them at his pleasure, yea, after his death they have no more power, and are accounted as dead. On the contrary, the officers of the kingdom receive their authority from the people in the general assembly of the states (or, at the least were accustomed so anciently to have done) and cannot be disauthorized but by them, so then the one depends on the king, the other of the kingdom, those of the sovereign officer of the kingdom, who is the king himself, those of the sovereignty itself, that is of the people of which sovereignty, both the king and all his officers of the kingdom ought to depend, the charge of the one has proper relation to the care of the king's person; that of the other, to look that the commonwealth receive no damage; the first sought to serve and assist the king, as all domestic servants are bound to do to their masters; the other to preserve the rights and privileges of the people, and to carefully hinder the prince, that he neither omit the things that may advantage the state, nor commit anything that may endamage the public.

Briefly, the one are servants and domestics of the king, and received into their places to obey his person; the other, on the contrary, are as associates to the king, in the administration of justice, participating of the royal power and authority, being bound to the utmost of their power to be assisting in the managing of the affairs of state, as well as the king, who is, as it were, president among them, and principal only in order and degree.

Therefore, as all the whole people is above the king, and likewise taken in one entire body, are in authority before him, yet being considered one by one, they are all of them under the king. It is easy to know how far the power of the first kings extended, in that Ephron, king of the Hittites, could not grant Abraham the sepulcher but in the presence, and with the consent of the people: neither could Hemor the Hevite, king of Sichem, contract an alliance with Jacob without the people's assent and confirmation thereof; because it was then the custom to refer the most important affairs to be dispensed and resolved in the general assemblies of the people. This might easily be practices in those kingdoms which were then almost confined within the circuit of one town.

But since the kings began to extend their limits, and that it was impossible for the people to assemble together all into one place because of their great numbers, which would have occasioned confusion, the officers of the kingdom were established, who should ordinarily preserve the rights of the people, in such sort notwithstanding, as when extraordinary occasion required, the people might be assembled, or at the least such an abridgment as might by the most principal members be a representation of the whole body. We see this order established in the kingdom of Israel, which (in the judgment of the wisest politicians) was excellently ordered. The king had his cupbearers, his carvers, his chamberlains and stewards. The kingdom had her officers, to wit, the seventy-one elders, and the heads and chief chosen out of all the tribes, who had the care of the public faith in peace and war.

Furthermore, the kingdom had in every town magistrates, who had the particular government of them, as the former were for the whole kingdom. At such times as affairs of consequence were to be treated of, they assembled together, but nothing that concerned the public state could receive any solid determination. David assembled the officers of his kingdom when he desired to invest his son Solomon with the royal dignity; when he would have examined and approved that manner of policy, and managing of affairs, that he had revived and restored, and when there was no question of removing the ark of the covenant.

And because they represented the whole people, it is said in the history, that all the people assembled. These were the same officers who delivered Jonathan from death, condemned by the sentence of the king, by which it appears, that there might be an appeal from the king to the people.

After that the kingdom was divided through the pride of Rehoboam. The council at Jerusalem composed of seventy-one ancients, seems to have such authority, that they might judge the king as well as the king might judge every one of them in particular. . . .

We read in another place, that Zedechias held in such reverence the authority of this council, that he was so far from delivering of Jeremy from the dungeon, whereunto the seventy-one had cast him, that he dare scarce remove him into a less rigorous prison. They persuading him to give his consent to the putting to death the prophet Jeremy, he answered, that he was in their hands, and that he might not oppose them in anything. The same king, fearing lest they might make information against him, to bring him to an account for certain speeches he had used to the prophet Jeremy, was glad to feign an untrue excuse. It appears by this, that in the kingdom of Judah this council was above the king, in this kingdom, I say, not fashioned or established by Plato or Aristotle, but by the Lord God Himself, being author of all their order, and supreme moderator in that monarchy. Such were the seven magi or sages in the Persian empire, who had almost a paralleled dignity with the king, and were termed the ears and eyes of the king, who also never dissented from the judgment of those sages. . . .

In the times of the emperors, there was the senate, the consults, the praetors, the great provosts of the empire, the governors of provinces, attributed to the senate and the people, all which were called the magistrates and officers of the people of Rome. And therefore, when that by the decree of the senate, the emperor Maximus was declared enemy of the commonwealth, and that Maximus and Albinus were created emperors by the senate, the men of war were sworn to be faithful and obedient to the people of Rome, the senate, and the emperors. Now for the empires and public states of these times (except those of Turkey, Muscovy and such like, which are rather a rhapsody of robbers, and barbarous intruders, than any lawful empires), there is not one, which is not, or hath not heretofore been governed in the manner we have described. And if through the conveniency and sloth of the principal officers, the successors have found the business in a worse condition, those who have for the present the public authority in their hands, are notwithstanding bound as much as in them lies to reduce things into their primary estate and condition.

In the empire of Germany, which is conferred by election, there are the electors and the princes, both secular and ecclesiastical, the counts, barons, and deputies of the imperial cities, and as all these in their proper places are solicitors for the public good, likewise in the Diets do they represent the majesty of the empire, being obliged to advise, and carefully foresee, that neither by the emperor's partiality, hate nor affection, the public state do suffer or be interested. And for this reason, the empire has its chancellor, as well as the emperor his, both the one and the other have their peculiar officers and treasurers apart. And it is a thing so notorious, that the empire is preferred before the emperor, that it is a common saying, "That emperor does homage to the empire." . . .

The kingdom of France heretofore preferred before all other, both in regard of the excellency of their laws and majesty of their estate, may pass with most as a ruling case. Now, although that those who have the public commands in their hands do not discharge their duties as were to be desired, it follows not though that they are not bound to do it. The king has his high steward of his household, his chamberlains, his masters of his games, cup-bearers, and others, whose offices were wont so to depend on the person of the king: after that the death of their master, their offices were void. And indeed at the funeral of the king, the lord high steward in the presence of all the officers and servants of the household, breaks his staff of office, and says, "Our master is dead, let every one provide for himself." On the other side, the kingdom has her officers, to wit, the mayor of the palace, who since has been called the constable, the marshals, the admiral, the chancellor, or great referendary, the secretaries, the treasurers and others, who heretofore were created in the assembly of the three estates, the clergy, the nobility, and the people.

Since that the Parliament of Paris was made sedentary, they are not thought to be established in their places before they have been first received and approved by that course of Parliament, and may not be dismissed nor disposed, but by the authority and consent of the same. Now all these officers take their oath to the kingdom, which is as much as to say, to the people in the first place, then to the king who is protector of the kingdom, the which appears by the tenure of the oath. Above all, the constable, who, receiving the sword from the king, has it girded unto him with this charge, that he maintain and defend the commonwealth, as appears by the words that the king then pronounces.

Besides, the kingdom of France has the peers (so called either for that they are the king's companions, or because they are the fathers of the commonwealth) taking their denominations from the several provinces of the kingdom, in whose hands the king at his inauguration takes his oath as if all the people of the kingdom were in them present, which shows that these twelve peers are above the king. They on the other side swear, "That they will preserve not the king, but the crown, that they will assist the commonwealth with their counsel, and therefore will be present with their best abilities to counsel the prince both in peace and war," as appears plainly in the patentee of their peership. . . .

We may also know, that those peers of France did often discuss suits and differences between the king and his subjects. Insomuch, that when Charles the Sixth would have given sentence against the Duke of Brittany they opposed it, alleging that the discussing of that business belonged properly to the peers and not to the king, who might not in any sort derogate from their authority.

Therefore it is that yet at this day the Parliament of Paris is called the court of peers, being in some sort constituted judge between the king and the people; yea, between the king and every private person, and is bound and ought to maintain the meanest in the kingdom against the king's attorney, if he undertake anything contrary to law.

Furthermore, if the king ordain anything in his council, if he treat an agreement with the princes his neighbors, if he begin a war, or make peace, as lately with Charles the Fifth the emperor, the Parliament ought to interpose their authority, and all that which concerns the public state must be therein registered; neither is there anything firm and stable which the Parliament does not first approve. And to the end that the counselors of that Parliament should not fear the king, formerly they attained not to that place, but by the nomination of the whole body of the court; neither could they be dismissed for any lawful cause, but by the authority of the said body.

Furthermore, if the letters of the king be not subsigned by a secretary of the kingdom, at this day called a secretary of state, and if the letters patent be not sealed by the chancellor, who has power also to cancel them, they are of no force or value. There are also dukes, marquesses, earls, viscounts, barons, seneschals, and, in the cities and good towns, mayors, bailiffs, lieutenants, capitols, consuls, syndics, sheriffs and others, who have special authority, through the circuit of some countries or towns to preserve the people of their jurisdiction. Time it is that at this day some of these dignities are become hereditary. Thus much concerning the ordinary magistrates.

Selection 11
An Apologist for Absolute Rule
Thomas Hobbes

Thomas Hobbes (1588–1679) was a political philosopher who lived and wrote during the period of the Puritan revolution in England. His great work, *Leviathan*, was published in 1651 at the peak of this uprising. Like that of Philippe Mornay, Hobbes' thought mirrors the political circumstances in which it was created. Forced to flee England because of his aristocratic associations, Hobbes longed for security and peace. His famous comment—that life was "nasty, brutish, and short"—reflects his own melancholy disillusionment with the events that he witnessed. Hobbes concluded that tranquility could best be attained under a monarch whose political power was unquestioned. In this selection from *Leviathan*, Hobbes discusses the reasons why power should be yielded up to the monarch.

CHAPTER XVII

Of the causes, generation, and definition of a commonwealth

Source: Thomas Hobbes, *Leviathan Or the Matter, Forme and Power of A Commonwealth Ecclesiasticall and Civil* (London: Andrew Crooke, 1651), Book I, ch. 17.

The final cause, end, or design of men, who naturally love liberty, and dominion over others, in the introduction of that restraint upon themselves, in which we see them live in commonwealths, is the foresight of their own preservation, and of a more contented life thereby; that is to say, of getting themselves out from that miserable condition of war, which is necessarily consequent, as hath been shown in Chapter XIII, to the natural passions of men, when there is no visible power to keep them in awe, and tie them by fear of punishment to the performance of their covenants, and observation of those laws of nature set down in the fourteenth and fifteenth chapters.

For the laws of nature, *as justice, equity, modesty, mercy,* and, in sum, *doing to others, as we would be done to,* of themselves, without the terror of some power, to cause them to be observed, are contrary to our natural passions, that carry us to partiality, pride, revenge, and the like. And covenants, without the sword, are but words, and of no strength to secure a man at all. Therefore notwithstanding the laws of nature, which every one hath then kept, when he has the will to keep them, when he can do it safely, if there be no power erected, or not great enough for our security; every man will, and may lawfully rely on his own strength and art, for caution against all other men. And in all places, where men have lived by small families, to rob and spoil one another, has been a trade, and so far from being reputed against the law of nature, that the greater spoils they gained, the greater was their honour; and men observed no other laws therein, but the laws of honour; that is, to abstain from cruelty, leaving to men their lives, and instruments of husbandry. And as small families did then; so now do cities and kingdoms which are but greater families, for their own security, enlarge their dominions, upon all pretences of danger, and fear of invasion, or assistance that may be given to invaders, and endeavour as much as they can, to subdue, or weaken their neighbours, by open force, and secret arts, for want of other caution, justly; and are remembered for it in after ages with honour.

Nor is it the joining together of a small number of men, that gives them this security; because in small numbers, small actions on the one side or the other, make the advantage of strength so great, as is sufficient to carry the victory; and therefore gives encouragement to an invasion. The multitude sufficient to confide in for our security, is not determined by any certain number, but by comparison with the enemy we fear; and is then sufficient, when the odds of the enemy is not of so visible and conspicuous moment, to determine the event of war, as to move him to attempt.

And be there never so great a multitude: yet if their actions be directed according to their particular judgments, and particular appetites, they can expect thereby no defence, nor protection, neither against a common enemy, nor against the injuries of one another. For being distracted in opinions concerning the best use and application of their strength, they do not help but hinder one another; and reduce their strength by mutual opposition to nothing: whereby they are easily, not only subdued by a very few that agree together; but also when there is no common enemy, they make war upon each other, for their particular interests. For if we could suppose a great multitude of men to consent in the observation of justice, and other laws of nature, without a common power to keep them all in awe; we might as well suppose all mankind to do the same; and then there neither would be, nor need to be any civil government, or commonwealth at all; because there would be peace without subjection.

Nor is it enough for the security, which men desire should last all the time of their life, that they be governed, and directed by one judgment, for a limited time; as in one battle, or one war. For though they obtain a victory by their unanimous endeavour against a foreign enemy; yet afterwards, when either they have no common enemy, or he that by one part is held for an enemy, is by another part held for a friend, they must needs by the difference of their interest dissolve, and fall again into a war amongst themselves.

It is true, that certain living creatures, as bees, and ants, live sociably one with another, which are therefore by Aristotle numbered amongst political creatures; and yet have no other direction, than their particular judgments and appetites: nor speech, whereby one of them can signify to another, what he thinks expedient for the common benefit: and therefore some man may perhaps desire to know, why mankind cannot do the same. To which I answer.

First, that men are continually in competition for honour and dignity, which these creatures are not: and consequently amongst men there ariseth on that ground, envy, and hatred, and finally war; but amongst these not so.

Secondly, that amongst these creatures, the common good differeth not from the private: and being by nature inclined to their private, they procure thereby the common benefit. But man, whose joy consisteth in comparing himself with other men, can relish nothing but what is eminent.

Thirdly, that these creatures, having not, as man, the use of reason, do not see, nor think they see any fault, in the administration of their common business; whereas amongst men, there are very many, that think themselves wiser, and abler to govern the public, better than the rest; and these strive to reform and innovate, one this way, another that way; and thereby bring it into distraction and civil war.

Fourthly, that these creatures, though they have some use of voice, in making known to one another their desires, and other affections; yet they want that art of words, by which some men can represent to others, that which is good, in the likeness of evil; and evil, in the likeness of good: and augment, or diminish the apparent greatness of good and evil; discontenting men, and troubling their peace at their pleasure.

Fifthly, irrational creatures cannot distinguish between *injury*, and *damage*: and therefore as long as they be at ease, they are not offended with their fellows: whereas man is then most troublesome, when he is most at ease: for then it is that he loves to shew his wisdom, and control the actions of them that govern the commonwealth.

Lastly, the agreement of these creatures is natural; that of men, is by covenant only, which is artificial: and therefore it is no wonder if there be somewhat else required, besides covenant, to make their agreement constant and lasting; which is a common power, to keep them in awe, and to direct their actions to the common benefit.

The only way to erect such a common power, as may be able to defend them from the invasion of foreigners, and the injuries of one another, and thereby to secure them in such sort, as that by their own industry, and by the fruits of the earth, they may nourish themselves and live contentedly; is, to confer all their power and strength upon one man, or upon one assembly of men, that may reduce all their wills, by plurality of voices, unto one will: which is as much as to say, to appoint one man, or assembly of men, to bear their person; and every one to own, and acknowledge himself to be author of whatsoever he that so beareth their person, shall act, or cause to be acted, in those things which concern the common peace and safety; and therein to submit their wills, every one to his will, and their judgments, to his judgment. This is more than consent, or concord; it is a real unity of them all, in one and the same person, made by covenant of every man with every man, in such manner, as if every man should say to every man, *I authorise and give up my right of governing myself, to this man, or to this assembly of men, on this condition, that thou give up they right to him, and authorise all his actions in like manner.* This done, the multitude so united in one person, is called a *commonwealth*, in Latin *civitas*. This is the generation of that great *leviathan*, or rather, to speak more reverently, of that *mortal god*, to which we owe under the *immortal God*, our peace and defence. For by this authority, given him by every particular man in the commonwealth, he hath the use of so much power and strength conferred on him, that by terror thereof, he is enabled to perform the wills of them all, to peace at home, and mutual aid against their enemies abroad. And in him consisteth the essence of the commonwealth; which, to define it, is *one person, of whose acts a great multitude, by mutual covenants one with another, have made themselves every one the author, to the end he may use the strength and means of them all, as he shall think expedient, for their peace and common defence.*

And he that carrieth this person, is called *sovereign*, and said to have *sovereign power;* and every one besides, his *subject.*

THREE

The Warrior

If we are to understand how the modern world was born, we must pay particular attention to the nature of war and its effects during the centuries from the mid-1300s to the late 1600s. During these years, the institutions and the outlook of medieval Europe were fundamentally transformed by a series of challenges to authority and tradition. Often the challenges were based on an effort to revive what was regarded as the better model of the ancient world—the ages of Greece, Rome, and the Bible. Just as often, however, change came because of new discoveries or ideas, and this is the case with warfare, which during the Renaissance passed through a great divide: the invention of gunpowder. Therefore, before we look at larger questions about war and its effects or about shifting attitudes toward the military, we must explore the succession of new techniques that made a battle in 1700 basically different from its predecessor in the 1300s.

GUNPOWDER AND ITS MILITARY CONSEQUENCES

We do not know who invented gunpowder, where, or when. There is no doubt that the Chinese had experimented with a mixture of potassium nitrate, sulfur, and charcoal to create explosions long before Europeans became interested in the compound. Although the Chinese applied it especially to fireworks and dazzling displays, they also developed its military uses, including primitive mines and hand grenades, during the Sung Dynasty (960–1279 A.D.). Yet at about the same time (the early 1300s) that the Chinese produced the first bombards, or simple cannons, Europeans were experimenting with similar weapons.

It is not clear whether the use of gunpowder in cannons was borrowed by the Europeans from China or is an example of simultaneous development in two widely separated parts of the globe. The traditional account of Western invention claims that a monk, experimenting with gunpowder, unexpectedly discovered its lethal properties. For those who disliked monks, the story made it easier to believe that the new substance was evil. What happened, according to tradition, is that the experimenter was pounding the gunpowder with a pestle in a narrow mortar so as to mix it and turn it into a finer powder. Leaving his tools unattended, he was startled to hear a loud bang and see his pestle hurtling across the room. The explosion in the small chamber had forced out the projectile at enormous speed, and for a number of years pestle-shaped objects were commonly fired from cannon. Pieces of artillery with large openings and a short, stubby shape are called "mortars" to this day.

Whatever the reasons for this breakthrough, once the projective force of gunpowder was appreciated, its career on the battlefield began. There are references to cannon being used in the 1310s, and the first drawing appeared in a manuscript in 1326. Given the enormous force generated by gunpowder, it was assumed that an extremely thick and strong barrel was necessary to contain the power and send the projectile along a specific path. The weapons were therefore heavy and cumbersome, useful mainly in sieges. On the battlefield they created alarm primarily with the noise of their discharge. They were expensive to make, difficult to cast, and could prove as dangerous to those firing them as to the enemy. Once they had proven their worth, however, as they had by the 1340s, when they were recognized as a new means of destroying defensive walls and also terrifying opponents, they became a fixture of warfare.

Over the centuries that followed, there was a steady effort to improve gunpowder weapons. Casting techniques were developed so that more reliable cannon, with standard-sized bores, could be produced. Standardization also affected the manufacture of cannonballs. In the early days, they were often stones chipped to an approximate ball shape or solid metal spheres of random sizes. As a result, they fitted loosely in the barrel, and emerged at totally unpredictable angles. Accuracy was impossible, and distance unreliable. Gradually, these problems were overcome, and lighter cannon, which could be moved around easily, were devised. By the 1600s, they had become essential not only in sieges, where their power could destroy all but the thickest walls, but also on the battlefield, where they were used for shock effect as well as to cause damage. And vicious new projectiles were invented—cannonballs linked together with a metal bar, "enhanced" with chains that swung wildly to mow people down, or packed into bags that burst and sent metal flying about when they landed.

Handguns were less destructive, but no less essential. The earliest ones to appear on the battlefield, in the mid-fifteenth century, also were cumbersome, and they took at least a minute to reload. Again, improvements over the following 150 years made them more powerful and quicker to reload, although their range and accuracy remained fairly limited because they suffered from the same lack of standardization as cannon in the manufacture of barrels and shot. Not until rifling became common in the nineteenth century were these problems finally overcome,*

---

* The technique of rifling—cutting a groove in the barrel of a gun so as to set a bullet spinning and thus improve its accuracy—was known in the Renaissance and used in expensive handguns. However, it was too costly for the mass production of infantry weapons, and there was some fear that humble sharpshooters might deliberately fire at officers and social superiors if they were capable of precise accuracy.

but in the meantime, it was easy to train a soldier to use a gun, and large numbers of men with guns were soon regarded as a formidable threat.

Cannon appeared sporadically, but ever more frequently, in the wars of the 1300s and 1400s, especially the so-called Hundred Years' War between the English and the French (1337–1453). They made castles far more vulnerable and began to have an impact on battles, although archers were still the main cause of the devastating English victories at Crécy (1346) and Agincourt (1415). By the time of the next major international conflict, the so-called Italian Wars (1494–1559), a struggle among the French, the Spanish, the Austrian Habsburgs, and various Italian states for control of Italy, the handgun was becoming one of the basic infantry weapons. A major reason that the Spaniards emerged from the Italian Wars as the most powerful nation in Europe, a position they held for decades, was their mastery of handgun tactics.

What the Spaniards did was to organize their infantry into huge squares of up to about 3000 soldiers, called *tercios*. At the center of the *tercio* were pikemen, who used their long weapons to fend off any attempts by cavalry to charge the square. Around the edge, arranged in rows which could wheel about in any direction, were the troops with guns. The theory was that in order to maintain a constant barrage of fire, they ought to shoot, at a signal, one row at a time. Immediately after shooting, the men in the front row were supposed to drop to their knees and begin reloading while the next row fired. This continued until the last row had fired, and then the front row was expected to have had enough time to reload. It did not often work exactly this way, but the *tercio* did become the most effective means of keeping up a steady stream of small-arms fire on the battlefield. For the tactic to work, strict discipline and large numbers were necessary; a well-drilled *tercio* could grind down all obstacles in its path as it moved slowly about a battlefield, stopping only to deliver its shattering barrages. Until 1643, when the French won a victory at Rocroi, no enemy was able to defeat the Spanish *tercios* in a pitched battle.

The only way to resist such power was to change strategy. When the Dutch revolted against their Spanish rulers, they managed to defend their independence throughout a long struggle (1568–1609) by avoiding pitched battles. Maurice of Nassau, their leader, was a student of military history and one of the pioneers of what is now called "guerilla warfare." Avoiding battles, he struck at the Spaniards through small engagements and raids. When their superior forces seemed about to occupy the Netherlands, he opened the dykes that protected his low-lying country from the sea and pushed the Spaniards back with floods. Flexibility and adaptability were used to counter massive power.

This strategy was developed further by the king of Sweden, Gustavus Adolphus, who was the most successful general of the Thirty Years' War (1618–1648) that devastated much of northern and central Europe. Although he never fought a Spanish army, Gustavus demonstrated that small, highly mobile units could defeat massive squares organized like *tercios*. Instead of continuous fire, he had all the men in his small units shoot at once in a single salvo. The shock effect was much greater, and if multiplied by many units, moving quickly, it disoriented and disrupted the huge, lumbering squares. The smaller units could move easily out of their enemy's range and, accompanied by the light, transportable cannon that

Map 5. Sites of major battles in 16th- and 17th-century Europe

Gustavus developed, could wreak havoc on their large targets. Even the cavalry waited for a salvo to have its disruptive effect before they charged.

The advantages of speed and flexibility were also recognized in naval warfare. The basic tactic until the late 1500s was for a captain to bring his vessel close enough to another ship to allow the soldiers he carried to board and capture the enemy. The more soldiers he carried, the better; the bigger the ship, the more powerful it was.

It was the Venetians who perfected this tactic, especially in their wars against the Turks in the Mediterranean, which culminated in a famous victory at Lepanto in 1571. Just seventeen years later, however, when the Spaniards sent an Armada of huge ships to invade England, they learned how effective small, maneuverable opponents could be. The speedy and mobile English fleet harassed the great Armada until its commanders panicked and fled. The idea gradually took hold that it was more effective to sink a ship than to capture it. Naval cannons were developed, and they came to be used in the sailor's equivalent of the salvo, the broadside.

Smaller and more mobile units, whether on land or at sea, still required a large number of total men. A major consequence of gunpowder, whether used by *tercios* or by versatile companies, was its effect on the size of armies. Because new methods made sieges both more elaborate and more common (for reasons discussed in the next paragraph), commanders were always demanding more troops. As these were recruited and the advantages of multiplying companies equipped with guns became apparent, so there was created a need for ever larger armies—not only for sieges but also, since they were available, on the field. Many of the forces fighting the battles of the Hundred Years' War had fewer than 10,000 men. By the time of the Italian Wars, the Spaniards could put 40,000 men into action. Gustavus Adolphus invaded Germany with 130,000 soldiers, and by the end of the 1600s Louis XIV of France had a standing army of 400,000 men. Moreover, those who did the actual fighting required increasingly elaborate logistical and technical support, which sometimes amounted to as many as five people per soldier.

The technical help was especially important in sieges, which took an increasingly large part of an army's time in the 1500s and 1600s. Castles fell easily to cannon, but towns, with extensive earthworks, tremendously thick walls, and carefully planned defenses, were a different matter. To capture territory, one had to capture towns. Yet cannonballs made little impression on six-foot-thick walls; the gunpowder itself had to be brought to the base of the wall and exploded so as to open a breach that the besiegers could attack. To reach the target, they had to dig a trench to protect those carrying the gunpowder. Since a defender could shoot right down a trench that was dug straight at a wall, a series of angled trenches was used to bring the attackers close. In response, builders of fortifications created obstacles as well as star-shaped bastions along the walls that multiplied the defenders' lines of fire. And the trench systems, in turn, grew ever more complicated. All this required high technical and engineering skills and a constantly increasing commitment of time and resources. As on the battlefield, sophisticated expertise and substantial manpower were becoming essential in siege warfare.

By 1700, armies were not just larger than they had been in 1300; their weapons, tactics, and organization were radically different. New kinds of discipline had been made necessary by gunpowder—both the *tercio* and the small company depended on highly trained leadership at all levels. Drilling had become mandatory, and the first military academies had been established. To control the enormous bodies of soldiers, a new hierarchy of command had emerged, which by the mid-1500s included the ranks and titles that are familiar to us today—lieutenant, major, colonel, and so forth. And among the products of the 1600s were standardized uniforms, large permanent armies that did not disband each winter, and regular military housing and barracks. Although these changes were not the result *only* of the invention of gunpowder, there is no doubt that they were made possible by the development of this new instrument for the conduct of war.

LINKS WITH SOCIAL, ECONOMIC, AND POLITICAL CHANGE

Almost every aspect of life in Renaissance Europe was affected by the military changes wrought by gunpowder. Examples of these consequences range from the design of houses, which could become more elegant once the builders realized that they could not be defended and therefore did not need fortifications, to the spread of disease, which was often carried by armies on the march. In turn, warfare felt the impact of the many social, economic, and political shifts of the period. Yet the most profound results of the vastly increased scale and complexity of war were felt in three areas: the status of nobles, the volume of economic activity and taxes, and the powers of monarchs. Although important, warfare was less central and less far-reaching in its effects on demographic, architectural, industrial, and other changes.

During the Middle Ages, a nobleman's status depended to a large extent on his military functions. As the lord and protector of a local area, he was responsible for recruiting and commanding a body of troops who were drawn from the area he ruled. His subjects served as footsoldiers with simple weapons. The more wealthy among them, known as "squires," were able to afford horses and armor. They formed a cavalry unit, whose most important members, knights on horseback, were the army's elite, interested only in fighting one another. A major reason for the destruction of the French cavalry at the battle of Agincourt in 1415 was their refusal to attack the English archers, whom they regarded as common men unworthy of their attention. But the growing effectiveness in the 1300s and 1400s of England's longbowmen, who could kill even an armored knight one hundred feet away, brought about a "leveling" of combat. They made all soldiers equally vulnerable, and this blurring of the distinctive status of the knight was only intensified by the indiscriminate power of guns.

The same process transformed another of the aristocracy's traditional functions, for in addition to their roles in recruitment and battle, nobles had to use their castles to defend the regions they controlled. Before the invention of gunpowder, a well-built castle was virtually immune to attack and could be captured only through a long and costly siege. Noblemen, therefore, had little to fear from a distant king; they were usually left alone to rule their regions and could think of their monarch as a somewhat more formidable equal. Cannon put an end to that immunity. Not only did gunpowder destroy the strategic value of the castle, but the new weapons demanded an expensive manufacturing process that only monarchs and exceptionally powerful aristocrats could afford.

The special role of the nobles in wartime was further undermined when they ceased to be the only source of manpower, as mercenary companies, consisting of soldiers hired from all parts of Europe, became a common basis for armies. The Swiss, for example, were famous as fighters and were easily enticed by good pay from their poor and rugged land. To this day, it is a Swiss Guard that protects the Pope in the Vatican. During the Renaissance, mercenary leaders (often known by their Italian name of *condottieri*) became major political figures in Italy and sometimes the lords of large areas they had won by conquest. Thus even the nobles' traditional responsibility as military commanders was endangered. Unless a great many of them banded together, they were increasingly unable to pose a military threat to the rulers who were gaining a monopoly over armed force. It is true that, accustomed to leadership, nobles were still essential as officers, but with common-ers giving orders as sergeants at the lower levels (and sometimes rising much higher if they were talented) and artillery and logistics experts gaining in importance, they could no longer feel uniquely qualified for warfare or entitled to their status because of their military skills.

Naturally, the members of the nobility resented these changes and continued to assert themselves. Indeed, their attempts to resist the growing power of kings and to retain their own customary authority were a source of conflict and upheaval in much of Europe for more than two hundred years until, in the late 1600s, nobles finally came to justify their superior social status primarily through government service and cultural distinction. Other motives were at work in this adaptation—the wish for a more cultivated lifestyle, inspired by Renaissance humanism; the acceptance of the rise of central governments; and the constant search for economic and political advantage—but an important motivation was the need to respond (in image as well as in reality) to the changing conditions of warfare and their effects on the nobility's traditional military role.

The chief reason the invention of gunpowder influenced the economic life of the Renaissance was the enormous growth in the size of armies. What is uncertain is whether the stimulus outweighed the destruction. On the positive side was the emergence of a new and enormous weapons manufacturing industry, with atten-dant advances in mining, metallurgy, and artisanal skills. The construction of immense city fortifications throughout Europe was a colossal boon to the building trade and its suppliers, from brickmakers to carpenters. Armies required clothing, food, transport, and shelter—all products that gave employment to artisans and ordinary laborers. The huge capital sums that were needed to pay the army's wages and bills helped bankers and the financial market. And merchants and traders could make fortunes as suppliers at every level of military organization. For hundreds of thousands of civilians, not to mention similar numbers of soldiers, warfare was essential to livelihood.

The employment was not always productive, however. Camp followers and maimed ex-soldiers were burdens, not economic assets. Armies were marching cities that devoured everything in their path. Entire regions could be devastated, picked clean of crops, farm animals, and food stores, by an army that settled in for just a few weeks. The destruction often differed only in details from the effects of famine or plague. Not until the Thirty Years' War did anyone conceive of a better system of maintaining troops, and even then it was as a means of self-enrichment. The imperial general Albrecht von Wallenstein, one of the wealthiest landowners in central Europe, used his own fertile territories in Bohemia to produce much of the food and beer for his army. He thus reduced the threat to civilian property from his troops and did so at a profit, because he received the market rate for the goods he supplied. Wallenstein was a solitary exception, however. More typical was his chief enemy, the Swede Gustavus Adolphus, who marched through Germany deliber-ately creating what he called a "swath of destruction" so that other armies would not be able to live off the land he had passed.

The economic balance sheet becomes difficult to compile when we consider that armies spread diseases as they moved and often drew into their ranks (sometimes by force if recruiting officers could not meet their quotas) civilians who could have led productive lives as wage earners and artisans. Did they provide more employment than they took away? Did they create more opportunities than they destroyed? Were the benefits of increased mobility they brought greater than the harm they caused as disrupters of communities? Did they employ surplus labor or divert vital resources? None of these questions can be answered unequivocally, because the experience varied by region and trade. Miners and bricklayers fared well, while the agriculture of heavily contested territories like the Netherlands and central Germany suffered. Everywhere, however, there was one burden that grew remorselessly because of war: taxation.

The chief beneficiaries of the military changes of this period were central governments, usually led by kings. As the overlord of all the nobles, the monarch had the greatest responsibility in a time of war. He or she—for there were many famous women leaders, from Italian princesses to Joan of Arc and Elizabeth I of England—determined foreign policy and thus the purpose and course of hostilities. When they gained almost total control over the power to make war because they alone had the resources to put a gunpowder army into the field, monarchs used their position not only to subdue rival nobles but also to expand their powers in many areas. And the reason they had the resources was that they could tax entire kingdoms, unlike the nobles, who had smaller regional bases.

General taxes had appeared in medieval Europe for the first time because of warfare—to pay for the Crusades—and once established, they never disappeared. Until the 1400s, however, they were fairly modest, less burdensome than the dues owed to local nobles and the tithes given to the Church. Monarchs still had a limited number of servants, small armies, and an adequate income from customs duties, legal fees, and the products of their private lands. As gunpowder made its first major impact in the fifteenth century, however, conditions began to change rapidly. The first small standing armies were set up in France and Spain, and in both countries taxes were created to meet these new expenses because the government could raise taxes without the bother of repeated constitutional consent from its subjects. The fifty-year period starting in the 1460s is often referred to as the "Age of the New Monarchy," when a series of determined kings—Louis XI in France (1461–1483), Ferdinand of Aragon in Spain (1479–1516), and Henry VII in England (1485–1509)—succeeded in expanding their powers and increasing their revenues. It was a process that continued, despite occasional interruptions, into modern times.

As the costs of war soared over the next two hundred years, so did the revenues of government and the size of the bureaucracies that were needed to collect taxes and to recruit, pay, and supply armies. By the 1600s, nobody could regard royal servants and finances as a minor burden. Kings employed thousands of officials and raised taxes in geometric increments. Between 1500 and 1640, the French royal revenue grew more than fivefold. And throughout this period France's military expenditures (not including the salaries of officials) amounted to one-third or more of the government's expenses. The need for money was so pressing that new schemes were constantly being sought to produce funds. In France, as in other countries, the most successful expedient was the sale of government offices, which were often created (without any real duties) in order to be sold. The inducement was that the purchaser of the office automatically became a nobleman and thus exempt from taxes. The result, however, was that the sales simultaneously diluted the special status of the nobility and shifted the growing tax burden onto a smaller section of the population. By the 1630s this device provided the French Crown with half its income. Although this proved to be the saturation point and revenues from the purchase of offices began to decline, the size of the bureaucracy and the amount of taxes continued to mushroom.

Kings used their armies to crush rebellions at home as well as to fight enemies abroad. And they applied their multiplying officials and resources to new interventions in the lives of their subjects. Whether censoring opinions or offering systematic relief for the poor, they were asserting their supremacy and demonstrating their authority throughout their kingdoms. It is no wonder that the 1600s have come to be regarded as the "Age of Absolutism," exemplified by the French King Louis XIV (1643–1715), who established more extensive and direct control over his kingdom than any previous European monarch. Even in states that adopted a constitutional system, with elections and representative assemblies—as in England—the central government was still the dominant force in the nation, for a parliament could impose its will just as effectively as an absolutist king. Of all the social, economic, and political developments that led to this outcome, none made a contribution to compare with the effects of war.

Next to these decisive transformations of European society, some of the other results of the new forms of Renaissance warfare may seem secondary, but their impact was far from trivial. Once the castle ceased to be defensible, for example, its shape altered dramatically. The crenellated towers gave way to graceful designs which created the great country houses that now adorn the European landscape. Gunpowder also was essential to the conquest of overseas empires. The extraordinary victories of Hernando Cortes and the other Spanish conquistadors as they overran entire civilizations in the New World depended largely on the remarkable weapons that enabled them to frighten the inhabitants, who vastly outnumbered them. In metallurgy, new techniques arose from weapons manufacture, and in banking, new ways of transferring large sums were devised, often to meet military expenditures. The catalog of the results of war could be extended into almost every corner of European history, but these few items alone should indicate the reasons that Western civilization could never be the same again. And the effects were felt far beyond Europe. When the Portuguese arrived in Japan in 1543, for example, they brought firearms with them. By the end of the 1500s, those weapons not only changed the construction of castles but also promoted the growing centralization of military and political power in feudal Japan. It was a transformation that was to be repeated throughout the world.

PERCEPTIONS

Although few contemporaries made the connections that historians now draw between warfare and other activities, the people of the Renaissance did realize that enormous changes were taking place, and they struggled to make sense of what they observed. For the scientist, the invention of gunpowder was one of the main reasons to celebrate the ingenuity and advances of the age. In a book published in 1620, for example, the Englishman Sir Francis Bacon gushed confidence:

> It is well to observe the force and virtue and consequences of discoveries, and these are to be seen nowhere more conspicuously than in those three which were unknown to the ancients . . . namely, printing, gunpowder, and the magnet. For these three have changed the whole face and state of things throughout the world.
>
> (*Novum Organum*, Book I, Aphorism 129)

Others saw the story differently. The Italian poet Ludovico Ariosto adopted the widely held view that gunpowder had put an end to knightly bravery. If one could kill an opponent from a distance, who would have the chance to display the bravery that was essential for virtue? In his most famous poem, *Orlando Furioso* (1516), Ariosto has his hero throw a gun into the sea with a bitter comment:

> "To ensure that no knight will ever again be intimidated by you, and that no villain will ever again boast himself the equal of a good man because of you, sink here. / O cursed, abominable device, constructed by the fiend Beelzebub in the forge of Hades when he planned to bring the world to ruin by you, back to hell from whence you came I consign you." So saying, he threw it to the deep.
>
> (Canto 9, lines 90–91)

This reaction can be linked to the growing unease of the nobles as the nature of war changed. The easy brashness of a twelfth-century knight, Bertrand de Born, no longer seemed so appealing when fighting ceased to be an activity in which the nobility had a clear-cut, unique, and valorous role:

> I tell you that my joy in eating, drinking, or sleeping is less than when I hear the cry, "Up and at 'em!"
> Or when I hear riderless horses whinny under the trees and groans of, "Help me! Help me!" And when I see both great and small fall on the grass and in ditches, And see the dead transfixed by spear shafts!
> Barons! Mortgage your castles, domains, and cities,
> But never, never, give up war!
>
> (*Sirventes*: "Be'm plai")

Instead, the nobility began to cultivate new virtues which set them apart from their inferiors—good manners, education, and courtesy. These had always been to some degree part of the knight's self-image, especially in his relations with women, but in the Renaissance they were give a new prominence. Dozens of handbooks and manuals of advice were written, but none was more influential than *The Book of the Courtier*, published in 1528 by the Italian Baldassare Castiglione. Two centuries earlier, it would have been hard to imagine that an essential mark of the gentleman was the ability to speak well:

> He should be one who is never at a loss for things to say that are good and well suited to those with whom he is speaking; . . . he should know how to sweeten and refresh the minds of his hearers, and move them discreetly to gaiety and laughter with amusing witticisms and pleasantries, so that, without ever producing tedium or satiety, he may continually give pleasure.
>
> (*The Book of the Courtier*, Book II, Chapter 41)

Among ordinary people, attitudes were similarly mixed, although the negatives generally outweighed the positives. For every soldier glad of a chance to make a livelihood or perhaps change his life, there were dozens whose families suffered deprivation or loss because of the military. Antiwar riots and popular demands for peace were far more common than enthusiastic mobilizations for war, even if thousands of ordinary people did prove willing to give their lives for their faith when they were swept by the enthusiasms of the Protestant Reformation and the Catholic Counter-Reformation in the sixteenth century. As these religious wars became more destructive, though, the regions crossed by armies could become virtual deserts; the resultant despair and attacks on soldiers by civilians were unmistakable evidence of the feelings of ordinary people. Much depended on how close the fighting came to home. When it remained distant, one could indulge in dreams of glory, as did the anonymous English writer of a book published in 1692:

> War is said to be a curse to a nation; 'tis true, but 'tis only so where the seat of war is, where all is committed to plunder, rapine, fire, flames, and utter destruction. But how many nations have raised their name, and rendered themselves famous and rich by war? And what have not advantageous wars brought into this nation? Our conquests . . . have for certain advanced our riches.

> (*The Present War No Burden to England*, 1692)

It was quite evident in the 1600s, however, that antiwar sentiments were becoming increasingly respectable, even in the court circles primarily responsible for maintaining hostilities. François Fenelon, an archbishop at the court of Louis XIV, wrote a novel for the king's grandson that was quite explicit in one passage:

> The evils of war never fail to drain a nation, and put it in danger of ruin, even while it is most victorious; with how great advantage soever they begin it, they are never sure to end it without being exposed to the most tragical chances of fortune. . . . And though you should hold victory chained in your camp, you destroy yourself in destroying your enemies. You dis-people your country, leave your ground uncultivated, interrupt commerce, nay, which is far worse, you weaken your laws and suffer manners to be corrupted.

> (*The Adventures of Telemachus*, 1699)

Many of the great literary and philosophical figures of the period expressed similar sentiments. The English poet John Milton asked, "What can war but endless war still breed?" ("Sonnet on the General Lord Fairfax," 1648), and in 1660 the influential political philosopher John Locke looked back in dismay at the "war and contention, all those flames that have made such havoc and desolation in Europe, and have not been quenched but with the blood of so many millions" (*The Tracts on Government*, ed. Philip Abrams, p. 160).

The most vivid index of changing perceptions is in the work of the great painters of the Renaissance and Baroque. Scenes such as Paolo Uccello's *Battle of San Romano* (Figure 11) were designed to emphasize the leadership of heroes—in this case the triumphant commander, wearing a splendid octagonal hat and riding a magnificent horse. This was painted in the mid-1450s. In the next century, a great monarch was still shown in this pose. Titian's portrait of the Emperor Charles V commemorates a major victory and shows him in full armor astride another great horse (Figure 4). Charles never went near the battlefield, but a ruler was thought of

Figure 11. Paolo Uccello, *Battle of San Romano* (detail). Completed around 1456 to celebrate a Florentine victory, this painting is a fascinating essay in perspective. The horses, spears, and bodies are seen at odd angles, but the dominant figure is the commander at the center with his splendid three-dimensional hat.

as being at his most glorious when he appeared as a warrior in this fashion. After the passage of another 150 years, the tradition was still alive, for King Louis XIV appeared on horseback as well as in splendid robes (Figure 9). And depictions of battles were a common decoration for palaces and public buildings.

Yet the brutality of religious war in the mid-1500s also inspired some remarkable protests. At the very time when the first pleas for toleration—cries for peace instead of aggression—were being heard, the Flemish artist Pieter Brueghel was producing his own indictment of the warriors. Although it was still not possible to do this openly, nobody could object to a biblical scene, so Brueghel set *The Massacre of the Innocents* in an immediately recognizable village of his own day (Figure 12). This was a time when the Catholic Spaniards were tightening their control over the Netherlands, where he lived, and his painting therefore puts before us a company of Spanish soldiers who are tearing babies away from mothers and slaughtering them. The judgment on the military was unmistakable. And Brueghel's dismay at violence and destruction in general is apparent in his depiction of the mythic figure of *Mad Meg* (Figure 13).

Brueghel was an outsider, a brilliant social critic, but never an establishment figure. Yet little more than half a century after his death in 1569, the most respected and admired artists of the day were following his lead. The devastations of the Thirty Years' War, which probably reduced the population of Germany by more than a

Figure 12. Pieter Brueghel the Elder, *Massacre of the Innocents*. Although ostensibly a biblical scene, this painting of the 1560s shows Brueghel's homeland, the Low Countries, in the harsh season of winter. As a company of the Spanish troops who had been sent to keep the people subdued looks on, soldiers tear babies and children from their mothers and kill them.

third, put the glories of battle in a new light. Even those who worked at the royal courts responsible for the fighting felt compelled to plead for different values, and in the 1620s and 1630s we can see an extraordinary change come over their work.

The Frenchman Jacques Callot, famous for his depiction of battle scenes, produced a harrowing series of etchings called *The Miseries of War* (Figure 14). Even though the Dutch were fighting for their independence at this very time, one of their artists, Jacques De Gheyn, showed the god of war, Mars, asleep, and the artist added a pointed caption: "Mars rests after crowning himself with glory; may he rest more gloriously from now on for the good of his people" (Figure 15). When the Flemish artist Peter Paul Rubens was asked to decorate the city of Antwerp to welcome as its new ruler one of the great heroes of the Thirty Years' War, the Infante Ferdinand, who had just defeated the Swedish army for the first time, he even dared to choose an antiwar message to greet him. The final tableau contrasted the benefits of peace with the ferocity of war and showed Ferdinand's predecessor, his aunt Isabella, trying to prevent new wars. Rather than encouraging a heroic ruler to further valor, an artist was asking him to abandon the military life.

Figure 13. Pieter Brueghel the Elder, *Mad Meg*. The scene dominated by Mad Meg, a gigantic woman from Netherlandish myth whom Brueghel presents as a symbol of avarice, demonstrates the destructiveness of war. As her followers battle devils near the entrance to Hell (the open mouth of the huge head of Satan on the left), we see that the landscape is ravaged, the sky is menacing, and the figure of Meg herself is heroic but also crazed.

When the king of Spain decided to decorate the chief public room in a new palace he built in the 1630s with commemorations of notable victories, the most famous painting he commissioned was anything but a glorification of war. Velazquez's *The Surrender of Breda* emphasizes the weariness, disillusion, and magnanimity of battle—the victor comforting the loser—not the feelings of triumph (Figure 16). The destruction and chaos of the Thirty Years' War—familiar throughout the continent because of the many depictions of the fighting, such as the engraving *The Siege of Magdeburg* (Figure 17)—were taking their toll. Rubens, who visited most of the leading courts of the time, expressed his dismay in an extraordinary painting, *The Horrors of War* (Figure 18), which shows the devastation Mars causes and the agony of the woman in black who, Rubens said, represents Europe herself. And in England, the greatest portraitist of the day, Antony van Dyck, was beginning to create new ways for nobles to have themselves painted. They no longer appeared as

A la fin ces Voleurs infames et perdus ,
Comme fruits malheureux a cet arbre pendus   *Monstrent bien que le crime (horrible et noire engeance)*
Est luy mesme instrument de honte et de vengeance ,   *Et que cest le Destin des hommes vicieux*
Desprouuer tost ou tard la iustice des Cieux . [1]

Figure 14. Jacques Callot, *The Miseries of War: The Hanging* (engraving). The engravings published by Callot in 1633, and entitled *Miseries of War*, were widely distributed. They emphasize the lack of discipline of the soldiers and the brutality caused by armies. In this example, looters are hanged for their crimes. The popularity of these engravings is an indicator of the growing resentment caused by the endless fighting.

heroes, but as rich, elegant, cultivated courtiers. The very image of the aristocrat (and thus of the warrior) had changed in response to the transformation of warfare.

Partly because of the growing distaste for violence, mirrored and encouraged by artists, political leaders began to try to bring armies under tighter control. Discipline improved rapidly in the second half of the 1600s, and battles became far less bloody. To reduce the deprecations of soldiers on civilians, who were, after all, the king's subjects, governments built barracks, improved pay, and took pains to ensure sufficient supplies, particularly food, for the troops. As a result, the military could come to be regarded as simply one aspect of society—a solid profession, universally familiar, but without special claims either to virtue or to censure.

It may seem ironic that the invention of gunpowder should at first have expanded the scale and ferocity of war yet eventually have paved the way for the more disciplined, less destructive military life of the late 1600s. Paradoxes are inevitable, however, when one deals with a phenomenon such as war, whose effects stretch into so many corners of European history. No important feature of Renaissance life was left untouched by the military changes of the period, and developments soon took society far beyond the immediate results of the new technology and tactics. Gradually, people came to understand how radically war was affecting them and realized that traditional assumptions about heroism and virtue were no longer beyond question. It was as they struggled to create a new context for warfare, and for its many political, economic, and social consequences, that Europeans began to shape what we can recognize as the modern state and the modern world's many-sided attitudes toward war.

Figure 15. After Jacques de Gheyn, *The Sleeping Mars* (engraving). It is significant that this antiwar engraving of Mars (god of war) asleep, with a caption that hopes he will remain asleep, was produced in the Netherlands during the 1620s, when the Dutch were fighting for their survival during the Thirty Years' War. The rising dismay over the constant warfare affected even a country struggling for its independence.

Figure 16. Diego Velazquez, *The Surrender of Breda*. Painted for a great hall commemorating Spanish victories in a new palace that was built in Madrid in the 1630s, this picture recalls the capture of the Dutch city of Breda in 1625. The disciplined Spaniards stand on the right, and their commander accepts the keys of the city from the tattered Dutch on the left. The commander's comforting gesture and the gloomy atmosphere suggest the agonies, not the triumphs, of battle.

Figure 17. *The Siege of Magdeburg in 1631* (engraving). Perhaps the most brutal episode of the Thirty Years' War was the seige of Magdeburg in 1631—shown in this engraving, as fire and artillery engulf the city. After the city surrendered, it was looted and much of the population was slaughtered.

Original Sources

Although humans have made war with one another since the beginning of recorded history, during the Renaissance the theory and practice of war was transformed. The invention of gunpowder revolutionized the development of weapons, and this, in turn, changed fighting and war's effects. Destruction became both more precise and more widespread.

These changes also affected attitudes toward war. No longer could warfare be glorified as a valiant act of chivalry. Chivalric gestures seemed easier, somehow, at the point of a sword rather than facing the barrel of a gun. By the end of the seventeenth century, war seemed radically different to people at every level of society.

I. EXPERIENCES OF WAR

War's reality is portrayed in this first section of the readings. Blaise de Monluc was a French nobleman with the perspective of one kind of eyewitness—that of a "warrior." In *Simplicissimus*, war's impact on the poor peasants is graphically dramatized. Finally, an otherwise anonymous field preacher of Prince Frederick Henry of Orange presents war from the point of view of an observer rather than a participant. Each contributes to our understanding of what the experience of war actually was during the Renaissance.

Selection 1
The Battle of Cerisoles, 14 April 1544
Blaise de Monluc

Blaise de Monluc, Marshal of the French Army, wrote his *Commentaries* after over half a century of experience in wars in France and Italy. The French King Henri IV regarded them as "the soldier's Bible" because of their mixture of shrewd observation and sound, practical advice.

I then took four lieutenants, namely le Breil (whom I have mentioned before), le Gasquet, Captain Lyenard and Captain Fabas, who was my own lieutenant. To Fabas and Lyenard I gave the right wing and myself with the two others took the left, leading towards the little house that was afterwards so much disputed; and it was ordered that the Swiss which were commanded by Monsieur de Boutieres (who a little before the rumour of the battle had been recalled from his own house)

Source: Blaise de Monluc, *The Habsburg-Valois Wars and the French Wars of Religion*, ed. by Ian Roy, trans. by Charles Cotton (London: Longmans, 1971), pp. 104, 106–109, 113.

and we should fight together in the vanguard. The battle was to be conducted by Monsieur d'Enghien, having under his cornet all the young lords that came from court, and the rearguard was commanded by Monsieur Dampierre wherein were four thousand Gruyeriens and three thousand Italians led by the Sieur de Dros and de Cros, together with all the guidons and archers of companies. . . .

Now I had discovered their German foot and their artillery, and as I was retiring Monsieur de Thermes and Signor Francisco Bernardino came and placed themselves on the right hand of our battalion and upon the skirt of the hill (which was very straight), and over against the battalion of the Italians; for their lancers were exactly opposite to our pikes. Monsieur de Boutieres with his company and that of the Count de Tende advanced on the left hand of our battle, and the Swiss were three or fourscore paces behind us and a little on the one side. In the meantime our arquebusiers that were conducted by Lyenard and Captain Fabas sometimes beat back the enemy as far as their main battle, and sometimes the enemy repelled them up to ours. I saw then that I must of necessity disarm our battalion of arquebusiers that made our flank on that side where Monsieur de Boutieres stood and give them to them, wherewith to make a charge; which they did, and with great fury beat them up to their battle, and it was high time, for their arquebusiers had almost gained the flank of our horse. I therefore ran up to them and we began a furious skirmish, which was great and obstinately fought, for all our squadrons were closed up together and it continued a long hour or more.

Now the enemy had placed their cannon by the side of the little house, which played directly into our battle. Monsieur de Mailly then advanced with ours and placing himself close by us, began to shoot at those of the enemy by the little house, for there where we maintained the skirmish he could not do it without killing our own men; when, looking towards our own battle, I saw Monsieur de Taix, who began to march with his pikes, charge directly towards the Italians, whereupon I ran up to him saying, "Whither do you go, sir, whither do you go, you will lose the battle; for here are all the Germans coming to fight you and will charge into your flank." The captains were the occasion of this, who ceased not to cry out to him, "Sir, lead us on to fight, for it is better for us to die hand to hand than stand still here to be killed with the cannon." 'Tis that which terrifies the most of anything and oftentimes begets more fear than it does harm. But however so it was that he was pleased to be ruled by me, and I entreated him to make his men kneel on one knee with their pikes down, for I saw the Swiss behind laid at their full length squat to the ground, so as hardly to be seen; and from him I ran to the arquebusiers. The enemy's arquebusiers by

this time were beginning to retire behind the house when, as I was going up to charge straight up to them, I discovered the front of the Germans' battle and suddenly commanded the captains Breil and Gasquet to retire by degrees towards the artillery, for we were to make room for the pikes to come up to the fight, and I went to our battle, where being come I said to my men these words:

Oh my fellow soldiers, let us now fight bravely, and if we win the battle we get a greater renown than any of our nation ever did. It was never yet read in history that ever the Gauls fought the Germans pike to pike but that the Germans defeated them, and to set this honourable mark upon ourselves that we were better men than our ancestors, this glory ought to inspire us with a double courage to fight so as to overcome or die and make our enemies know what kind of men we are. Remember, comrades, the message the King sent to us and what a glory it will be to present ourselves before him after the victory. "Now, sir," said I to Monsieur de Taix, "it is time to rise," which he suddenly did, and I began to cry out aloud: "Gentlemen, it may be there are not many here who have ever been in a battle before, and therefore let me tell you that if we take our pikes by the hinder end and fight at the length of the pike, we shall be defeated; for the Germans are more dexterous at this kind of fight than we are. But you must take your pikes by the middle as the Swiss do and run headlong to force and penetrate into the midst of them, and you shall see how confounded they will be." Monsieur de Taix then cried out to me to go along the battle and make them all handle their pikes after this manner, which I accordingly did, and now we were all ready for the encounter.

The Germans marched at a great rate directly towards us and I ran to put myself before the battle, where I alighted from my horse, for I ever had a lackey at the head of the battalion ready with my pike. And as Monsieur de Taix and the rest of the captains saw me on foot they all cried out at once, "Get up, Captain Monluc, get up again and you shall lead us on to the fight." To whom I made answer that if it was my fate to die that day, I could not die in a more honourable place than in their company, with my pike in my hand. I then called to Captain la Burte, who was sergeant major, that he should always be stirring about the battalion when we came to grapple, and that he and the

sergeants behind and on the sides should never cease crying "Put home, soldiers, put home," to the end that they might push on one another.

Selection 2

Simplicius Simplicissimus

Christoph von Grimmelshausen

The Thirty Years' War (1618–1648) was one of the most brutal of this entire period. Grimmelshausen's classic work, *Simplicissimus*, which remained unpublished until 1837, vividly portrays what this destruction meant in human terms—even to a participant that he termed the "most simple of the simple." Although fictionalized, this account was based on Grimmelshausen's first-hand observations.

CHAPTER 4

How Simplicissimus's palace was stormed, plundered, and ruinated, and in what sorry fashion the soldiers kept house there

Although it was not my intention to take the peace-loving reader with these troopers to my dad's house and farm, seeing that matters will go ill therein, yet the course of my history demands that I should leave to kind posterity an account of what manner of cruelties were now and again practised in this our German war: yea, and moreover testify by my own example that such evils must often have been sent to us by the goodness of Almighty God for our profit. For, gentle reader, who would ever have taught me that there was a God in Heaven if these soldiers had not destroyed my dad's house, and by such a deed driven me out among folk who gave me all fitting instruction thereupon? Only a little while before, I neither knew nor could fancy to myself that there were any people on earth save only my dad, my mother and me, and the rest of our household, nor did I know of any human habitation but that where I daily went out and in. But soon thereafter I understood the way of men's coming into this world, and how they must leave it again. I was only in shape a man and in name a Christian: for the rest I was but a

Source: H. J. C. von Grimmelshausen, *The Adventurous Simplicissimus* (London: William Heinemann, 1912), pp. 28–32.

beast. Yet the Almighty looked upon my innocence with a pitiful eye, and would bring me to a knowledge both of Himself and of myself. And although He had a thousand ways to lead me thereto, yet would He doubtless use that one only by which my dad and my mother should be punished: and that for an example to all others by reason of their heathenish upbringing of me.

The first thing these troopers did was, that they stabled their horses: thereafter each fell to his appointed task: which task was neither more nor less than ruin and destruction. For though some began to slaughter and to boil and to roast so that it looked as if there should be a merry banquet forward, yet others there were who did but storm through the house above and below stairs. Others stowed together great parcels of cloth and apparel and all manner of household stuff as if they would set up a frippery market. All that they had no mind to take with them they cut in pieces. Some thrust their swords through the hay and straw as if they had not enough sheep and swine to slaughter: and some shook the feathers out of the beds and in their stead stuffed in bacon and other dried meat and provisions as if such were better and softer to sleep upon. Others broke the stove and the windows as if they had a never-ending summer to promise. Houseware of copper and tin they beat flat, and packed such vessels, all bent and spoiled, in with the rest. Bedsteads, tables, chairs, and benches they burned, though there lay many cords of dry wood in the yard. Pots and pipkins must all go to pieces, either because they would eat none but roast flesh, or because their purpose was to make there but a single meal.

Our maid was so handled in the stable that she could not come out; which is a shame to tell of. Our man they laid bound upon the ground, thrust a gag into his mouth, and poured a pailful of filthy water into his body: and by this, which they called a Swedish draught, they forced him to lead a party of them to another place where they captured men and beasts, and brought them back to our farm, in which company were my dad, mother, and our Ursula.

And now they began: first to take the flints out of their pistols and in place of them to jam the peasant's thumbs in and so to torture the poor rogues as if they had been about the burning of witches: for one of them they had taken they thrust into the baking oven and there lit a fire under him, although he had as yet confessed no crime: as for another, they put a cord round his head and so twisted it tight with a piece of wood that the blood gushed from his mouth and nose and ears. In a word, each had his own device to torture the peasants, and each peasant his several torture. But as it seemed to me then, my dad was the luckiest, for he with a laughing face confessed what others must out with in the midst of pains and miserable lamentations: and such honour without doubt fell to him because he was the householder. For they set him before a fire and bound him fast so that he could neither stir hand nor foot, and smeared the soles of his feet with wet salt, and this they made our old goat lick off, and so tickle him that he well nigh burst his sides with laughing. And this seemed to me so merry a thing that I must needs laugh with him for the sake of fellowship, or because I knew no better. In the midst of such laughter he must needs confess all that they would have of him, and indeed revealed to them a secret treasure, which proved far richer in pearls, gold, and trinkets than any would have looked for among peasants. Of the women, girls, and maidservants whom they took, I have not much to say in particular, for the soldiers would not have me see how

they dealt with them. Yet this I know, that one heard some of them scream most piteously in divers corners of the house; and well I can judge it fared no better with my mother and our Ursel than with the rest. Yet in the midst of all this miserable ruin I helped to turn the spit, and in the afternoon to give the horses drink, in which employ I encountered our maid in the stable, who seemed to me wondrously tumbled, so that I knew her not, but with a weak voice she called to me, "O lad, run away, or the troopers will have thee away with them. Look to it well that thou get hence: thou seest in what plight . . ." And more she could not say.

CHAPTER 5

How Simplicissimus took French leave, and how he was terrified by dead trees

Now did I begin to consider and to ponder upon my unhappy condition and prospects, and to think how I might best help myself out of my plight. For whither should I go? Here indeed my poor wits were far too slender to devise a plan. Yet they served me so far that towards evening I ran into the woods. But then whither was I to go further? for the ways of the wood were as little known to me as the passage beyond Nova Zembla through the Arctic Ocean to China. 'Tis true the pitch-dark night was my protection: yet to my dark wits it seemed not dark enough; so I did hide myself in a close thicket wherein I could hear both the shrieks of the tortured peasants and the song of the nightingales; which birds regarded not the peasants either to show compassion for them or to stop their sweet song for their sakes: and so I laid myself, as free from care, upon one ear, and fell asleep. But when the morning star began to glimmer in the East I could see my poor dad's house all aflame, yet none that sought to stop the fire: so I betook myself thither in hopes to have some news of my dad; whereupon I was espied by five troopers, of whom one holloaed to me, "Come hither, boy, or I will shoot thee dead."

But I stood stock-still and open-mouthed, as knowing not what he meant or would have; and I standing there and gaping upon them like a cat at a new barn-door, and they, by reason of a morass between, not being able to come at me, which vexed them mightily, one discharged his carbine at me: at which sudden flame of fire and unexpected noise, which the echo, repeating it many times, made more dreadful, I was so terrified that forthwith I fell to the ground, and for terror durst not move a finger, though the troopers went their way and doubtless left me for dead; nor for that whole day had I spirit to rise up. But night again overtaking me, I stood up and wandered away into the woods until I saw afar off a dead tree that shone: and this again wrought in me a new fear: wherefore I turned me about posthaste and ran till I saw another such tree, from which I hurried away again, and in this manner spent the night running from one dead tree to another. At last came

blessed daylight to my help, and bade those trees leave me untroubled in its presence: yet was I not much the better thereby; for my heart was full of fear and dread, my brain of foolish fancies, and my legs of weariness, my belly of hunger, and mine eyes of sleep. So I went on and on and knew not whither; yet the further I went the thicker grew the wood and the greater the distance from all human kind. So now I came to my senses, and perceived (yet without knowing it) the effect of ignorance and want of knowledge: for if an unreasoning beast had been in my place he would have known what to do for his sustenance better than I. Yet I had wit enough when darkness again overtook me to creep into a hollow tree and there take up my quarters for the night.

Selection 3
Journal of a Field Preacher of Prince Frederick Henry of Orange (1645)

By 1645, the Revolt of the Netherlands, or Eighty Years' War, was coming to a close. This account of war's effects on soldiers and villagers is taken from the journal of a field preacher (or army chaplain) of the Dutch leader, Prince Frederick Henry. It shows that although this war had been fought spasmodically for many years, in 1645 it was no less bloody and inhuman.

Monday

Oct. 2. We were able to cross the River Schelde without loss of time, for a nobleman had fled with his goods to Ghent and failed to destroy the bridges behind him. Thus we came in the Land called Aalst. The people here, completely unaware of our presence, were easily surprised and subdued. A few of our cavalrymen went into the taverns and had several drinks with the peasants, asking them if they knew of any troops in the area. They'd heard of a few soldiers from Lorraine and of the French Army, but knew nothing about the

army of the Prince of Orange. A few of our other soldiers walked into a peasant's house, and found there a great fire burning, over which hung various pots and pans. Next to them were beef, fowl, cabbage, parsnips, turnips, and a large pot of cooked peas (being the normal trimmings of a peasant wedding feast). They also found much good, strong beer; realizing that a wedding feast had been underway, and that the groom, bride, and guests had all fled, these hungry, uninvited wedding guests, who were driven there out of hunger, discussed the matter and decided to eat the entire meal themselves. . . .

The church was also plundered by the soldiers, who saw a variety of paintings, among others one with large writing on it: MARIA, REFUGE FOR THE SINNERS. . . .

Source: Schrick van Vlaenderen en Brabandt, Aenghedaen door sijn Hoogheydt Frederick Hendrick, Prince van Oraengien (Middelburg, 1645), unpaged. Trans. by Craig Harline.

Tuesday

Oct. 3. His Highness marched by night across the bridge over the Schelde. . . . We passed through many lovely pasturelands near the river, and arrived in a village named Selderoode, which is situated almost on a mountain, and dense with trees and bushes. In the churchyard of this village we found, in the middle of the night, countless women and children from this and surrounding villages. These women and children were weeping bitterly; it was a sorry spectacle to behold, and a pitiful sound to hear. We tried to persuade them to take shelter in the church, although this church was almost too small for all those women and children. But they refused to enter the church, fearing (they said), that the French would come and burn the church with them inside of it. We answered to the contrary, but they would not budge. I tried every argument I could muster, the mercy and charity of our Prince, the honor of our officers [and so forth]. We promised them that no harm would come to them, and that a few of our number would accompany them to safety in Ghent the next day. Then the women learned that I was a preacher. . . . They believed me, and proceeded like lambs to the church, beseeching their guards to let no one in the church while they were there. . . . I cannot express how I felt when those women pleaded with me and surrounded me, wetting my hands with their kisses and sobs. My heart broke, tears streamed down my face to see all this sorrow and to hear the pitiful wailings of these helpless women and young children. . . .

We set off again; around midday the army arrived in the Land of Waas. It is an exceptionally beautiful, fruitful land, full of trees. During our march from Melle to Steken, one could not see much further than one hundred rods because of the natural growth and the planted trees. . . . We marched about a mile into this land and came upon an impressive castle surrounded by a moat. . . . This castle was plundered by the soldiers; after most such pillaging, I went inside to have a look around. Feathers flew above the roof of the castle like thick, snowy clouds, for the soldiers ripped open any beds they found, shook out the feathers, and took the casing or stuffed it full of loot. Everyone was able to find here any utensils he needed, for the castle was full of them. I was sorry to see, here and in other places, contracts, rent-rolls, wills, and other papers belonging to the lord of the castle scattered everywhere. The soldiers could profit little from such carelessness; thus, whenever I had a chance, I would gather the papers up and stash them away, hoping that the rightful owners would find, after restoring order to their dwellings, that a few of their rent-rolls or debt books had survived the onslaught.

II. COURT LIFE, GENTLEMEN, AND GENTLEWOMEN

Although the brutality of war was clearly defined in the preceding readings, the political and military leadership of the Renaissance paid tribute to ideals and values that were rather different from what this reality suggests. These new ideals and values were to have a lasting impact on the way the warrior was regarded.

Selection 4
"The Perfect Gentleman"
Giovanni della Casa

Giovanni della Casa (1503–1556) was renowned as a bishop, poet, diplomat, and orator. "The Perfect Gentleman" is a selection from his book of manners or "courtesy" book, *Galateo*. The book's primary purpose—similar to that of the contemporary newspaper column, "Miss Manners"—was to demonstrate proper models of behavior.

There is no doubt, but who so disposes himself to live, not in solitary and desert places, as hermits, but in fellowship with men and in populous cities, will think it a very necessary thing to have skill to put himself forth comely and seemly, in his fashions, gestures, and manners. The lack of these parts does make those other virtues lame, and little or nothing can they work to good effect without other helps, whereas this civility and courtesy, without other relief or patrimony, is rich of itself and has substance enough, as a thing that stands in speech and gestures alone.

And that you may now more easily learn the way unto it, you must understand it behooves you to frame and order your manners and doings, not according to your own mind and fashion but to please those with whom you live, and after that direct your doings. And this must be done by discretion and measure. For who so applies himself too much to feed other men's humours in his familiar conversation and behaviour with men, is rather to be thought a jester, a juggler, or flatterer than a gentleman well taught and nurtured. As contrariwise, whoso has no care or mind to please or displease, is a rude, untaught, and uncourteous fellow. Forasmuch then, as our manners have

Source: Della Casa, "Galatea," in *The Portable Renaissance Reader*, ed. by J. B. Ross and M. M. McLaughlin (New York: Viking Press, Inc., 1953), pp. 340–343, 345–347.

some pleasure in them when we respect other men and not our own pleasure, if we diligently search forth what those things be that most men do generally like or dislike, we shall in such sort wisely and easily find out the means and ways to choose and eschew those fashions and manners we are to leave or take, to live amongst men.

We say then, that every act that offends any of the common senses, or overthwarts a man's will and desire, or else presents to the imagination and conceit matters unpleasant, and that likewise which the mind does abhor, such things I say be naught, and must not be used. For we must not only refrain from such things as be foul, filthy, loathsome, and nasty, but we must not so much as name them. And it is not only a fault to do such things but against good manner by any act or sigh to put a man in mind of them. And therefore it is an ill-favoured fashion that some men use, openly to thrust their hands in what part of their body they list.

Likewise, I like it ill to see a gentleman settle himself to do the needs of nature in presence of men, and after he has done to truss himself again before them. Neither would I have him (if I may give him counsel), when he comes from such an occupation, so much as wash his hands in the sight of honest company, for that the cause of his washing puts them in mind of some filthy matter that has been done apart. And by the same reason, it is no good manner when a man chances to see, as he passes the way (as many times it happens) a loathsome thing that will make a man to cast his stomach, to turn unto the company and show it them. And much worse I like it, to reach some stinking thing unto a man to smell unto it, as it is many a man's fashion to do with importunate means, yes, thrusting it unto their nose, saying "Foh, see I pray you, how this does stink," where they should rather say, "Smell not unto it, for it has an ill scent."

And as these and like fashions offend the senses to which they appertain, so to grind the teeth, to whistle, to make pitiful cries, to rub sharp stones together, and to file upon iron do much offend the ears and would be left in any case. Neither must we refrain from those things alone, but we must also beware we do not sing, and specially alone, if we have an untuneful voice, which is a common fault with most men; and yet, he that is of nature least apt unto it, does use it most.

So there be some kind of men that in coughing and sneezing make such noise that they make a man deaf to hear them; some others use in like things so little discretion that they spit in men's faces that stand about them. Besides these there be some that in yawning bray and cry like asses. And yet such, with open mouth, will ever say and do what they list, and make such noice, or rather roaring, as the dumb man does, when he strives with himself to speak. All these ill-favored fashions, a man must leave, as loathsome to the ear and the eye. . . .

And when you have blown your nose, use not to open your handkerchief, to glare upon your snot, as if you had pearls and rubies fallen from your brains, for these be slovenly parts, enough to cause men, not so much not to love us, as if they did love us, to unlove us again. . . .

Likewise do they very ill that now and then pull out a letter out of their pocket to read it, as if they had great matters of charge and affairs of the commonwealth committed unto them. But they are much more to be blamed that pull out their knives or their scissors, and do nothing else but pare their nails, as if they made no account at all of the company and would seek some other solace to pass the time away. This fashion too must be left, that some men use, to sing between the teeth, or play the drum with their fingers, or shuffle their feet. For these demeanours show that a body is careless of any man else. . . .

In speech a man may err many ways. And first in the matter itself, that is in the talk, which may not be vain or filthy. For they that do hear it will not abide it; as you talk they take no pleasure to hear but rather scorn the speech and the speaker both. Again, a man must not move any question of matters that be too deep and too subtle, because it is hardly understood of the most. And a man must watchfully foresee that the matter be such as none of the company may blush to hear it, or receive any shame by the tale. Neither must he talk of any filthy matter, albeit a man would take a pleasure to hear it; for it ill becomes an honest gentleman to seek to please but in things that be honest.

Neither in sport nor in earnest must a man speak anything against God or His saints, how witty or pleasant soever the matter be. Wherein the company that Giovanni Boccaccio has brought to speak in his novels and tales has erred so much that methinks every good body may justly blame them for it. . . .

And they do as much amiss, too, that never have other things in their mouth than their children, their wife, and their nurse. "My little boy made me so laugh yesterday; hear you, you never saw a sweeter babe in your life. My wife is such a one, Cecchina told me; of truth you would not believe what a wit she has." There is none so idle a body that will either intend to answer or abide to hear such foolish prittle-prattle. For it irks a man's ears to hearken unto it. . . .

Neither must a man boast of his nobility, his honour or riches, much less vaunt of his wit, or gloriously rehearse too much of his deeds and valiant acts, or what his ancestors have done, nor upon every occasion, fall in rehearsal of such things, as many men do. For in such case a man would wean they seek either to contend with the company (if they be, or will take upon them to be, as good gentlemen and of as much wealth and worthiness as they be), or else to overcrow them (if they live in meaner condition and calling, than they do), and as it were to upbraid them their poor and mean condition of life. . . .

We say that those be good manners and fashions which bring a delight or at least offend not their senses, their minds and conceits with whom we live. And of these we have spoken enough. But you must understand with all this that men be very desirous of beautiful things, well proportioned and comely. And of counterfeit things foul and ill-shapen, they be as squeamish again on the other side. And this is a special privilege given to us, that other creatures have no capacity to understand what beauty or measure means. And, therefore, as things not common with beasts but proper to ourselves, we must embrace them for themselves and hold them dear; and yet those, much more, that draw nearest to the knowledge of man as which are most apt and inclined to understand the perfection which nature has left in man. . . .

Selection 5
"The Court Lady"
Baldassare Castiglione

Baldassare Castiglione's *Book of the Courtier*, published in 1528, was one of the most influential manuals of advice written during the Italian Renaissance. In it, Castiglione (1478–1529) recreated Italian court life and set forward ideals for the "perfect courtier" and "court lady" which greatly influenced norms of behavior among the elite. This selection focuses on appropriate roles for women; the narrative female voice is that of the Duchess Elisabetta Gonzaga.

. . . Frisio replied: "Surely it is out of place and beside the purpose to speak of women now, particularly when more remains to be said of the Courtier, for we ought not to mix one thing with another."

"You are greatly mistaken," replied messer Cesare Gonzaga, "because just as no court, however great, can have adornment or splendor or gaiety in it without ladies, neither can any Courtier be graceful or pleasing or brave, or do any gallant deed of chivalry, unless he is moved by the society and by the life and charm of ladies: even discussion about the Courtier is always imperfect unless ladies take part in it and add their part of that grace by which they make Courtiership perfect and adorned."

Signor Ottaviano laughed, and said: "There you have a little sample of the kind of bait that makes men fools."

Source: Baldassare Castiglione, *Book of the Courtier*, trans. by Charles S. Singleton (Garden City, N.Y.: Doubleday Anchor, Inc., 1959), pp. 204–212.

Then the Magnifico, turning to the Duchess, said: "Since it is your pleasure, Madam, I will say what I have to say, but with great fear that I shall give no satisfaction. Certainly, it would cause me far less toil to imagine a lady worthy of being the queen of the world than to imagine a perfect Court Lady, because I do not know where to find my model for the latter; whereas, for the Queen, I should not need to go very far, since it would be enough for me to set forth the divine accomplishments of a lady whom I know and, in contemplating those accomplishments, set all my thoughts to expressing clearly in words what many see with their eyes; and if I could do no more, I should have performed my task by merely uttering her name."

Then said the Duchess: "Do not exceed bounds, signor Magnifico, but hold to the order given, and describe the Court Lady so that such a noble lady may have someone capable of serving her worthily."

The Magnifico continued: "Then, Madam, in order to show that your commands can induce me to attempt what I do not even know how to do, I will speak of this excellent Lady as I would wish her to be; and when I have fashioned her to my taste, and since then I may not have another, like Pygmalion I will take her for my own. And, though signor Gasparo has said that the same rules which serve for the Courtier serve also for the Lady, I am of a different opinion; for although some qualities are common to both and are as necessary for a man as for a woman, there are yet others that befit a man and to which a woman ought to be a complete stranger. I say this of bodily exercises; but above all I think that in her ways, manners, words, gestures, and bearing, a woman ought to be very unlike a man; for just as he must show a certain solid and sturdy manliness, so it is seemly for a woman to have a soft and delicate tenderness, with an air of womanly sweetness in her every movement, which, in her going and staying, and in whatever she says, shall always make her appear the woman without any resemblance to a man.

"Now, if this precept be added to the rules which these gentlemen have taught the Courtier, then I think she ought to be able to follow many such and adorn herself with the best accomplishments, as signor Gasparo says. For I hold that many virtues of the mind are as necessary to a woman as to a man; also, gentle birth; to avoid affectation, to be naturally graceful in all her actions, to be mannerly, clever, prudent, not arrogant, not envious, not slanderous, not vain, not contentious, not inept, to know how to gain and hold the favor of her mistress and of all others, to perform well and gracefully the exercises that are suitable for women. And I do think that beauty is more necessary to her than to the Courtier, for truly that woman lacks much who lacks beauty. Also she must be more circumspect, and more careful not to give occasion for evil being said of her, and conduct herself so that she may not only escape being sullied by guilt but even by the suspicion of it, for a women has not so many ways of defending herself against false calumnies as a man has. But since Count Ludovico has set forth in great detail the chief profession of the Courtier, and has insisted that this be arms, I think it is also

fitting to state what I judge that of the Court Lady to be, and when I have done this I shall think to have discharged the greater part of my assignment.

"Leaving aside, then, those virtues of the mind which she is to have in common with the Courtier (such as prudence, magnanimity, continence, and many others), as well as those qualities that befit all (such as kindness, discretion, ability to manage her husband's property and house and children, if she is married, and all qualities that are requisite in a good mother), I say that, in my opinion, in a Lady who lives at court a certain pleasing affability is becoming above all else, whereby she will be able to entertain graciously every kind of man with agreeable and comely conversation suited to the time and place and to the station of the person with whom she speaks, joining to serene and modest manners, and to that comeliness that ought to inform all her actions, a quick vivacity of spirit whereby she will show herself a stranger to all boorishness; but with such a kind manner as to cause her to be thought no less chaste, prudent, and gentle than she is agreeable, witty, and discreet: thus, she must observe a certain mean (difficult to achieve and, as it were, composed of contraries) and must strictly observe certain limits and not exceed them.

"Now, in her wish to be thought good and pure, this Lady must not be so coy, or appear so to abhor gay company or any talk that is a little loose, as to withdraw as soon as she finds herself involved, for it might easily be thought that she was pretending to be so austere in order to hide something about herself which she feared others might discover; for manners so unbending are always odious. Yet, on the other hand, for the sake of appearing free and amiable she must not utter unseemly words or enter into any immodest and unbridled familiarity or into ways such as might cause other to believe about her what is perhaps not true; but when she finds herself present at such talk, she ought to listen with a light blush of shame. . . .

"And since words that have no subject matter of importance are vain and puerile, the Court Lady must have not only the good judgment to recognize the kind of person with whom she is speaking, but must have knowledge of many things, in order to entertain that person graciously; and let her know how in her talk to choose those things that are suited to the kind of person with whom she is speaking, and be careful lest, unintentionally, she might sometimes utter words that could offend him. Let her take care not to disgust him by indiscreet praise of herself or by being too prolix. Let her not proceed to mingle serious matters with playful or humorous discourse, or mix jests and jokes with serious talk. Let her not show ineptitude in pretending to know what she does not know, but let her seek modestly to do herself credit in what she does know—in all things avoiding affectation, as has been said. In this way she will be adorned with good manners; she will perform with surpassing grace the bodily exercises that are proper to women; her discourse will be fluent and most prudent, virtuous, and pleasant; thus she will be not only loved but revered by everyone and perhaps worthy of being considered the equal of this great Courtier, both in qualities of mind and of body."

Having spoken thus far, the Magnifico paused and was silent as if he had ended his talk. Then signor Gasparo said: "Truly, signor Magnifico, you have greatly adorned the Lady and given her excellent qualities. Yet it seems to me that you have held much to generalities, and mentioned some things in her so great that I believe you were ashamed to expound them; and, rather than explain them, you have wished they were so, like those persons who sometimes desire things that are impossible and miraculous. Hence, I would have you set forth to us a little better what the bodily exercises proper to a Court Lady are, and in what way she ought to converse, and what those many things are of which you say it is fitting that she should have knowledge; and whether you mean that prudence, magnanimity, continence, and the many other virtues you have named are supposed to help her merely in the management of her house, children, and family (which, however, you do not wish to be her principal profession), or

rather in her conversation and graceful practice of these bodily exercises; and by your faith, take care not to set these poor virtues to such menial tasks that they will be ashamed."

The Magnifico laughed and said: "Signor Gasparo, you cannot help showing your ill will toward women. But, truly, I thought I had said quite enough and especially to such an audience as this; for I think there is none here who does not recognize that, as for bodily exercises, it is not seemly for a woman to handle weapons, ride, play tennis, wrestle, and do many other things that are suited to men."

Then the Unico Aretino said: "With the ancients it was the custom for women to wrestle naked with men, but we have lost that good practice, along with many others."

Messer Cesare Gongzaga added: "And, in my time, I have seen women play tennis, handle weapons, ride, hunt, and engage in nearly all the exercises that a cavalier can." . . .

Then signor Gasparo said, laughing: "Since you have granted letters and continence and magnanimity and temperance to women, I am quite surprised that you do not wish them to govern cities, make laws, lead armies, and let the men stay at home to cook or spin."

The Magnifico replied, also laughing: "Perhaps that would not be so bad either." Then he added: "Don't you know that Plato, who certainly was no great friend to women, put them in charge of the city and gave all martial duties to the men? Don't you believe that many women could be found who would know how to govern cities and armies as well as men do? But I have not given them these duties, because I am fashioning a Court Lady, not a Queen. I know full well that you would like tacitly to renew the false aspersion which signor Ottaviano cast on women yesterday, representing them as very imperfect creatures, incapable of any virtuous action, and of very little worth and of no dignity compared to men; but, in truth, both you and he would be making a very great mistake in thinking so." . . .

Selection 6
Life of Federigo, Duke of Urbino

Vespasiano da Bisticci

Federigo of Urbino was greatly admired in the Renaissance, for to many of his peers he embodied those ideals publicized later by Castiglione. This account of Federigo as a military leader illustrates the qualities that Renaissance aristocrats revered.

Although the life of M. Federigo, duke of Urbino, of the house of Montefeltro, has been written in the historical genre, since I have nevertheless written like this of other worthy men who lived in this period, I cannot refrain from writing down certain things worth remembering. He began military life as a young man, in imitation of Scipio Africanus, under the tutelage of Nicolo Piccinino, a very distinguished military leader of the time. Federigo had many singular qualities, and his era had no other of his stature, so distinguished he was in all ways. In military matters, his strength of will and intellect, conjoined with unparalleled prudence, made him triumph using judgment more than force. In all matters, thus, he was prudent, and this prudence led to the capture of innumerable cities in the Kingdom and throughout Italy. He was never defeated in battle. One could say that his victories were without number and the places captured unparalleled in number.

For all his victories he was honored, as anyone can see who will read the story of his life: there are treated all his worthy deeds, and therefore, I will not expatiate, except for brief comments on some things worth remembering that his excellency accomplished, beginning with the battle of St. Fabianus. The duke was ill with fever, yet had begun the battle. It lasted for several hours, and it was thought that the king's forces might be routed. The duke—though ill—realized the danger, and recognizing that the peasants' forces were superior, mounted his horse and rode to the middle of the camp. He began to restore the courage which his soldiers had lost, since the victory had not been theirs. And due to his usual prudence, there was reason for them to believe that the advantage had

been to the men of the king as much as to their opponents. Had he not come, in spite of the forcefulness of the leaders who were there, they would have been routed without any escape, and by his presence, he was the reason, as noted, for their survival. . . .

I shall not fail to mention, among his other virtues, his fidelity to vows, in which he was never delinquent. Witness to this is provided by all those to whom he made a vow, for he never broke his word. Witnesses would be King Alfonso and King Ferdinando: he was in their service for more than 32 years. Not only did he keep to what he had promised them in writing but also to what he had said. When it seemed, once, that Bartolomeo of Bergamo was about to harm the people of Florence, the duke of Urbino had finished his term of service to King Ferdinando and was free to attach himself to anyone he wanted, yet he did not tarnish his loyalty. The Venetians, who were promoting all measures by which they could attain their will through the order that had been given to support the passage of Bartolomeo of Bergamo, long thinking of all the things through which they could obtain what they had long desired—rule over Italy—recognized that everything depended on the duke of Urbino, for whatever party had him on its side would be the winner. . . .

At this time, the duke finished his term of service with King Ferdinando. The Venetians sent their ambassador to the duke, who was in camp between Imola and Faenza. There were also present the representatives of his majesty the King, of the State of Milan and of the Florentines. The ambassador of the Venetians joined them and said that he wanted to speak to the duke, since they knew that he had finished his term of service and that he could legitimately act in any way he wished. When the group made its request of the duke on behalf of the leaders of Venice, the duke

Source: Vespasiano da Bisticci, *Vite di Uomini Illustri del Secolo XV*, ed. by Ludovico Frati (Bologna: Romagnoli-Dall'Acqua, 1893), pp. 280–284. Trans. by A. Keaney.

said that he wished to say that he was in the presence of the representatives of the league, that it was good that his service was finished, but, as he said, in terms of his loyalty, his service was now over and that he was under obligation to his majesty the King.

When the ambassador saw that he could not obtain what he wanted, he left and went to Cervia and there wrote a letter to the duke of Urbino, offering him 100,000 ducats in time of war, and 60,000 in time of peace. The duke was not willing to read the letter when it arrived, but sent it to the representative of the league. This done, he dismissed his master of horse without any reply, having told the ambassador and the representatives what was his desire, which was to be in the pay of the service of his majesty the King, as he had been to that day. And thus he showed that his word was inviolable and that he observed not only what he was obliged to, but what he was not.

I will not fail to describe how Volterra was acquired by his Lordship only through his prudence. Because of the site of the place, it could not have been taken through force of arms, nor had it proved possible by men of old or more recent times. When the duke of Urbino was in the service of the king and the Florentines, the people of Volterra had revolted because of certain differences with the Florentines and were governing themselves. The king heard what the people of Volterra had done and quickly wrote to the duke that, at any request of the Florentines, he should ride with his own forces and those of the league, and, if the people he had in Romagna were not enough, he should utilize twelve squadrons of his own troops. The king had commanded them to obey the duke as if he [the Duke] were acting on the king's behalf. The letter received; the duke immediately wrote to Florence of his commission by the king. He added in the letter that it was desirable to approach the enterprise slowly and to take their time; that it would be easy to get into and difficult to get out of; if it were not successful, he thought the state might be lost. They replied that they would ask him when it came time. Some days later, they decided to undertake the enterprise against Volterra. They quickly advised the duke and sent Bongiovanni Gianfigliazzi with

money to get him to come to Volterra immediately. When he learned from Bongiovanni what the Signoria wanted, the duke prepared to ride with as many cavalry as he could. Before going, he wrote to Piero dei Felici, who was his agent in Florence, not, however, to ask for money from the Florentines during the war with Volterra, for he wanted them to understand that he was serving voluntarily and not for any financial reward. The people of Volterra sought from all the lords and powers in Italy help to prevent them from falling into the hands of the Florentines. But they found none available, because the Pope had sent some cavalry squadrons to help the Florentines. There were no powers in Italy which were not involved, given the conditions which then prevailed.

When the duke arrived at Volterra, he immediately took a position in the weakest spot in the area. Although it was called weak, it was, in fact, so strong that it could not be attacked from that side or from any other. He drew up his forces and those of the Pope in places which apparently could be attacked, although in fact they could not be. Remaining in his camp, he gave all possible indications that he would attack the city, but none the less he waited with his usual prudence to see if they would arrive at an accord, since there could be no other remedy. Often he sent soldiers inside to talk with those governing, and to see if he could get some indication of a way of agreement from soldiers of the other side, demonstrating to them that the people of Volterra, being alone in this defense (as they were), were not sufficient to resist the Florentine forces. Nonetheless, while he was working for an accord, the siege continued on the ground, and the duke attacked however he could, even at night. In this way, with his usual caution, he began to deal with some enemy soldiers and caused them to desert, and thus learn what his situation was. When the people of Volterra saw that they could not get help from anywhere, they began to listen to him, to find a way to an accord. This lasted for several days. At Florence there was great doubt that they could take another route and they begged the duke to see a way, with God as help, that he could free them from the clear danger in which they found themselves. He consoled them, saying not to doubt for a moment that he would soon get them out of it. The soldiers complained to the Signoria, saying that it would be a great risk for them to stay more than a year and that the Signoria should seek to make an accord to relieve them of this burden and to send them to the hospital: "the Signoria should show favor to your soldiers, but you are doing the opposite." Every day seemed 1000 days to the duke, until the accord was made, because by his nature he was turned toward the road of peace.

The people of Volterra were themselves besieged and surrounded. Although the inhabitants were not prevented from entering and leaving the city, one risked his life by entering a besieged city. Recognizing this clear danger, they began to negotiate for peace. They sent to the camp for a safe-conduct. When they arrived, the duke recognized their danger and immediately started negotiations for an accord. Those discussions lasted some days. Finally, respecting person and property, they concluded by handing the territory over to the Florentines. They were deprived of all the provisos they had before—to elect a mayor and the Sig-noria—and they were subject to the new provisions.

In agreement with the representatives of Florence, the duke entered the territory, and commanded that no one be bold enough to touch anything, under threat of hanging. But mercenaries of the duke of Milan arrived and began to pillage the land. Immediately the duke, sword in hand, came running—he and the Florentine representatives—to stop the pillage, but it was not possible to prevent this great evil. After the mercenaries, the ordinary soldiers began to do the same, and naturally it was such a great disorder that it could not be halted. The duke of Urbino did whatever he could but could not wrest control from their hands. It was one of the greatest disappointments that the duke ever had, so much so that from his displeasure and grief he could not contain his tears. Everything could have had a good end, if this rioting had not followed, as was realized by the representatives and all who were present.

III. PERCEPTIONS OF WAR

The different ways in which Renaissance warfare was perceived, understood, or justified are as valuable for us to study as the ways in which various individuals experienced war. Thomas More imagined how war might be avoided in an ideal society. Prince William of Orange, known as "the Silent," called on the Dutch people to rise against the Duke of Alva, hated governor of their monarch Phillip II of Spain. Finally, Peter Paul Rubens was most interested in laying bare the connection between the reality of war and his understanding of it as an artist.

Selection 7
Utopia, Book Two
Thomas More

Thomas More, Lord Chancellor of England under Henry VIII, was beheaded for treason in 1535 and canonized 400 years later. His description of an imaginary land—Utopia—was a best-seller when it was published in 1516 and has been called a defense of both communism and democracy.

OF THEIR MILITARY DISCIPLINE

They detest war as a very brutal thing; and which, to the reproach of human nature, is more practised by men than by any sort of beasts: they, in opposition to the sentiments of almost all other nations, think that there is nothing more inglorious than that glory that is gained by war; and, therefore, though they accustom themselves daily to military exercises and the discipline of war, in which not only their men, but their women, likewise, are trained up, that, in cases of necessity, they may not be quite useless: yet they do not rashly engage in war, unless it be either to defend themselves or their friends from any unjust agressors, or, out of good-nature or in compassion, assist an oppressed nation in shaking off the yoke of tyranny. They, indeed, help their friends not only in defensive but also in offensive wars; but they never do that unless they had been consulted before the breach was made, and, being satisfied with the grounds on which they went, they had found that all demands of reparation were rejected, so that a war was unavoidable: this they think to be not only just when one neighbour makes an inroad on another by public order and carry away the spoils, but

Source: Thomas More, *Utopia*, trans. by Bishop Burnet (London: Jones and Bumford, 1808), pp. 159–177.

when the merchants of one country are oppressed in another, either under pretence of some unjust laws, or by the perverse wresting of good ones; this they count a juster cause of war than the other, because those injuries are done under some colour of laws. This was the only ground of that war in which they engaged with the Nephelogetes against the Aleopolitanes, a little before our time: for the merchants of the former having, as they thought, met with great injustice among the latter, which, whether it was in itself right or wrong, drew on a terrible war, in which many of their neighbours were engaged; and their keenness in carrying it on being supported by their strength in maintaining it, it not only shook some very flourishing states and very much afflicted others, but, after a series of much mischief, ended in the entire conquest and slavery of the Aleopolitanes; who, though, before the war, they were, in all respects, much superior to the Nephelogetes, were yet subdued; but, though the Utopians had assisted them in the war, yet they pretended to no share of the spoil.

But, though they so vigorously assist their friends in obtaining reparation for the injuries they have received in affairs of this nature; yet, if any such frauds were committed against themselves, provided no violence was done to their persons, they would only, on their being refused satisfaction, forbear trading with such a people. This is not because they consider their neighbours more than their own citizens; but, since their neighbours trade every one upon his own stock, fraud is a more sensible injury to them than it is to the Utopians, among whom the public, in such a case, only suffers: as they expect nothing in returns for the merchandise they export but that in which they so much abound, and is of little use to them, the loss does not much affect them; they think, therefore, it would be too severe to revenge a loss attended with so little inconvenience either to their lives or their subsistence, with the death of many persons: but, if any of their people are either killed or wounded wrongfully, whether it be done by public authority, or only by private men: as soon as they hear of it, they send ambassadors, and demand, that the guilty persons may be delivered up to them; and if that is denied, they declare war; but if it be complied with, the offenders are condemned either to death or slavery.

They would be both troubled and ashamed of a bloody victory over their enemies; and think it would be as foolish a purchase, as to buy the most valuable goods at too high a rate. And in no victory do they glory so much, as in that which is gained by dexterity and good conduct, without bloodshed. In such cases they appoint public triumphs, and erect trophies to the honour of those who have succeeded; for then do they reckon that a man acts suitably to his nature, when he conquers his enemy in such a way, as that no other creature but a man could be capable of, and that is, by the strength of his understanding. Bears, lions, boars, wolves, and dogs, and all other animals employ their bodily force one against another, in which, as many of them are superior to men, both in strength and fierceness, so they are all subdued by his reason and understanding.

The only design of the Utopians in war is to obtain that by force, which if it had been granted them in time, would have prevented the war; or if that cannot be done, to take so severe a revenge on those that have injured them, that they may be terrified from doing the like for the time to come. By these ends they measure all their designs, and manage them so, that it is visible that the appetite

of fame or vain-glory, does not work so much on them, as a just care of their own security.

As soon as they declare war, they take care to have a great many schedules, that are sealed with their common seal, affixed in the most conspicuous places of their enemies country. This is carried secretly, and done in many places all at once. In these they promise great rewards to such as shall kill the Prince, and lesser in proportion to such as shall kill any other persons, who are those on whom, next to the Prince himself, they cast the chief balance of the war. And they double the sum to him, that instead of killing the person so marked out, shall take him alive, and put him in their hands. They offer not only indemnity, but rewards, to such of the persons themselves that are so marked, if they will act against their countrymen: by this means those that are named in their schedules, become not only distrustful of their fellow-citizens, but are jealous of one another: and are much distracted by fear and danger; for it has often fallen out, that many of them, and even the Prince himself, have been betrayed by those in whom they have trusted most: for the rewards that the Utopians offer, are so unmeasurably great, that there is no sort of crime to which men cannot be drawn by them. They consider the risque that those run, who undertake such services, and offer a recompence proportioned to the danger; not only a vast deal of gold, but great revenues in lands, that lie among other nations that are their friends, where they may go and enjoy them very securely; and they observe the promises they make of this kind most religiously. They very much approve of this way of corrupting their enemies, though it appears to others to be base and cruel; but they look on it as a wise course, to make an end of what would be otherwise a long war, without so much as hazarding one battle to decide it. They think it likewise an act of mercy and love to mankind, to prevent the great slaughter of those that must otherwise be killed in the progress of the war, both on their own side, and on that of their enemies, by the death of a few that are most guilty; and that in so doing, they are kind even to their enemies, and pity them no less than their own people, as knowing that the greater part of them do not engage in the war of their own accord, but are driven into it by the passions of their Prince.

If this method does not succeed with them, then they sow seeds of contention among their enemies, and animate the Prince's brother, or some of the nobility, to aspire to the crown. If they cannot disunite them by domestic broils, then they engage their neighbours against them, and make them set on foot some old pretensions, which are never wanting to princes, when they have occasion for them. These they plentifully supply with money though but very sparingly with any auxiliary troops; for they are so tender of their own people, that they would not, willingly, exchange one of them, even with the prince of their enemies country.

But as they keep their gold and silver only for such an occasion, so, when that offers itself, they easily part with it; since it would be no inconvenience to them, though they should reserve nothing of it to themselves. For besides the wealth that they have among them at home, they have a vast treasure abroad; many nations round about them, being deep in their debt: so that they hire soldiers from all places for carrying on their wars; but chiefly from the Zapolets, who live five hundred miles east of Utopia. They are a rude, wild, and fierce nation, who delight in the woods and rocks, among which they were born and bred up. They are hardened both against heat, cold, and labour, and know nothing of the delicacies of life. They do not apply themselves to agriculture, nor do they care either for their houses or their cloaths: cattle is all that they look after; and for the greatest part, they live either by hunting, or upon rapine; and are made, as it were, only for war. They watch all opportunities of engaging in it, and very readily embrace such as are offered them. Great numbers of them will frequently go out, and offer themselves for a very low pay, to serve any that will employ them: they know none of the arts of life, but those that lead to the taking it away; they serve those that hire them, both with much courage and great fidelity; but will not engage to serve for any determined time, and agree upon such terms, that the next day they may go over to the enemies of those whom they serve, if they offer them a greater encouragement, and will, perhaps, return to them

the day after that, upon a higher advance of their pay. There are few wars in which they make not a considerable part of the armies of both sides: so it often falls out, that they who are related, and were hired in the same country, and so have lived long and familiarly together, forgetting both their relations and former friendship, kill one another upon no other consideration, than that of being hired to it for a little money, by princes of different interests; and such a regard have they for money, that they are easily wrought on by the difference of one penny a day, to change sides. So entirely does their avarice influence them; and yet this money, which they value so highly, is of little use to them; for what they purchase thus with their blood, they quickly waste on luxury, which among them is but of a poor and miserable form.

This nation serves the Utopians against all people whatsoever, for they pay higher than any other. The Utopians hold this for a maxim, that as they seek out the best sort of men for their own use at home, so they make use of this worst sort of men for the consumption of war; and therefore they hire them with the offers of vast rewards, to expose themselves to all sorts of hazards, out of which the greater part never returns to claim their promises; yet they make them good, most religiously, to such as escape. This animates them to adventure again, whenever there is occasion for it; for the Utopians are not at all troubled how many of these happen to be killed; and reckon it a service done to mankind, if they could be a means to deliver the world from such a lewd and vicious sort of people, that seem to have run together, as to the drain of human nature. Next to these, they are served in their wars, with those upon whose account they undertake them, and with the auxiliary troops of their other friends, to whom they join a few of their own people, and send some man of eminent and approved virtue to command in chief. There are two sent with him, who, during his command, are but private men, but the first is to succeed him if he should happen to be either killed or taken; and, in case of the like misfortune to him, the third comes in his place; and thus they provide against all events, that such accidents as may befal their generals, may not endanger their armies. When they draw out troops of their own people, they take such out of every city as freely offer themselves, for none are forced to go against their wills, since they think, that if any man is pressed that wants courage, he will not only act faintly, but, by his cowardice, dishearten others. But if an invasion is made on their country, they make use of such men, if they have good bodies, though they are not brave; and either put them aboard their ships, or place them on the walls of their towns, that being so posted, they may find no opportunity of flying away; and thus either shame, the heat of action, or the impossibility of flying, bears down their cowardice; they often make a virtue of necessity, and behave themselves well, because nothing else is left them. But as they force no man to go into any foreign war against his will, so they do not hinder those women who are willing to go along with their husbands; on the contrary, they encourage and praise them, and they stand often next their husbands in the front of the army. They also place together those who are related, parents, and children, kindred, and those that are mutually allied, near one another; that those whom nature has inspired with the greatest zeal for assisting one another, may be the nearest and readiest to do it; and it is matter of great reproach, if husband or wife survive one another, or if a child survives his parent; and therefore when they come to be engaged in action, they continue to fight to the last man; if their enemies stand before them: and as they use all prudent methods to avoid the endangering their own men, and if it is possible let all the action and danger fall upon the troops that they hire; so if it becomes necessary for themselves to engage, they then charge with as much courage, as they avoided it before with prudence: nor is it a fierce charge at first, but it encreases by degrees; and as they continue in action, they grow more obstinate, and press harder upon the enemy, insomuch that they will much sooner die than give ground; for the certainty that their children will be well looked after, when they are dead, frees them from all that anxiety, concerning them, which often masters men of great courage; and thus they are animated by a noble and invincible resolution. Their skill in military affairs encreases their courage: and the wise sentiments which, according to the laws of their country, are instilled into them in

their education, give additional vigour to their minds: for as they do not under-value life so as prodigally to throw it away, they are not so indecently fond of it, as to preserve it, by base and unbecoming methods. In the greatest heat of action the bravest of their youth, who have devoted themselves to that service, single out the general of their enemies, set on him either openly or by ambuscade; pursue him everywhere, and, when spent and wearied out, are relieved by others, who never give over the pursuit, either attacking him with close weapons when they can get near him, or with those which wound at a distance, when others get in between them: so that, unless he secures himself by flight, they seldom fail at last to kill or to take him prisoner. When they have obtained a victory, they kill as few as possible, and are much more bent on taking many prisoners, than on killing those that fly before them: nor do they ever let their men so loose in the pursuit of their enemies, as not to retain an entire body still in order; so that if they have been forced to engage the last of their battalions, before they could gain the day, they will rather let their enemies all escape than pursue them, when their own army is in disorder; remembering well what has often fallen out to themselves that when the main body of their army had been quite defeated and broken, when their enemies imagining the victory obtained have let themselves loose into an irregular pursuit, a few of them that lay for a reserve, waiting a fit opportunity, have fallen on them in their chace, and, when straggling in disorder, and apprehensive of no danger, but counting the day their own, have turned the whole action, and, wresting out of their hands a victory that seemed certain and undoubted, while the vanquished have suddenly become victorious.

It is hard to tell whether they are more dextrous in laying or avoiding ambushes they sometimes seem to fly when it is far from their thoughts; and when they intend to give ground, they do it so, that it is very hard to find out their design. If they see they are ill posted, or are like to be overpowered by numbers, they then either march off in the night with great silence, or by some stratagem delude their enemies: if they retire in the daytime, they do it in such order that it is no less dangerous to fall upon them in a retreat, than in a march. They fortify their camps with a deep and large trench; and throw up the earth that is dug out of it for a wall; nor do they employ only their slaves in this, but the whole army works at it, except those that are then upon the guard; so that when so many hands are at work, a great line and a strong fortification is finished in so short a time, that it is scarce credible. Their armour is very strong for defence, and yet is not so heavy as to make them uneasy in their marches; they can even swim with it. All that are trained up to war, practise swimming: both horse and foot make great use of arrows, and are very expert: they have no swords, but fight with a poll-ax that is both sharp and heavy, by which they thrust or strike down an enemy; they are very good at finding out warlike machines, and disguise them so well, that the enemy does not perceive them, till he feels the use of them; so that he cannot prepare such a defence as would render them useless; the chief consideration had in the making them, is, that they may be easily carried and managed.

If they agree to a truce, they observe it so religiously, that no provocations will make them break it. They never lay their enemies country waste, nor harm their corn, and even in their marches they take all possible care, that neither horse nor foot may tread it down, for they do not know but that they may have use for it themselves. They hurt no man whom they find disarmed, unless he is a spy. When a town is surrendered to them, they take it into their protection: and when they carry a place by storm, they never plunder it,

but put those only to the sword that oppose the rendering of it up, and make the rest of the garrison slaves, but for the other inhabitants, they do them no hurt; and if any of them had advised a surrender, they give them good rewards out of the estates of those that they condemn, and distribute the rest among their auxiliary troops, but they themselves take no share of the spoil.

When a war is ended, they do not oblige their friends to reimburse their expences; but they obtain them of the conquered, either in money, which they keep for the next occasion, or in lands out of which a constant revenue is to be paid them; by many increases, the revenue which they draw out from several countries on such occasions, is now risen to above 700,000 ducats a year. They send some of their own people to receive these revenues, who have orders to live magnificently, and like princes, by which means they consume much of it upon the place; and either bring over the rest to Utopia, or lend it to that nation in which it lies. This they most commonly do, unless some great occasion, which falls out but very seldom, should oblige them to call for it all. It is out of these lands that they assign rewards to such as they encourage to adventure on desperate attempts. If any prince that engages in war with them, is making preparations for invading their country, they prevent him, and make his country the seat of the war; for they do not willingly suffer any war to break in upon their island; and if that should happen, they would only defend themselves by their own people; but would not call for auxiliary troops to their assistance.

Selection 8
William of Orange Justifies the Dutch Revolt (1572)

By the time William, Prince of Orange, called on the inhabitants of the north Netherlands to rise against the hated governor of Philip II, King of Spain, hundreds of citizens of the Low Countries had already been exiled or put to death. William believed that Philip now ruled unjustly and provided justification for those who supported guerilla warfare against the Spanish.

William, by God's grace prince of Orange, count of Nassau . . . Lieutenant general of his Royal Majesty in Holland, Zeeland, Friesland, and Utrecht, wishes for each and every estate, lord, knight, nobleman, captain, bailiff, sheriff, steward, burgomaster, alderman, rentmaster, guild member, tradesman, civic guard, and citizen and all good residents of these Netherlands, of whatever station, freedom and deliverance from the current enslavement by cruel, foreign, bloodthirsty oppressors.

From the depths of our heart we anguish over the numerous and excessive acts of violence, burdens, taxes of ten, twenty, and thirty percent, and still more burdens, seizures, executions, expulsions, confiscations, and still more intolerable inflictions, intimidations, and oppressions which the enemy at large together with his Spaniards, bishops, inquisitors and other hangers-on inflicts each day, and more and more, on you, your wives, your daughters, and souls, bodies, and goods. After so many years, this grows but steadily worse in the name of His Royal Majesty, but without his knowledge, in violation of his oath, and contrary to these lands' liberties and privileges (in truth, however, at the instigation of Cardinal Granvelle and the Spanish Inquisitors, whose purpose it is to carry out the decretals of the Council of Trent and the Spanish Inquisition). These events are already so well-known and infamous, especially to you

who see, fear, and suffer them yourselves that I need not give any broader account of them.

It is also well-known to you and to the rest of the world with what dispatch, expense, difficulties, and worries we have worked throughout these last four years in order to restore to each and every one of you, and to our beloved fatherland, your former freedom, prosperity, and wealth, and to deliver you from the foreign tyrants and oppressors, for the sake of our own conscience and the execution of our oath, which binds and obligates us to you for the true service of the King, the liberties of this country and the deliverance of the oppressed; and also to enable you to enjoy the freedom of your consciences and of the word of God, in proper obedience and true constant service to his Royal Majesty, without having to bear any longer these fears, anxieties, persecutions, slayings, and robberies by the tyrants, the Spanish foreigners, the inquisitions, bishops, and the edicts.

We (as a member of the community of the Netherlands) would long since have helped you and brought you to that favorable condition, with God's grace, if you had not been made blind and deaf by the inordinate fear, the vain hopes, and false temptations instilled in you by governors who were put in place by the enemy and are truly betrayers of the fatherland and sworn servants of the tyrant; if until now you had not been negligent for so long in helping and supporting us to attain your own welfare and deliverance. We hope that you now understand this better and will give us more help, particularly since you now see the great possibilities which we have at this time and which draw you on, and you know that we have not

Source: *Correspondance de Guillaume le Taciturne, Prince d'Orange*, vol. 6, ed. by L. P. Gachard (Brussels: C. Muquardt, 1854), pp. 297–300. Trans. by Sherrin Marshall.

faltered but have ceaselessly sought by all feasible means to achieve these aims. For now, various lords and friends stand ready to offer us renewed help and aid on sea and on land. Indeed, the enemy has already suffered notable losses from ourselves and our helpers, who have entered this country and taken over various cities, harbors, and districts which have placed themselves in our hands for their deliverance on behalf of his Royal Majesty. . . . For it is greatly to be feared that if you do not take advantage of this favorable situation, when our common enemy suffers from a shortage of troops, with many sick, and a shortage of ships and supplies, and when we already hold so many waterways that the enemy finds it difficult to move about, then God will never again grant such a great opportunity. For you will have shamefully and evilly scorned and wasted the means which He sends to you so that you can now readily attain

the freedom of His word and your consciences and of your fatherland, your lives, wives, children, and the restoration of those privileges, rights, and goods, which you lost so shamefully and scandalously (all in the true service of the King). We ask God in His grace to spare you all these evils and to give us and you His blessing, and strength and prosperity. With these, after expelling the tyrannical oppressors, together we shall see the Netherlands in their ancient freedom, exercised again without any violence, with proper obedience to the King and security for your consciences, and according to the advice of the States General. To attain this, if you will help by giving yourselves over into our hands, we wish to contribute all our strength, but if you do not do so and bring shame, violence, and grief upon yourselves, we wish no blame laid upon us. (Signed William of Nassau)

Selection 9
Letter on "The Horrors of War"
Peter Paul Rubens

In this famous letter, Rubens offered rare insights into the artist's meaning and intent. His letter explicitly described the symbols and images—frequently classical in their themes— detailed in his painting (Figure 18).

. . . The principal figure is Mars, who has left the open temple of Janus (which in time of peace, according to Roman custom, remained closed) and rushes forth with shield and blood-stained sword, threatening the people with great disaster. He pays little heed to Venus, his mistress, who, accompanied by her Amors and Cupids, strives with caresses and embraces to hold him. From the other side, Mars is dragged forward by the Fury Alekto, with a torch in her hand. Nearby are monsters personifying Pestilence and Famine,

those inseparable partners of War. On the ground, turning her back, lies a woman with a broken lute, representing Harmony, which is incompatible with the discord of War. There is also a mother with a child in her arms, indicating that fecundity, procreation, and charity are thwarted by War, which corrupts and destroys everything. In addition, one sees an architect thrown on his back with his instruments in his hand, to show that that which in time of peace is constructed for the use and ornamentation of the City, is hurled to the ground by the force of arms and falls to ruin. I believe, if I remember rightly, that you will find on the ground under the feet of Mars a book as well as a drawing on paper, to imply that he treads underfoot all the arts and letters. There ought also

Source: R. S. Magurn (ed. and trans.), *The Letters of Peter Paul Rubens* (Cambridge, Mass.: Harvard University Press, 1955), pp. 408–409.

Figure 18. Peter Paul Rubens, *The Horrors of War*. The dismay at the violence of the Thirty Years' War pervades Rubens's painting as well as the letter in which he explains its details.

to be a bundle of darts or arrows, with the band which held them together undone; these when bound form the symbol of Concord. Beside them is the caduceus and an olive-branch, attribute of Peace; these also are cast aside. That grief-stricken woman clothed in black, with torn veil, robbed of all her jewels and other ornaments, is the unfortunate Europe, who, for so many years now, has suffered plunder, outrage, and misery, which are so injurious to everyone that it is unnecessary to go into detail.

FOUR
The Dissenter

Every society has its dissenters—and always has. The very first were probably Adam and Eve, soon followed by Cain, and after them men and women in every generation who, at least in secret, and sometimes openly, dissented from an authority that stood over them. We all live under some kind of authority, and the reasons a few of us decide to question it, to reject it, or to persuade others to join us are rarely easy to define. Thus, although we may be able to explain the actions of a specific Renaissance dissenter, we would soon find that motives changed from individual to individual and from group to group. What was of universal significance in this period, however, was that for the first time in Western history dissent achieved respectability and permanence—and this breakthrough changed the nature of social and political relations once and for all.

DISSENT BEFORE LUTHER

There were many outsiders in medieval society—people who did not fit, for various reasons, within its accepted and familiar contours. All communities create their own structures and instinctively favor certain groups over others; the towns and villages of Europe during the Middle Ages were no exceptions. Jews, for example, suffered resentment, disabilities, and persecution because they did not conform to the faith of Christian Europe. Beggars and lepers were two other groups, not insignificant in number, who were poorly treated; because they seemed out of the ordinary, or at least unlike the majority, they were feared, shunned, and despised. Even women were often treated as if they were different in some shameful way, incapable of attending university, owning property, or inheriting a title (though in some areas of northern Europe the last two were possible). Only a minority of the population—adult Christian males—always seemed unexceptional. They were the rulers and leaders of society, and they set the standard by which orthodoxy was measured. Others seemed, in one way or another, not to "belong." They were relegated to an "outsider" status that is all too common not just in large societies but even in communities as small as a high school class.

For most members of these groups in medieval Europe, the situation of being second-class citizens was so familiar that it was almost never openly challenged. There were very occasional complaints, but in general we can only imagine what resentment such people felt over the injustice and unfairness of their situation. And their silence was understandable, considering the reaction that erupted whenever discontent was expressed openly. Dissenters were hardly less unpopular in the Middle Ages—or less determinedly punished—than they had been in the Garden of Eden.

The central authority that towered above all others in the Middle Ages was the Church. It was the source of values and moral guidance, and it provided structure and purpose for the life of every individual. The richest institution in Europe, blessed with vast properties and endowments it had received from the faithful, it also had its own laws, which made its clergy both distinct and immune from the normal system of justice. All intellectual life revolved around these clergymen, who included most of Europe's scholars and even a good proportion of its literate people. Their academic subject, theology, was considered the "queen of the sciences."

It took enormous courage to challenge so mighty and embracing a presence. How could a lone individual, or even a group, dare to claim a better understanding of some crucial issue than this all-knowing institution? Remarkably enough, quite a few did. Perhaps the most spectacular were the inhabitants of a remote and rugged area of central France who were known as the "Albigensians." They were unmistakably heretics—people who rejected the authority and the very organization of the Church. They believed that a huge and eternal struggle against evil, in which an ascetic life was the only defense, determined salvation, and most of them denied the existence of hell. Gaining thousands of adherents in the early 1200s, the Albigensians created what was essentially an independent region of France with its own set of beliefs. Their fate, however, revealed what open dissenters could expect.

The head of the Church, the Pope, considered the threat of the Albigensians so serious that he launched a crusade against them, even though crusades were supposed to be holy wars only against non-Christians. This case, he felt, warranted an exception, and he persuaded kings and nobles (since the Church itself had no troops) to send an army against them. The result was a wholesale slaughter. The heresy was destroyed, and most traces of dissent were wiped out.

This is not to say that criticism was impossible or that every argument for change was immediately crushed. An Italian contemporary of the Albigensians, for example, a young man named Francis from the town of Assisi, felt that the Church had abandoned the message of humility, simplicity, and poverty that Christ had preached. It had become too rich, too worldly, too materialistic. At first, he was viewed with considerable suspicion, for he seemed to be challenging almost all current practices and beliefs, but eventually, the power and validity of his message were recognized. Francis was allowed to found a new group within the Church, the Franciscans, who practiced a life of poverty, and he himself was canonized as St. Francis.

Such success stories were rare, however. By and large, people were either content to accept official teachings, or—deterred by examples like those of the Albigensians—they kept their disagreements to themselves. As a result, the one significant type of resistance or opposition the Church faced came not from individual believers, but rather from the only other major authority in the Middle Ages: secular governments. With money and power at stake, this rivalry was often intense. Again and again, but increasingly in the 1200s and 1300s, nobles and kings stood up to bishops and popes, resisting their demands for money, their control over valuable ecclesiastical appointments, and their claim to judge all actions and policies. One monarch, Henry II of England, had a troublesome archbishop killed in 1170. Over a century later, in 1302, the king of France intimidated a Pope who was causing him problems by sending troops into his residence.

Essentially, however, these were political conflicts. They did not involve attacks on the central teachings of the Church. Late in the 1300s, however, attempts were made to link the two—to use political support as a means of helping dissenting ideas to establish themselves. The first effort was made in England, where a clergyman named John Wycliffe, who taught at Oxford University and was also a respected figure at the royal court, began to argue that the Church had become too remote from the people. He demanded a simplification of doctrines, more reliance on the Bible (which he wanted translated from Latin into English so as to make it easier to understand), and less power for priests. Many of his views, including his questioning of the authority of the Pope, were branded heretical, but even though Wycliffe was forced to leave Oxford when he offended his chief protector, his aristocratic patrons did keep him unharmed until his death in 1384. His followers, known as "Lollards," were ordinary people and therefore not so lucky. They managed to survive as an underground movement in the countryside until the Protestant Reformation exploded over a hundred years later, but on the whole, they experienced exactly the kind of repression that was the standard response to dissent in this period.

An admirer of Wycliffe, a Bohemian priest named Jan Hus, started a broader and more defiant movement in his homeland. Hus was a distinguished churchman and scholar. He served as rector (the equivalent of president) of the Charles University in Prague, one of Europe's best-known institutions, and he was the main preacher at a fashionable chapel in Prague. Like Wycliffe, he argued that priests were not a holy and privileged group, set apart from laypeople, but that the Church was made up of all the faithful. To emphasize this equality, he rejected the custom of allowing the congregation at a mass only to eat the wafer, which symbolized Christ's body, but not to drink the wine, which symbolized his blood. In a dramatic gesture, he shared the cup of wine with all worshippers, thus reducing the distinctiveness of the priest. His followers adopted a chalice, or a cup, as the symbol of their movement.

Hus was not hesitant about defying the leadership of the Church. Denounced for the positions he had taken, he replied by questioning the authority of the Pope himself:

> If a Pope is wicked, then like Judas he is a devil and a son of perdition and not the head of the Church militant. If he lives in a manner contrary to Christ, he has entered the papacy by another way than through Christ.

In 1415 Hus was summoned to the Council of Constance, an official gathering of Church leaders from all of Europe. Although he had been guaranteed safe passage if he came to answer accusations of heresy, the promise was broken. He was condemned, handed over to the secular authorities, and executed. His followers, however, unlike the Lollards in England, refused to retreat in the face of persecution.

A new leader, Jan Zizka, known as "John of the Chalice," raised an army in 1420 and led a successful campaign against the Emperor, who was also King of Bohemia and the head of the effort that was now mounted against the Hussites. The resistance lasted twenty years, outliving Zizka but sustained by Bohemian nobles, and eventually the Hussites were allowed to remain within a special church, the Utraquist Church,* in which both cup and wafer were shared by all worshippers at mass. Hus's other demands, however, such as the surrender of all personal possessions by the clergy (an echo of St. Francis), were rejected. Those who tried to fight on for these causes were defeated in battle, and so, after a long struggle, the dissent came to an end, having made only a minor dent in the unity of the Church.

Yet the lessons that could be drawn from the experiences of the Albigensians, of Wycliffe, and of Hus were clear. On the one hand, dissatisfaction with official teachings was not insignificant. Charismatic leaders could find a following for unorthodox ideas if they could tap the resentment that did exist over the authoritarian and materialistic outlook of the Church. On the other hand, it was impossible for dissent to survive if it could not win support from nobles, princes, or other leaders of society. Even with such help, the Hussites had to limit their demands; without it, they could have gained nothing. A hundred years after Hus's death, a new reformer arose who had learned these lessons, and he was to transform the very nature of dissent itself.

LUTHER

That reformer, Martin Luther, born in 1483, was the first rebel against the Church who succeeded in making dissent respectable—not to his enemies, of course, but to a significant segment of European society. His achievement was unprecedented and had far-reaching consequences. He showed that it was possible to express views that challenged authority, to win the support both of large masses and of the political leadership that ensured his survival, and then to establish the dissident position as a new orthodoxy. Once this door had been opened, it could never again be slammed shut.

The conditions for Luther's revolt were ideal. Like Hus, he lived in the Holy Roman Empire, a fragmented area of northern and central Europe ruled over by a weak central government. Each region had considerable autonomy and, therefore, the possibility of going its own way. Moreover, the Empire, lacking strong political leadership, was an easy prey to the financial demands of the papacy. Both resentment of the Church and opportunities for independent action were thus available to a religious reformer. And Luther had precisely the passion and the determination that were needed.

* The name comes from the Latin word *utraque,* meaning "both."

Figure 19. Enguerrand Charonton, *The Avignon Pietà*. The powerful spirituality of Europeans on the eve of the Reformation is reflected in this 1460 depiction of Mary's grief over the crucified Christ. The mourners around the dead body convey an emotion that would have been echoed by those who saw the painting.

Luther came from a fairly comfortable family. His father was a miner and wanted the best education for young Martin. While Luther was studying to become a lawyer, however—then, as now, a career that promised social mobility—he determined instead to enter the Church. He was convinced that he was deeply sinful, and he thought that by becoming a monk he would not only gain access to the guidance he needed to save himself from hell but also be able to devote himself single-mindedly to that cause. And he was a dedicated monk, doing everything that was prescribed for salvation. As he later described these years:

> I was a good monk, and I kept the rule of my order so strictly that if ever a monk got to heaven by the way he practiced his religion it was I. If I had continued any longer, I would have killed myself with vigils, prayers, reading, and other work.

Yet nothing seemed to help. Under the influence of Christian humanists such as Erasmus, however, Luther was beginning to wonder whether the Church was setting the right example or teaching the right doctrine. To find his own way to spiritual peace, he turned, as did the Christian humanists, to a closer study of the original message of Christ and St. Paul in the Bible.

In 1511 Luther's monastery, aware of how bright he was, appointed him to teach at the University of Wittenberg. It was in his studies, as he prepared his lectures and classes, that he finally found—in the Bible itself—the answer that had not emerged from the official teachings of the Church. A number of years later, he described what happened:

> My situation was that, although an impeccable monk, I stood before God as a sinner troubled in conscience, and I had no confidence that my merit would assuage him. Night and day I pondered until I saw the connection between the justice of God [which punishes the wicked] and the statement [in the Bible] that "the just shall live by faith." Then I grasped that the justice of God is that by which, through grace and sheer mercy, God justifies us through faith. Thereupon I felt myself to be reborn and to have gone through open doors into paradise.

The solution to his anxieties was not to work harder at the official rituals of the Church, but rather to rely on his faith and trust in God.

Never someone to keep his ideas to himself, Luther preached this message of comfort whenver he gave a sermon in Wittenberg. Nobody was much concerned about what he was saying—nor did it seem inconsistent with accepted beliefs—until, in 1517, he concluded that the representatives of the Pope who were selling indulgences were acting contrary to good Christian doctrine. Indulgences were remissions of the punishment for sin that were supposed to be earned by confession and contrition. They had begun to be thought of differently as a result of the Crusades. Anyone who died on a Crusade expected to be admitted directly to heaven; if one was unable to join up, however, one could still get the benefits by paying for someone else to go. By the 1500s, this device had deteriorated, in the propaganda of its salespeople, into a simple selling of forgiveness, and Luther was furious that poor people were wasting money on what he regarded as a false promise. One overcame sin, he felt, only through faith and repentance. Since that was surely standard doctrine, he laid it out in ninety-five theses that he offered to discuss with other theologians. The result was that the sale of indulgences dropped off, and Luther found himself bitterly attacked. It was at that point that his dissent began.

Over the next three years Luther worked out the implications of his ideas. In essence, he said, salvation rested on just two foundations: faith in God and faith in His word, the Bible. Nothing else was really needed, certainly not an elaborate structure of rituals and regulations. Like Hus, Luther believed that there should be no distinction between clergymen and laypeople, and he rejected the authority of the Pope. As he developed these beliefs, which he eventually published in three short books in 1520, he encountered increasingly sharp criticism from official spokesmen, including the accusation that he was another Hus. Luther was so confident that he was right, however, that opposition merely drove him to further extremes, until finally he denounced all who stood against him, calling the Pope anti-Christ and denying the power of the Church and its traditions.

At this point, however, the forces of repression began to gather strength. Ominously, in light of Hus's fate, it was again the Holy Roman Emperor who took action. Luther was summoned to defend himself at a meeting of the Empire's leaders, a Diet, in the city of Worms in 1521. And, as before, a promise of safe conduct was offered, although this time the dissenter's supporters made sure that he would be safe by abducting him to a secure place immediately after the meeting.

Figure 20. Lucas Cranach, *Portrait of Martin Luther* (1525). The simplicity, power, and determination of the reformer were captured in the many portraits his friend Lucas Cranach painted. Here he is in his early forties, four years after the Diet of Worms.

Luther himself did not withdraw an inch. As he put it in a famous speech to the Emperor:

> Unless I am refuted by scripture and plain reason, I do not accept the authority of Popes and councils for they have contradicted each other. My conscience is captive to the word of God. I cannot and will not recant anything, for to go against conscience is neither right nor safe. Here I stand, I cannot do otherwise. May God help me.

To which the Emperor replied equally decisively, in terms that echoed the voice of authority and repression in all ages:

> I am determined to stake on this cause my kingdoms, my friends, my blood and my body, my life and my soul. A single monk who goes counter to all Christianity for a thousand years must be wrong. I am determined to proceed against him as a notorious heretic.

And so the battle was joined.

The clear danger to Luther was that he might go the way of Hus, and his supporters the way of the Albigensians and the Hussites. His protest had struck a

Figure 21. *Charles V at the Diet of Augsburg, 1530* (engraving). At another meeting of the Diet of the Holy Roman Empire, in the city of Augsburg in 1530, the Lutherans tried to persuade Charles V (seated under the canopy) to accept their doctrines. The "Confession" they presented to him became the basis of the new church's doctrines, but Charles found it no more acceptable than the ideas he had heard from Luther in Worms nine years before.

nerve, and by the time of the confrontation at Worms, he had thousands of admirers. Their open backing for his ideas—which had been spread quickly by the newly invented printing press—showed how deeply the position of the dissenter appealed to many elements in Luther's society. A number of princes, moreover, were delighted at the opportunity to defy both Emperor and Pope, and after Worms, Luther's prince, the Elector of Saxony, hid him in the fortress at Wartburg to protect him from retribution. Never one to remain idle, Luther translated the New Testament into German during his eleven months at Wartburg, but he soon returned to the fray, because there were now religious reformers who were going much further than he thought proper. Some were rejecting all religious discipline, denying even the need to rely on the Bible (since the Holy Spirit within each believer might be enough to secure salvation), and advocating radical social policies. By 1525, their demands for change had helped provoke a series of peasant revolts in the Empire, and Luther now had to worry that his disciples might seem so

Figure 22. *Lutheran Broadside* (woodcut). The favorite propaganda of both sides in the religious disputes of the sixteenth century was the savage broadside—a single sheet that could easily be posted in a public place or passed around with a nasty cartoon that the illiterate could understand. In this example, Luther's critics are animals, and the Pope, in the center, is labeled the Antichrist.

extreme that political leaders would be frightened into helping the Church repress his movement completely.

Luther's caution about going beyond his basic doctrinal reforms was certainly not appreciated by his more radical followers. One fiery preacher, Thomas Müntzer, pulled no punches:

> Martin Luther declares that poor people get enough from their faith. He claims that the word of God is sufficient. Does he not realize that men whose every moment is consumed in earning a living have no time to read the word of God? The princes bleed the people and count as their own the fish in the streams, the birds in the air, and the grass in the fields. Dr. Martin Liar says amen to all of this. What courage has he, this Dr. Pussyfoot, the new Pope of Wittenberg, Dr. Easychair?

Luther faced the basic dilemma of the dissenter. He had won support, but now others wanted to go much further. If he could not find a respectable basis for his ideals which permitted him to reject these extremists, they might drive away those among his allies who feared too much upheaval. Isolating the rebels, the orthodox would be able to crush them forever.

From the start, Luther had attacked his radical critics, like Müntzer, as viciously as they had attacked him. Yet he had been sympathetic to the peasants, who said he had inspired one of their key demands: the right to choose their own preachers.

When, however, their other demands (which derived from a long history of peasant grievances) and uprisings threatened to undermine traditional social and political authorities, he made the crucial decision which ensured the future of his dissent.

The critical shift appears unmistakably if one compares Luther's statements before and after the peasant revolts. First, when he was concerned about injustice:

> Since it depends on each person's conscience to know what he must believe, and no harm is done to secular authority, this authority should keep silent, and busy itself with its own affairs and let each one believe this or that as he chooses and not use force with anyone on this account. One should not seek to triumph over heretics by fire but by writings.

A few years later, when he was more worried about peasant violence:

> If the peasant is in open rebellion, then he is outside of the law, for rebellion is not simply murder, but is like a great fire which attacks and lays waste the whole land. So does rebellion turn all upside down like a great disaster. Therefore, anyone who can smite, slay, or stab secretly or openly, should remember that nothing is more poisonous, hurtful, or devilish than a rebel.

Luther had thrown his lot in with the princes who had stood by him against the Emperor. He urgently wanted the world to change, but not in a way that would challenge the political and social leadership of the time.

Luther's forcefulness in convincing important segments of the nobility and many town governments that he had a more appealing version of Christianity than the traditional Church would not by itself have ensured the survival of his movement. The decisive achievement that gave his dissent the respectability and permanence that his predecessors had lacked was his ability to maintain these alliances despite the radical implications of his ideas. Although he did not compromise his basic concerns, he was still able to thread a path between conformity and anarchy. What he taught, therefore, seemed both new and yet not too upsetting.

In a tradition-bound society, this was an extraordinary accomplishment. It made the princes ready, despite the enmity of the Emperor, to fight for Luther's views; it induced them to protest the official rejection of those views; and it then made them willing to accept the title of "Protestant"—a remarkable admission of open unorthodoxy by essentially conservative people. In the end, their determination, tested on the battlefield, was to ensure the acceptance of the new Lutheran Church even by the Emperor. Once dissent crossed this threshold, its status was transformed.

This is not to say that it swept all before it. The traditional Church still had enormous assets: its comfortable familiarity, its belief in giving its adherents as much support as possible to help them to salvation (as opposed to the lonely individual responsibility demanded by the Protestants), its devotion to the poor and unfortunate, and its gorgeous and appealing rituals, which were the antithesis of the severity of Protestantism. In the end, the Church was to hold on to more of its faithful than it was to lose, yet there was no question by 1600 that its monopoly was lost.

DISSENT BEYOND RELIGION

The immediate beneficiaries of the new situation were the founders of other Protestant churches. When the Swiss city of Geneva, for instance, tried to become independent of its ruler, a bishop, in the 1530s, it naturally combined religious with political revolt. Although the citizens were deeply conservative, they were willing to break with the Roman Church and then to invite a reformer, John Calvin, to create a new church for them. If carried out under the right auspices, such breaks with tradition had become perfectly acceptable, even to people who were instinctively suspicious of deviations from orthodoxy in any other area. The result was the creation, by the mid-1500s, of Calvinist churches in Geneva, the Empire, Scotland (where the members were called "Presbyterians"), France, and Hungary and other Protestant churches in England, Poland, and Switzerland.

Although it was easier to win recognition for these new churches once Luther had shown it was possible, dissent in general remained as unpopular as ever. Against the ordinary person who, inspired by the reformers, attempted to express individual beliefs, the repression was as severe as it had always been. When a Dutchwoman named Elizabeth Dirks tried to apply the new teachings and interpret the Bible for herself, she was hauled up before the authorities of the Catholic Church in 1549:

Official: "What do you think of our mass?"
Elizabeth: "My Lord, I have no faith in your mass but only in that which is the word of God."
Official: "What do you think about the Holy Sacrament?"
Elizabeth: "I never in my life read in Scripture about a Holy Sacrament, but only of the Supper of the Lord."
Official: "Shut your mouth; you speak with a haughty tongue."
Elizabeth: "No, my Lord, I speak with a free tongue."
Official: "Do priests have the power to forgive sins?"
Elizabeth: "No, my Lord, how should I believe that? I say that Christ is the only priest through whom sins are forgiven."
Official: "So far we have treated you gently. Since you won't confess, we will put you to torture. Take hold of her."

Two months later, Elizabeth Dirks was condemned to death and drowned in a sack. That her fate was shared by tens of thousands of individuals who challenged traditional authorities in the 1500s and 1600s merely confirms that tolerance was still severely limited. The dissent of large movements like Lutheranism and Calvinism had learned to survive by moderating demands for social change and by becoming identified with otherwise respectable elements in society. Elizabeth Dirks, and thousands like her, had neither of these advantages (Figure 23). They remained within small groups, each with its own set of beliefs, and although they were often called "Anabaptists" (after a practice, common to many of them, of rebaptising their adherents so that they could understand, as adults, the sacrament that was being administered), no two of these sects were the same. Persecuted not only by Catholics but also by other Protestants, they nevertheless developed a respect for the individual conscience that was unique to the age. Above all, they refused to protect themselves with the dogmatism, aggressiveness, and intolerance that became characteristic of those dissenters, like Luther, who established their own churches.

Yet the destruction of the monopoly on truth that had belonged to the medieval Church had significant consequences. Now there were competing orthodoxies (not to mention the steadfast independence of the Anabaptists), and it was no longer so

Figure 23. *Execution of the Münster Radicals* (engraving). The execution of dissenters was a common sight in the sixteenth century. Here the leaders of a group of radical reformers, who took over the city of Münster in 1535, are burned at the stake after the capture of the city by a combined Catholic-Lutheran army—a unique joint campaign that was mounted because both faiths feared extreme reformers more than one another.

easy to define what was universally true. Some of Europe's most sensitive observers saw the implications of what had happened and argued for toleration—for the view that dissent was no longer punishable in an age of uncertain truth. Two Frenchmen in particular made stirring pleas for new attitudes that the world has struggled to accept ever since.

One, Sebastian Castellio, was appalled at the persecutions he witnessed, and in 1554 he put the issue with a simplicity that is unanswerable:

To kill a heretic is not to crush a doctrine. It is to kill a man.

The other Frenchman, the writer Michel de Montaigne, emphasized (in an essay published in 1580) the horror of the viciousness performed in the name of Christian belief:

> We willingly describe as pious only those actions that accord with our feelings. Thus there is no hostility that outdoes Christian hostility. Our faith does wonders when it encourages our leaning toward hatred, cruelty, ambition, avarice, slander, rebellion. Against that inclination, and toward goodness, kindness, moderation it neither walks nor flies, except by a miracle, when some rare nature appears. Our religion is supposed to destroy vices; in fact, it covers them, fosters them, provokes them.

For a long time these were voices in the wilderness, but the idea of toleration which they conveyed—and which now appeared, for the first time, as a noble ideal to set against the belief in orthodoxy and unity—injected a powerful new standard of behavior into European culture.

Indeed, the notion that religious convictions should not be imposed, but ought to be decided for themselves by all individuals, could be taken in other directions as well. Within a few years, those who disputed the established Church authorities were beginning to dispute standard political and social arrangements as well. This was exactly what Luther had feared and rejected. Yet the connection could not be repressed merely because it failed in the peasant revolts of the 1520s. Half a century later, the followers of Calvin in France and the Netherlands explicitly linked religious dissent with demands for broader change.

Luther's revolt had already implied that there might be such an association, even though he himself had vehemently denied it. After all, he was giving the individual, rather than the Church, responsibility for a central human concern—salvation. Might people not wish to extend that responsibility and independence into other areas of life? Moreover, by emphasizing the primacy of faith, Luther implied that there might be justification for resisting wicked rulers who sought to force one's conscience. There was some reason to expect, therefore, that those of Luther's critics who predicted that social upheaval would follow religious upheaval were going to be right.

The two countries where that connection first became obvious were France and the Netherlands. In both, the Protestants were primarily followers of Calvin. As they faced growing persecution in the mid-1500s, however, they gradually discarded Calvin's insistence (which echoed Luther's) on obeying political authorities. What happened, they asked, when an evil ruler prevented believers from exercising their faith? The answer seemed clear: rebellion in the name of religion. In France, the Calvinists fought over thirty years of civil war (Figure 24) until the Edict of Nantes (1598) recognized their right to worship unharmed; in the Netherlands, they led a revolt which, beginning in 1568 and continuing for eighty years, finally created a new state, the United Provinces (usually known by the name of its leading province, Holland), where, by and large, all creeds were tolerated.

The victories of these Calvinists, who had established themselves by 1600 as a major presence in Europe, confirmed the respectability that dissent could now achieve. Breaking openly with tradition and defying established authority were no longer unthinkable; indeed, protest could succeed. Within states, however, diversity was usually regarded as dangerous. It was still thought best to have—in a phrase

Figure 24. François Dubois, *St. Bartholomew's Day Massacre.* The most notorious blood-bath of the religious wars was the massacre on St. Bartholomew's day of unsuspecting Protestants who had gathered for a wedding in Paris in 1572. After men, women, and children were hung, stabbed, or shot, many of their corpses were dragged to the river and thrown in, because it was felt necessary to "cleanse" the city of the pollution of heresy.

common at the time—"one king, one faith." The acceptance the Lutherans won in the Empire, for example, was not for individuals but for princes. At the Peace of Augsburg in 1555, each independent city and principality in the Empire was given the right to decide whether its citizens would be Catholics or Lutherans; dissenters would have to move to a territory that accepted them. In France, the toleration for the Calvinists was grudging and was chipped away until, in 1685, it was revoked altogether. The Calvinists had simply never developed sufficient political power to survive. And in many areas dissent continued to be crushed. In 1618, for instance, the Bohemians again rebelled against the Emperor, this time as Protestants, but they were again subdued by superior force. Only in the United Provinces, where the government in fact led the fight against persecution, was there real toleration for all faiths, from Judaism to Catholicism.

Yet the ripple effects of these upheavals in the central institution of European life, religion, did not stop with politics. Very soon, dissent over faith inspired campaigns for change not only in government but also in society at large. The Empire's peasants had already suggested, in the 1520s, that they wanted improvements in their economic and social, as well as their religious, situation. And the

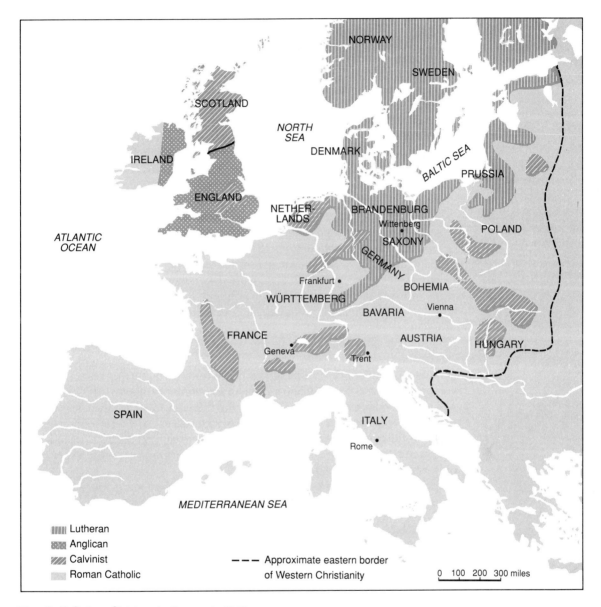

Map 6. Religious divisions in Europe in 1600

demands were soon to go beyond the redress of grievances, for the Reformation raised doubts about dozens of the comfortable assumptions of European society.

It had never seemed necessary, for example, for ordinary people to learn how to read. But how else were they now going to study the Bible for themselves? The determination that everyone should have access to the Bible brought fundamental literacy and further schooling not only to men who had never had such education before but also—even more upsetting—to thousands of women in Protestant areas. Although many continued to view women as strictly subordinate to men, there was a growing emphasis in the 1600s and 1700s—almost always associated with Protestantism—on marriage as a partnership, on families reading the Bible together, and on equality between men and women in their home life. Moreover, anyone who took female subservience for granted had to reconcile that opinion with the independent role women played in the Reformation—as preachers, teachers, and active promoters of religious causes. We have seen the example of Elizabeth Dirks, and there were countless others. A number of the most important early Calvinists in France were women aristocrats, and they helped ensure noble support—and thus survival—for the movement in its early days.

These kinds of consequences were taken further by a number of dissenters who, starting with strong religious faith, went on to challenge inequities and injustices in all areas. They began to wonder whether a country that persecuted people for their beliefs might not need to be changed in more than its attitude toward heresy. If dissenters had a stake in their society, were they not entitled to criticize its failings and try to make it a better place? This outlook led to the first major social and political revolution in modern times, the Puritan Revolution of the 1640s and 1650s in England.

That this cataclysm often goes by the name of "Puritan"—and thus is identified with the most extreme critics of the official Church of England—indicates the importance of religion in inspiring the many reforms that were attempted. The revolutionaries executed England's king; abolished the monarchy, the aristocracy, and the traditional Church; discussed giving the vote to all adult males; tried to replace the legal system with biblical law; closed all theaters; ended almost completely the censorship of the press; permitted virtually all beliefs to be practiced openly; and at one time or another considered transforming just about every major social institution in the land.

Perhaps the most remarkable of the programs for change was put forward in 1652 by a preacher named Gerrard Winstanley. He wanted to abolish private property and have people live together in communes, sharing everything:

> I affirm and challenge anyone to disprove that the earth was made to be a common treasury of livelihood for all, without respect for persons, and was not made to be bought and sold; and that mankind is the lord over the beasts, birds, fishes and the earth, and was not made to acknowledge any of his own kind to be his teacher and ruler. This being a truth, as it is, then none ought to be lords or landlords over another, but the earth is free for every son and daughter of mankind to live upon.

Winstanley attracted a group of followers, known as "Diggers," because they started to dig up some public land in order to establish a little community inspired by his ideas. However, the authorities could not allow so profound an assault on the traditions of society, even in the midst of a revolution. The settlement was destroyed, and the Diggers were dispersed.

By its very nature, dissent fails more often than it succeeds. It usually starts as a small and fragile voice, and the odds are that it will be suppressed. Once Luther had demonstrated that it could be respectable, though, it could never again be totally silenced. Moreover, it soon moved, from its beginnings in religion, to the political and social forms that remain familiar to this day. And although individual dissenters like Winstanley might fail, their ideas continued to challenge society long after they themselves were gone. In Winstanley's case, the attempt to abolish private property was to be picked up two centuries later by Karl Marx.

Thanks to the events of the Renaissance, therefore, dissenters have become essential figures in our history. And the possibility that they might actually promote the health of the societies they live in—that pluralism might be helpful rather than harmful—was already recognized in this period, by the poet John Milton, who lived through the Puritan Revolution and wrote in 1644:

> Books which are likely to taint life and doctrine cannot be suppressed without the fall of learning. A wise man can gather gold out of the drossest volume, and a fool will be a fool with the best book. Where there is much desire to learn, there will be much arguing, many opinions. What some lament, we should rejoice at. Let Truth and Falsehood grapple; who ever knew Truth put to the worse, in a free and open encounter?

Ever since, the modern world has been striving to learn the leasson that Milton was trying to teach. And it is to the period of the Renaissance that we owe his understanding both of dissent and of its consequences.

Original Sources

A number of dissenters in the century before Luther—of whom Wycliffe and Hus are perhaps the best known—foreshadowed the thinking of Luther and later reformers such as Calvin. There were connections between these earlier forms of dissent and the spread of Lutheranism, since many early Lutherans were to be influenced by the message of earlier dissenters. Communication between the different areas of Europe, eastern and western, was made easier by growing trade, and later in the 1400s a new invention, the printing press, became an essential stimulus to communication. Additionally, the rise of Christian humanism brought intellectuals from numerous countries into correspondence with one another through their common language—Latin.

It is important to note that not all those who were labeled as "dissenters" had as their principal motivation conscious dissent from the organized religious structure of the time. The Jews, for example, were outsiders in the Christian world and persecuted for centuries prior to Luther's appearance on the scene, as the first selection demonstrates. Others were on the margins of society throughout this period, such as those condemned as sorcerers and witches. Although the most brutal and widespread "witch hunts" did not occur until the seventeenth century, witches had long been greatly feared and considered to have special malevolent powers. Historians have debated for many years the extent to which witchcraft was "real," that is, an actual historical phenomenon rather than the result of the tortured imaginings of fanatical witchhunters. There seems to be no doubt that witches were identified as dissenters, and some really were just that. However, the vast majority of those condemned as witches were innocent victims who were tormented because of their persecutors' fear and ignorance. The same was true for the Jews.

I. DISSENT BEFORE LUTHER

The first two selections exemplify types of "dissent" before Martin Luther. The first indicates how Jews were treated; the second is a letter by the Czech reformer Jan Hus, written after his imprisonment for heresy.

Selection 1

A Letter on Spanish Massacres of Jews

Written by a well-known philosopher and rabbi, Hasdai Crescas, this letter describes an experience that was all too common in Renaissance and early modern times. In this case the victims were Jews, who were easy (and frequent) targets for those who were inclined to think of the "outsider" as the cause of any problems that troubled society. It was often assumed, for example, that economic difficulties or plagues had to be the fault of such outsiders, and the result sometimes became as violent as the massacres described here. The emotion Crescas displays was heightened by the fact that his own son was killed in the massacres. A hundred years later, the dislike of Jews was to lead to their expulsion from Spain.

[Saragossa, 19 October 1391]

If I were to tell you here all the numerous sufferings we have endured you would be dumbfounded at the thought of them; I will therefore set before you only in brief detail the table of our disaster set with poisonous plant and wormwood, giving you a bare recital of the facts so that you may satiate yourselves on the bitterness of our wormwood and drink from the wine of our grief. As I suppose that you have been told the story already, I will recount it as briefly as possible, commencing as follows:

On the day of the New Moon of the fateful month Tammus in the year 5151 [July 1391] the Lord bent the bow of the enemies against the populous community of Seville where there were between 6,000–7,000 heads of families, and they destroyed their gates by fire and killed in that very place a great number of people; the majority, however, changed their faith. Many of them, children as well as women, were sold to the Moslems, so that the streets occupied by Jews have become empty. Many of them, sanctifying the Holy Name, endured death, but many also broke the holy Covenant.

Source: Franz Kobler, ed., *Letters of Jews through the Ages: A Self-Portrait of the Jewish People*, vol. 1: *From Biblical Times to the Renaissance* (New York: Hebrew Publishing Co., 1952), pp. 272–275. (Reprinted by permission of the Publishers, Hebrew Publishing Company, P.O. Box 157. Rockaway Beach, NY 11693. Copyright 1952. All rights reserved.)

From there the fire spread and consumed all the cedars of Lebanon [Jewish scholars, here Jews generally] in the holy community of the city of Cordova. Here, too, many changed their faith, and the community became desolate.

And on the day of misery and punishment, on which the sufferings were intensified, the wrath of the Lord was discharged on the holy city; the source of learning and the word of the Lord, namely the community of Toledo, and in the temple of the Lord the priests and the learned were murdered. In that very place the Rabbis, the descendants of the virtuous and excellent R. Asher of blessed memory, together with their children and pupils, publicly sanctified the Holy Name. However, many who had not the courage to save their souls changed their faith here, too.

The country trembled even on account of these three communities, apart from the others in their neighborhood to the number of 70. And withal, we were in the greatest danger here, and had to be on the alert day and night. On the 7th of the month Ab the Lord destroyed mercilessly the community of Valencia, in which there were about a thousand heads of families; about 250 men died, sanctifying the name of the Lord; the others fled into the mountain; some of these saved themselves but the majority changed their faith.

From there the plague spread over the communities of glorious Majorca, which is situated on the shore of the sea. On the day of the New Moon of

Ellul, the bloodthirsty villains came there, profaned, plundered and robbed them and left them like a net in which there are no fish. There died, sanctifying the Holy Name, about 300 persons, and about 800 took refuge in the royal castle; the others changed their faith.

On the following Sabbath the Lord poured out his fury like fire, destroyed His sanctuary and profaned the crown of His teaching, namely the community of Barcelona, which was destroyed on that day. The number of murdered amounted to 250 souls; the rest fled into the castle, where they were saved. The enemies plundered all streets inhabited by Jews and set fire to some of them. The authorities of the province, however, took no part in this; instead, they endeavoured to protect the Jews with all their might. They offered food and drink to the Jews, and even set about punishing the wrongdoers, when a furious mob rose against the better classes in the country and fought against the Jews who were in the castle, with bows and missiles, and killed them in the castle itself. Amongst the many who sanctified the Name of the Lord was my only son, who was a bridegroom and whom I have offered as a faultless lamb for sacrifice; I submit to God's justice and take comfort in the thought of his excellent portion and his delightful lot. Amongst them were many who slaughtered themselves and others who threw themselves down from the tower and whose limbs were already broken before they had reached halfway down the tower. Many also came forth and sanctified the name of the Lord in the open street. All the others changed their faith, and only few found refuge in the towns of the princes; a child

could register the names of these. However, there were precisely the most esteemed. Consequently, because of our many sins, there is none left in Barcelona today who still bears the name of Jew.

In the town of Lerida, too, many died and others changed their faith. There were only a few people who saved their lives.

In the town of Gerona, where knowledge of the Law could be found combined with humility, the Rabbis of that place sanctified the Name of the Lord publicly, and few only changed their faith. The majority of the community escaped to the houses of the citizens and are today in the castle.

In a word, in the state of Valencia not one single Jew remained, with the sole exception of the place called Murviedro. In the province of Catalonia, too, not one single Jew remained except in the towns of the princes and administrators, who nowhere attacked them.

For us, however, who are still in the country of Aragon, there is no more trouble and complaint, because the Lord has taken pity on us and has preserved the remnant of us in all these places after vehement supplication, although nothing but our bodies is left us after the distribution of our belongings. In spite of this, fear fills our hearts, and our eyes are directed towards the Father in heaven, that He may be merciful to us and may heal us of our wounds, and keep our feet from wavering. May this be His will, Amen.

'I am the man that hath seen affliction by the rod of His wrath,' Hasdai ben Abraham ben Hasdai ben Judah Crescas, who writes here in Saragossa, on the 20th day of the month Marheshvan in the year 5152 of the creation.

Selection 2
"To All Faithful Czechs" (1415)

Jan Hus

This letter was written during Hus's imprisonment in Constance and in awareness of his impending death. In it, the theologian denies the right of Church Councils to condemn him, his works, and his thought. Notice Hus's reliance on the ultimate authority of scripture and his identification with the martyred St. Catherine of Alexandria.

Constance, Franciscan prison
26 June 1415

Master Jan Hus, in hope a servant of God, to all faithful Czechs who love God and will love Him, sends his wish and unworthy prayer that they would live in God's grace, die in it, and dwell with God for ever!

Faithful and beloved of God!

I have tried once more to call to your attention that the proud and avaricious Council, full of all abomination, condemned my Czech books, having neither heard nor seen them, even if it had heard them, it would not have understood them. For there were Italians, French, English, Spaniards, Germans, and others of other languages in that Council—unless perhaps Bishop John of Litomyšl might have understood them somewhat. For he was there along with other Czechs, the provocators, with the Prague and Vyšehrad chapters from whom had originated the calumny against the truth of God and of our Bohemian land. I hold that land, in the hope of God, as the land of the best faith, knowing of her desire for the Word of God and for morals.

O, had you seen that Council which calls itself the most holy, and that cannot err, you would surely have seen the greatest abomination! For I have heard it commonly said by the Swabians that Constance or Kostnice,* their city, would not for thirty years rid itself of the sins which that Council has committed in their city. They say, further-more, that all have been scandalized by that Council, and others spat when they saw the abominal things.

I say to you that when I stood before that Council the first day,† seeing that there was no order in it whatever, I said aloud, when they were all quiet: "I had supposed that there would be greater reverence, goodness, and better order in this Council than there is!" At that time the presiding cardinal‡ said, "What do you say? You spoke more humbly at the castle!" And I answered, saying, "Because at the castle nobody shouted at me, and here all are shouting!"

Because that Council conducted itself in such a disorderly way, it has done more harm than good. Therefore, faithful and in God dear Christians, do not allow yourselves to be terrified by their decrees, which, I hope in God, will profit them nothing. They will fly away like butterflies, and their decrees will turn into a spiderweb. They wanted to frighten me, but could not overcome God's power in me. They did not dare to oppose me with Scripture, as those gracious lords hears, who, despite all shame, stood bravely by the truth—The Czechs, Moravians, and the Poles; but especially Lord Wenceslas of Dubá and Lord John of Chlum. For they were present there, since King Sigismund himself permitted them to be in the Council. They heard it when I said: "I ask for instruction; and if I have written anything wrong, I wish to be instructed therein." Then the presiding cardinal said: "As you wish to be instructed, here is your instruction: you must recant, as fifty masters of the Holy Scriptures have so concluded!"

Source: Matthew Spinka, *The Letters of John Hus* (Manchester, England: Manchester University Press, 1972), pp. 195–197.
* The Czech form of the name.

† 5 June, but it was more likely on 8 June.
‡ Pierre d'Ailly.

Yea! what a fine instruction! So St Catherine,* a young maiden, should have retreated from the truth and faith in the Lord Jesus Christ because fifty masters stood up against her! Nevertheless, that dear maiden remained steadfast unto death and brought the masters to the Lord God, whom I, a sinner, am unable to bring!

I am writing this to you that you may know that they did not defeat me by any Scripture or any proof, but that they sought to seduce me by deceits and threats to recant and abjure. But the merciful Lord God, Whose law I have extolled, has been and is with me, and I hope that He will be with me to the end and will preserve me in His grace until death.

The letter was written on Wednesday after St John the Baptist,† in prison and in chains, in the expectation of death; but by reason of God's secret counsels I cannot say whether it is my last letter. For the Almighty God can yet set me free.

---

* This refers to the story of St. Catherine of Alexandria. Emperor Maximin promised a great reward to any philosopher who would convert her to paganism. She withstood them all.

† 26 June.

II. LUTHER AND HIS TIMES

The appearance of Martin Luther altered the nature of dissent during the Renaissance. After Luther, it was no longer possible to ignore questions of religious and civil disobedience, since the two became increasingly intertwined and central to European identity.

Selection 3
The Freedom of a Christian
Martin Luther

This brief pamphlet demonstrates that Luther's rejection of the doctrine of "good works" in favor of what he termed the "righteousness of faith" occurred as early as 1520.

Martin Luther's treatise on christian liberty [the freedom of a christian]

Many people have considered Christian faith an easy thing, and not a few have given it a place among the virtues. They do this because they have not experienced it and have never tasted the great strength there is in faith. It is impossible to write well about it or to understand what has been written about it unless one has at one time or another experienced the courage which faith gives a man when trials oppress him. But he who has had even a faint taste of it can never write, speak, meditate, or hear enough concerning it. It is a living "spring of water welling up to eternal life," as Christ calls it in John 4 [:14].

As for me, although I have no wealth of faith to boast of and know how scant my supply is, I nevertheless hope that I have attained to a little faith, even though I have been assailed by great and various temptations; and I hope that I can discuss it, if not more elegantly, certainly more to the point, than those literalists and subtile disputants have previously done, who have not even understood what they have written.

To make the way smoother for the unlearned—for only them do I serve—I shall set down the following two propositions concerning the freedom and the bondage of the spirit:

Source: Martin Luther, *Luther's Works: Career of the Reformer I,* vol. 31, ed. by Harold J. Grimm (Philadelphia: Fortress Press, 1957), pp. 343–350. (Reprinted from *Luther's Works,* Volume 31, edited by Harald J. Grimm, copyright 1957 Fortress Press. Used by permission of Augsburg Fortress.)

A Christian is a perfectly free lord of all, subject to none.

A Christian is a perfectly dutiful servant of all, subject to all.

These two theses seem to contradict each other. If, however, they should be found to fit together they would serve our purpose beautifully. Both are Paul's own statements, who says in I Cor. 9 [:19], "For though I am free from all men, I have made myself a slave to all," and in Rom. 13 [:8], "Owe no one anything, except to love one another." Love by its very nature is ready to serve and be subject to him who is loved. So Christ, although he was Lord of all, was "born of woman, born under the law" [Gal. 4:4], and therefore was at the same time a free man and a servant, "in the form of God" and "of a servant" [Phil. 2:6–7].

Let us start, however, with something more remote from our subject, but more obvious. Man has a twofold nature, a spiritual and a bodily one. According to the spiritual nature, which men refer to as the soul, he is called a spiritual, inner, or new man. According to the bodily nature, which men refer to as flesh, he is called a carnal, outward, or old man, of whom the Apostle writes in II Cor. 4 [:16], "Though our outer nature is wasting away, our inner nature is being renewed every day." Because of this diversity of nature the Scriptures assert contradictory things concerning the same man, since these two men in the same man contradict each other, "for the desires of the flesh are against the Spirit, and the desires of the Spirit are against the flesh," according to Gal. 5 [:17].

First, let us consider the inner man to see how a righteous, free, and pious Christian, that is, a spiritual, new, and inner man, becomes what he is. It is evident that no external thing has any influence in producing Christian righteousness or freedom, or in producing unrighteousness or servitude. A simple argument will furnish the proof of this statement. What can it profit the soul if the body is well, free, and active, and eats, drinks, and does as it pleases? For in these respects even the most godless slaves of vice may prosper. On the other hand, how will poor health or imprisonment or hunger or thirst or any other external misfortune harm the soul? Even the most godly men, and those who are free because of clear con-

sciences, are afflicted with these things. None of these things touch either the freedom or the servitude of the soul. It does not help the soul if the body is adorned with the sacred robes of priests or dwells in sacred places or is occupied with sacred duties or prays, fasts, abstains from certain kinds of food, or does any work that can be done by the body and in the body. The righteousness and the freedom of the soul require something far different since the things which have been mentioned could be done by any wicked person. Such works produce nothing but hypocrites. On the other hand, it will not harm the soul if the body is clothed in secular dress, dwells in unconsecrated places, eats and drinks as others do, does not pray aloud, and neglects to do all the above-mentioned things which hypocrites can do.

Furthermore, to put aside all kinds of works, even contemplation, meditation, and all that the soul can do, does not help. One thing, and only one thing, is necessary for Christian life, righteousness, and freedom. That one thing is the most holy Word of God, the gospel of Christ, as Christ says, John 11 [:25], "I am the resurrection and the life; he who believes in me, though he die, yet shall he live"; and John 8 [:36], "So if the Son makes you free, you will be free indeed"; and Matt. 4 [:4], "Man shall not live by bread alone, but by every word that proceeds from the mouth of God." Let us then consider it certain and firmly established that the soul can do without anything except the Word of God and that where the Word of God is missing there is no help at all for the soul. If it has the Word of God it is rich and lacks nothing since it is the Word of life, truth, light, peace, righteousness, salvation, joy, liberty, wisdom, power, grace, glory, and of every incalculable blessing. This is why the prophet in the entire Psalm [119] and in many other places yearns and sighs for the Word of God and uses so many names to describe it.

On the other hand, there is no more terrible disaster with which the wrath of God can afflict men than a famine of the hearing of his Word, as he says in Amos [8:11]. Likewise there is no greater mercy than when he sends forth his Word, as we read in Psalm 107 [:20]: "He sent forth his word, and healed them, and delivered them from destruction." Nor was Christ sent into the world for any other ministry except that of the Word. Moreover, the entire spiritual estate—all the apostles, bishops, and priests—has been called and instituted only for the ministry of the Word.

You may ask, "What then is the Word of God, and how shall it be used, since there are so many words of God?" I answer: The Apostle explains this in Romans 1. The Word is the gospel of God concerning his Son, who was made flesh, suffered, rose from the dead, and was glorified through the Spirit who sanctifies. To preach Christ means to feed the soul, make it righteous, set it free, and save it, provided it believes the preaching. Faith alone is the saving and efficacious use of the Word of God, according to Rom. 10 [:9]: "If you confess with your lips that Jesus is Lord and believe in your heart that God raised him from the dead, you will be saved." Furthermore, "Christ is the end of the law, that every one who has faith may be justified" [Rom. 10:4]. Again, in Rom. 1 [:17], "He who through faith is righteous shall live." The Word of God cannot be received and cherished by any works whatever but only by faith. Therefore it is clear that, as the soul needs only the Word of God for its life and righteousness, so it is justified by faith alone and not any works; for if it could be justified by anything else, it would not need the Word, and consequently it would not need faith.

This faith cannot exist in connection with works—that is to say, if you at the same time claim to be justified by works, whatever their character—for that would be the same as "limping with two different opinions" [I Kings 18:21], as worshiping Baal and kissing one's own hand [Job 31:27–28], which, as Job says, is a very great iniquity. Therefore the moment you begin to have faith you learn that all things in you are altogether blameworthy, sinful, and damnable, as the Apostle says in Rom. 3 [:23], "Since all have sinned and fall short of the glory of God," and, "None is righteous, no, not one; . . . all have turned aside, together they have gone wrong" (Rom. 3:10–12). When you have learned this you will know that you need Christ, who suffered and rose again for you so that, if you believe in him, you may through his faith become a new man in so far as your sins

are forgiven and you are justified by the merits of another, namely, of Christ alone.

Since, therefore, this faith can rule only in the inner man, as Rom. 10 [:10] says, "For man believes with his heart and so is justified," and since faith alone justifies, it is clear that the inner man cannot be justified, freed, or saved by any outer work or action at all, and that these works, whatever their character, have nothing to do with this inner man. On the other hand, only ungodliness and unbelief of heart, and no outer work, make him guilty and a damnable servant of sin. Wherefore it ought to be the first concern of every Christian to lay aside all confidence in works and increasingly to strengthen faith alone and through faith to grow in the knowledge, not of works, but of Christ Jesus, who suffered and rose for him, as Peter teaches in the last chapter of his first Epistle (I Pet. 5:10). No other work makes a Christian. Thus when the Jews asked Christ, as related in John 6 [:28], what they must do "to be doing the work of God," he brushed aside the multitude of works which he saw they did in great profusion and suggested one work, saying, "This is the work of God, that you believe in him whom he has sent" [John 6:29]; "for on him has God the Father set his seal" [John 6:27].

Therefore true faith in Christ is a treasure beyond comparison which brings with it complete salvation and saves man from every evil, as Christ says in the last chapter of Mark [16:16]: "He who believes and is baptized will be saved; but he who does not believe will be condemned." Isaiah contemplated this treasure and foretold it in chapter 10: "The Lord will make a small and consuming word upon the land, and it will overflow with righteousness" [Cf. Isa. 10:22]. This is as though he said, "Faith, which is a small and perfect fulfilment of the law, will fill believers with so great a righteousness that they will need nothing more to become righteous." So Paul says, Rom. 10 [:10], "For man believes with his heart and so is justified."

Should you ask how it happens that faith alone justifies and offers us such a treasure of great benefits without works in view of the fact that so many works, ceremonies, and laws are prescribed in the Scriptures, I answer: First of all, remember what has been said, namely, that faith alone, without works, justifies, frees, and saves; we shall make this clearer later on. Here we must point out that the entire Scripture of God is divided into two parts: commandments and promises. Although the commandments teach things that are good, the things taught are not done as soon as they are taught, for the commandments show us what we ought to do but do not give us the power to do it. They are intended to teach man to know himself, that through them he may recognize his inability to do good and may despair of his own ability. That is why they are called the Old Testament and constitute the Old Testament. For example, the commandment, "You shall not covet" [Exod. 20:17], is a command which proves us all to be sinners, for no one can avoid coveting no matter how much he may struggle against it. Therefore, in order not to covet and to fulfil the commandment, a man is compelled to despair of himself, to seek the help which he does not find in himself elsewhere and from someone else, as stated in Hosea [13:9]: "Destruction is your own, O Israel: your help is only in me." As we fare with respect to one commandment, so we fare with all, for it is equally impossible for us to keep any one of them.

Now when a man has learned through the commandments to recognize his helplessness and is distressed about how he might satisfy the law— since the law must be fulfilled so that not a jot or title shall be lost, otherwise man will be condemned without hope—then, being truly humbled and reduced to nothing in his own eyes, he finds in himself nothing whereby he may be justified and saved. Here the second part of Scripture comes to our aid, namely, the promises of God which declare the glory of God, saying, "If you wish to fulfil the law and not covet, as the law demands, come, believe in Christ in whom grace, righteousness, peace, liberty, and all things are promised you. If you believe, you shall have all things; if you do not believe, you shall lack all things." That which is impossible for you to accomplish by trying to fulfil all the works of the law— many and useless as they all are—you will accomplish quickly and easily through faith. God our

Father has made all things depend on faith so that whoever has faith will have everything, and whoever does not have faith will have nothing. "For God has consigned all men to disobedience, that he may have mercy upon all," as it is stated in Rom. 11 [:32]. Thus the promises of God give what the commandments of God demand and fulfil what the law prescribes so that all things may be God's alone, both the commandments and the fulfilling of the commandments. He alone commands, he alone fulfils. Therefore the promises of God belong to the New Testament. Indeed, they are the New Testament.

Since these promises of God are holy, true, righteous, free, and peaceful words, full of goodness, the soul which clings to them with a firm faith will be so closely united with them and altogether absorbed by them that it not only will share in all their power but will be saturated and intoxicated by them. If a touch of Christ healed, how much more will this most tender spiritual touch, this absorbing of the Word, communicate to the soul all things that belong to the Word. This, then, is how through faith alone without works the soul is justified by the Word of God, sanctified, made true, peaceful, and free, filled with every blessing and truly made a child of God, as John 1 [:12] says: "But to all who . . . believed in his name, he gave power to become children of God."

From what has been said it is easy to see from what source faith derives such great power and why a good work or all good works together cannot equal it. No good work can rely upon the Word of God or live in the soul, for faith alone and the Word of God rule in the soul. Just as the heated iron glows like fire because of the union of fire with it, so the Word imparts its qualities to the soul. It is clear, then, that a Christian has all that he needs in faith and needs no works to justify him; and if he has no need of works, he has no need of the law; and if he has no need of the law, surely he is free from the law. It is true that "the law is not laid down for the just" [I Tim. 1:9]. This is that Christian liberty, our faith, which does not induce us to live in idleness or wickedness but makes the law and works unnecessary for any man's righteousness and salvation. . . .

Selection 4
The *Twelve Articles* of the Swabian Peasants (1525)

Luther's "Reformation" did not cause the uprising of the peasants, although once fundamental beliefs in the sphere of religion had been called into question, other issues could be raised more readily—even before dissent became widespread. It seemed to many contemporaries who read the articles reproduced here that the peasants *had* been influenced by Luther, and strains of Luther's thought seemed implicit in their writings. Thus Luther had to decide quickly whether he wished to support them or not. As his "Friendly Admonition to Peace" makes clear, he chose the side of what he and the majority regarded as legitimate rule.

To the Christian reader peace, and the grace of God through Christ.

There are many antichristians who have lately taken occasion of the assembling of the peasants to cast scorn upon the Gospel, saying, Is this the fruit of the new Gospel? Is no one to be obedient, but are all to rebel and balk, to run together with force and gather in crowds in order to reform, to overthrow, or perhaps to slay the spiritual and temporal lords? To all these godless and wicked critics the following articles make answer, in order, first, to remove this reproach from the Word of God, and second, to justify in a Christian way the disobedience, nay, the rebellion of the peasants.

First, the Gospel is not a cause of rebellion and disturbance, because it is a message about Christ, the promised Messiah, whose words and life teach nothing but love, peace, patience and unity; and all who believe in this Christ become loving, peaceful, patient and harmonious. This is the foundation of all the articles of the peasants (as will clearly appear), and they are directed to the hearing of the Word of God and to life in accordance with it. How, then, can the antichristians call the Gospel a cause of revolt and disturbance? But the fact that some antichristians and enemies of the Gospel resist these demands and requests is not the fault of the Gospel, but of the devil, the deadliest enemy of the Gospel, who arouses opposition in his own by means of unbelief. Hereby the

Source: Martin Luther, *The Works of Martin Luther with an Introduction and Notes*, vol. 4, (Philadelphia: Muhlenberg Press, 1931), pp. 210–216.

Word of God, which teaches love, peace, and unity, is suppressed and taken away.

Second, It follows evidently that the peasants, desiring in their articles this Gospel for doctrine and life, cannot be called disobedient and rebellious; but if it be the will of God to hear the peasants, earnestly crying to live according to His Word, who will blame the will of God? Who will meddle in His judgment? Nay, who will resist His majesty? Did He not hear the children of Israel, crying to Him, and release them out of the hand of Pharaoh, and can He not today deliver His own? Yea, He will deliver them, and that quickly! Therefore, Christian reader, read the following articles with care, and afterwards judge.

Here follow the articles.

THE FIRST ARTICLE

First, It is our humble petition and request, as also the will and intention of all of us, that in the future we should have authority and power so that a whole community should choose and appoint a pastor, and also have the right to depose him, if he should conduct himself improperly. The pastor thus chosen should preach to us the Holy Gospel purely and clearly, without any human addition, doctrine, or commandment; for to proclaim to us continually the true faith gives us cause to pray to God for His grace to instil and confirm this true faith within us, and if His grace is not instilled in us, we always remain flesh and blood, which availeth nothing, since it stands clearly in the Scriptures that only through true faith can we come to God, and only through His mercy can we be saved. Therefore we need a leader and pastor; and thus our demand is grounded on the Scriptures.

THE SECOND ARTICLE

Second, Since the tithe is appointed in the Old Testament and fulfilled in the New, we will none the less gladly pay the just tithe of grain, but in a proper way. Since men ought to give it to God and distribute it to those that are His, it belongs to the pastor who clearly proclaims the Word of God, and we will that, for the future, this tithe be gathered and received by our church-provost, whom a community appoints; that out of it there shall be given to the pastor, who shall be chosen by an entire community, a modest, sufficient maintenance for him and his, with the consent of the whole community; that the remainder shall be distributed to the poor and needy who are in the same village, according to the circumstances and with the consent of the community. Anything that then remains shall be kept, so that if the needs of the land require the laying of a war-tax, no general tax may be laid upon the poor, but it shall be paid out of this surplus.

If it should happen that there were one or more villages that had sold their tithes to meet certain needs, they are to be informed that he who has the tithes in this way from a whole village is not to be deprived of them without return, but we will come to agreement with him, in proper way, form, and manner, to buy them back from him on suitable terms and at a suitable time. But in case anyone has not bought the tithes from any village, and his forbears have simply appropriated them to themselves, we will not, and ought not, and intend not, to pay him anything further, but will keep them for the support of the aforesaid, our chosen pastor, and for distribution to the needy, as the Holy Scriptures contain, no matter whether the holders of the tithes be spiritual or temporal. The small tithe we will not give at all, for God the Lord created cattle for the free use of men, and we regard this an improper tithe, which men have invented; therefore we will not give it any longer.

THE THIRD ARTICLE

Third, It has been the custom hitherto for men to hold us as their own property; and this is pitiable, seeing that Christ has redeemed and bought us all with the precious shedding of His blood, the lowly as well as the great, excepting no one. Therefore, it agrees with Scripture that we be free and will to be so. Not that we would be entirely free; God does not teach us that we should desire no rulers. We are to live in the commandments, not in the free self-will of the flesh; but we are to love God, recognize Him in our neighbor as our Lord, and do all (as we gladly would do) that God has commanded in the Lord's Supper; therefore, we ought to live according to His commandment. This commandment does not teach us that we are not to be obedient to the rulers, but we are to humble ourselves, not before the rulers only, but before everyone. Thus to our chosen and appointed rulers (appointed for us by God) we are willingly obedient in all proper and Christian matters, and we have no doubt that, as true and real Christians, they will gladly release us from serfdom, or show us in the Gospel that we are serfs.

THE FOURTH ARTICLE

Fourth, It has been the custom hitherto that no poor man has had the power to be allowed to catch game, wild fowl, or fish in running water; and this seems to us altogether improper and unbrotherly, selfish, and not according to the Word of God. In some places the rulers keep the game to spite us and for our great loss, because the unreasoning beasts wantonly devour that property of ours which God causes to grow for the use of man; and we have to endure this and keep quiet about it, though it is against God and neighbor. When God the Lord created man, He gave him authority over all animals, over the birds in the air, and over the fish in the water. Therefore it is our request that if anyone has waters, he offer satisfactory documentary evidence that the waters have been wittingly sold to him; in that case we do not wish to take them from him by force; on the contrary, Christian consideration must be shown, for the sake of brotherly love. But he who cannot bring sufficient proof of this shall surrender them to the community in a proper manner.

THE FIFTH ARTICLE

Fifth, We are also aggrieved in the matter of wood-cutting, for our lords have appropriated all the woods to themselves alone, and when the poor man needs any wood, he must buy it at a double price. It is our opinion that woods held by lords, spiritual or temporal, who have not bought them, should revert to an entire community, and that a community be free, in a regular way, to allow anyone to take home what he needs for firewood without payment, and also to take for nothing any that he needs for wood-working, though with the consent of him whom the community shall choose to supervise this. If there are no woods that have not been thus honestly purchased, a brotherly and Christian agreement should be reached about them; but if the property had first been appropriated and afterwards sold, the agreement shall be made in accordance with the facts in the case, and according to brotherly love and the Holy Scriptures.

THE SIXTH ARTICLE

Sixth, We have a heavy grievance because of the services which are increased from day to day, and grow daily. We desire that this matter be properly looked into and that we be not so heavily burdened, but that gracious regard he had to us, as our ancestors rendered services only according to the Word of God.

THE SEVENTH ARTICLE

Seventh, We will not henceforth allow ourselves to be further oppressed by the lords, but a man shall possess his holding in accordance with the terms on which it has been granted, according to the agreement between lord and peasant. The lord shall not compel him further, or force him to more services, or demand anything else from him for nothing, so that the peasant may use and enjoy his holding unburdened and peacefully; but if the lord needs more services, the peasant shall be willing and obedient, though at such times as may not work the peasant injury, and he shall perform the services for proper pay.

THE EIGHTH ARTICLE

Eighth, We are greatly aggrieved, as many of us have holdings, because the said holdings will not support the rents, and the peasants suffer loss and ruin. (We ask) that the lords have honorable men inspect the said holdings, and fix a fair rent, so that the peasant shall not labor for nothing, for every laborer is worthy of his hire.

THE NINTH ARTICLE

Ninth, We are aggrieved by the great wrong of continually making new laws. Punishment is inflicted on us, not according to the facts in the case, but at times by great ill-will, at times by great favor. In our opinion we should be punished by the ancient written law, and the cases dealt with according to the facts, and not according to favor.

THE TENTH ARTICLE

Tenth, We are aggrieved because some have appropriated to themselves meadows out of the common fields, which once belonged to a community. We would take these back again into the hands of our communities, unless they have been honestly purchased; but if they have been unjustly purchased, we should come to a kindly and brotherly agreement about them, according to the facts in the case.

THE ELEVENTH ARTICLE

Eleventh, We would have the custom called Todfall entirely abolished. We will not suffer it, or allow widows and orphans to be so shamefully robbed, against God and honor, as now happens in many places, under many forms, and that by those who ought to guard and protect them. They have skinned and scraped us, and though they had little authority, they have taken that. God will no longer suffer it; it shall be entirely done away; no man shall henceforth be bound to give anything of it, whether little or much.

CONCLUSION

Twelfth, It is our conclusion and final opinion that, if one or more of the articles here set forth were not to be in agreement with the Word of God (though we think this is not the case), these articles, when they are shown to us by the Word of God to be improper, we will recede from, if this is explained to us with arguments of Scripture. If some of the articles were conceded to us, and it were afterwards found that they were unjust, they shall be from that hour null and void, and have no more force; likewise, if in the Scriptures, with the truth, more things were discovered that were against God and injurious to our neight, we will, and we have determined to, use forbearance and practice and exercise ourselves in all Christian doctrine. Therefore we will pray to God the Lord, for He, and none other can give us this. The peace of Christ be with us all.

Selection 5
Friendly Admonition to Peace Concerning the Twelve Articles of the Swabian Peasants (1525)
Martin Luther

This is Luther's response to the *Twelve Articles*.

The peasants who have now banded together in Swabia have put their intolerable grievances against the rulers into twelve articles, and undertaken to support them with certain passages of Scripture, and have published them in printed form. The thing about them that pleases me best is that, in the twelfth article, they offer to accept instruction gladly and willingly, if there is need or necessity for it, and are willing to be corrected, in so far as that can be done by clear, plain, undeniable passages of Scripture, since it is right and proper that no one's conscience should be instructed or corrected, except by divine Scripture.

Now, if that is their serious and sincere meaning—and it would not be right for me to interpret it otherwise, because in these articles they come out boldly into the open, and show no desire to shun the light—then there is good reason to hope that things will be well. As one who am counted among those who now deal with the divine Scriptures here on earth, and especially as one whom

Source: Martin Luther, *The Works of Martin Luther with an Introduction and Notes*, vol. 4, (Philadelphia: Muhlenberg Press, 1931), pp. 219–231. (Reprinted from *The Works of Martin Luther*, Volume 4, copyright 1931, Muhlenberg Press. Used by permission of Ausburg Fortress.)

they mention and call upon by name in the second document, it gives me the greater courage and confidence in openly publishing my instruction, which I do in a friendly and Christian spirit, as a duty of brotherly love, in order that, if any misfortune or disaster shall come out of this matter, it may not be attributed to me, or blamed on me, because of my silence. But if this offer of theirs is only pretence and show (and without doubt there are some of that kind of people among them; for it is not possible that so great a crowd should all be true Christians and have good intentions, but a large part of them must be using the good intentions of the rest for their own selfish purposes and seeking their own advantage), then without doubt, it will accomplish very little, or contribute, in fact, to their great injury and eternal ruin.

Because this matter, then, is great and perilous, concerning, as it does, both the kingdom of God and the kingdom of the world (for if this rebellion were to proceed and get the upper hand, both kingdoms would be destroyed and there would be neither worldly government nor Word of God, but it would result in the permanent destruction of all Germany), therefore it is necessary to speak boldly and to give advice without regard to anyone. It is also necessary that we be willing listeners and allow things to be said to us, so that our hearts may not be hardened and our ears stopped, as has happened before now, and we may not get the full vigor of God's wrath. For the many terrible signs that are seen both in heaven and earth, point to a great disaster and a mighty change in Germany. Although, sad to say, we care little about this. Nevertheless, God goes on His way, and some time He will make our hard heads soft.

TO THE PRINCES AND LORDS

We have no one on earth to thank for this mischievous rebellion, except you princes and lords; and especially you blind bishops and mad priests and monks, whose hearts are hardened, even to the present day, and who do not cease to rage and rave against the holy Gospel, although you know that it is true, and that you cannot refute it. Besides, in your temporal government, you do nothing but flay and rob your subjects, in order that you may lead a life of splendor and pride, until the poor common people can bear it no longer. The sword is at your throats, but you think yourselves so firm in the saddle that no one can unhorse you. This false security and stubborn perversity will break your necks, as you will discover. I have often told you before to beware of the saying, in Psalm cvi, Effundit contemptum super principes, "He poureth contempt upon princes." You are striving after it, and want to be smitten over the head, and no warning or exhorting will help you to avoid it.

Well, then, since you are the cause of this wrath of God it will undoubtedly come upon you, if you do not mend your ways in time. The signs in heaven and the wonders on earth are meant for you, dear lords; they bode no good for you, and no good will come to you. A great part of God's wrath has already come, and God is sending so many false teachers and prophets among us, so that through error and blasphemy we may richly deserve hell and everlasting damnation. The rest of it is now here, for the peasants are mustering, and this must result in the ruin, destruction, and desolation of Germany by cruel murder and bloodshed, unless God shall be moved by our repentance to prevent it.

For you ought to know, dear lords, that God is doing this because this raging of yours cannot and will not and ought not be endured for long. You must become different men and yield to God's Word. If you do not do this amicably and willingly, then you will be compelled to it by force and destruction. If these peasants do not do it for you, others will. Even though you were to beat them all, they would still be unbeaten, for God will raise up others. It is His will to beat you, and you will be beaten. It is not the peasants, dear lords, who are resisting you; it is God Himself who is resisting you in order to visit your raging upon you. There are some of you who have said that they will stake land and people on the extirpation of Lutheran teaching. What would you think, if you were to turn out to be your own prophets, and your land and people were already staked? Do not jest with God, dear lords! The Jews, too, said, "We have no king," and it became so serious that they had to be without a king forever.

To make your sin still greater, and ensure your merciless destruction, some of you are beginning to blame this affair on the Gospel and say it is the fruit of my teaching. Well, well! Slander away, dear lords. You did not want to know what I taught, and what the Gospel is; now there is one at the door who will soon teach you, unless you amend your ways. You, and everyone else, must bear me witness that I have taught with all quietness, have striven earnestly against rebellion, and have diligently held and exhorted subjects to obedience and reverence toward even your tyrannous and ravenous rule. This rebellion cannot be coming from me. But the murder-prophets, who hate me as much as they hate you, have come among these people and have gone about among them for more than three years, and no one has resisted them save me alone. If, therefore, God is minded to punish you, and allows the devil, through his false prophets, to stir up the people against you, and if it is, perhaps, His will that I shall not be able to prevent it any longer; what can I or my Gospel do? Not only has it suffered your persecution and murdering and raging; it has also prayed for you and helped protect and maintain your rule over the common people. If I had any desire to be revenged on you, I could laugh in my sleeve, and become a mere onlooker at the doings of the peasants, or even join in with them and help make matters worse; but from this may my God preserve me, as He has done hitherto.

Therefore, my dear lords, enemies or friends, I beg submissively that you will not despise my faithfulness, though I am a poor man. I beg that you will not make light of this rebellion. Not that I believe or fear that they will be too strong for you, or that I would have you be afraid of them on that account. But fear God and have respect for His wrath! If it be His will to punish you as you have deserved (and I am afraid that it is), then He would punish you, even though the peasants were a hundred times fewer than they are. He can make peasants out of stones and slay a hundred of you by one peasant, so that all your armor and your strength will be too little.

If it is still possible to give you advice, my lords, give a little place to the will and wrath of God. A cart-load of hay must give way to a drunken man; how much more ought you to leave your raging and your obstinate tyranny and deal reasonably with the peasants, as though they were drunk or out of their mind. Do not begin a struggle with them, for you do not know what the end of it will be. Try kindness first, for you do not know what God wills to do, and do not strike a spark that will kindle all Germany and that no one can quench. Our sins are before God; therefore we have to fear His wrath when even a leaf rustles, let alone when such multitude sets itself in motion. You lose nothing by kindness; and even though you were to lose something, it can afterwards come back to you ten times over in peace, while in conflict you may, perhaps, lose both life and goods. Why run into danger, when you can get more by another, and a good way?

The peasants have put forth twelve articles, some of which are so fair and just as to take away your reputation in the eyes of God and the world and fulfil the Psalm about pouring contempt upon princes. Nevertheless, almost all of them are framed in their own interest and for their own good, though not for their best good. I should, indeed, have put forth other articles against you that would have dealt with all Germany and its government.

I did this in my book To the German Nobility, when there was more at stake; but you made light of that, and now you must listen to and put up with these selfish articles. It serves you right, as people to whom nothing can be told.

The first article, in which they ask the right to hear the Gospel and choose their pastors, you cannot reject with any show of right, though, to be sure, it contains some selfishness, since they allege that these pastors are to be supported by the tithes, and these do not belong to them. Nevertheless, the sense of the article is that permission should be given for the preaching of the Gospel, and this no ruler can or ought oppose. Indeed no ruler ought to prevent anyone from teaching or believing what he pleases, whether Gospel or lies. It is enough if he prevents the teaching of sedition and rebellion.

The other articles recite physical grievances, such as Leibfall, imposts and the like; and they, too, are fair and just. For rulers are not instituted in order that they may seek their own profit and self-will, but in order to provide for the best interests of their subjects. Flaying and extortion are, in the long run, intolerable. What good would it do if a peasant's field bore as many gulden as stalks or grains of wheat, if that only meant that the rulers would take all the more, and make their splendor all the greater, and squander the property on clothing, eating, drinking, building, and the like, as though it were chaff? The splendor would have to be checked and the expenditure stopped, so that a poor man too could keep something. You have gathered further information from their broadsides, in which they present their grievances sufficiently.

TO THE PEASANTS

So far, dear friends, you have learned only that I admit it to be (sad to say!) all too true and certain that the princes and lords, who forbid the preaching of the Gospel and oppress the people so unbearably, are worthy, and have well deserved, that God put them down from their seats, as men who have sinned deeply against God and man. And they have no excuse. Nevertheless, you, too, must have a care that you take up your cause with a good conscience and with justice. If you have a good conscience, you have the comforting advantage that God will be with you, and will help you through. Even though you were worsted for a while, and though you suffered death, you would win in the end, and would preserve your soul eternally with all the saints. But if you have not justice and a good conscience, you will be worsted; and even though you were to win for a while, and were to slay all the princes, yet in the end you would be lost eternally, body and soul. This is, therefore, no joking matter for you; it concerns your body and soul eternally. The thing that is most necessary to consider and that must be most seriously regarded, is not how strong you are and how completely wrong they are, but whether you have justice and a good conscience on your side.

Therefore, dear brethren, I beg you, in a kindly and brotherly way, to look diligently to what you do, and not to believe all kinds of spirits and preachers, now that Satan has raised up many evil spirits of disorder and of murder, and filled the world with them. Only listen and give ear, as you offer many times to do. I will not spare you the earnest warning that I owe you, even though some of you, poisoned by the murderous spirits, will hate me for it, and call me a hypocrite. That does not worry me; it is enough for me if I save some of the good-hearted and upright men among you from the danger of God's wrath. The rest I fear as little, as they despise me much; and they shall not harm me. I know One Who is greater and mightier than they are, and He teaches me in Psalm iii, "I am not afraid, though many thousands of people set themselves against me." My confidence shall outlast their confidence; that I know for sure.

In the first place, dear brethren, you bear the name of God and call yourselves a "Christian band" or union, and allege that you want to live and act "according to the divine Law." Now you know that the name, Word, and titles of God are not to be assumed idly or in vain, as He says in the second Commandment, "Thou shalt not bear the name of the Lord Thy God in vain," and adds "For God will not let him be guiltless who bears His name in vain." Here is a clear, plain text, which applies to you, as to all men. Without regard to your great numbers, your rights, and your terror, it threatens you, as well as us and all others, with God's wrath. He is, as you also know, mighty enough and strong enough to punish you as He here threatens, if His name is borne in vain; and so you have to expect no good fortune, but only misfortune, if you bear His name falsely. Learn from this how to judge yourselves; and accept this kindly warning. For Him Who once drowned the whole world in the Flood and sank Sodom with fire, it is a simple thing to slay or to defeat so many thousand peasants. He is an almighty and terrible God.

In the second place, it is easy to prove that you are bearing God's name in vain and putting it to shame; nor is it to be doubted that you will, in the end, encounter all misfortune, unless God is untrue. For here stands God's Word, and says through the mouth of Christ, "He who takes the sword shall perish by the sword." That means nothing else than that no one, by his own violence, shall arrogate authority to himself; but as Paul says, "Let every soul be subject to the higher powers with fear and reverence."

How can you get over these sayings and laws of God, when you boast that you are acting according to divine law, and yet take the sword in your own hands, and revolt against the "higher powers" that are ordained of God? Do you not think that Paul's judgment in Romans xiii will strike you, "He that withstands the ordinance of God shall receive condemnation"? That is "bearing God's name in vain"; alleging God's law and withstanding God's law, under His name. O have a care, dear sirs! It will not turn out that way in the end.

In the third place, you say that the rulers are wicked and intolerable, for they will not allow us the Gospel, and they oppress us too hard by the burdens thay lay on our temporal goods, and they are ruining us body and soul. I answer: The fact that the rulers are wicked and unjust does not excuse tumult and rebellion, for to punish wickedness does not belong to everybody, but to the worldly rulers who bear the sword. Thus Paul says in Romans xiii, and Peter, in I Peter iii, that they are ordained of God for the punishment of the wicked. Then, too, there is the natural law of all the world, which says that no one may be judge in his own cause or take his own revenge. The proverb is true, "He who resists is wrong," and the other proverb, "He who resists makes strife." The divine law agrees with this, and says, in Deuteronomy xxxii, "Vengeance is mine, I will repay, saith the Lord." Now you cannot deny that your rebellion proceeds in such a way that you make yourselves your own judges, and avenge youselves, and are unwilling to suffer any wrong. That is contrary not only to Christian law and the Gospel, but also to natural law and all equity.

If your undertaking is to prosper, when you have against you the divine and Christian law of the Old and New Testaments, and also the natural law, you must produce a new and special command of God, confirmed by signs and wonders, which bid you do these things. Otherwise God will not allow His Word and ordinance to be broken by your violence. On the contrary, because you boast of the divine law and yet act against it, He will let you fall and be punished terribly, as men who dishonor His name; and then He will condemn you eternally, as was said above. For the word of Christ in Matthew vii, applies to you; you see the mote in the eye of the rulers, and see not the beam in your own eye. Also the saying of Paul in Romans iii, "Let us do evil that good may come; whose damnation is just and right." It is true that the rulers do wrong when they suppress the Gospel and oppress you in temporal things; but you do much more wrong when you not only suppress God's Word, but tread it under foot, and invade His authority and His law, and put yourselves above God. Besides, you take from the rulers their authority and right; nay, all that they have. For what have they left, when they have lost their authority?

I make you the judges, and leave it to you to decide who is the worse robber, the man who takes a large part of another's goods, but leaves him something, or the man who takes everything that he has, and his living besides. The rulers unjustly take your property; that is the one side.

On the other hand, you take from them the authority, in which their whole property and life and being consist. Therefore, you are far greater robbers than they, and intend to do worse things than they have done. "Nay," you say, "we are going to leave them enough to live on." If anyone wants to believe that, let him! I do not believe it. One who dares go so far as to take away, by force, the authority, which is the main thing, will not leave it at that, but will take the other, and the smaller thing, that depends upon it. The wolf that eats a whole sheep will also eat its ear. And even though you were so good as to leave them enough to live on, nevertheless, you would take the best thing they have, namely, their authority, and make yourselves lords over them; and that would be too great a robbery and wrong. God will hold you the greatest robbers.

Can you not imagine it, or figure it out, dear friends? If your enterprise were right, then any man might become judge over another, and there would remain in the world neither authority, nor government, nor order, nor land, but there would be only murder and bloodshed; for as soon as anyone saw that someone was wronging him, he would turn to and judge him and punish him. Now if that is unjust and intolerable when done by an individual, neither can it be endured when done by a band or a crowd. But if it can be endured from a band or a crowd, it cannot be prevented with right and justice when individuals attempt it; for in both cases the cause is the same, namely, a wrong. And what would you do yourselves, if disorder broke out in your band, and one man set himself against another and took his own vengeance on him? Would you put up with that? Would you not say that he must let others, whom you appointed, do the judging and avenging? How, then, do you expect to stand with God and the world, when you do your own judging and avenging upon those who have injured you; nay, upon your rulers, whom God has ordained?

Now, all this has been said concerning the common, divine and natural law which even heathen, Turks, and Jews have to keep, if there is to be any peace or order in the world. Even though you were to keep this whole law, you would do no better and no more than heathen and Turks. For not to be one's own judge and avenger, but to leave this to the authorities and the rulers, makes no man a Christian; it is a thing that must eventually be done whether willingly or not. But because you are acting against this law, you see plainly that you are worse than heathen or Turks, to say nothing of the fact that you are not Christians. But what do you think that Christ will say to this? You bear His name, and call yourselves a "Christian assembly," and yet you are so far from Christian, and your actions and lives are so horribly contrary to His law, that you are not worthy to be called even heathen or Turks, but are much worse than these, because you rage and struggle against the divine and natural law, which all the heathen keep.

See, dear friends, what kind of preachers you have and what they think of your souls. I fear that some prophets of murder have come among you, who would like, by your means, to become lords in the world, and do not care that they are endangering your life, property, honor, and soul, temporally and eternally. If, now, it is really your will to keep the divine law, as you boast, then do it. There it stands! God says, "Vengeance is mine; I will repay;" and again, "Be subject not only to good lords, but also to the wicked." If you do this, well and good; if not, you may, indeed, cause a calamity, but it will finally come upon yourselves. Let no one be in doubt about this! God is just, and will not endure it. Be careful, therefore, with your liberty, that you do not run from the rain and fall in the water, and thinking to gain freedom of body, lose body and goods and soul eternally. God's wrath is there; fear it, I advise you! The devil has sent false prophets among you; beware of them!

And now we would go on, and speak of the law of Christ, and of the Gospel, which is not binding on the heathen, as the other law is. For if you boast that you are Christians and are glad when you are called Christian, and want to be known as Christians, than you must allow your law to be held up before you rightly. Listen, then, dear Christians, to your Christian law! Your Supreme Lord Christ, whose name you bear, says, in Matthew vi, "Ye shall not resist evil, but if any one compels you to go one mile, go with him two miles, and if anyone takes your cloak, let him have your coat, too; and if anyone smites you on one check, offer him the other also." Do you hear, "Christian assembly"? How does your undertaking agree with this law? You will not endure it when anyone does you ill or wrong, but will be free, and suffer nothing but good and right; and Christ says that we are not to resist any evil or wrong, but always yield, suffer it, and let things be taken from us. If you will not bear this law, then put off the name of Christian, and boast of another name that accords with your actions, or Christ Himself will tear His name from off you, and that will be too hard for you.

Thus says Paul, too, in Romans xii, "Avenge not yourselves, dearly beloved, but give place to the wrath of God." Again, he praises the Corinthians, in II Corinthians xi, because they suffer it gladly if a man smite or rob them; and in I Corinthians vi, he rebukes them because they went to law about property, and did not endure the wrong. Nay our Leader, Jesus Christ, says, in Matthew vii, that we are to wish good to those who wrong us, and pray for our persecutors, and do good to those who do evil to us. These are our Christian laws, dear friends! Now see how far the false prophets have led you away from them, and yet they call you Christians, though they have made you worse than heathen. For from these sayings, a child easily grasps that it is Christian law not to strive against wrongs, not to grasp after the sword, not to protect oneself, not to avenge oneself, but to give up life and property, and let who takes it take it; we have enough in our Lord, who will not leave us, as He has promised. Suffering, suffering; cross, cross! This and nothing else, is the Christian law! But now you battle for temporal goods, and will not let the coat go after the cloak, but want to recover the cloak. How, then, will you die, and give up your life, or love your enemies, or do good to them? O worthless Christians! Dear friends, Christians are not so common that so many of them can get together in one crowd. A Christian is a rare bird! Would to God that the majority of us were good, pious heathen, who kept the natural law, not to mention the Christian law! . . .

III. THE SPREAD OF DISSENT AND ITS IMPLICATIONS

Once underway, the spread of religious dissent proved impossible to contain. Catholic princes attempted to curtail the spread of Protestantism, while Protestant rulers fought back vigorously.

Meanwhile, those outsiders identified as "dissenters" by both groups struggled to survive. They included less acceptable forms of Protestantism, such as those espoused by Anabaptists. Jews were labeled as deviant, as were witches, and all were persecuted mercilessly. Not until the end of early modern times did principles of toleration emerge and have a lasting effect.

Selection 6
The Beehive of the Romish Church
Philip Marnix

John Calvin and his followers brought the rationale and arguments of Martin Luther into new areas of Europe in a second wave of reform that went beyond what Luther had said and done. In this selection, Philip Marnix, Lord of St. Aldegonde, utilizes the form of satire to demonstrate loathing for the Roman Catholic faith and its practices. First published in French in 1567, *The Beehive* was translated into Dutch two years later and into English just after that. It parodies a defense of the Church which one of the faithful might have made.

CHAPTER III

Of the qualitie and sundrie sortes of Bees

Those Bees *Ergo,* are of sundry qualities, but are in a manner all brought into two sortes of species, according to the description of *Plinie.* For the one are domesticall or house Bees, and be conversant among people. The other are strange and odde, terrible to see to, more teastie or angry, and with a sharper sting, but withall, more diligent in their Beehive. And albeit they are conversant also amongst people, and frankely bestowe their honie, yet be they more solitarie and stranger than the other, and therefore are called with the Greeke word *Monachi,** that is to say, dwelling solitarie or by themselves, and are knowne from other, by a

hoode which they weare on their heads. Wee will terme the first tame Bees; and these wilde Bees.

Furthermore, they are both divided into foure manner of sortes or kindes, after the description of *Aristotle* and *Columella.* Of which the very best are thick and round: they make the most hony, & keepe company next to their king, amongst which the most excellent are of a sanguine colour, as though they had redde scarlet wings. Those tend on the king, and are commonly by his side, being of both kindes, wilde and tame: the other are of manifold and sundry sortes with more varietie: but how much the neerer they approch to the king, so much the thicker and rounder they commonly grow.

The second kinde or sort resemble and are like to Waspes, Horseflies and Hornets: they make not so much hony as the first, because they come not of so good a kind. Notwithstanding, they labour earnestly, and bring also much hony into the hive. They are in a manner of the condition and nature of Horseflies and Hornets, saving that they love not so well to flie and seize on horses and kine, as they

Source: Philip Marnix, Lord of St. Aldegonde, *The Beehive of the Romish Church*, trans. by George Gilpin the Elder (London: John Dawson, 1623), pp. 352–357.
* Monks.

doe on sheepe. Wherein they digresse cleane from the nature of the ordinarie Honybees, which doe carefully shunne the sheepe, for feare, lest they should intangle themselves, & sticke in their fleeces. But those have a good remedie for that, for they first bite away their wool, after that their skinne, and lastely doe sucke their blood, to which they are wonderfully addicted. There are also amongst these, which are as profitable in the Bee hive, as any other, by reason of their fearcenesse, for they have very fearce & murthering stinges, in so much as those beeing stoung by them, can hardly escape death. For the wound cannot be remedied with any thing, but with golden salve; they are of the generation of *waspes*, which *Aristotle* and *Plinie* doe name in Greeke *Ichneumones*, which may be interpreted Inquisitours, so after the Latin phrase *Inquisitores*, & after the saying of *Plinie* are so called, because with great industrie and diligence, they know to seeke and catch the flies, and bite off their heads, permitting them to live of that which remaines; howbeit, these our *Ichneumones* do most covet the wool and bloode of sheepe, & are marvellous bloodthirstie. They are likewise of both kinds some tame, some wilde: But the wild are alwayes more fearce & deadly. They are bredde or ingendred, after the same order which *Aristotle* doth declare of his *Ichneumones:* namely, they take very venimous Spiders, named *Phalangiae* (which are found plentifully in *Spaine* at the old Inquisitors walles & postes), and carrie those to their holes: and after they have greased them a good with filth and durte (whereunto ours use commonly Popes grease) then doe they set or broode over them, and after that sort increase their kinde.

The third sorte is by *Arlem* named Pheres, which signifies asmuch as theeves & rovers, because they are of an exceeding theevish disposition, and have a great large and broad belly commonly blacke to see to. These devoure great store of honie, and love exceedingly wel the smacke of Prebendes and fat beneficed hony, which the Bee Apothecaries doe terme in Latin *Veneficia:* And therefore are called *Veneficiari*, or veneficed. They are for the most part tame, yet there are found not a few, which are of the wilde

and strange disposition. And they are separated amongest them selves, each over a severall office and charge, according as the king hath appointed them. For some have nothing else to doe, but with an irksome buzzing by day and night doe swarme in their hive. But they know their rule, how and when they shall swarme, and are for that cause called *Regulares*, or by a Greeke word *Canonici*.

Touching the wilde sorte of Bees, some are called fathers, or with a *Chaldean* word *Abbas*, because they beare rule over the other Bees, like a father over his children. Some keepers, or after the Italian and French phrase, *Gardians*. Some are called the first, or in Latine *Priores*. Some Controllers, or in Latin *Provinciales:* each after his state and calling, and according to the rule and dominion which hee beareth over the other common Bees, which common Bees make the fourth and last heape or kind of Bees, according to *Aristotles* declaration, and are named in Greeke *Cephenes* and in Latin *Fungi*, that is after our language Buzzardes or Drones. These are the most unprofitable Bees, and yet the most in number: they have no sting, and will not worke, but live on the labour of the other, and chiefly the wilde Bees amongst the which some flie swarming from doore to doore, to find out baightes to fill their bagges: and therefore are called *Mendicantes*, that is to say, beggars, or begging bees: because they are of the begging order of Bees. But the tame Drones doe not flie so from house to house, but tarry in their Bee hive, and there get their commons with swarming, without labouring, or doing any good. For when they would doe any good, then doe they commonly misse, and are also for that cause called Missebees, or Massebees.

CHAPTER IV

Of the nature of Bees: of their ingendring, and procreation

Further, concerning the nature of these Bees, there is a difference betwixt male and female, especially amongst the wilde. And they love to goe together, yet doe they not ingender the one of the other, but be most altogether ingendred and made of their king, like as *Aristotle* and *Plinie* doe plainely shew: for without this king, they cannot bring forth their like, notwithstanding they can brood up these foresaid wormes named *Clerus*, after they have been first ingendred by the king if *Plinie* be credible, in the sixteenth chapter of the forenamed booke of his Historie.

CHAPTER V

What the rule and being of these Bees are touching their king

In their rule they resemble the common sort of hony Bees, for they have all one king, and cannot abide without asking, whom they call *Papa*, as if one should say, *Pater Apum*, that is to say, The father of Bees, whereof it cometh, that we call all these Bees in the Dutch tongue *Papen*, and with us *Papistical Priests*. For the Bees are called in Latine *Apes*.

This king hath a sting in like maner, but he doth not occupie himselfe abroad, because all other bees are prest to do him service, in whatsoever pleaseth him to commande. And like as this king of Honiebees hath a spot on his head: so likewise doth he carrie a token or marke on his head, like a triple crowne: howbeit, all the other Bees (as hath beene said) doe beare in like manner a round white spot in the middle of their heads, in manner of a crownet. They flie all at once about this king,

and shew themselves very meeke & obedient towards him. He goeth seldome abroad, but when hee doth determine to goe forth any whither, it may bee perceived long before, by the swarming and humming of the forerunners. For whensoever he goeth out, the whole swarme followeth round about him, and oftentimes they carrie him on their shoulders, like as the honie Bees doe carrie their king.

He hath likewise certaine loyterers by him, and serviteurs which gard him and some other of the very best, which be of a ruddie or sanguine colour, and remaine always next to his side, and are for that cause named *Laterales*, or a *Latere*. In summe, each one would faine be next, for that is reputed for great honour: where he settles, there is the host of the whole swarme and staple of the honie and honnie combe: and such as dwell many hundreth miles thence, bend notwithstanding their flight thitherwardes: whosoever hath him to friend, shall in like manner finde friendship of all the whole swarme: when they lose him, then is all their porridge spilt, and sporte at an end: For they creepe pensively to their selles and closets, and there buzze, or swarme so long and so much, till they have gotten another. And if by mishap it chaunceth, that there be two or three kings, (like as hath often beene seene,) then falles out great schismes and troubles among them, and they bee at mortall warres together: yea, cease not, till the one or the other be dispatcht and made away: like as *Virgil* hath finely set forth.

Selection 7
Letter from a Dutch Anabaptist Martyr (1573)
Janneken

The Bloody Theater or Martyr's Mirror was first compiled by the Dutchman Thieleman van Bracht early in the seventeenth century. It catalogs the accounts of interrogations, tortures, and deaths of the faithful, with excerpts taken for the most part from contemporary archives. Although historians have made guesses as to this woman's identity—her name may have been Janneken Muntsdorp—no certainty is possible, so this may be regarded as the letter of an otherwise anonymous woman who writes movingly to her infant daughter on the eve of her execution.

Testament written by Janneken, while in prison at Antwerp, addressed to her daughter, A.D. 1573.

May the true love of God, and the wisdom of the Father, strengthen you in every virtue, my dearest child. May the God of heaven and of earth, the God of Abraham, of Isaac, and of Jacob, the Lord of Israel, preserve you in every virtue and strengthen your understanding in his truth. I commend you, my dear infant, to God, who is great and terrible, who alone is wise; may he preserve you and keep you; grow up in his fear. And if he should call you hence while young, it would meet my cordial prayer, because you are yet young, and I must leave you in this wicked world.

But since the Lord has so ordained it, that I must leave you here, deprived of both father and mother, I will therefore commend you to the Lord, to do with you what seems meet in his sight; he will provide for you, if you only fear God, for he is a father to the orphan and a protector to the widow.

I, your dear mother, in prison, cannot help or provide for you, because I had to leave your father for the Lord's sake, with whom I lived but six months. Then we were both apprehended and separated, because we sought to work out our souls' salvation. They took him from me, and I knew not whether I was *encient* [pregnant] or not; I had yet to remain in prison and see him go on

Source: Thieleman von Bracht, *The Bloody Theater or Martyr's Mirror*, trans. by Daniel Rupp (Lancaster, Pa: David Miller, Inc., 1837), pp. 895–898.

before, which caused me great distress. But after patiently spending my time solitarily, and carrying you nine months under my breasts, I bore you, after many excrutiating throes; they then took me away from you, and I am now waiting here every morning to meet death, and will soon follow your dear father. Hence, I write this to you as a memento of your dear mother.

Since I have been condemned to die, and have to leave you here, I take this method to remind you, that, if you come to the years of discretion, you would fear and serve God diligently; examine and learn why and for whose sake we both were put to death, and be not ashamed to confess us before the world—for we did not suffer as evildoers. Therefore, be not ashamed of us, for it is the way in which the prophets and apostles had to go before us—for there is no other way in which we can be saved.

Therefore, my dear one, for whom I had great sorrow and anxiety of mind, if you attain the years of discretion examine well into this way, although you may expect much tribulation and affliction on it and be exposed to many imminent dangers, as we may see and read if we examine the scriptures—for they mention many of the sufferings of Christ in this way: but the world seek to be free from all these, by turning the back upon Christ. But, my dear child, if we desire to reign with Christ we must also suffer with him—we must bear the cross—and this is the cross that Christ would have us to bear, namely: that we should walk in his footsteps, and help to bear his reproach; for Christ himself declared: YE SHALL BE

HATED AND PERSECUTED FOR MY NAME'S SAKE! Nay, he went himself this despised way, before us, and gave us an example that we are to follow his footsteps: because, for his sake we must forsake all—father, mother, sister, brother, husband, wife, children; nay *one's own life.*

Now I have to forsake all this for the Lord, which the world is not worthy to suffer—for had we remained in the world, we need not have done all this; for when we agreed with the world, committed idolatry and all manner of unrighteousness, the world was then perfectly satisfied with us: but, because we sought to fear God and to avoid such an ungodly course of life, knowing that God could not thus approbate our conduct, we immediately strove to avoid such things, and are turned from idols to the living God, and sought to live a life of faith, in all quietness; because we did so, the world immediately molested us, persecuted us unto death, and we had to be a prey for every one and become an open spectacle to all the world.

They seek to murder and burn us—we are driven from pillar to post, and exposed at stakes— and our flesh they give to worms to feed upon: therefore, my dear child, is fulfilled in your father and mother, what was foretold that should befall us. But not every one is chosen to suffer, nor need all anticipate to suffer—but the Lord has chosen us to suffer; so, then, if you arrive at the years of understanding, follow the example of your father and mother. This I desire of you, for you are yet quite young. I wrote this when you were but one month old; and since I am soon, by the help of the Lord, to make my sacrifice, I leave this to you that you might do what I desire of you, and always cleave to those who fear God, and not look upon the vain things of this world—upon the multitude who are on the downward road to ruin, which leads to hell; but look upon the small flock of Israel, that has not liberty of conscience in any place, but has to flee from place to place, so that you may afterwards inherit the kingdom of your Father—for, if you seek your salvation, you may readily perceive the road which leads to life and the road which leads to hell. First seek the kingdom of Heaven, and all other things shall be added to you that you stand in need of.

I would further entreat, always live honestly when you have come to the years of understanding, so that none will have cause of complaint towards you. Be always faithful and true, and take advantage of none; always keep your hands pure, and always be willing to work with your own hands, for Paul says: He that will not work shall not eat; and Peter says: He that would live long and see good days, must keep his tongue from speaking evil.

Therefore, my dear Janneken, do not accustom yourself to evil speaking; do not indulge in vain and vulgar conversation, nor tell falsehoods, for liars shall not inherit the kingdom of Heaven—for it is written: A lying mouth kills the soul. Therefore, be careful to avoid all such things, and do not run about in the streets like other ill-bred children; rather take your book and read, and seek what will promote your salvation.

Be subject to those with whom you may live: if they speak ill of those who give you bread, do you speak well of them, and be always doing something. Do not exalt yourself, but compare yourself with the humble; always honor seniors, wherever you may be.

I will leave you. If it should have pleased the Lord to continue me with you to raise you, I would have spared no pains to do so; but it appears it is not the will of the Lord to do so. And if I could have been permitted to remain with you for some time, still God might have taken me away—so that you would have been deprived of my aid and advice personally, even as it was the case with me and your father: for we were permitted to remain together but for a short time, though the Lord had so united us that we would not have separated, voluntarily, for the whole world—nevertheless, we had to separate, to do the will of the Lord; thus I have to leave you, also, May the Lord, your creator, take you under his paternal protection, and it is his will that he takes me from you. I have now to travel this way through, upon which the prophets, Christ, and the apostles walked, and to the martyrs, and thousands of others who laid off their mortal garb, died for Christ's sake, and are now resting and waiting under the altar till their number be fulfilled, of whom your dear father is one. And I am now ready to follow him—for I have already been sentenced, even to death, according to all human appearances. But if it should not be the will of the Lord, though I am condemned to die, he can, nevertheless, ransom me, and restore you, my dear child, to me, even as he restored Abraham's son Isaac. The God who preserved Daniel in the lion's den, and delivered the three children from the burning furnace, can release me from the hand of man.

My dear child, if it were not so, still I know that he is faithful and true. Therefore, my dear, be content. Though you be deprived of father and mother, remember that you have a Father in heaven, who will, undoubtedly, provide for you. As soon as you grow up, strive to learn to read and write—for it is an advantage to him who fears God—so that, in case of necessity, you will be able to write a letter, and be able to read this and any others which your father left on record. Read both, and remember *us*. Dear Janneken, we did not leave many earthly possessions and I have very little to give you; but what I have, I leave you. We nevertheless leave you a good example, how you are to fear God: this is better than many temporal possessions. Only follow us, and you will be rich enough. True, you are poor here—but if you fear God, and eschew sin , you will inherit much, as the apostle says to the Hebrews: My son, despite not the chastening of the Lord, for those who are without chastisement are bastards, and not heirs. Therefore, my dear, cease not to fear God on account of the cross, for a christian need not look for any thing else, in this world, than tribulation and persecution—because we have to enter the kingdom through much tribulation and suffering; for Paul says: All that would live godly in Christ Jesus, must suffer persecution; and Christ says: He that will not take his cross upon himself and follow me, is not worthy of me: for the servant is not above his lord, nor the disciple more than his master. If they called the master of the house Beelzebub, how much more will they call those of the household? If they have persecuted the master, they will also persecute us; they have hated him they will also hate us, because they have not known my Father, says the Lord almighty. For his kingdom was not of this world; if it had been, the world would have loved him—but because it was not, they hated him. Thus it is at the present day, because our kingdom is not of this world: hence, they hate us. But it is much better for us to be rejected and hated of the world, than to lament forever in future. And those who refuse to bear the cross, shall never inherit eternal life—for we know of a truth, that all those who would live godly in this world must suffer persecution: they must become a prey to all men.

The prophets and apostles have set us an example, by walking in the same road before us—nor did Christ, for our sakes, shun himself, but suffered death for us, and how should he not then give us all things? Therefore I entreat you, my dear, strive to walk in this way—for this is the only way to life; there is no other way whereby men can be saved than through Jesus Christ, as Paul says: Other foundation cannot be laid than that which is laid, which is Jesus Christ, through whose streams we are healed and through whose blood we are purchased—for we are not purchased with silver or gold, but with the precious shed blood of Christ, and he has called us as the first begotten of Christ.

All those who have died in sin and have reformed, and have risen with Christ into a new life, so that they do not live any more to themselves but belong to the Lord, and whether they live or die, live and die to the Lord. These, then, do belong to the Lord—they are his own: for, my dear, what shall the death of Christ avail those who still live in sin, and do not repent of their ungodly life in which they live, such as drunkards, murderers, fornicators, idolaters, liars, backbiters, who cannot please God? Their works are only of the devil. To all such, the Lord says that they shall not inherit the kingdom of God except they do reform; and if they do, it avails them nothing that Christ did. True, they desire to sin, in reliance upon the mercy of God: they say nothing of his justice—he is all mercy when you hear them. But, bear in mind he is also just—we dare not sin in reliance upon his grace; for if we do all we possibly can, and observe all he commands us, we have still to confess we are unprofitable servants and have merited nothing, but are worthy of eternal death. And if he were not merciful, we could not be saved: hence, we dare not presume to sin in dependence upon his grace, but we must always strive to observe the things he commanded us.

We can merit nothing—we must be saved by grace: therefore, always fear God, for the fear of the Lord is the beginning of wisdom; and he that fears the Lord will do right—he shall prosper in this world and the world to come. Always cleave to those who fear the Lord sincerely. Do not conform to this world, and do not lead a dissolute life—for the world and all in it will perish. Have no communion with the unfruitful works of darkness, but rather much more reprove them; and be renewed in life, so that you may proclaim the virtues to which God has called you.

Ah! my most beloved, that you might learn to know the truth when you grow up, and follow your dear father and mother, who have gone on before you; for your dear father testified with his own blood that this is the truth, and I trust to seal it with my blood, although flesh and blood must remain suspended to posts and stakes, inasmuch as I assuredly know we shall meet again. Follow us, my dear, so that you may come there also, when we shall see each other again; then will the Lord say to you: Come thou blessed of my Father, inherit the kingdom prepared for you from the foundation of the world.

Then we shall not be deprived of our joy. If they have separated us here, and we had to leave you, I am, nevertheless, persuaded that it was the will of the Lord; for if it had pleased the Lord, he might have ordered it otherwise. Therefore, remain satisfied he knows what he intends with you, because I have to leave you. Always act honorably, and be complaisant towards every one. When you are grown, let your discretion be manifest to all men.

I leave you among my friends, and hope that my father and step-mother, my brothers and sisters, will do much for your comfort as long as they live: obey them in all things not contrary to the will of God. All that I am to receive, thirty guilders, I bequeath to you: if there should be any more, I bequeath the same—but whether there will I know not, for I have been confined a long time in this place, and I know not what the expenses may be; but I trust that my sister Grietjen will do the best in this matter. I do not know what is coming to you from your father, for I know very little about his parent's circumstances, because they live far from home. But if they should hear of you, my friends may do that for you which seems best.

Now, my dear Janneken, you who are yet so very young and little, I leave you this letter, and a gold *real* which I had with me in prison; these things I leave you, as a *testament* and as a *memento*. Read this letter carefully when you arrive at years of understanding, and preserve it as long as you live, in remembrance of me and your father, so that you may be edified by it. I bid you good night, and kiss you cordially with the kiss of peace. Follow me and your father, and be not ashamed to confess us before the world—for we are not ashamed to confess our father before the world, and this adulterous generation: hence, I entreat you not to be ashamed to confess our faith, for it is the true evangelical faith—there will never be any other.

Rejoice, that we did not die as evil-doers. Should they attempt to put you to death, do not be deterred from fearing God; for if you strive to do good, none can prevent you from fearing God. Seek peace, and follow after it—then you shall receive the crown of life. May you receive this crown, and may the despised Jesus be your bridegroom; this is my sincere prayer. Always remember your father, and your mother, who wrote this with her own hand for your edification. Always keep this gold real with you, and this letter as an everlasting testament. I bid you good night. I trust to seal this letter with my own blood at the stake.

I now commend you to the Lord, and the word of his grace. I expect to meet you. Follow me, my dear child. Farewell.

Written August 10th, A. D. 1573, at Antwerp.

This is the testament that I wrote in prison for my daughter Janneken, whom I bore and brought forth in these bonds.

By me, your dear mother

JANNEKEN MUNSTDORP,

A prisoner for the sake of the Lord.

Selection 8
"When My Children Were Sent to the Lizards" (1493)

Samuel Usque

Samuel Usque's autobiography and extended meditation on the fate of the Jews in Portugal (his homeland) and Spain is not well known, although it provides an extraordinarily touching, yet factual account of horrors to which he was himself an eyewitness.

This dreadful tempest was soon followed by the lash of an even rougher storm. The Portuguese king, eager to find some logical excuse to vex me, called for an investigation to see if the number of my people who had entered his kingdom exceeded the stipulated six hundred families. Since the haste with which my children had left Castile did not allow time for a census, or for anyone to wait and see if there was sufficient number, they found that they had exceeded the number. The king claimed the excess as his captives and slaves; he could thus vex the Jews at will and carry out his evil designs against them. Their willingness to redeem themselves for the price at which the rest had entered, or a higher price, proved of no avail.

To my misfortune, the island of São Thomé had recently been discovered. It was inhabited by lizards, snakes and other venomous reptiles, and was devoid of rational beings. Here the king exiled condemned criminals, and he decided to include among them the innocent children of these Jews. Their parents had seemingly been condemned by God's sentence.

When the luckless hour arrived for this barbarity to be inflicted, mothers scratched their faces in grief as their babies, less than three years old, were taken from their arms. Honored elders tore their beards when the fruit of their bodies was snatched before their eyes. The fated children raised their piercing cries to heaven as they were mercilessly torn from their beloved parents at such a tender age.

Several women threw themselves at the king's feet, begging for permission to accompany their children; but not even this moved the king's pity.

Source: Samuel Usque, *Consolation for the Tribulations of Israel*, trans. by Martin A. Cohen (Philadelphia: Jewish Publication Society, 1965), pp. 201–202.

One mother, distraught by this horrible unexampled cruelty, lifted her baby in her arms, and paying no heed to its cries, threw herself from the ship into the heaving sea, and drowned embracing her only child.

Thus those innocent souls were removed from their parents' sweet tenderness by such inhumanities and delivered into the power of merciless enemies. O brothers, who could describe to you the hidden and visible anguish which cloaked all my children—the sighs, the tears, the bloody and febrile groans which were heard in all their houses; for there are no words of consolation to relieve a pain so great, though each one had good reason to hope for consolation.

This monstrous cruelty would have induced many people to take their own lives before the time allotted them by God's will, if others would not have suffered by their absence. But husbands feared their beloved wives would be widowed and alone among enemies, while wives were restrained by the hope of seeing their children again.

Finally, when those innocent children arrived at the wilderness of São Thomé, which was to be their grave, they were thrown ashore and mercilessly left there. Almost all were swallowed up by the huge lizards on the island, and the remainder, who escaped these reptiles, wasted away from hunger and abandonment. Only a few were miraculously spared that dreadful misfortune.

O Lord, whose power encompasses the dominion of the entire universe, how shall I fortify my heart and soul with patience so that the great force and onslaught of such tribulations does not shatter it? Consider that "You have oppressed us and broken us in a land of dragons, and have covered us with a shadow of death," as my son David had once foreseen and lamented (Ps. 44.20). In addition to the misfortunes in England, your threats against me were again executed here: "Your children shall be delivered to other peoples, and when your eyes see this they shall continually shed tears, and you shall have no strength to be able to bear it" (Deut. 28.32). "Because I shall set the teeth of beasts against them and the fury of serpents against the people" (Deut. 32.24). "And at this time I shall not hear when you call Me and are afflicted" (Jer. 11.11). Therefore "gird yourself with sackcloth, O daughter of My people, and wallow in ashes. Make your mourning, as for an only son, and a most bitter lamentation" (Jer. 6.26). Now since I have suffered such harsh punishments from Your anger, help me now, O Lord, and delay not.

Selection 9
Auto-de-fé in Seville, Spain

If the state could turn against Anabaptists with ferocity, countries that espoused an ever-fiercer and more stringent Catholicism—notably Spain—could and did direct their vehemence against numerous groups, among them Jews and converts from Judaism (Marranos), who were often suspected of false conversion. Note also that any view regarded as deviant on virtually any subject could cause its proponent to be burned at the stake.

Report of the persons who were brought as penitents to the public auto-de-fé, held by the Holy Court of the Inquisition upon Sunday the 3rd day of May in the year 1579.

First: Orbrian, a native of Flanders, inhabitant of the city of Xeres de la Frontera, a binder by trade, in his thirtieth year. He had burnt different paintings with the picture of our Lord Jesus Christ and other saints thereon and had put his faith entirely in the teachings of Luther, considering them to be the truth. He had also ventured to teach others. He, showing great stubbornness on account of this, was condemned and handed over to the arm of secular justice, so that he be burnt alive and all his goods and chattels be confiscated.

Second: Juana de Perez, a Portuguese, a woman of forty, domiciled at Riamonto. She was of the Jewish faith and held it through many years, practising its commands and ceremonies and also instructing other persons therein. She was confessed and been reconciled to Holy Church. Will be punished by taking the veil and perpetual seclusion. Her goods and chattels will be confiscated.

Third: Juan de Color, a black, from Rafao, slave of Juan de la Romo, in his thirty-fifth year. He reviled the name of Our dear Lady and other saints when pronounced in his presence. He has, likewise, despised Her miracles. He has been reconciled and punished by taking the habit and two years of imprisonment. Thereafter he is to be restored to his master.

Fourth: Ginos Raros, Englishman, master gunner on the galleon *Granada* in his fortieth year. He has fought with the Catholic Christians in the following of Juan Alquino and has comported himself by land and sea as is the custom among Lutherans. He has been reconciled, and punished with the habit and perpetual prison. The first twelve years he is to serve on the galleys and pull the oars.

Fifth: Fernando Morisco, in his twenty-second year. He has fled from a galleon into Barbary and has disavowed his Holy Faith. He committed robbery on a galliot against God's commandment and was therefore taken prisoner as a corsair. He has been reconciled. He has been punished with the habit and perpetual prison. He is to spend the first year on a galley.

Sixth: Joanna Macozuo, a virgin, domestic and sick-nurse in a nunnery at Seville. She has confessed to having been tempted repeatedly and having visions of the Evil One through which she came to believe various things that are against our Holy

Source: Victor von Klarvill (ed.), *The Fugger Newsletters: Being a Selection of Unpublished Letters from the Correspondents of the House of Fugger during the Years 1568–1605*, trans. by Pauline de Chary (New York: Putnam's Sons, 1924), pp. 30–34.

Catholic Faith. Whereas she doubted, she has been permitted to return to the Faith. But the habit was taken from her. She is to remain for two years wherever she may be ordered to betake herself, and there fast on Fridays for one year.

Seventh: Luis Morino desired to sail with others to Barbary but has been reconciled. He was punished with the habit and four years' imprisonment. There he is to be instructed in the tenets of the Faith and punished with one hundred strokes of the rod.

Eighth: Alfonso Morisco from the Kingdom of Granada. Like offence, like punishment.

Ninth: Voror Morro, slave of Juan Matthias has incited the aforementioned. Was punished with one hundred strokes of the rod.

Tenth: Thomas Morro. Like offence, like punishment.

Eleventh: Maria, a virgin, daughter of Juana de Perez. She has, in company with others, given herself up to Jewish practices. She was subjected to penance so that she should recant. She has confessed and is to remain six years in prison.

Twelfth: Lorenzo Martin in his thirtieth year. He has said that one should confess to God and not to man. That it is mockery to confess to priests and that the speech and faith of Moors and Christians are alike. He has been subjected to penance and will be kept three months in prison.

Thirteenth: Juan Corineo, a Moor, wanted to sail to Barbary and has said: "Our dear Lady did not conceive as a virgin." Has been punished with one hundred strokes of the rod.

Fourteenth: Fray Juan de Spinosa, of the Order of the Holy Trinity. Has said Mass and heard Confession without having been ordained. Has been subjected to penance, so that he be detained six years in a cloister of the Order. As long as he lives, he will not be ordained.

Fifteenth: Juan de Montis, a Moor, has married twice. One hundred strokes of the rod and ten years on a galley.

Sixteenth: Juan Garcia and Fernando Domos, like offence, like punishment.

Seventeenth: Consalvo de Noguera and Bartholomeo Gonzales for a like offence one hundred strokes of the rod and four years on a galley.

Eighteenth: Pedro Galigo, like offence, like punishment.

Nineteenth: Francis Gonzales, inhabitant of Cadiz, one hundred strokes of the rod and three years on the galley, and Maria de Soto, both on account of marrying twice. She recanted on the pillory and was banished from the district for three years.

Twentieth: Pedro Fernandez, a Portuguese, for bearing false witness in matters of marriage and Rodrigo Fernandez for a like reason one hundred strokes of the rod each.

Twenty-first: Ines de Campo for bearing false witness in matters of faith, three hundred strokes of the rod and banishment for six years from Seville. Her daughter Isabella de Palareos for like reason two hundred strokes of the rod and banishment for six years from Seville.

Twenty-second: Fernando Copos, a Portuguese, and Juana de Ramora have averred that fornication is no sin. Have renounced and disclaimed their crime. They were publicly shamed by being led through the town.

Twenty-third: Isabella Sanchez, Carolona Vandola, Phillippa de Color, a seamstress, Alfonse de Sansiago, Caspar Sanchez, like offence, like punishment.

Twenty-fourth: Francisco Berocano has said that it is no sin if a woman goes to a man and they copulate. Has disavowed his words as frivolous.

Twenty-fifth: Isabella Diaz, a Portuguese, has said that it is no sin to sleep with a strange man. Same punishment.

Twenty-sixth: Diego de Robloz has greatly blasphemed God. Three hundred strokes of the rod and three years on the galleys.

Twenty-seventh: Victorio Rigo has blasphemed God. Two hundred strokes of the rod.

Twenty-eighth: Antonio Martin and Juana Batista, a Moorish woman. Like offence, like punishment.

Twenty-ninth: Sebastian Garcia. For a like reason put into the pillory with a rope round his neck.

Thirtieth: Juan Francis for a like reason put into the pillory with his tongue tied and a rope round his neck. Likewise, Elena Nigra, Juliana Morisca, Anna de Cranco, a Mulatto, and Martha, a Mulatto.

Thirty-first: The Baccalaureate Andreas Perez, priest of San Salvador in Seville, was on account of various misdemeanours, necromancy and invocation of the Devil, subjected to penance and imprisoned for one year, under deprivation of priesthood.

Thirty-second: Andreas Conseno, a peasant, has said that one must not confess one's mortal sins to priests, because they are men. Has recanted in a public *auto de fé* and received one hundred strokes of the rod.

Thirty-third: Fernando Anias, an embroiderer in silks has said: "It is of no account to God whether we fast or not—neither should we worship the pictures." Has forsworn his crime in public *auto de fé*.

Thirty-fourth: Casparo Sanchez has said that God is not present in the Host.

Thirty-fifth: Francisco Roman has said that it is not needful to pray for the souls in purgatory. Both have forsworn their crime.

Thirty-sixth: Juan Francisco has oft-times blasphemed God and said that this was no sin. Has forsworn his crime.

Thirty-seventh: Juan Garcia has uttered divers blasphemies, with regard to Our dear Lady. His tongue was pinioned, a cross was given into his hand and a cord placed round his neck and he was beaten two hundred times with a rod.

Thirty-eighth: Juan Astruez, a locksmith, Juan Lipiotol and Fernando Gil have said that they were relations of the Inquisitors. Since this is not true, they have had a rope placed round their necks and have been exposed to public shame.

Vale! I rejoice that this is at an end.

Selection 10
Chronicler's Report on Witches Burned at the Stake

Were there really witches? As this selection points out, the common people certainly thought so. Taken from a contemporary chronicle, it claims to give a factual account of the activities of witches burned at the stake in 1580 and the dire deeds to which they had confessed. Although this chronicle cannot be considered to be historically accurate, it does offer a good example of the real anxieties of the populace, which made the witch hunts possible. Did the coming of the Protestant Reformation and the subsequent upheaval make the witch hunts easier to justify? That is one possible historical explanation, though there were other reasons for the fears witches aroused (see Figure 25).

Hear Oh Christians, what is now sung to you; listen eagerly to what has recently happened—

Source: Robert M. Kingdon (ed.), *Transition and Revolution: Problems and Issues of European Renaissance and Reformation History* (Minneapolis, Minn.: Burgess Publishing Company, 1974), pp. 211–213; taken from *Zwo Newe Zeittung. Was man fur Hexen oder Unholden verbrendt hat, von dem siebenden Hornung an biss auff den zwentzigsten Howmonat diss MDLXXX. Jars, auch darbey angeseigt, an was ohrt und enden, auch was sie bekendt haben, etc.* (Hof, 1580).

great misery and a miracle! Behold an evil deed, this year, as I will show. They executed many witch-women, as I will shortly show, and what they did; behold the great wonder.

In 1580 I was amazed that on 7 February in Wurzach nine witches were executed. They confessed to many miserable deeds, as I will explain. At Biberach, I tell you, they burned five of them at the same time. At Kirth they burned four all at once without hesitation; they were all old and very

Figure 25. Hans Baldung Grien, *Witches* (woodcut). The image of the witch was quite vivid among sixteenth-century Europeans. In this woodcut by Hans Baldung Grien, they are hags cavorting around a fiendish brew. One of the reasons they aroused fear is that they seemed to have arcane knowledge (represented by the bizarre writing on the urn) at a time when few women were educated.

rich, and had caused much misery, as I will describe later. In Allgäu I must report that they burned nine at once openly at Wanga, and three more at Isny. And at Fissach they burned eleven at the end of the same month. Three fled to Lindau thinking they would be safe there. At Rottenburg on the Neckar and at Horb they burned nine. And at Dreiburg on the Walde and at Rottweil they burned a goodly number of witches, nearly thirty in all, who had wretchedly killed many small children. Constance on Lake Constance burned two on the 6th of May, who confessed an evil crime. At Überlingen they burned three who with great sorrow confessed many crimes, as I will tell later. Mr. Lazarus von Schwendi burned many of them. At Kuppenen they burned six and three more nearby. In the Wanzenau in the city of

Keisersberg they burned one on St. Vitus Day and others still lie in prison. At Burgau on the day after St. John's Day they burned six. They could not refrain from burning an unrepentant man-witch and another woman. At Rastatt they burned seven and five in Baden, who had done strange things to men, women, and children with magic and poison. And in the Margravate Baden they took away the wife of a tile maker, carrying her magically through the air together with a child. They found her on the second day at Gersbach, miserably bound to the child. She had lost her wits; her reason was taken from her along with the child. At Rastatt, as I said, they were busy burning. A rain and thunderstorm brought misery and wretchedness to that place, and it sounded as if armored men and horses were up there. Furthermore I must tell what they confessed; I cannot remain silent.

Listen Oh men and women! Three hundred plainly came together in the Black Forest and they resolved on a crime by which they should cause frost throughout the land on Holy Pentecost. They prayed to the devil for help and counsel. At once they buried three pails of corn, wine, and grain in three places. There was a young maid there from Wurzach, who was the daughter of a witch. They looked and found the pails deep in the woods, full of all kinds of fruit. They seized her at once and said the devil had taught her to harm man, woman, and child. They then confessed how the witches came together; I cannot keep from telling you this. The devil came to them quickly and told them to make a storm so that no one would bring sickles to the fields for thirty German miles around.

And they said that they wanted it to start in that place on the day of Christ's Ascension. But God used his power to protect so that the storm went no farther than five German miles, starting in the Black Forest and having a width of one-half mile. It destroyed most of the grain in the fields at Biberach. Finally they confessed openly that with their own hands they had ruined the fruit of the trees at Breisach and a great many grapes at Kestenholtz. May God have mercy, for they quickly confessed how they had harmed 200 children, both rich and poor, and had made them dumb; and they had killed many poor men's cattle in their stalls.

Afterward they confessed that on a Saturday night the devil held an assembly at a castle high on a mountain one German mile from Colmar. Large and small came together there. Nearly 500 persons came from many lands and from far away, riding on cats and on calves. Many of them were dead, and yet they too had strange adventures at that place. They danced and jumped over sticks and stones. And each one brought along his lover-demon, who had strange names. I must tell you what these lovers commanded them to do. They told them to make a huge storm. With their strange help it could happen. So they tried five times to make a hail which was to wreak destruction. They couldn't make a storm as large as they wanted, but a rainstorm came that did much harm to houses, mills, grain, and corn, which drowned in the fields of many pious folk. Shortly afterward they confessed that if they hadn't been caught so quickly, they would have made a storm for forty German miles around, that would have caused much more damage. They would have ruined so much grain and wine so far around that no pious upright man could have made even half a measure of wine or brought even half a bushel of grain into his barn. And whatever cattle and men were in the fields would have been hit with hail stones weighing five or even seven pounds. They were indeed so angry that they went crazy, and no one knew what they might have gone on to freeze with frost: corn, wine, and fruit in the fields. But the frost was prevented at Villingen.

So throughout you have heard how 114 witches in all were convicted and executed, who confessed such things as they did in many a place. Oh God, grant us a pious magistracy who may truly root out such godless folk at any time, and grant us eternal salvation.

Selection 11
Debate on the Nature of Witchcraft: Correspondence Between Johann Weyer and Johann Brenz (1565)

Johann Brenz (1499–1570) was a Protestant Reformer who preached against the fear of witchcraft, since he believed its perils to be greatly exaggerated. Johann Weyer (1515?–1588), a physician at the court of Julich-Cleves, came to the conclusion that those accused as witches usually deserved sympathy rather than punishment. The only dangerous witches, he felt, were those who used poisons. The exchange of letters between the two reveals how biblical interpretation was used commonly in all sorts of situations and how two enlightened, well-educated men of this time could define and differentiate various forms of witchcraft.

Johann Weyer to Dr. Johann Brenz, Doctor of Sacred Scripture and Provost at Stuttgart:

I wish you happiness, grace, and good fortune together with my friendly greeting, worthy Brenz, through Him who loved us and with His blood cleansed all who deny themselves, receive Christ and walk in His footsteps and follow Him.

For good reasons I have always regarded you highly and held you in highest honor for the great energy, skill, and fear of God which you have displayed in your efforts to rid the church of idolatry and to cleanse it of false teaching. But now even more should you be praised and honored on account of a wonderfully learned and pious sermon which you recently delivered and had printed. For in that sermon you teach elegantly and truly that idolatry should not be held to be the sin of heathen alone, when they make gods and pray to them, but also the sin of men who attribute what belongs to God alone to the devil and his horde, the magicians, witches, and covenanters with the devil. As when men, after an accident or misfortune, neglect God's help, as if there were no longer a God who could help, and fall away from God, no longer calling on Him in need; but seek elsewhere for

help and salvation, with the devil or his followers. This too is a shameful and cursed idolatry. Therefore, you were rightfully angry about the people in the Duchy of Württemberg whose wine and fruit were destroyed by a terrible hail. In their stubborn faithlessness, instead of coming to recognize their own sins through such punishments, and instead of truly repenting and reforming their lives and living according to God's word, they fell into superstition. They hold that such misfortunes come not from the Lord God on account of their sins, but from witches, whom they wish burned. Rightly have you punished and thumped these fellows. Verily you instructed and taught your congregation and dear flock rightly by displaying witnesses from Holy Scripture and also by showing the natural causes of hail so that it is in no way a work or creation of the devil or of his followers, the witches and magicians, but that it is God the true author and ruler's creation and work, and that he sends such things to mankind that the godless may thereby be punished, led to recognize their sins, and encouraged to repentance and improvement of life. But also that the pious may be tested through such hail and storms whether they will remain steadfast in the true faith. I say truly that your teaching of how men should react to such evils in certainty and with a good conscience, and how they may avoid misfortune, is not poor or despicable advice but true and godly. I understand your teaching and opinion very well, dear Brenz, and I do not doubt that you serve the Christian congregation best with such a glorious and consoling sermon.

Source: Robert M. Kingdon (ed.), *Transition and Revolution: Problems and Issues of European Renaissance and Reformation History* (Minneapolis, Minn.: Burgess Publishing Company, 1974), pp. 220–226; taken from *Zwo Newe Zeittung. Was man fur Hexen oder Unholden verbrendt hat, von dem siebenden Hornung au biss auff den zwentzigsten Howmonat diss MDLXXX. Jars, auch darbey angeseigt, an was ohrt und enden, auch was sie bekendt haben, etc.* (Hof, 1580). Trans. by Erik Midelfort.

The seriousness and industry that suffuse your work are especially needed in this area of great darkness and confusion, for the conjurers blind the eyes of many, especially those who praise the gospel most highly, including great lords and nobles as well as the comman man, but even more importantly those like you whose office and calling require them to teach healthy, pure doctrine to others. They have made much confusion. But the good and gracious God, who leaves no pious man unrewarded, will reward you richly.

As to the first part of your sermon, I must confess that it seems sufficient to me (for which I thank you very much). As to the second part, however, I have a criticism and objection at a point in which we do not agree. Therefore I could not omit explaining myself and describing my position briefly so that if you teach me that I have erred anywhere, I can improve and change my opinions, which are contained for all to see in my *Six Books on the Delusions of Demons (De praestigiis daemonum)*, and especially in Book Six. Witches have no power to make hail, storms, and other evil things, but they are deceived by the devil. For when the devil, with the permission and decree of God, can make hail and storms, he goes to his witches and urges them to use their magic and charms, so that when the trouble and punishment come, the witches are convinced that they and the devil have caused it. Thus the witches cannot make hail and other things, but they are deluded and blinded by the devil himself to whom they have given themselves. In this way they think that they have made hail and storms. Not on that account but for their godless lives should they be punished severely. All of this you teach openly. And to confirm and strengthen your position you also cite the Imperial Law with these words: "There are many who practice evil arts to disturb and poison the elements. And they spare not the life of innocent persons but cause them great harm. Therefore when such people oppose nature they should be punished, with death." You also confirmed and strengthened your teaching with the law of Moses, by which, as Moses said: "Thou shalt not suffer a witch to live (Exodus 22:18).

Now, dear Brenz, so that the truth may appear openly from a friendly comparison, I ask that I may present freely my opinions. Do not take offense at this or blame me, for I will not present anything willful, unreasonable, frivolous, immoderate, or outrageous (as God is my witness, who knows everything). First you admit that witches have no power at all to cause hail or storms, even though their senses are so deluded by the devil that they believe and confess that they have awakened or caused storms and other such evils. The law, however, does not speak of those who cannot work such magic, but of those who do use the evil magical arts, which our witches cannot learn or understand because they are stupid, uneducated, dull, foolish, and crazy, and also because of their age and sex. And the law states clearly that it has those in mind who disturb and poison the air, which again our witches cannot do, as you explicitly teach. For no one can do that. Thus such witches are not referred to in this law for they cannot harm human life. I argued this extensively in my book. Since I find that you agree sufficiently with me in your sermon, I do not wish to explain myself at length or use a lot of words. For if witches could physically harm someone or be dangerous, then they are not simply witches or sorcerers, and they should be called poisoners instead. And they deserve the punishment meted out by Moses, Imperial law, and common law. Yet just because there is no agreement in that matter, one should not on that account conclude that Imperial law teaches or confirms that our witches must be punished. Indeed the law says not one word about them. Our witches have been corrupted in their phantasy by the devil and imagine often that they have done evil things that didn't even happen or caused natural occurrences that actually did not take place. In their confessions, especially under torture, they admit to doing and causing many things which are impossible for them and for anyone. One should not believe them when they confess that they have bound themselves to the devil, given themselves to his will, promised to follow his evil goals, just as we do not believe their confession that they make hail and storms, disturb and poison the air, and other impossible deeds. For both are confessed by one man at the same time and in the same way. Why should we believe such ridiculous confessions, brought us by the devil, more than others? Why approve a confession which is totally false and deluded, especially when made by an old, feeble, and captive woman, who is not to be trusted anyway? Therefore put no trust in such false and unfounded confessions, for they are started and fostered by the devil who is a liar and a father of lies. A person who is driven by the devil and almost always possessed by him confesses whatever the devil forcefully impresses on her senses, and she believes thoroughly whatever she confesses and says. Yes the devil always rules the tongues of witches so that they say much that they did not intend, which can be seen in women possessed by the devil, who, when released from the devil's bondage, are reminded of what they said earlier, and they are ashamed. I saw this the first time in a nun who lay sick in the hospital; when she came to her senses, she confessed to me the same horrible deeds that others confess with torture and torment. She had been plagued by the devil in this way in her cloister. She was later sacrificed, despite the fact that she was possessed by the devil, and despite the law's insistence that in criminal cases proof must be as bright and clear as the noonday sun. Even if an old woman, in deep depression, gives herself to the devil, one should not immediately condemn her to the fire but instead have regard for her confused, burdened, and depressed spirits and use all possible energy to convert her that she may avoid evil, and give herself to Christ. In this way we may bring her to her senses again, win her soul, and save her from death, as St. James teaches. For every man who sins, or is unjust, or hates his brother, is not of God but of the devil, as St. John says. And the fornicators, adulterers, idolaters, voluptuaries, drunkards, calumniators, and slanderers, and the avaricious will not inherit or possess the Kingdom of God. When such persons devote themselves criminally to the devil's service, and are unfaithful to God the Lord, they are not condemned to flames at once, even if they have seduced other persons into taking part in their evil deeds, thereby sinning more grievously. They fully deserve God's revenge and punishment, which is much harder and stricter than temporal punishment; nor can they escape it un-

less they repent and cordially convert. For then they are released from pain and punishment, just as those whom Paul described, who abandon their faith in the last times, and follow seductive spirits and devil's doctrine. I would say the same concerning heretics, who are seduced by the devil's false words and persuasions, and who are unjust to God and to others. At the Last Judgment they will not be severely punished if they repent, confess their error, and abandon it. That such persons should be sharply restrained in some cases I do not deny; nor would I oppose it. But clearly it is even more imperative for magistrates not to proceed too harshly or too quickly with the many old women who are naturally feeble and silly and are deceived, seduced, and sometimes even possessed by the devil; for they are considered witches although they are harmless. Those who kill these poor, duped, crazy, but innocent women anger God most of all. I do not doubt that they will have to suffer harsh punishment from Christ for the gruesome cruelty and tyranny that they exercise against these women, like the bloodthirstiest hangmen, unless they do true penance and obtain a merciful God. A vice or sin, committed or conceived in the heart, is punished by God the Lord, who is a searcher of men's hearts and who knows our thoughts. For a man who desires the wife of another is an adulterer in his heart and cannot escape the punishment of God. But the magistrate must not punish him as an adulterer even if he confesses openly his deepest will and thoughts, for the sword is not entrusted to the magistracy for such cases.

Now, if a troublemaker or quarreler is to be punished, as the will and consensus of mankind agree, it is first necessary and required that he really deserve punishment by displaying a reasonable and understanding human will. He must have intentionally planned, with will, mind, and spirit, to commit some crime or heinous deed against the commonwealth; and he must have been able to do the deed; and he must have begun to commit at least part of the crime, or have made an attempt. It were well to distinguish clearly such men from those who, in the weakness of their mind, imagine that they are committing some evil or believe that they have already completed some deed which actually never occurred and was impossible to do. Otherwise one would have to attribute criminal will and consent to fools, children, and the mentally ill, who often persuade themselves that they have done evil and in their folly confess that they are guilty of crimes. What have witches done in consenting to and applauding the plans of the devil for causing trouble and misfortune (at God's decree)? Nothing more than people who, when in trouble, wickedly and jealously wish bad luck to others, and who rejoice and are happy, with willing and consenting minds, when misfortune occurs, as we often see. The secular laws occasionally deal with this matter, teaching that all other things being equal, women sin less than men in doing certain crimes because their mind and understanding are weak. Therefore, they ought also to be less severely punished, as I demonstrate in Book Six, Chapter Ten. And God specially commanded that poor widows be faithfully protected and cared for, because they are old women, as Holy Scripture testifies. I know of no better or more secure way of punishing and chastising the witches than having them taught the law of God's Word by a true and pious teacher, so that they may withstand the devil and his deeds, and his blandishments, and if repentant thus find the free acceptance of the whole community again. Yet because they did give in to the devil and did not completely oppose him, some argue that they have earned and indeed deserve a sharper punishment; in that case then send them for a while into miserable exile or fine them according to the gravity of their crime and sin; but spare their lives.

Regarding the law of Moses in Exodus 22, which you apply to this case, I answer that in the Hebrew text the word is *Mechasepha* which the Seventy Translators [the editors of the Septuagint] rendered as *pharmakoùs où peribiósete*, that is, thou shalt not suffer the poisoner (as the Hebrews called it) to live or to survive; and in this way the Seventy Translaters interpreted and explained the intent and meaning of the law. And the word *Casaph*, and other words with that as a root, can hardly be interpreted in the Greek translation as meaning anything other than poisoning. There-

fore this decree does not concern our witches, who poison no one and use no poisons in their business. They cannot be punished on that basis. Yet others foolishly persuade themselves that the witches should be killed and burned because this word *Mechasepha*, in the Old Testament, is translated into German as sorceress. Here one should note the teaching of Josephus, who was a born Jew. He interpreted the law this way: "No Israelite should possess anything deadly or poisonous, prepared for harmful use. Those who are found with such things should be killed and thus suffer what they planned to do to others, and the prepared poison should be exhibited."

For this reason no one will easily convince me that anyone at the time of Moses had ever seen or heard of the kind of diabolical nonsense and delusion with which our witches have long been troubled and fooled. Moses and the books of the Old Testament actually speak of only four kinds of sorcery and magic. The first were the diviners or tricksters of Pharoah, who dazzled the eyes of the king with their devil's art, and could make a fog before his eyes so that he believed certain things existed which actually did not. Our witches cannot bring such things to pass, and do not want to. Moses called them *Hartumim*, if I remember correctly, for I am at the hunting lodge Betsburg, fifteen miles from my library at Cleves, and cannot consult a Hebrew Bible. Secondly, there are the *Mechasepha* or poisoners, who kill or otherwise grievously harm men and cattle, using perhaps poison or other evil medicines. Third are those who practice all kinds of divination, and they are called by various names: *Kasam* (Deut. 15; Jeremiah 17), *Onen* (Deut. 18; 2 Chron. 31; Jeremiah 17; Micha 5), *Nahas* (Deut. 18; 2 Chron. 33), *Ob* (Deut. 18; Isaiah 19; 1 Kings 28; 4 Kings 23; and elsewhere), *Jidoni* (Deut. 18; Levit. 19 & 20; 4 Kings 23; Isaiah 19). [Fourthly] the Hebrews used the word *Habar* for magicians who mumble secret words which supposedly contain great mystery and power. David uses this word and also *Lahas* (Psalm 58) when he speaks of the adders that stop their ears against the voice of the charmer. Whatever the meaning of these words, they do not imply the kind of foolishness employed by our old women. When the decree of Moses is rightly used against poisoners, they really ought to be punished according to its terms. And I have never defended those whom the *Lex Cornelia de sicariis et veneficis* condemns (*Digest*, Book 46, Title 8).

I have been glad to send you my opinion, dear Brenz, because I trust that you will respond to my writing with a favorable answer. May the merciful God give grace and spirit that you may follow faithfully your Christian calling, for the honor of God, the building of his Church, and so that souls may be saved.

Betsburg, 10 October 1565

RESPONSE OF JOHANN BRENZ TO JOHANN WEYER

[Brenz praises Weyer's work but insists on one point of disagreement.]

Yet it must be noted clearly that these persons who have broken the laws deserve a dreadful punishment and are reasonably and rightly condemned. Regarding the imperial law, I see very well that it uses language like this: "Whoever uses evil and inappropriate arts to infect or disturb the elements," etc. And I insist now as before that it is not within the ability of the devil himself or of any man to cause the disturbance of the elements. It is in God's power alone. Yet I do not doubt that the said law only uses the language of the common man and simply expresses the opinion which magicians and witches also have regarding themselves. For they are persuaded by the devil that they can disturb the elements with their arts. To this I can hear your response that in this case the law is punishing only an intention and a false persuasion. But this is not so, for the law "regards the completed and certain attempt as equivalent to the crime itself." For these poor, wretched women do not only intend to disturb the elements with their cooking and other arts, but they do all they can with the greatest energy, collecting herbs, cooking them with their charms over a fire, and all those things that they learned from the devil and

his followers. Here the law is right in punishing the "completed attempt" as I indicated. . . . [Brenz gives several examples in which attempted murder and attempted fornication are punished.] Thus one can conclude that regardless of whether witches and sorcerers can disturb the elements or cause harm to men with their charms and magic, yet their intentions do not remain only evil thoughts and desires, but produce a full attempt at the crime itself. For this reason the stern seriousness of the law should not be rejected or discarded in this case. And I believe also that the law of Moses in Exodus 22 has the same meaning. It is true, of course, that the word *Casaph* is translated as *pharmakos* or poison. But the *pharmakos* is not only a person who gives someone a poisoned drink, but also he who by mistake gives a safe drink to a person for whom he had prepared a poisoned drink. Thus when the witches and magicians thoroughly intend and plan to harm the fruits, meadow, cattle, or other persons by using either poison or other illicit means, they cannot be held guiltless. . . .

It is, however, necessary to know that one has to have really thorough knowledge and sound witnesses in these cases so that one does not go too far in accusing and punishing those who break these laws. If the matter is understood rightly, one has to distinguish, as you correctly say, between the evil-minded, impudent, willful knaves and the melancholy or mentally ill, or those who err solely from simplicity or superstition. For who could be so merciless and stubborn that he would want to prosecute these last-mentioned persons? . . . It is a great virtue and sign of virtue to take care of the poor orphans, to sympathize with them and have mercy on them. May the dear Lord further you in your new calling and office since you desire that the poor, troubled women should be taken from the hangman and saved from fiery punishment either through your medical healing or through my theological healing. . . . Stuttgart, on the day of the holy martyr Stephen, 1565.

Selection 12
"Of Vanity"
Michel de Montaigne

Michel de Montaigne (1533–1592) has been acclaimed as one of the greatest French writers. Much of his work was in the form of essays on various subjects. Religious controversy prompted by the Reformation and Wars of Religion formed the backdrop of Montaigne's entire life. His writings are filled with calls for toleration, and as this selection notes, "The laws which condemn us not to be able, themselves accuse us for not being able." It seems fitting to close this unit with a selection from Montaigne, since his wry awareness of his own shortcomings and foibles as well as those of the world around him typifies the skepticism and open-mindedness that the Renaissance eventually, though only slowly, inspired.

Yes, I confess, I see nothing, even in a dream or a wish, that I could hold myself to; variety alone satisfies me, and the enjoyment of diversity, at least if anything satisfies me. In traveling, I am encouraged by the very fact that I can stop without loss, and that I have a place where I can turn aside from it comfortably.

I love private life because it is by my own choice that I love it, not because of unfitness for public life, which is perhaps just as well suited to my nature. I serve my prince the more gaily because I do so by the free choice of my judgment and my reason, without personal obligation, and because I am not thrown back on his service and constrained to it by being unacceptable and unwelcome to every other party. So with the rest. I hate the morsels that necessity carves for me. Any advantage on which I had to depend exclusively would have me by the throat.

Let one oar row in water, the other on the shore.

A single cord never keeps me in place.

"There is vanity," you say, "in this amusement." But where is there not? And these fine precepts are vanity, and all wisdom is vanity. . . . These exquisite subtleties are only fit for preaching; they are arguments that would send us all saddled into the other world. Life is a material and corporeal movement, an action which by its very essence is imperfect and irregular; I apply myself to serving it in its own way. . . .

Source: Donald M. Frame (trans. and ed.), *Montaigne's Essays and Selected Writings* (New York: St. Martin's Press, 1963), pp. 369–371.

What is the use of these lofty points of philosophy on which no human being can settle, and these rules that exceed our use and our strength? I often see people propose to us patterns of life which neither the proposer nor his hearers have any hope of following, or, what is more, any desire to follow. . . .

It would be desirable that there should be more proportion between the command and the obedience; and a goal that we cannot reach seems unjust. There is no man so good that if he placed all his actions and thoughts under the scrutiny of the laws, he would not deserve hanging ten times in his life—even such a man that it would be a very great loss and very unjust to punish and destroy him. . . . And one man might not offend the laws at all, who would not for all that deserve in any degree to be praised as a virtuous man, and whom philosophy would very justly cause to be whipped: so confused and uneven is this relationship.

There is no question of our being good men according to God; we cannot be so according to ourselves. Human wisdom has never yet come up to the duties that she has prescribed for herself; and if she ever did come up to them, she would prescribe herself others beyond, to which she would aim and aspire, so hostile to consistency is our condition. Man ordains that he himself shall be necessarily at fault. He is not very clever to cut out his own duty by the pattern of a different nature than his own. To whom does he prescribe what he expects no one to do? Is it wrong of him not to do what it is impossible for him to do? The laws which condemn us not to be able, themselves accuse us for not being able. . . .

FIVE

The Merchant

In the Europe of the 1300s one would have found few of the economic behaviors and attitudes characteristic of the modern system we call "capitalism." Even by the end of the period this book covers—around 1700—much that is familiar to us in the worlds of commerce, finance, and industry still lay ahead: mechanized factories, widely accessible stock markets, rapid transportation, instant communications, vast multinational corporations, and the discipline of economics itself. Yet many of the essential elements of the modern system had developed during the intervening centuries, notably in Italy, the Netherlands, and England. The classic figure of the merchant took on new roles and in so doing changed social and political, as well as economic, relationships. A snapshot of three cities that can serve as exemplars at each stage of this process will suggest the nature of the transformation and how it came about.

VENICE AROUND 1450

No city in the 1300s was more closely identified with commerce than Venice. The very commitment of its citizens to trade, however, made them exceptional in a Europe that was fragmented into hundreds of self-sufficient regions, most of which were devoted overwhelmingly to agriculture and had few outside contacts. Barter was still a crucial means of exchange in this rural world—if you needed a new plough, for example, you might offer to trade the blacksmith a lamb for it. Money was a rare commodity, and few would have known what finance or long-distance transactions meant. Given the dominance of agriculture, one's social standing relative to others was determined, at birth, by a web of rights and obligations that depended on land and its products. Put simply, the more land you owned, the higher you were in the social hierarchy.

Into this structure of relationships and values, the merchant—even the city— fitted uneasily at best. It was taken for granted that landowners were far superior to those (however rich) who dirtied their hands in trade, and yet such people, and the nonrural places where they lived, were becoming ever more important in the European economy. In cities, new ways of earning a living were being created, often accompanied by social attitudes (such as a respect for wealth) that did not sit well with traditional norms. Nowhere, however, were these new patterns of behavior and outlook being developed with more vigor than in Venice.

Almost from the day it was settled—according to legend, by refugees from the barbarian invasions that destroyed the Roman Empire—the cluster of islands in a lagoon off the northeast coast of Italy that was to be called Venice shaped the character of its inhabitants by its topography. They built the only city in medieval Europe that had no walls, protected as it was by the sea that surrounded it. That the Venetians would become sailors was inevitable. That they should have won, by a combination of trading skill, shrewd organization, and naval effectiveness, a maritime empire in the eastern Mediterranean and a land empire in northern Italy was simply, in their eyes, a reward for their commercial and political astuteness and the fulfilment of their ambition to bring back to life the empire that once had been centered on the city of their ancestors, Rome. The source of their power, however, was not so much the military might that had been crucial to the ancient Romans, but rather a remarkable aptitude for political stability and commercial success.

Essential to the political stability—which kept Venice free from significant unrest throughout the more than 700 years of its existence as an independent republic—was the willingness of the one hundred and fifty or so families who emerged as the city's rulers to assume active roles in commerce as well as government. It was from these patrician families that the city's principal officials (including its leader, the doge) were elected; nevertheless, they would have considered it unthinkable that trade could be beneath their dignity. They had privileges, to be sure, but their commitment to public service and their sense of themselves as integral members of their community gave a status to economic activity, at the heart of a great empire, that it had nowhere else in Europe. Unlike powerful families elsewhere, who even in cities tended to cut themselves off from the less privileged, Venice's patricians jostled elbows with their fellow citizens at the fish market and took an active part in commerce. They could behave like aristocrats, and in fact in the 1500s they built magnificent country villas and ran farms on the Italian mainland that were the envy of nobles as far away as England (Figure 26). Yet they also kept a close involvement in trade, which set them apart, as aristocrat-merchants, from both the typical merchant and the typical aristocrat of the time.

Given this combination of interests, it is no surprise that they should have welcomed enterprising newcomers to their city with open arms. For example, despite occasional bouts of persecution, Venice managed to maintain a thriving Jewish quarter—called the "ghetto," from the Italian word for "foundry," which had been on the site and which gave its name to all such quarters—with elegant synagogues served by rabbis whom even doges sometimes came to hear preach. Such diversity of people was one of Venice's great strengths. The city took superb advantage of its location to attract Greeks, Germans, Turks, Slavs, and Armenians, who established communities that helped promote trade with their homelands. And it was precisely this network of contacts, extending throughout Europe and the

Figure 26. Andrea Palladio, *Villa Barbaro*, Maser (1565). The stunning country villas the architect Andrea Palladio built for Venice's patricians, not far from the city, influenced the style of the European mansion for centuries. And yet, although they evoked ancient buildings and were magnificently decorated, they remained characteristic of the practical Venetians in that they were used to run agricultural estates. This villa, completed in 1565, was adorned by one of the leading artists of the day, Paolo Veronese, but its lower floor served as a workshop and storehouse for farm equipment.

Middle East, that enabled Venice to become the chief importer of spices and other products from the East and their principal distributor throughout Europe. Nor was it accidental that the Continent's most famous traveler before Columbus should have been a Venetian, Marco Polo, who shaped for centuries the image of China and much of Asia.

Venice's wealth, location, unusual setting, and unique architecture, which blended artistic traditions from the Muslim, Orthodox, and Western worlds, also made it the most famous tourist center in Europe. Pilgrims on their way to the Holy Land mingled with those who had come for the exotic goods in the shops or for the exotic sights to create a flood of visitors who not only widened the city's connections but also enriched its economy. Yet the prosperity also was the result of a spirit of innovation which was vital to the development of the role of the merchant in Renaissance Europe. Political and social stability, diversity of population, geographic advantages, and wide-ranging contacts may have been important, but they were merely prerequisites to success. The root of Venice's ability to win markets and dominate trade routes was a willingness to experiment with new commercial practices and industrial activities which, gathering momentum from around 1300 onward and supported by government policies, helped expand opportunities for its craftsmen and traders.

The first of these devices was financial. Long-distance trade, the republic's lifeblood, demanded large investments. Consider the requirements for importing and distributing a shipment of pepper—a highly lucrative product, worth a great deal per ounce—that was picked up from a port in the Middle East. It would not have been cheap to start with, because it would have been brought to the port by caravan from an area on the far side of Asia where it had been grown. A further substantial sum of money would have had to be spent to bring the pepper to Venice: for a ship, a crew, and possibly an agent and warehouse in the Middle Eastern port. Then there would have been the costs of finding buyers for the shipment; of the

Figure 27. Canaletto, *Campo di Rialto*. Although it was painted around 1758, long after Venice's most prosperous days were over, this depiction of the square near the Rialto Bridge, where the bankers set up their tables and benches under the arcade, shows that the scene remained familiar for centuries.

paperwork; of the new voyages to bring it to its final destinations, which might range from Paris to Hamburg; and perhaps also of storage until it could all be sold. To assemble the capital that would be needed for such a venture would almost certainly have called for a syndicate or partnership of some kind. Only a group of investors could have financed it, because no one of them could have afforded the total cost or the risk of losing so large an investment. Indeed, Shakespeare's play *The Merchant of Venice* is about just such a situation—and the consequences when a ship did get lost.

It was to sustain large-scale activities like these that the Venetians, together with businessmen who had to raise funds in the other major cities of Europe, developed a whole series of new financial methods. The most important was the bank, which is said to have taken its name from the benches, or *banchi*, set up by financiers near the Rialto Bridge, the main trading center in Venice (Figure 27). Here people with surplus resources to invest could find ventures into which they could put their funds. The "bankers" acted essentially as middlemen, who were paid a commission to exchange different currencies and to bring investors together with appropriate enterprises. In ever larger amounts, these bankers accumulated the capital that Venice's trade required.

To make the system work, however, one had to be able to transfer funds to distant places without incurring the danger of transporting large amounts of cash. The solution was the letter of transfer or credit, the distant ancestor of today's check. The bankers linked up with agents in other commercial centers, who would honor letters brought by the traders which specified how much had to be paid to the bearer. Thus our pepper importer would appear at the Middle Eastern port with a letter of credit from a Venetian banker for the cost of the pepper. That sum (or a new letter of credit) would then be given by the banker's agent, as payment, to the trader who had brought the shipment across Asia. These letters—also known as "bills of exchange" or "promissory notes" (that is, notes promising payments)—began to take on value themselves and became a kind of paper money. Backing them, though, was a currency that the government took great pains to support: the ducat. Named after the doge, and based on a precious metal content that had universal value, this Venetian coin was regarded for centuries as one of the most reliable in Europe, because the city's economic stability, and thus its commerce, required that its financial instruments remain not only flexible (thanks to the banks and letters of credit) but also totally dependable.

And yet Venice's prosperity was not merely the result of the shrewdness and innovations of its traders. Venice also was widely admired as a center of superb craftsmanship, sought after by both tourists and consumers of luxuries throughout Europe. Its printers and publishers produced the most beautiful and popular books of the age. And to this day, Venetian glass and leather remain highly prized, sold in shops that attract buyers from many parts of the world, as they did during the Renaissance.

What amazed visitors was the combination of financial wizardry, artistic achievement, and a shopper's delight. One German traveler's description is filled with wonder at what he saw in 1497:

> One reaches a small square called the Rialto. Here the merchants assemble every day at ten o'clock for their business. Leading from the Rialto are long streets where the merchants have shops, such as goldsmiths and jewellers selling pearls and precious stones. One street contains tailors, cobblers, rope-sellers, linen and cloth dealers, and others, trading there without number. We went to the chief church of St. Mark through many narrow streets, in some of which were apothecaries, in some bookbinders, in others all kinds of merchants pursuing a thriving trade. St. Mark's is a very beautiful church, covered with marble stones and with gold. The Doge's Palace is very fine and is daily being made more beautiful. Since it was in my mind to travel, I had to see that my money was not stolen. I was therefore taken with the help of the German merchants to a gentleman of Venice who traded in all countries, who gave bills of exchange for Alexandria, Damascus, Beirut, Antioch, Constantinople, and other towns. When I presented these bills to the person to whom they were made out, although I could not speak with him, he would stare at me and disappear into the back of his house, returning at once and paying me my money. I was told this by the gentleman in Venice, and in truth they keep to it.

Perhaps the most remarkable of Venice's achievements was the organization of a manufacturing enterprise that can be considered the first real assembly-line factory in European history—the Arsenal (Figure 28). The key to the durability of the Venetian empire, apart from its political stability and wealth, was its control of the seas. Consequently, the republic's leaders had to apply their formidable adminis-

Figure 28. *The Venice Arsenal*, detail from Jacopo de Barbari, *View of Venice* (engraving). In this bird's-eye view of Venice in 1500, the Arsenal occupies a prominent place. The many sheds around the U-shaped stretch of water where the ships were assembled are clearly visible, as in the long white building, ending in a white tower and dotted with windows, where the huge strands of hemp were twisted into rope.

trative and economic skills to naval matters. And this they did by creating the most elaborate industrial complex of the age, a massive shipbuilding and armaments center that was capable of building and outfitting a warship in the course of one day. At its height in the 1500s, the Arsenal employed over 5000 people, and their regular wages and well-planned benefits (including pensions, sick pay, and family assistance) were a source of work and steady income that helped significantly to maintain the economic and social stability of this city of about 100,000 inhabitants.

The Arsenal operated under a carefully structured division of labor. Every employee had a specific skill, and many were specially trained for their tasks. Thus there was one building, hundreds of feet long, that was devoted entirely to the manufacture of rope. Everyone who worked there was an expert in some aspect of the process that transformed the raw material, hemp, into the immensely long, twisted strands of rope that were essential for a ship's sails. The sails, in turn, were the responsibility of another department, staffed by women as well as men, who cut and sewed dozens of cloths and canvases for the ships every day. In the armaments division, the workers not only manufactured cannon but also devised methods for moving huge weights, such as cannonballs, with levers and pulleys that Galileo was to marvel at as a means of understanding the principles of mechanics. A good indication of the seriousness with which the Venetian government regarded the welfare of the Arsenal is the fact that it wanted one of the leading mathematicians and physicists of the day to serve as a consultant to this enterprise.

The atmosphere that was fostered in Venice, in other words, bore little relation to the outlook of the fragmented world and the isolated communities of rural Europe. International contacts, a vigorous entrepreneurial spirit, complex organizational skills, and a reliance not just on money but on highly sophisticated techniques for handling capital set this city apart. And yet, although in the 1400s and 1500s Venice still seemed an exceptional place, the behavior and attitudes it promoted were harbingers of the future. By the time we come to the heyday of our next exemplar, Amsterdam, we are entering an age in which it was becoming clear that what we now call "capitalism"—the organization of economic life around the accumulation and investment of money, or capital—was becoming a decisive force on the European scene.

AMSTERDAM AROUND 1600

The similarities between Venice and Amsterdam have struck many observers. Although in the Dutch case water is not quite so visible and serves as a means of transportation in an essentially landed area rather than as the natural adjunct of dozens of islands, it has often been remarked that the two cities are unusual in sharing so great a reliance on the canals in their midst. Both places moreover, flourished as a result of their involvement in long-distance maritime trade and international finance. And both were exceptionally open and welcoming to people of diverse backgrounds and cultures. These analogies are important and relate to the cities' economic roles, but the differences are significant, too, and reflect the expansion of the European economy by the early 1600s.

Two major transformations in particular had taken place since the glory days of Venice a hundred years before. First, trade was now conducted across the entire world. The discovery of America and the opening up of sea routes around Africa to the Far East—the source of the pepper and spices that had been coming to Venice via overland caravans—revolutionized the patterns of international commerce. It was not that the old routes ceased functioning, but that now a cheaper means of transport, by sea, was available to the East, and new routes and new goods (notably silver) were available to the West. As overseas colonies grew, they also offered new markets, which were supplied by Europeans from home. Italians continued to do well in this changing economic landscape, but increasingly after 1600 two northern maritime powers, the Netherlands and England, with easy access to the Atlantic and aggressive merchant communities, took over the leadership of international finance and trade. They even began to dominate shipping in the Mediterranean, the Venetians' home area, and the result was another of the transformations of the age: the shift of the center of European enterprise and economic activity away from the Mediterranean, where it had largely been situated for some two thousand years, to the North.

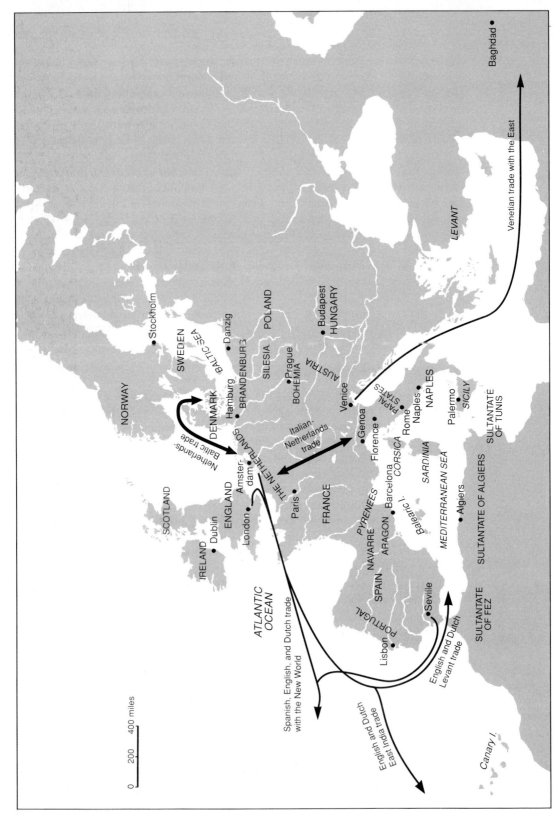

Map 7. Major trade routes around 1600

Baghdad

Venetian trade with the East

LEVANT

Stockholm

SWEDEN

BALTIC SEA

Danzig

NORWAY

POLAND

SILESIA

BRANDENBURG

Budapest
HUNGARY

Hamburg

DENMARK

Prague
BOHEMIA

AUSTRIA

Venice

PAPAL STATES

Naples
NAPLES

Palermo
SICILY

SULTANATE OF TUNIS

Netherlands-Baltic trade

THE NETHERLANDS

Amsterdam

Italian-Netherlands trade

Genoa

Florence

Rome

CORSICA

SARDINIA

MEDITERRANEAN SEA

SULTANATE OF ALGIERS

Algiers

SCOTLAND

ENGLAND

London

Paris

FRANCE

PYRENEES

NAVARRE

ARAGON

Barcelona

Balearic I.

IRELAND

Dublin

ATLANTIC OCEAN

SPAIN

PORTUGAL

Lisbon

Seville

SULTANATE OF FEZ

English and Dutch Levant trade

Spanish, English, and Dutch trade with the New World

English and Dutch East India trade

Canary I.

0   200   400 miles

170

Where the Netherlands were concerned, the need to thrive at the expense of the South was quite direct, for in the late 1500s the Dutch had launched a long struggle for independence from their rulers, the Spanish. By 1648, they had succeeded in that effort and had created a new nation, basically Protestant (unlike Spain), consisting of seven provinces along the North Sea and around a large inlet known as the Zuider Zee. With a population of little more than a million, the Dutch had always had to be enterprising. Their agriculture was perhaps the most efficient in Europe, making superb use of limited space and—because much of their land was below sea level—expanding that space with dykes and other feats of engineering that reclaimed land from the sea. A major source of livelihood was fishing, because the main schools of herring—a cheap fish that was eaten throughout northern Europe—congregated off the Dutch coast. This, in turn, promoted high skills in shipbuilding and seamanship that were to be crucial to the Dutch economy. Equally important was the country's urbanization, for it has been estimated that less than half the population—the lowest percentage in Europe—lived in rural areas by the mid-1600s. Wage earners, who included women and children as well as men, were very poorly paid, but at least in the cities they were more likely to be literate and to contribute to the commercial life that was the heart of Dutch prosperity.

Until the mid-1500s, the main financial center in northern Europe had been the port of Antwerp. As the struggle between Spain and the Netherlands intensified, however, Antwerp became a casualty of the wars—it was looted by Spanish troops in 1576 and then blockaded by Dutch ships. As a result, the international bankers and financiers who had helped make Antwerp rich looked for a more secure city, not too far away, to which they could move their operations. What they found was Amsterdam, the chief port of Holland, the richest and most powerful of the provinces that were winning their independence from Spain.

Amsterdam in 1600, as it became the most prosperous financial center of Europe, was a city of some 65,000 people; it was nearly to triple in size by 1650 (Figure 29). Like Venice, it was tolerant of diverse faiths and cultures and a hospitable place for any group that seemed productive and enterprising. It also was a lively hub of artistic and intellectual activity. Unlike the Venetians, however, its inhabitants often gave visitors an impression of sobriety, even austerity, and of public decorum; it would have been unimaginable for Amsterdam to have become a magnet for tourists. Yet everyone was struck by the wealth, ingenuity, dignity, and orderliness the city displayed:

> I went to Amsterdam, a city at present for riches, trade, shipping, fair streets, and pleasant habitations, scarce yielding to any other of the world. The whole town is built upon piles driven down into the earth. By this means they build houses in the sea, and lay foundations in places where no solid bottom is found. The *Stadthuis* [town hall] is the noblest building. The hospital for the sick hath a great revenue. Besides, there are great sums of money collected for the poor, so that there is not a beggar to be seen in the streets.
>
> (Edward Browne, *An Account of Several Travels*, 1677)

The welfare system depended on sending those beggars who did appear on the streets to workhouses, where they were given unskilled work, such as making sacks. Conditions in these workhouses were usually terrible, with long hours and little food, but they did at least save the city's poor from the starvation and homelessness that was common elsewhere in Europe.

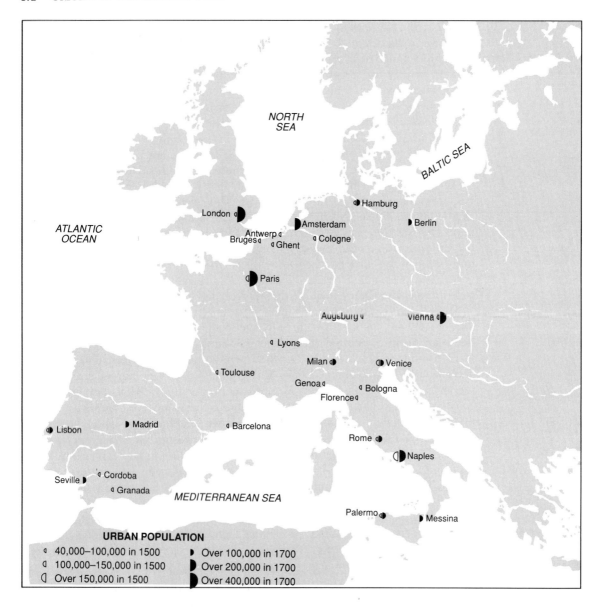

NORTH
SEA

BALTIC SEA

ATLANTIC
OCEAN

Hamburg

London

Berlin

Amsterdam

Antwerp
Bruges   Ghent   Cologne

Paris

Augsburg   Vienna

Lyons

Milan   Venice

Toulouse

Genoa   Bologna

Florence

Lisbon   Madrid   Barcelona

Rome

Naples

Seville   Cordoba
Granada   MEDITERRANEAN SEA

Palermo   Messina

URBAN POPULATION

◁ 40,000–100,000 in 1500   ▶ Over 100,000 in 1700
◁ 100,000–150,000 in 1500   ▶ Over 200,000 in 1700
◁ Over 150,000 in 1500   ▶ Over 400,000 in 1700

Map 8. Growth of cities, 1500–1700. Half circles are omitted for those cities whose population was below 40,000 in 1500 or below 100,000 in 1700.

What gave Amsterdam its air of single-minded economic purpose was that it was overwhelmingly a shipping and commercial center, unlike both Venice and London, which also were homes of governments. The capital of the Netherlands was The Hague, and Amsterdammers were therefore more exclusively concerned with economic matters than were Venetians or Londoners. Indeed, one of their problems in the 1600s was to persuade the central government to support their

Figure 29. *Amsterdam Harbor* (engraving, 1660s). This engraving was made during Amsterdam's richest years. So many ships were loaded or unloaded along the canals that dozens had to wait in the harbor outside the city. The flatness of the countryside and the windmills in the background make the scene unmistakably Dutch.

interests—which called for peace, toleration, free trade, and aeeess to all markets— instead of pursuing war with Spain or trying to impose strict Calvinism, which tended to be the agenda of the more rural areas of the Netherlands. On the other hand, the prosperity of their countrymen, and particularly their skills in fishing, shipping, and agriculture, provided an abundant source of investment for the city's financial and trading ventures.

Like Venice, Amsterdam also became an important craft and industrial center, noted especially for its fine jewellery, its textiles, and such major enterprises as the refining of salt. Here, as in Venice, women could achieve considerable success as shopkeepers and in various crafts; although men still dominated commerce, small enterprises were often family ventures. Yet it was in the larger world of finance and commerce that the Dutch merchants demonstrated the ingenuity and skill that made Amsterdam the richest city in Europe. For a small country, with few resources, the only way to prosper in the cut-throat world of international trade was to undersell the competition. To do this, one had to have sufficient funds, readily and cheaply available, to make expensive enterprises possible. Moreover, in order to keep the costs down, one needed extremely efficient means of shipping goods— preferably the most efficient in Europe. It was to these two goals that the merchants of Amsterdam devoted themselves and on which their success was based.

Raising large amounts of money in 1600 was no easy task, especially when the funds were used to outfit the long-distance voyages (or even some fairly short ones) on which trade depended, because the risks of shipwreck, piracy, and enemy action at sea were always considerable. One response to the problem was insurance, and the Dutch, like the Venetians, were pioneers in this means of protecting investors against losses. More reassuring, however, were measures that spread the risk. The Venetians and others had long traded in syndicates—partnerships that enabled individuals to avoid having to fund ventures on their own. The Dutch now expanded this practice dramatically, creating a radically different system of financing major enterprises. What they did was to establish the first joint-stock companies, the ancestors of the modern, publicly owned corporation.

Two companies in particular, one for trade with the East Indies and the other for the West Indies, were structured so as to attract the maximum investment with the least risk. The way they worked was that a group of merchants got together and announced the preparation of a voyage to the Far East. For such an enterprise, an entire fleet of ships would be needed, plus the funds to buy pepper, spices, and other commodities. It also would cost money, once the fleet came home, to warehouse the cargo until it could be sold. A shipload of pepper, for example, might take a year to sell in its entirety, and in the meantime, the proceeds could not be distributed. To finance a venture of this scale, dozens of investors were needed; what the company did, therefore, was to offer shares in the enterprise. If you put up, say, two percent of the investment, you would get two percent of the profits. Moreover, you would not have to spend time managing the expedition. The company itself would take care of hiring the fleet, selling the imports, and so forth. It also hired the agents in the East Indies, built warehouses, and maintained contacts both with the sources of the goods and with the markets where they were sold. The investors needed none of these skills; they merely obtained shares, both of the original capital, or stock, of the company and of its profits. The total stock was jointly held by these shareholders—hence the name "joint-stock company."

Within a short time, as the company's activities became continuous and it became clear that each year there would be both investments and profits, the shares that were sold were of the company itself rather than of a voyage. The directors would distribute a set portion of the annual profits per share, and the value of these "stocks" would be determined by how good this return was. So successful was this mechanism that in 1611 Amsterdam established the first stock exchange, a place where people could make money not so much as a result of specific trading ventures but by speculating on the future success of an entire company.

Another source of financial security was the Bank of Amsterdam, established in 1609. This bank, whose assets were guaranteed by the city, had as its members all local merchants. By depositing there whatever money they earned, they were assured that their funds would always be available, in local currency. Eventually, the bank used these deposits to make loans, at the lowest interest rates in Europe. What this meant was that those who wanted to start new enterprises could do so more cheaply than anywhere else. The bank thus became a vital means of providing Dutch merchants with secure finances and the lowered costs that enabled them to undersell their competition.

This aim was served, too, by their shipping industry. In addition to relying on low wages, the Dutch used their country's long experience at sea to organize a fleet of extraordinary efficiency. A remarkable production line along a river near Amsterdam (not unlike the Venice Arsenal, though less devoted to military ends) turned out a stream of ships (Figure 30). And it was well known that the Dutch could transport goods with a smaller crew than could any of their rivals. Their specialty, the *fluyt*, was a slow and ungainly vessel, used only within Europe, but it soon came to dominate the continent's lucrative carrying trade, from the Baltic to the Mediterranean, because it held more goods than other cargo ships and demanded fewer sailors. By the mid-1600s it was estimated that the Dutch owned three-quarters of the merchant ships in Europe, and it was clear that they controlled

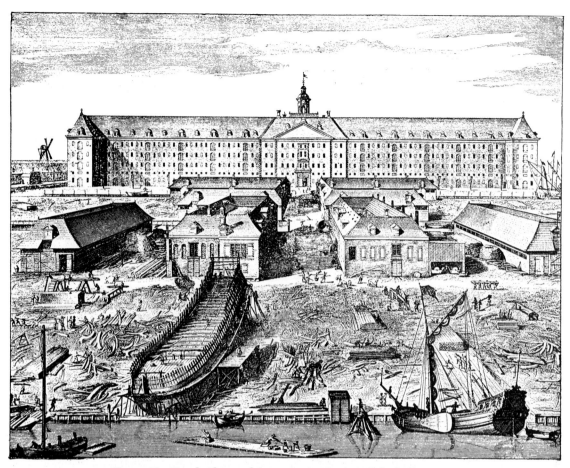

Figure 30. *Dutch Shipyard* (engraving). The Dutch built the most efficient ships in the world in the seventeenth century, and they could turn them out more quickly and in greater numbers than anyone else. Their chief assembly line, with the inevitable windmill not too far away, was a few miles from Amsterdam.

transportation even within other countries like France, let alone international trade.

Unable to compete, their neighbors decided to fight efficiency with repression. A new view of economic activity, which later came to be called "mercantilism," was on the rise in the 1600s. It started from the premise (which, of course, was false) that the amount of wealth in the world was fixed. It was therefore the responsibility of political leaders to increase their country's share of the total pie, and the way to do this was not only to encourage their own merchants but also to put obstacles in the way of foreigners. Governments imposed tariffs on imports, forbade the use of foreign ships in domestic trade, and used tolls and subsidies to give their own people a competitive advantage. The chief target, the Dutch, tried to keep trade as free as possible, and many of the measures against them in fact proved self-defeating. Eventually, however, the larger countries around the Netherlands resorted to wars which undermined Dutch dominance of international trade, although not the efficiency and vigor with which they maintained, for centuries, high prosperity at home and a lucrative empire overseas.

LONDON AROUND 1690

The city that benefited from the decline of Amsterdam and became the world's new financial center was London. Again, like both Venice and Amsterdam, it proved to be a place remarkably open to diverse beliefs and cultures. In 1656, following a ban that had lasted over 300 years, Jews were allowed to settle in England again, and in 1690 an Act of Toleration permitted the free exercise of all faiths. A major argument in favor of readmitting the Jews was that they had skills as merchants and financiers that would help English trade, and it was precisely this kind of encouragement to all means of expanding commerce that enabled London to dominate both shipping and finance as thoroughly as had Amsterdam. Although the dominant faith in both cities was Protestantism, it was openness, location, and innovation (as in Catholic Venice), not religious belief, that promoted economic success.

The role of the merchant was by now firmly established at the forefront of European society. London in 1690 was a city of around half a million, teeming with men and women engaged in a dizzying variety of crafts and businesses, from water pipelines to coffee houses. Newspapers, though often totally inaccurate, were an accepted part of daily life, as was overseas trade and the sale of stocks. What was unprecedented was the degree to which the worlds of politics, finance, and industry were coming to be mingled. Great merchants were major figures, and they played important roles not just within a city, as they had in Venice or Amsterdam, but also in the affairs of a far-flung kingdom with a population of nearly six million.

Perhaps the most remarkable indication of the merchants' prominence was the creation of the Bank of England. In the Netherlands, the Bank of Amsterdam, like other such banks that had appeared in Italy, was a city institution that provided important services for the local merchant community. What the Londoners did was to establish a national bank, in which both mercantile and landed wealth was put at the disposal of the government. Here political, aristocratic, and commercial leaders all came together in a joint enterprise that demonstrated the new economic coherence and power not just of a city but of a large territorial state.

Essential to this coherence was a social and a geographic unity that was unique among the major states of Europe. In all other countries, the traditional disdain of the landed classes for any hint of manual labor had led to codes of conduct that dismissed any kind of trading activity as beneath the dignity of an aristocrat. In Spain, poorer nobles, known as *hidalgos*, preferred to beg rather than taint their honor by engaging in commerce. The French used a special word, *dérogeance*, to indicate the shame that would be visited on a landed family that stooped to such activities. Only the English developed, over the course of the sixteenth century, a set of values that blurred these traditional distinctions.

The reasons the pattern differed in England had to do with political as well as social conditions. Ever since the time of Norman Conquest, in 1066, when the whole country had been conquered by a foreign ruler, the king had made sure to keep lands, and thus real power, in every area of the country. Uniquely in Europe, therefore, the English king was able to rely on the cooperation of local landowners to exercise his authority throughout his realm. This cooperation led, eventually, to a reliance on a representative institution, Parliament, which in the 1500s became an essential part of the central government. As this happened, representatives of every city and county were brought together, with increasing frequency, to discuss major policies and to approve the raising of taxes.

What was crucial was that, unlike other such assemblies, Parliament had just two houses, or chambers. In the House of Lords there sat about a hundred great landowners, the only families considered nobles in England, and about two dozen bishops. The House of Commons, however, included everybody else, which meant merchants from cities as well as nonnoble landowners. These two groups, which on the Continent would have been separated by a basic social divide and kept in different political assemblies, not only worked together in the House of Commons in the 1500s but also began to intermarry, moving in different generations quite easily from one status to the other. If, for instance, a wealthy merchant bought a country estate, his son could join the landowning class and leave trade. Then, because in England (unlike most of Europe) only the eldest son was entitled to inherit land, his younger sons might return to merchant life.

This fluidity had significant consequences for England's economic development. When, in the late 1500s, the London merchant community needed funds to launch overseas trading and colonial ventures, it was able to attract investments in its joint-stock companies by landowners, who on the Continent would never have deigned to become involved in trade in this way. Moreover, aristocrats were willing to set up industrial enterprises, such as mines and glassworks, on their lands. And in general, the old distinction between land and commerce, though certainly still significant, did not have the force in England that it did elsewhere in Europe. Indeed, it was for that reason that it proved so astonishingly easy to create the Bank of England in 1694.

The purpose of this bank, unlike the Bank of Amsterdam, was to raise money from the public that could be lent to the government. The government paid interest, which was the attraction, and the loan was secured by future tax income. In essence, what was being established was a mechanism for managing the national debt. Eventually, the promissory notes the Bank of England issued (the equivalent of the letters of credit that the Venetian bankers had written centuries earlier) became England's currency. To get started, however, the enormous sum of one million pounds—which today would be the equivalent of at least a billion dollars—had to be secured. Incredibly enough, more than a million pounds were raised in just twelve days from the London and landed communities. Nothing could have demonstrated more vividly the centrality of the merchant in English life.

Equally telling was the unity of England's economy. No longer were local areas isolated from one another. Instead, the resources of the entire country—a far larger and more diverse complex of people and places than the hinterlands of Venice or Amsterdam—could be marshalled for common enterprises. This was what the mercantilists had sought, and it became clear in the late 1600s that government policy, especially a series of wars fought with the Dutch, was intended to help commerce wherever possible. Yet this sense of purpose would not have been possible if it had not become apparent that all the regions of the country were indeed held together in a single economic system.

This coherence was demonstrated by the experiences of William Stout, a young man from Lancaster—in the northwest corner of England, about as far away from London as one could get without crossing into Scotland—who opened a general store in 1687. He later described how he set about filling it with merchandise:

> So soon as I had taken a shop, I applied to get what money was due by my father's will, which was fifty pound. I sold some land, in all, 119 pound, and I borrowed twelve pound which I repaid the following [year]. And I borrowed of my sister 10 pounds which I kept many years. All this money was got ready, and I fit the shop. [Since] several of our neighbours, shopkeepers, determined to go to London, and my brother Josias offering to lend me a horse, I made ready for the journey. We all got well to London in five days, and there I applied to tradesmen I was recommended to and bought goods. The ketch then lading for Lancaster, I got all my goods on board, and was then ready to return [overland] by way of Sheffield. I brought with me from London to Sheffield about twenty pounds, which I laid out in Sheffield and Birmingham manufactories.

What was clear from this journey was that even in the most remote areas, someone involved in trade knew about, and used, the resources of the entire country. Many goods came from London, but other localities were known for special products. Thus Stout went to Sheffield to get cutlery, for which it was already famous (and remains so to this day), and in similar fashion he was to obtain gloves, hats, and socks from different places, each known to be centers of production for these particular items.

The scale and coherence of England's economy, for all its domination by London (in which it has been estimated that some twenty percent of the country's population lived at some point in their lives), indicated that the old identification of a merchant with a specific city, and with its narrow interests, was giving way to an integration of the trader's world into every aspect of national life. The creation of the Bank of England was both a political and an economic undertaking, made possible by the understanding that commerce was no longer a distinct, peripheral activity, but essential to the well-being of the state. The merchant, in other words, had moved from the edge to the very heart of society.

Original Sources

The revitalization of economic life that occurred at the time of the Renaissance affected every aspect of life. To cite just one example, following the Black Death (ca. 1348), Italian merchants possessed excess capital, since many markets had closed. This new wealth made possible expanded patronage of the arts.

It has been argued that the Renaissance in artistic, cultural, and intellectual life affected only three to five percent of the Italian population—the very wealthiest. The life of the merchant, however, offered great opportunities for social mobility. In European cities, the merchant was at the center of economic and social ferment and, by the end of the Renaissance era, had moved to a central role in society as a whole.

I. CITY LIFE

The rise and enhanced importance of cities are two of the most noteworthy differences between the Middle Ages and the Renaissance. Towns had developed during the Middle Ages, but they were smaller and less consequential in economic terms than Renaissance and early modern cities. As the text chapter points out, geographic location had much to do with a city's expansion and success. Venice, Amsterdam, and London—each situated on the water—were all world centers of trade by 1700, the end of the period covered here. Economically secure residents of cities were proud to term themselves "citizen." The poor, however, were always on the margins of city life and often were regarded by the town magistrates and governors as dangerous liabilities.

Selection 1
How One Citizen Regarded His City

During the Renaissance, the individuality of men and women was shaped in part through identification with their places of residence. Citizens took enormous pride in their city-states. In this selection, Giovanni Villani (d. 1348) writes enthusiastically of what he sees as Florence's outstanding qualities.

MORE ON THE GREATNESS AND STATE AND MAGNIFICENCE OF THE COMMUNE OF FLORENCE

Since we have spoken about the income and expenditure of the Commune of Florence in this period, I think it is fitting to mention this and other great features of our city, so that our descendants in days to come may be aware of any rise, stability,

Source: Robert S. Lopez (ed.), *Medieval Trade in the Mediterranean World: Illustrative Documents* (New York: Columbia University Press, 1990), pp. 71–74

and decline in condition and power that our city may undergo, and also so that, through the wise and able citizens who at the time shall be in charge of its government, [our descendants] may endeavor to advance it in condition and power, seeing our record and example in this chronicle. We find after careful investigation that in this period there were in Florence about 25,000 men from the ages of fifteen to seventy fit to bear arms, all citizens. And among them were 1,500 noble and powerful citizens who as magnates gave security to the Commune. There were in Florence also some seventy-five full-dress knights. To be sure, we find that before the second popular government now in power was formed there were more than 250 knights; but from the time that the people began to rule, the magnates no longer had the status and authority enjoyed earlier, and hence few persons were knighted. From the amount of bread constantly needed for the city, it was estimated that in Florence there were some 90,000 mouths divided among men, women, and children, as can readily be grasped [from what we shall say] later; and it was reckoned that in the city there were always about 1,500 foreigners, transients, and soldiers, not including in the total the citizens who were clerics and cloistered monks and nuns, of whom we shall speak later. It was reckoned that in this period there were some 80,000 men in the territory and district of Florence. From the rector who baptized the infants—since he deposited a black bean for every male baptized in San Giovanni and a white bean for every female in order to ascertain their number—we find that at this period there were from 5,500 to 6,000 baptisms every year, the males usually outnumbering the females by 300 to 500. We find that the boys and girls learning to read [numbered] from 8,000 to 10,000, the children learning the abacus and algorism from 1,000 to 1,200, and those learning grammar and logic in four large schools from 550 to 600.

We find that the churches then in Florence and in the suburbs, including the abbeys and the churches of friars, were 110, among which were 57 parishes with congregations, 5 abbeys with two priors and some 80 monks each, 24 nunneries with some 500 women, 10 orders of friars, 30 hospitals with more than 1,000 beds to receive the poor and the sick, and from 250 to 300 chaplain priests.

The workshops of the *Arte della Lana* were 200 or more, and they made from 70,000 to 80,000 pieces of cloth, which were worth more than 1,200,000 gold florins. And a good third [of this sum] remained in the land as [the reward] of labor, without counting the profit of the entrepreneurs. And more than 30,000 persons lived by it. [To be sure,] we find that some thirty years earlier there were 300 workshops or thereabouts and they made more than 100,000 pieces of cloth yearly; but these cloths were coarser and one half less valuable,

because at that time English wool was not imported and they did not know, as they did later, how to work it.

The *fondachi* of the *Arte di Calimala*, dealing in French and Transalpine cloth, were some twenty, and they imported yearly more than 10,000 pieces of cloth, worth 300,000 gold florins. And all these were sold in Florence, without counting those which were reexported from Florence.

The banks of money-changers were about eighty. The gold coins which were struck amounted to some 350,000 gold florins and at times 400,000 [yearly]. And as for deniers of four petty each, about 20,000 pounds of them were struck yearly.

The association of judges was composed of some eighty members; the notaries were some six hundred; physicians and surgical doctors, some sixty; shops of dealers in spices, some hundred.

Merchants and mercers were a large number; the shops of shoemakers, slipper makers, and wooden-shoe makers were so numerous they could not be counted. There were some three hundred persons and more who went to do business out of Florence, and [so did] many other masters in many crafts, and stone and carpentry masters.

There were then in Florence 146 bakeries. And from the [amount of the] tax on grinding and through [information furnished by] the bakers we find that the city within the walls needed 140 *moggia* of grain every day. By this one can estimate how much was needed yearly, not to mention the fact that the larger part of the rich, noble, and well-to-do citizens with their families spent four months a year in the country, and some of them a still longer period.

We also find that in the year 1280, when the city was in a good and happy condition, it needed some 800 *moggia* of grain a week.

Through [the amount of] the tax at the gates we find that some 55,000 *cogna* of wine entered Florence yearly, and in times of plenty about 10,000 *cogna* more.

Every year the city consumed about 4,000 oxen and calves, 60,000 mutton and sheep, 20,000 she-goats and he-goats, 30,000 pigs.

During the month of July 4,000 *some* of melons

came through Porta San Friano, and they were all distributed in the city. . . .

[Florence] within the walls was well built, with many beautiful houses, and at that period people kept building with improved techniques to obtain comfort and richness by importing designs of every kind of improvement. [They built] parish churches and churches of friars of every order, and splendid monasteries. And besides this, there was no citizen, whether commoner or magnate, who had not built or was not building in the country a large and rich estate with a very costly mansion and with fine buildings, much better than those in the city—and in this they all were committing sin,

and they were called crazy on account of their wild expenses. And yet, this was such a wonderful sight that when foreigners, not accustomed to [cities like] Florence, came from abroad, they usually believed that all of the costly buildings and beautiful palaces which surrounded the city for three miles were part of the city in the manner of Rome—not to mention the costly palaces with towers, courts, and walled gardens farther distant, which would have been called castles in any other country. To sum up, it was estimated that within a six-mile radius around the city there were more than twice as many rich and noble mansions as in Florence.

Selection 2
The Ideal of Florentine Republicanism

A later and more sophisticated view of Florence's eminence was expressed by Florentine Councillor Coluccio Salutati in 1403. Here, Salutati challenges a Milanese humanist, Antonio Loschi, who was employed by the Duke of Milan. The Duke's goal was military conquest of northern and central Italy, and Salutati engaged in a "war of words" with Loschi to demonstrate that Florence's strength was founded on its love of liberty.

Anyway, let us now listen to this new violent and crazy prophet [Antonio Loschi]: "We will see your famous perseverance and Roman strength in defending a base liberty, or rather a most cruel tyranny. You are accustomed to go proudly in your Roman name and declare yourselves sons of Rome. How great is your impudence in this will have to be recorded."

We will see, you say: rather you have seen, are seeing, and will see more than Roman Perseverance and the courage of the people of Florence in defending sweetest freedom, which, as was said, is a gift from heaven which surpasses all the wealth of the world. All the people of Florence have made up their minds to defend it like life itself, even more than life, with their wealth and with the sword; to leave to their children this great inheritance we have received from our fathers; to leave it, with the aid of God, strong and unblemished. So much do we love this which you call

Source: Eugenio Garin (ed.), *Prosatori Latini del Quattrocento* (Milan: Riccardo Ricciardi, n.d.), pp. 15–23. Trans. by A. Keaney.

base—you silliest of all men—this freedom which only someone who has not known it, like you, does not appreciate. This freedom which you Lombards alone—I don't know whether by their nature, custom, or both—seem neither to love nor to desire. But you alone consider base and abhor what is the highest gift of God. I think in this you will not be able to find a single ally, even under the lordship of your prince, so great and natural is the love of freedom. Therefore it seems to me that you, not through humility but through guilt, can be, even should be, called a slave of slaves. But why do I call you a slave? From the fact that you are so pleased with your slavery that you are not ashamed to call freedom base, and—even more stupidly—do not hesitate to call it a most cruel tyranny. . . . Have you by chance ever known any freedom, in Italy or elsewhere, purer and freer than that of Florence—a freedom which can, I will not say be surpassed, but even paralleled? . . .

I am well aware that freedom, the guardian of the laws, is burdensome and can appear to be slavery: it appears so to unbridled youth which lusts to run about freely under the guide of the passions, and so I well understand how you and people like you not only do not comprehend what freedom is but abhor its name and its substance. Livy is witness to this when, in his firm style, he records the traitorous plot to restore the kings: "There were," he writes, "among the youth of Rome some adolescents of no low status who had enjoyed uncontrolled license under the kings, of the same age as and companions to the young Tarquins, used to living by royal customs. They considered equality of rights license and complained that the freedom of others was directed toward enslaving them." These and things like these which that great man wrote, I think that you, given the curiosity men have about things they desire, have long mediated on until you consider freedom, the sweetest of gifts, the most cruel tyranny. You call base to the utmost degree a good so great that there can be nothing more beautiful than it. The stupidity and falsity of all this I would leave to you yourself to judge, if you represented a single person. I am instead constrained to show it to all our readers.

Because you seem to me to deny that the people of Florence are of Roman descent, tell me, please, where have you found the contrary? Because you don't want to concede what all of Italy, you excepted, concedes—what no one outside of you, horrible beast, ever contradicted and what the city of Rome and Roman leaders never deny at any time. They consider us to be and call us sons, flesh of their flesh, bone of their bone. And because you shamefully have called into doubt all of this with supreme stupidity, I want to relate what I think of the origin of so great a city. I will use as confirmation the great writers whom I can adduce so that I can take away from you the possibility of being delirious and offer you the opportunity to think correctly.

When relating the origin of the city of Florence, which is an obscure event, buried by the great antiquity of time, doubtless one might be led to believe, as usually happens, that this most glorious people, this most celebrated city, are descended from a small, but not ignoble, source. But since it is known that the most ancient population of Fiesole came into this city, either in war, as is the

tradition, or in peace, and that being mountain dwellers they were led by the beauty of the place to abandon their own settlements, there can be no doubt but that our city has a beginning even more impressive than could have been thought. Nor should it cause surprise that the population fled here. In fact, who knows—tell me—of the first beginning of Rome? We read that Evander and the Arcadians, because they were called to Italy by the Fates through the authority of Carmenta, coming in by the river Tiber, found in the place where Rome was founded, a city called in Latin Valentia. The Arcadians, translating the meaning of the name in Greek, said Rome instead of Valentia. For this reason, some have thought that the name of Rome was derived from this. The founder of the city was really called Romus and not Romulus, from which comes Roma and not Romula. But who could ever know who was the founder of that most ancient village called Valentia? Who could assign the true beginning of that village? As it is our hereditary fate that our first origin remains unknown, so is it the case with Rome. This remains the most valid argument for its antiquity.

Further, that our city had Roman founders is inferred from very firm conjectures. In fact there is a living tradition, rendered uncertain because of its age, that the city of Florence was a Roman work. In the city there is a Capitol, and near the Capitol a Forum: there is a Circus and a place called the Baths. There is a section called Parione, a place called Capacia, a temple, once famous, of Mars, who the pagans believed was the found of the Roman race: that temple is not in the Greek or Etruscan style, but in the Roman. And I will add a further sign of our origin; it no longer survives but existed up to the last third of the fourteenth century. Near the Ponte Vecchio, there was visible an equestrian statue of Mars, which the people preserved in memory of the Roman race and which the violence of the waters carried away together with three bridges, seventy years ago. There still remain the arches and the traces of the aqueduct made in the custom of our fathers who by means of such constructions brought sweet waters for general use. Since there are all these traces of Roma, since there are Roman names, and imitations of Roman customs, who will dare to say that the founders of all this were not Romans, when there survives so solid a documentation of this celebrated tradition? There still exist the round towers, the defences of the city gates now joined to the bishop's residence, and there are such that one who has visited Rome will not only support this claim but will swear that they are Romans—and not only because of the material which is the same with which were made the walls of Rome (that is to say, bricks and stones) but also because of their shape.

It is not then surprising that, based on so many elements, the tradition has remained constant and inextinguishable that our city was a Roman construction. . . . Thus it is the height of stupidity to doubt that Florence was the work of the Romans. . . .

To turn now to your arguments, you add: "We will see that empty and windy boasting and Florentine insolence, and we will learn how much the praise you people usurp, more than any mortal being, corresponds to true valor." You call "windy" and "empty" Florentine insolence. And who will be able to say that the Florentine government made any boasts in the letters it sent all around the world. Boasting looks to the future,

and this we leave to you and those like you. In fact it is characteristic of Florentine seriousness not to go boasting emptily for the future, as you do, with your divinations: these we postpone to another occasion. If, as I believe, the intention of boasting and insolence is to glorify one's own merits, there is no prince in Italy nor people in the world which can, with greater justice and truth, glorify itself for its undertakings in war and peace (and which, anyway, has ever put less importance on exalting itself) than Florence. On the other side, there is no glory less empty and windy than that which comes from proper merits. The things which this people has accomplished by fighting in defence of its own liberty, as has happened many times, or to remain loyal to its agreements, as it has always done, will it not perhaps be legitimate to record, without offending anyone, as an exhortation and example to others? And perhaps empty and windy is boasting founded on truth. If I wanted to collect here the acts and words of your leader (for the moment I ignore yours), those undertakings of which he boasts insolently, the result would be, believe me, that nothing like that could be imputed to the people of Florence in public or in private, except that, unlike your habit, they don't go inventing lies. . . .

Selection 3
The Poor Demand Relief from Taxes (1369)

Civic pride and love of liberty were not the only factors central to the identity of Florence. The state demanded upkeep. Wealthy merchants and other solvent city-dwellers were obliged to pay taxes, but the poor often believed that disproportionate tax burdens fell on them—rather than on those who could best afford to pay. This appeal, taken from a document in the Florentine archives, lays out their case and its rationale.

Lord priors of Florence! You should do something about the taxes which the poor people of Florence must pay, the forced loans and the extra levies. . . . If you don't do something, you will discover that no one in Florence will be able to save you. There will be an uprising if these forced loans

Source: Gene Brucker (ed.), *The Society of Renaissance Florence: A Documentary Study* (New York: Harper & Row, Inc., 1971), pp. 233–234.

and special levies are not reduced, for there is great privation here. People are living in misery since they earn little and prices have been so high for thirteen months and more. Just think about those who have three or four or five children, and who are assessed two or three florins, and who have to live from the labor of their hands and those of their wives. . . . How can they stay here and live? . . .

II. ECONOMIC LIFE
AND THE IMPLICATIONS OF FISCAL POLICY

Economic fortune and social mobility were closely intertwined during the Renaissance. It was possible, even in a single generation, for a family or individual to rise from poverty to great wealth, and family members would document such occurrences. Of course, the reverse also was true, but slides from wealth to destitution were recorded far less frequently.

Economic practices rooted in trade and commerce extended beyond the city's walls to the countryside. Arguments were put forth in favor of the expansion of trade beyond borders. For nations whose prosperity rested on commerce, these justifications carried enormous weight. It also should be noted that the expansion of trade helped further the growth of colonial empires. Trade provided a rationale for exploration, as well as encouragement for settlers to go abroad.

Selection 4
The Mercantile Career of Paolo Morelli

Following Paolo Morelli's death in 1374, his son Giovanni described Paolo's success. In this selection from Giovanni's diary, it can be seen that Paolo overcame enormous obstacles and built a vast fortune.

[Giovanni Morelli describes the business career of his father Paolo (1335–1374).] His brothers all died of the plague in the great epidemic of 1363; they all died within the space of twenty days. . . . Two [brothers] were involved in the woad trade and in dyeing: they had investments of some 15,000 florins [in these enterprises]. . . . The third brother . . . was a usurer and he did little else. He lent money in Florence and in the *contado* [the rural district around the city], to poor laborers and also to great and powerful men. . . .

Paolo, young, inexperienced, and alone . . . frightened by the death of his [brothers] and in fear of his own life, found himself in great confusion as a result of the need to collect credits worth thousands of florins. Many of the creditors and the employees of the company, who had their affairs in their heads, had died. Paolo had to search for these credits in Florence and the *contado*, and beyond, in Arezzo, Borgo [S. Sepulcro], Siena,

Pisa, and in other foreign parts. He also had to retrieve merchandise and sell it and take charge of everything. . . . He had to recover capital investments, and the usurious loans made by Calandro in various parts of Florence and the *contado*. Concerning this, he was involved in litigation with the bishop and with prominent citizens of Florence. . . . In addition to this, he was engaged in the manufacture of woolen cloth, as a partner of Tommaso di Guccio and others. He was also involved in *Monte* investments, in exchange and letters of credit, in the importation of French wool, and many other enterprises. . . .

He administered all of his affairs prudently . . . and if it had pleased God to give him another ten years of life, he would have become rich and would have amassed a fortune of 50,000 florins. . . . But just when his affairs were flourishing, he rendered his soul to God, on June 14, 1374. He had been married for ten years and six months. . . . In his testament, he bequeathed property worth 20,000 florins. . . . He was buried with great honors in S. Croce, in the tomb with his father and brothers. . . .

Source: Gene Brucker (ed.), *The Society of Renaissance Florence: A Documentary Study* (New York: Harper & Row, Inc., 1971), pp. 14–15.

Figure 31. *Merchants Clearing Accounts* (from a 15th-century French miniature). This sixteenth-century depiction of merchants clearing accounts gives a sense of the increasingly complicated exchanges among businessmen that were necessary as commerce expanded during Renaissance and early modern times.

Figure 32. Jan Gossaert, *Portrait of a Merchant* (1530). We can gain a sense of the early modern merchant not only from his writings but also from the art of the age. This splendid portrait suggests both the wealth of the subject and the growing importance to his profession of the paperwork that dominates his walls as well as his desk.

Selection 5
Insolvencies at the Exchange at Antwerp (1570)

The Fuggers of Augsburg were great Renaissance bankers. Their confidential agents provided them with some of the most detailed eyewitness accounts of the Renaissance era. This report documents a number of bankruptcies and demonstrates the interconnectedness of banking houses throughout Europe.

From Antwerp, the 9th day of December 1570

Here the Genoese have arranged a competition at the Exchange and because of it two Genoese houses have gone bankrupt this week: they are Giovanni Grimaldi and then Pedro Francesco et Pedro Christophoro Spinola, who have behind them all the Germans here. It has always been regarded as a well-established business, and has long traded in this town. The creditors keep of good cheer. It is, however, to be feared that it may

Source: Victor von Klarvill (ed.), *The Fugger Newsletters: Being a selection of unpublished letters from the Correspondents of the House of Fugger during the years 1568–1605,* trans. by Pauline de Chary (New York: Putnam's Sons, 1924), pp. 13–14.

be with this as with other bankruptcies. At first there is ever enough on hand, but in the end no one can obtain anything. The Spinola did show their books to the creditors, but would not deliver them, saying that their agent in Spain is still in a good position. They assert that they are not in difficulties on this account, and also that this came upon them unexpectedly. Therewith the creditors have to be content for the nonce. But they have had the books sealed up and have delivered them to a notary for custody. This bankruptcy has put an end to credit among the Genoese. Within the space of a few years many bankruptcies have taken place, but I have never seen such excitement on the Exchange as there is regarding this. They are owing a large amount, but no one knows how much, for their books have not as yet been balanced. Grimaldi are said to be indebted for 80,000 ducats.

It will probably not end with these two, but they will drag down others of their nation with them.

Herewith your Honour has a list of the Genoese who have become insolvent at Cambray, where these days is held the Besançon payment. This may truly be called a competition. Time will show which of these scoundrels wins the booty, and perhaps the gallows will be their summer dwelling.

The following bankruptcies are reported in letters from Lyons of the 29th day of November: Nicolo Giustiniani & Stefano Rizierola, Tomaso Spinola, fu de Niro, Giovanni Antonio & Girolamo Grimaldi, Jacopo Fiesco & Antonio Lescaro di Messina, Antonio & Tommaso de Franchi di Palermo. Bills have been protested—to Giovanni Francesco & Antonio Fornari di Genova, 11,000 scudi and Gentili di Napoli, for the same amount.

Selection 6
English Cloth for the Continent

The wars that plagued Europe throughout the Renaissance era created economic dearth as well. This Fugger agent in London, writing at the end of the sixteenth century, reveals guarded optimism over the speculation in cloth and other goods.

London, July 5, 1598

As for the peace between us and Spain it is universally talked of even at Court. All depends upon what Her Majesty's representatives bring back from France, and their return is awaited with great eagerness. If they bring good news, then various great Lords and Earls of the Council will be sent to France to continue negotiations with that country.

Two vessels have just come from Zante and two from Patras laden with currants and muscatel and two from San Lucar with 200 casks of wine. They say that the Earl of Cumberland has taken the island of Teneriffe in the Canaries. Whether this is true time will show.

Source: George T. Matthews (ed.), *The Fugger Newsletters* (New York: Capricorn Books, Inc., 1959), p. 232.

Three vessels have arrived this week from Venice laden with currants, muscatel and the like.

Up to now the English merchants have not yet decided what place to select for their cloth trade, for the deputies they sent for this purpose to Holland have not yet returned. Last Thursday four ships with the usual cargoes left here for Staden and Hamburg, but they are still lying off the mouth of the Thames, as an express messenger was sent after them yesterday to stop them. The reason is this, that the Merchant Adventurers have heard that they are not wanted at Hamburg and will not be allowed to send foreign goods there. How this will be settled we shall know in time. A finer crop of corn stands in the fields than has been seen for twenty years, thank God. May the Almighty grant a continuance of fine weather so that we may be freed from the scarcity!

Selection 7
The Freedom of the Seas (1609)

Hugo Grotius

The Dutch were foremost among the nations of traders in the seventeenth century. It was a Dutch lawyer and political theorist, Hugo Grotius, who penned the most eloquent defense of freedom of the seas. The sea, Grotius wrote, "belonged" to no one. His work provided a legal rationale for the expansion of the great Dutch trading enterprises, the West and East India Companies.

By the Law of Nations navigation is free to all persons whatsoever

My intention is to demonstrate briefly and clearly that the Dutch—that is to say, the subjects of the United Netherlands—have the right to sail to the East Indies, as they are now doing, and to engage in trade with the people there. I shall base my argument on the following most specific and unimpeachable axiom of the Law of Nations, called a primary rule or first principle, the spirit of which is self-evident and immutable, to wit: Every nation is free to travel to every other nation, and to trade with it.

God Himself says this speaking through the voice of nature; and inasmuch as it is not His will to have Nature supply every place with all the necessaries of life, He ordains that some nations excel in one art and others in another. Why is this His will, except it be that He wished human friendships to be engendered by mutual needs and resources, lest individuals deeming themselves entirely sufficient unto themselves should for that very reason be rendered unsociable? So by the decree of divine justice it was brought about that one people should supply the needs of another, in order, as Pliny the Roman writer says, that in this way, whatever has been produced anywhere should seem to have been destined for all. Vergil also sings in this wise:

Source: Hugo Grotius, *The Freedom of the Seas, or The Right which belongs to the Dutch to Take Part in the East India Trade*, ed. by James Brown Scott, trans. by Ralph Van Deman Magoffin (New York: Oxford University Press, 1916), pp. 7–10, 61–64, 72–76.

"*Not every plant on every soil will grow,*"

and in another place:

"*Let others better mould the running mass Of metals,*" etc.

Those therefore who deny this law, destroy this most praiseworthy bond of human fellowship, remove the opportunities for doing mutual service, in a word do violence to Nature herself. For do not the ocean, navigable in every direction with which God has encompassed all the earth, and the regular and the occasional winds which blow now from one quarter and now from another, offer sufficient proof that Nature has given to all peoples a right of access to all other peoples? Seneca thinks this is Nature's greatest service, that by the wind she united the widely scattered peoples, and yet did so distribute all her products over the earth that commercial intercourse was a necessity to mankind. Therefore this right belongs equally to all nations. Indeed the most famous jurists extend its application so far as to deny that any state or any ruler can debar foreigners from having access to their subjects and trading with them. Hence is derived that law of hospitality which is of the highest sanctity; hence the complaint of the poet Vergil:

"*What men, what monsters, what inhuman race,*
What laws, what barbarous customs of the place,
Shut up a desert shore to drowning men,
And drive us to the cruel seas again."

And:

"*To beg what you without your want may spare—*
The common water, and the common air."

We know that certain wars have arisen over this very matter; such for example as the war of the Megarians against the Athenians, and that of the Bolognese against the Venetians. Again, Victoria holds that the Spaniards could have shown just reasons for making war upon the Aztecs and the Indians in America, more plausible reasons certainly than were alleged, if they really were prevented from traveling or sojourning among those peoples, and were denied the right to share in those things which by the Law of Nations or by Custom are common to all, and finally if they were debarred from trade.

We read of a similar case in the history of Moses, which we find mentioned also in the writings of Augustine, where the Israelites justly smote with the edge of the sword the Amorites because they had denied the Israelites an innocent passage through their territory, a right which according to the Law of Human Society ought in all justice to have been allowed. In defense of this principle Hercules attacked the king of Orchomenus in Boeotia; and the Greeks under their leader Agamemnon waged war against the king of Mysia on the ground that, as Baldus has said, high roads were free by nature. Again, as we read in Tacitus, the Germans accused the Romans of "preventing all intercourse between them and of closing up to them the rivers and roads, and almost the very air of heaven." When in days gone by the Christians made crusades against the Saracens, no other pretext was so welcome or so plausible as that they were denied by the infidels free access to the Holy Land.

It follows therefore that the Portuguese, even if they had been sovereigns in those parts to which the Dutch make voyages, would nevertheless be doing them an injury if they should forbid them access to those places and from trading there.

Is it not then an incalculably greater injury for nations which desire reciprocal commercial relations to be debarred therefrom by the acts of those who are sovereigns neither of the nations interested, nor of the element over which their connecting high road runs? Is not that the very cause which for the most part prompts us to execrate robbers and pirates, namely, that they beset and infest our trade routes?

By the Law of Nations trade is free to all persons whatsoever

If however the Portuguese claim that they have an exclusive right to trade with the East Indies, their claim will be refuted by practically all the same arguments which already have been brought forward. Nevertheless I shall repeat them briefly, and apply them to this particular claim.

By the law of nations the principle was introduced that the opportunity to engage in trade, of which no one can be deprived, should be free to all men. This principle, inasmuch as its application was straightway necessary after the distinctions of private ownerships were made, can therefore be seen to have had a very remote origin. Aristotle, in a very clever phrase, in his work entitled the Politics, has said that the art of exchange is a completion of the independence which Nature requires. Therefore trade ought to be common to all according to the law of nations, not only in a negative but also in a positive, or as the jurists say, affirmative sense. The things that come under the former category are subject to change, those of the latter category are not. This statement is to be explained in the following way.

Nature had given all things to all men. But since men were prevented from using many things which were desirable in every day life because they lived so far apart, and because, as we have said above, everything was not found everywhere, it was necessary to transport things from one place to another; not that there was yet an interchange of commodities, but that people were accustomed to make reciprocal use of things found in one another's territory according to their own judgment. They say that trade arose among the Chinese in about this way. Things were deposited at places out in the desert and left to the good faith and conscience of those who exchanged things of their own for what they took.

But when movables passed into private ownership (a change brought about by necessity, as has been explained above), straightway there arose a method of exchange by which the lack of one person was supplemented by that of which another person had an oversupply. Hence commerce was born out of necessity for the commodities of life, as Pliny shows by a citation from Homer. But after immovables also began to be recognized as private property, the consequent annihilation of universal community of use made commerce a necessity not only between men whose habitations were far apart but even between men who were neighbors; and in order that trade might be carried on more easily, somewhat later they invented money, which, as the derivation of the word shows, is a civic institution.

Therefore the universal basis of all contracts, namely exchange, is derived from nature; but some particular kinds of exchange, and the money payment itself, are derived from law; although the older commentators on the law have not made this distinction sufficiently clear. Nevertheless all authorities agree that the ownership of things, particularly of movables, arises out of the primary law of nations, and that all contracts in which a price is not mentioned, are derived from the same source. The philosophers distinguish two kinds of exchange using Greek words which we shall take the liberty to translate as "wholesale" and "retail" trade. The former, as the Greek word shows, signifies trade or exchange between widely separated nations, and it ranks first in the order of Nature, as is shown in Plato's Republic. The latter seems to be the same kind of exchange that Aristotle calls by another Greek word which means retail or shop trade between citizens. Aristotle makes a further division of wholesale trade into overland and overseas trade. But of the two, retail trade is the more petty and sordid, and wholesale the more honorable; but most honorable of all is the wholesale overseas trade, because it makes so many people sharers in so many things.

Hence Ulpian says that the maintenance of ships is the highest duty of a state, because it is an absolutely natural necessity, but that the maintenance of hucksters has not the same value. In another place Aristotle says: "For the art of exchange extends to all possessions, and it arises at first in a natural manner from the circumstance

that some have too little, others too much." And Seneca is also to be cited in this connection for he has said that buying and selling is the law of nations.

Therefore freedom of trade is based on a primitive right of nations which has a natural and permanent cause; and so that right cannot be destroyed, or at all events it may not be destroyed except by the consent of all nations. For surely no one nation may justly oppose in any way two nations that desire to enter into a contract with each other.

The Dutch must maintain their right of trade with the East Indies by peace, by treaty, or by war

Wherefore since both law and equity demand that trade with the East Indies be as free to us as to any one else, it follows that we are to maintain at all hazards that freedom which is ours by nature, either by coming to a peace agreement with the Spaniards, or by concluding a treaty, or by continuing the war. So far as peace is concerned, it is well known that there are two kinds of peace, one made on terms of equality, the other on unequal terms. The Greeks call the former kind a compact between equals, the latter an enjoined truce; the former is meant for high souled men, the latter for servile spirits. Demosthenes in his speech on the liberty of the Rhodians says that it was necessary for those who wished to be free to keep away from treaties which were imposed upon them, because such treaties were almost the same as slavery. Such conditions are all those by which one party is lessened in its own right, according to the definition of Isocrates. For if, as Cicero says, wars must be undertaken in order that people may live in peace unharmed, it follows that peace ought to mean not an agreement which entails slavery, but an undisturbed liberty, especially as peace and justice according to the opinion of many philosophers and theologians differ more in name than in fact, and as peace is a harmonious agreement based not on individual whim, but on well ordered regulations.

If however a truce is arranged for, it is quite clear from the very nature of a truce, that during its continuance no one's condition ought to change for the worse, inasmuch as both parties stand on the equivalent of a *uti possidetis*.

But if we are driven into war by the injustice of our enemies, the justice of our cause ought to bring hope and confidence in a happy outcome. "For," as Demosthenes has said, "every one fights his hardest to recover what he has lost; but when men endeavor to gain at the expense of others it is not so." The Emperor Alexander has expressed his idea in this way: "Those who begin unjust deeds, must bear the greatest blame; but those who repel aggressors are twice armed, both with courage because of their just cause, and with the highest hope because they are not doing a wrong, but are warding off a wrong."

Therefore, if it be necessary, arise, O nation unconquered on the sea, and fight boldly, not only for your own liberty, but for that of the human race. "Nor let it fright thee that their fleet is winged, each ship, with an hundred oars. The sea whereon it sails will have none of it. And though the prows bear figures threatening to cast rocks such as Centaurs throw, thou shalt find them but hollow planks and painted terrors. 'Tis his cause that makes or mars a soldier's strength. If the cause be not just, shame strikes the weapon from his hands."

If many writers, Augustine himself among them, believed it was right to take up arms because innocent passage was refused across foreign territory, how much more justly will arms be taken up against those from whom the demand is made of the common and innocent use of the sea, which by the law of nature is common to all? If those nations which interdicted others from trade on their own soil are justly attacked, what of those nations which separate by force and interrupt the mutual intercourse of peoples over whom they have no rights at all? If this case should be taken into court, there can be no doubt what opinion ought to be anticipated from a just judge. The praetor's law says: "I forbid force to be used in preventing any one from sailing a ship or a boat on a public river, or from unloading his cargo on the bank." The commentators say that the injunction must be applied in the same manner to the sea and to the seashore. Labeo, for example, in commenting on the praetor's edict, "Let nothing be done in a public river or on its bank, by which a landing or a channel for shipping be obstructed," said there was a similar interdict which applied to the sea, namely, "Let nothing be done on the sea or on the seashore by which a harbor, a landing, or a channel for shipping be obstructed."

Nay more, after such a prohibition, if, namely, a man be prevented from navigating the sea, or not allowed to sell or to make use of his own wares and products, Ulpian says that he can bring an action for damages on that ground. Also the theologians and the casuists agree that he who prevents another from buying or selling, or who puts his private interests before the public and common interests, or who in any way hinders another in the use of something which is his by common right, is held in damages to complete restitution in an amount fixed by an honorable arbitrator.

Following these principles a good judge would award to the Dutch the freedom of trade, and would forbid the Portuguese and others from using force to hinder that freedom, and would order the payment of just damages. But when a judgment which would be rendered in a court cannot be obtained, it should with justice be demanded in a war. Augustine acknowledges this when he says: "The injustice of an adversary brings a just war." Cicero also says: "There are two ways of settling a dispute; first, by discussion; second, by physical force; we must resort to force only in case we may not avail ourselves of discussion." And King Theodoric says: "Recourse must then be had to arms when justice can find no lodgment in an adversary's heart." Pomponius, however, has handed down a decision which has more bearing on our argument than any of the citations already made. He declared that the man who seized a thing common to all to the prejudice of every one else must be forcibly prevented from so doing. The theologians also say that just as war is righteously undertaken in defense of individual property, so no less righteously is it undertaken in behalf of the use of those things which by natural law ought to be common property. Therefore he who closes up roads and hinders the export of merchandise ought to be prevented from so doing *via facti*, even without waiting for any public authority.

Since these things are so, there need not be the slightest fear that God will prosper the efforts of those who violate that most stable law of nature which He himself has instituted, or that even men will allow those to go unpunished who for the sake alone of private gain oppose a common benefit of the human race.

Selection 8
Advice to Planters in New Netherland

A new emphasis on colonization was one outgrowth of the expansion of trade. The directors of the Dutch West India Company managed the province of "New Netherland," which was founded in 1626. It lasted until it was taken over by the English in 1664, following war with Holland; after that it was renamed "New York." This selection is from a report by Cornelius van Tienhoven, Secretary of the Province.

Information relative to taking up land in New Netherland, in the form of colonies or private boweries (1650)

If any man be disposed to begin either by himself or others, Colonies, Bouweries or Plantations in New Netherland, lying in the Latitude of one and forty degrees and a half, he shall first have to inform himself fully of the situation of the lands lying on rivers, havens and Bays, in order thus to select the most suitable and particularly the most convenient grounds: It is therefore to be borne in mind that the lands in New Netherland are not all level & flat and adapted to raising of grain, inasmuch as they are, with the exception of some few flatts, generally covered with timber, in divers places also with large & small stones.

In order, then first to describe those lands which are actually the most convenient and best adapted for early occupancy, where and how located, I shall enumerate the following places, and commend the remainder to the consideration of proprietors of this country.

I begin then at the most easterly corner of Long Island, being a point situate on the Main Ocean, inclosing within, westward, a large inland sea adorned with divers fair havens and bays, fit for all sorts of craft; this Point is entirely covered with Trees, without any flatts and is somewhat hilly and

stoney, very convenient for Cod fishing, which is most successfully followed by the Natives during the Season.

This Point is also well adapted to secure the trade of the Indians in Wampum (the mine of New Netherland) since in and about the abovementioned sea and the islands therein situate, lie the cockles whereof Wampum is made from which great profit could be realized by those who would plant a Colonie or hamlet on the aforesaid hook for the cultivation of the land, for raising all sorts of cattle, for fishing, and the Wampum trade.

It would be necessary, in such case, to settle on the aforesaid land some persons thoroughly conversant with agriculture and others with the fishery.

Oyster bay, so called from the great abundance of fine and delicate oysters which are found there. This bay is about a short mile across, or in width at the mouth; deep and navigable, without either rocks or sands, runs westward in proportion, and divides itself into two rivers, which are broad and clear, on which said rivers lie fine maize lands, formerly cultivated by the Indians, some of which they still work; they could be had for a trifle. This land is situate on such beautiful bay, and rivers that it could at little cost be converted into good farms fit for the plough; there are here, also, some fine hay valleys.

Martin Gerritsen's bay or *Martinnehouck*, is much deeper and wider than Oyster bay, and runs westward in, divides into three rivers, two of

Source: E. B. O'Callaghan (ed.), *The Documentary History of the State of New York*, vol. 4 (Albany, N.Y.: Charles van Benthuysen, 1851), pp. 27–36.

which are navigable; the smallest stream runs up in front of the Indian village called Martinne houck, where they have their plantations. This tribe is not strong, and consists of about 30 families. In and about this bay there were formerly great numbers of Indian Plantations, which now lie waste and vacant. This land is mostly level and of good quality, well adapted for grain and rearing of all sorts of cattle; on the rivers are numerous valleys of sweet and salt meadows; all sorts of river fish are also caught there.

Schout's bay, on the East river, also very open and navigable, with one river running into it; on said river are also fine maize lands, level and not stony, with right beautiful valleys. Beyond said river is a very convenient hook of land, somewhat large, encircled by a large valley and river, where all descriptions of cattle can be reared and fed, such convenience being a great accommodation for the settlers, who otherwise must search for their cattle frequently several days in the bush.

The country on the East river between Greenwich and the island Manhattans, is for the most part covered with trees, but yet flat and suitable land, with numerous streams and valleys, right good soil for grain, together with fresh hay and meadow lands.

Wiequaeskeck, on the North river, five miles above New Amsterdam is very good and suitable land for agriculture, very extensive maize land, on which the Indians have planted—proceeding from the shore and inland 'tis flat and mostly level, well watered by small streams and running springs. This land lies between the Sintinck and Armonck streams situate between the East and north rivers.

In the Bay of the North river, about two miles from Sandy Hook, lies an inlet or small bay; on the south shore of said bay, called Neyswesinck, there are also right good maize lands which have not been cultivated by the natives for a long time. This district is well adapted for raising and feeding all sorts of cattle, and is esteemed by many not ill-adapted for fisheries; a good trade in furs could also be carried on there, and 'tis likewise accessible to all large vessels coming from sea, which are often obliged to lie to or anchor behind Sandy Hook,

either in consequence of contrary winds, or for want of a pilot.

The district inhabited by a nation called Raritangs, is situate on a fresh water river, that flows through the centre of the low land which the Indians cultivated. This vacant territory lies between two high mountains, far distant the one from the other. This is the handsomest and pleasantest country that man can behold, it furnished the Indians with abundance of maize, beans, pumpkins, and other fruits. This district was abandoned by the natives for two reasons; the first and principal is, that finding themselves unable to resist the Southern Indians, they migrated further inland; the second, because this country was flooded every spring like Renselaer's colonie, frequently spoiling and destroying their supplies of maize which were stored in holes under ground.

Through this valley pass large numbers of all sorts of tribes, on their way north or east, this land is therefore not only adapted for raising grain and rearing all description of cattle, but also very convenient for trade with the Indians.

On both sides of the South bay and South river also lie some handsome lands, not only suitable but very convenient for agriculture and trade.

I have already stated where the first Colonists should, in my opinion, settle, regard being had to the convenience of those lands in the possession of which other nations being anticipated, they would not be able to extend their pretended limits further, and great peace and security would be afforded to the inhabitants. I shall here further state the time when those emigrating hence to and arriving in New Netherland will take up land, and how each shall afterwards earn a living and settle in the most economical manner according to the fashion of the country.

Boors and others who are obliged to work at first in Colonies ought to sail from this country in the fore or latter part of winter, in order to arrive with God's help in New Netherland early in the Spring, as in March, or at latest in April, so as to be able to plant during that summer, garden vegetables, maize and beans, and moreover employ the whole summer in clearing land and building cottages as I shall hereafter describe.

All then who arrive in New Netherland must immediately set about preparing the soil, so as to be able, if possible to plant some winter grain, and to proceed the next winter to cut and clear the timber. The trees are usually felled from the stump, cut up and burnt in the field, unless such as are suitable for building, for palisades, posts, and rails, which must be prepared during winter, so as to be set up in the spring on the new made land which is intended to be sown, in order that the cattle may not in any wise injure the crops. In most lands is found a certain root, called red Wortel, which must, before ploughing, be extirpated with a hoe, expressly made for that purpose. This being done in the winter, some plough right around the stumps, should time or circumstances not allow these to be removed; others plant tobacco, maize and beans, at first. The soil even thus becomes very mellow, and they sow winter grain the next fall. From tobacco, can be realized some of the expenses incurred in clearing the land. Then maize and beans help to support both men and cattle. The farmer having thus begun, must endeavour, every year, to clear as much new land as he possibly can, and sow it with such seed as he considers most suitable.

It is not necessary that the husbandman should take up much stock in the beginning, since clearing land and other necessary labor do not permit him to save much hay and to build barns for stabling. One pair of draft horses or a yoke of oxen only is necessary, to ride the planks for buildings or palisades or rails from the land to the place where they are to be set.

The farmer can get all sorts of cattle in the course of the second summer when he will have more leisure to cut and bring home hay, also to build barns and houses for men and cattle.

Of the building of houses at first

Before beginning to build, it will above all things be necessary to select a well located spot, either on some river or bay, suitable for the settlement of a village or hamlet. This is previously properly surveyed and divided into lots, with good streets according to the situation of the place. This hamlet can be fenced all round with high palisades or long boards and closed with gates, which is advantageous in case of attack by the natives who heretofore used to exhibit their insolence in new plantations.

Outside the village or hamlet other land must be laid out which can in general be fenced and prepared at the most trifling expense.

Those in New Netherland and especially in New England, who have no means to build farm houses at first according to their wishes, dig a square pit in the ground, cellar fashion, 6 or 7 feet deep, as long and as broad as they think proper, case the earth inside with wood all round the wall, and line the wood with the bark of trees or something else to prevent the caving in of the earth; floor this cellar with plank and wainscot it overhead for a ceiling, raise a roof of spars clear up and cover the spars with bark or green sods, so that they can live dry and warm in these houses with their entire families for two, three and four years, it being understood that partitions are run through those cellars which are adapted to the size of the family. The wealthy and principal men in New England, in the beginning of the Colonies, commenced their first dwelling houses in this fashion for two reasons; firstly, in order not to waste time building and not to want food the next season; secondly, in order not to discourage poorer laboring people whom they brought over in numbers from Fatherland. In the course of 3 @ 4 years, when the country became adapted to agriculture, they built themselves handsome houses, spending on them several thousands.

After the houses are built in the above described manner or otherwise according to each person's means and fancy, gardens are made, and planted in season with all sorts of pot herbs, principally parsnips, carrots, and cabbage, which bring great plenty into the husbandman's dwelling. The maize can serve as bread for men, and food for cattle.

The hogs, after having picked up their food for some months in the woods, are crammed with corn in the fall; when fat they are killed and furnish a very hard and clean pork; a good article for the husbandman who gradually and in time begins to purchase horses and cows with the produce of his grain and the increase of his hogs, and instead of a cellar as aforesaid, builds good farm houses and barns.

Of the necessary Cattle

The cattle necessary in a Colonie or private Bouwery in New Netherland, are good mares and sound stallions.

Yoke oxen for the plough, inasmuch as in new lands full of roots, oxen go forward steadily under the plough, and horses stand still, or with a start break the harness in pieces.

Milch cows of kindly disposition and good bulls, sheep, sows, etc. Fowls are well adapted to Bouweries.

These Cattle are abundant in New Netherland and especially in New England and to be had at a reasonable price, except sheep which the English do not sell and are rare in New Netherland.

Prices of Cattle

In New Netherland;

A young mare with her 2d or third foal costs	fl. 150 to 160 =		$60
A 4 to 5 year old stallion about	130	=	52
A milch cow with her 2d or 3d calf	100	=	40
A year old sow	20 to 24	=	8 to 10
A sheep, being an ewe	20 to 24		

In New England;

A good mare sells for	fl. 100 to 120	
A stallion	100	
A milch cow		60 to 70
A yearling sow		12 to 14

Sheep are not sold here.

It is to be observed that in a Colonie each Farmer has to be provided by his Landlord with at least one yoke of oxen or with two mares in their stead two cows, one or two sows, for the purpose of increase, and the use of the farm and the support of his family.

If the above cattle multiply in course of time with God's blessing the Bouweries can be fully stocked with necessary cattle, and new Bouweries set off with the remainder, as is the practice in Renselaer's Colonie and other places, as so on *de novo*, so as to lay out no money for stock.

All farming implements necessary for the land must be also procured, except wagon and plough which can be made there.

And as it is found by experience in New Netherland that farmers can with difficulty obtain from the soil enough to provide themselves with necessary victuals and support, those who propose planting Colonies must supply their farmers and families with necessary food for at least two to three years, if not altogether it must be done at least in part.

Necessary supplies for the farmer

If no wheat or rye can be had for bread, maize can be always had in season from the Indians at a reasonable price. The skepel costs ordinarily 10 @ 15 stivers when bought from the Indians.

Meat	Vinegar
Pork	Pease, and
Butter or Oil instead	Beans.

Salad oil and vinegar are not easy to be had in that country except at an excessively high price from the Dutch traders.

All this being arranged it must be noted what description of people are best adapted for agriculture in New Netherland and to perform the most service and return the most profit in the beginning.

First, a person is necessary to superintend the working men; he ought to be acquainted with farming.

Industrious country people, conversant with the working and cultivation of land, and possessing a knowledge of cattle.

It would not be unprofitable to add to these some Highland boors, from the Veluwe, Gulick, Cleef, and Berg.

Northerners are a people adapted to cutting down trees and clearing land, inasmuch as they are very laborious and accustomed to work in the woods.

Northerners can do almost anything, some can build much, others a little, and construct small craft which they call yawls.

Carpenters who can lay brick.

Smiths conversant with heavy work, curing cattle and provided with suitable medicines.

One or more surgeons, according to the number of the people, with a chest well supplied with all sorts of drugs.

One or more Coopers.

A Clergyman, Comforter of the sick, or precentor who could also act as Schoolmaster.

A Wheelwright.

All other tradesmen would [be required] in time; the above mentioned mechanics are the most necessary at first. In order to promote population through such and other means, the people must be provided with Freedoms and Privileges so as to induce them to quit their Fatherland, and emigrate with their families beyond the sea to this far distant New Netherland. And as poor people have no means to defray the cost of passage and other expenses, it were desirable that wealthy individuals would expend some capital, to people this country or at their own expense remove themselves like the English of New England, with funds and a large body of working men, and provide those without means, with land, dwelling, cattle, tools and necessary support; and that, until they could derive the necessary maintenance from the soil and the increase of cattle, after which time they would be able to pay yearly a reasonable quit rent to their Lords and Masters from the effects in their possession.

By the population and cultivation of the aforesaid lands those who shall have disbursed funds for the removal of the laboring classes the purchase of cattle and all other expenses, would, in process of some years, after God had blessed the tillage, and the increase of the cattle, derive a considerable revenue in grain, meat, pork, butter, and tobacco, which form at first the earliest returns, in time can be improved by industry, such as the making pot and pearl ashes, clapboards, knees for ship building, staves, all sorts of pine and oak plank, masts for large ships, square

timber, and ash and hickory planks in which a staple trade could be established. The English of New England put this in practice, as is to be seen, after the land had been first brought to proper condition; they sell their provisions at the Caribbean Islands, staves at Madeira and the Canaries, Masts and Fish in Spain and Portugal, and bring in return all sorts of commodities, so much of which returns as they do not consume are again distributed by them throughout all the Islands known and inhabited in the Northern part of America. So that through the variety of the returns, which of necessity was received, a profitable trade is already established in New England, which can also be right well set on foot by the Netherlanders, if the population of the country were promoted.

The following is the mode pursued by the West India Company in the first planting of Bouweries

The Company, at their own cost and in their own ships conveyed several boors to New Netherland, and gave these the following terms:—

The farmer, being conveyed with his family over sea to New Netherland, was granted by the Company for the term of six years a Bouwery, which was partly cleared, and a good part of which was fit for the plough.

The company furnished the farmer a house, barn, farming implements and tools, together with four horses, four cows, sheep and pigs in proportion, the usufruct and enjoyment of which the husbandman should have during the six years, and on the expiration thereof return the number of cattle he received. The entire increase remained with the farmer. The farmer was bound to pay yearly one hundred guilders ($40) and eighty pounds of butter rent for the cleared land and bouwery.

The county people who obtained the above mentioned conditions all prospered during their residence on the Company's lands.

Afterwards the cattle belonging to the Company in New Netherland were distributed for some years among those who had no means to purchase stock.

The risk of the Cattle dying is shared in common and after the expiration of the contract, the Company receives, if the Cattle live, the number the husbandman first received, and the increase which is over, is divided half and half, by which means many people have obtained stock and even to this day, the Company have still considerable cattle among the Colonists, who make use on the above conditions of the horses in cultivating the farm; the cows serve for the increase of the stock and for the support of their families.

The foregoing is what is necessary to be communicated at present respecting the establish-

ment of one or more Colonies and relative to supplies. What regards the government and preservation of such Colonies; and what persons ought to be in authority there and who these ought to be, I leave to the wise and prudent consideration of your noble High Mightinesses. Meanwhile I pray the Creator of Heaven and Earth to endow your High Mightinesses with the Spirit of grace and wisdom, so that all your High Mightinesses' deliberations may tend to the advantage of the Country and its Inhabitants.

III. SOCIAL VALUES, NORMS, AND DEVIANCE

Throughout history, family life has shaped many social ideals and realities. The Renaissance was no different. Images of family life during the Renaissance illustrate some of the merchant's needs and beliefs, whether these pertained to faith in God or to making money.

During the Renaissance and early modern era, the state increasingly attempted to solve social ills by formulating laws aimed at controlling these problems. Activities which had not been regulated during the Middle Ages now became subject to the state's or city's scrutiny and its decrees. The extent to which such laws succeeded in their objectives is questionable. For good or ill, however, much social legislation with which we still live today originated during the Renaissance era.

Selection 9
A Mother's Advice to Her Merchant Son

Alessandra Macinghi negli Strozzi's life provides a good illustration of the perils faced by both women and men in Renaissance Italy and the fortitude with which such challenges were met. After her husband, Matteo Strozzi, died in exile in 1435, Alessandra completed the rearing of her seven children. Until her death in 1470, she corresponded with her eldest son, Filippo, a successful merchant who carried on the family's business in Naples. This letter mixes maternal concern with hard-headed business advice.

To Filippo degli Strozzi, in Naples.
In the name of God, 24 August 1447.

Dearest son. Recently I had your letter of July 16, to which I will make this reply. First I inform you that we have arranged for our Catherine to be married to the son of Parente di pier Parenti: he is worthy and virtuous, an only child, rich, 25 years

Source: Alessandra Strozzi, *Lettere di una gentildonna fiorentina del secolo XV ai figliuoli esuli*, ed. by Cesare Guasti (Florence: Casa Editrice G. C. Sansoni, 1877), pp. 3–9. Trans. by A. Keaney.

old, and has a silk workshop. He has a little political influence. For a dowry, I'm giving him 1000 florins, that is 500 which he has to have in May 1448 from the bank of Monte; the other 500 I have to give him—money and household goods—when he gets married. This will be, I believe, in November, God willing. This money is partly from you, partly from me. If I had not made this decision, there would be no marriage this year: however, whoever takes a wife wants money and I didn't find anyone willing to wait to have a dowry in 1448, and part in 1450. So giving him this 500—

money and goods—I will give him also the 500 of 1450, if she lives.

This was the correct decision to have taken. She was 16 years old, and we couldn't postpone marriage for her. We might have found a husband of higher status and family but that would have cost 1400 or 1500 florins. That would have been ruinous for you and me, and I don't know how the girl would have been happy. All things considered, I decided to make a good arrangement for the girl and not worry about other things.

She will have good status as a young woman of Florence: she has a mother-in-law and a father-in-law who are happy only when they are concerned with her happiness. O, I am not talking about Marco, her husband, who always says to her: ask for whatever you want. When she was engaged, he had cut for her a coat of soft, velour silk, and a robe of the same material: and it was the prettiest material there was in Florence: he had it done in his shop. He had made for her a garland of feathers with pearls, which came to 80 florins; and her hair-do beneath, and there were two plaits of pearls which came to 60 or more florins. When she goes out, she will have on her back more than 400 florins. And he ordered a crimson velvet bridal outfit, with long sleeves, lined with martens. And a red robe embroidered with pearls. He can't do enough of these things. She's lovely, and he wants her to appear even more so. In truth, there is no other in Florence like her: she has all the qualities, in the eyes of many. My God give her health and happiness for a long time, as is my desire.

For now I would not want to send Matteo abroad. Although he is small, I wouldn't have anybody with me, and I could fare poorly without him—at least so long as Caterina is going to get married. Then I think I will be too alone. For now, I am not minded to send him. If he wants to be good, I'll keep him here. He can't be drafted as a soldier until he's 16, and he was 11 in March. I've taken him from the abacus and he's learning to write. I can keep him in the shop, and he will stay there for this winter. Afterwards, we'll see what he wants to do. May God give him the strength which he needs.

About my dealings with the Commune, I inform you that I owe 240 florins and I am being given trouble by no less than 4 offices which have to cash the money for the Commune. For 6 months I have had nothing else to do but to go first to this office, then to that. Now, through the grace of God, I have reached an agreement with them until February: I pay, in all, 9 or so florins a month. It is expected that the new tax will come out at the end of October. Since if they oblige me, as they are saying, by paying the special tax on widows and wards, I won't have two florins. But perhaps I won't owe so much. Now that the duke is dead, the rumor is that we won't pay as much, unless the king of Aragon becomes a nuisance. He's already started near Monte Varchi, at a town called Cennina. They've already been there three weeks, and they're still apt to stay there. There was a farmer there who said that they could live for a year on the grain and stuff left there. It's said that if he recovers it, more than 40000 florins will be spent. May God provide for our needs.

Caterina says that you should send her a bit of that soap. And if there's a good water or something else to make her pretty, she asks you to send it quickly and with a person you trust, so that it won't be spoiled.

Don't be surprised if I don't write to you frequently: I am totally taken up with Caterina's business. I will be relieved when Matteo will have learned to write: but don't worry about me. Make sure to write to me occasionally if only to say that you and Niccolo are fine. I don't know how you're handling the business you have in hand, as careful as you are. God knows how displeased I was when I found I couldn't come when you were at Livorno: things like that we say mouth-to-mouth, not in a letter. May it please God that I see you safe before I die. Above all, my son, conduct yourself well, so that you may give me some consolation, since this past year your sad ways gave me so much pain. And consider your position and what Niccolo has done differently from you, that you might be worthy to kiss the ground where he puts his feet. And I say the same through love of you, that you are more obligated to him than to your father or mother, when I think what he has done for you: no one else would have done it. So be aware of it and be grateful for the kindness you and your wife have received and welcome it continuously. I don't want to spend more time in talking, that you have to listen to me every day, since you're not a child, in July you'll be 19 and that's enough. Above all, set some mony aside. It doesn't occur to me to say more. May God guard you from evil. I am not witing to Niccolo about Caterina since he has been told by Giovanni and Antonio. Greet him for me. And if you are in charge of money, handle yourself so as to receive honor. And keep your hands clean, so that I won't have more grief than I've already had.

Selection 10
A Dutch Merchant's Exhortation to His Children (1646)

Louis de Geer (b. 1587) emigrated to Holland during the Revolt of the Netherlands and amassed a fortune in textiles, ironworks, tin, and copper. Moneylending, during the Thirty Years' War, also proved lucrative. Toward the end of his life, De Geer summed up his philosophy and principles. He demonstrates that the role of faith still mattered enormously even in what was by now a highly secularized world.

Children, I prayed God in the year 1619, that He should rule over you, the unborn as well as those already born, and allow you to be reared in his fear, so I vowed—so far as God heard my prayer—to give for each child two hundred guilders yearly: God heard my prayer and notwithstanding my many sins and crimes, awakened my joy in you and allowed it to grow.

Now I write to you, this fatherly exhortation, that you also will feel forever in God's debt, and that

Source: Sherrin Marshall, *The Dutch Gentry 1500–1650*, trans. by Sherrin Marshall (Westport, Conn.: Greenwood Press, Inc., 1987), p. 91. (*Reprinted by permission of Greenwood Publishing Group, Inc., Westport, Conn., from The Dutch Gentry, 1500–1650, edited and translated by Sherrin Marshall. Copyright by Greenwood Publishing Group, Inc., and published in 1987 by Greenwood Press.*)

you will carry forward this charitable eulogy, always to remember the poor and behave righteously, and not think that your means lessen through such giving, but on the contrary, they will expand and grow, as seed that a fruitful Farmer sows.

This said story has moved me to purchase annuities for each child in the sum of 210 guilders yearly, with the understanding that the surplus 10 guilders should be for the poor of Leeuwarden. . . . You can dispose yourselves of the money, and God pray that he so rules your hearts, that he implants in you the love for the poor . . . that you will hear forever the voice of our Lord Matt. Chapter 25, verse 34 and following. There also God . . . for his dearest Son Jesu Christi, who with the Father and the H. Spirit in eternity . . . Amen. Amen. Your Father, Louys de Geer.

Figure 33. Petrus Christus, *St. Eligius as a Goldsmith* (1449). Renaissance goldsmiths played a vital part not only in training artists but also in finance. Because of the value of the merchandise they made and sold, their shops—like the one here, with customers looking in the window, as one can see in the circular mirror—were sources of capital as well as goods. In addition to providing such items as the ring he is handing to the young woman, the goldsmith might well have been a source of investment for the traders in his city.

Selection 11
The City Fathers of York (England) Regulate Trade

This passage from the York City Housebooks represents a typical concern of the York "city fathers." Their court met several times a month and regulated the affairs of all social groups within the city in a paternalistic manner. In this excerpt, dated October 13, 1626, the apprenticeships mentioned are apprenticeships for poor boys that the city funded.

It is ordered betwixt the company of milliners & pinners that the pinners shall not from & after Candlemas next sell any thread buttons or silk buttons nor any other buttons but tin brass and Jet And the milliners shall not from & after candlemas next sell any pins but such as they can make themselves.

Source: York City Archives, B. 35 (*City of York House Book 1625–1637*), folio 24r; courtesy of Diane Willen.

And now it is ordered that John Crawen shall have xx [shillings] given him out of the Chamber to take Paul Dobbison apprentice to the trade of a glover for viii years.

And that Robert Tildesley shall have likewise given him xx [shillings] to take William Fawcett apprentice for viii years. And albeit Robert Tildesley be not a freeman yet the said Fawcett being a freemans son to have his freedom when his apprenticeship is ended.

Selections 12, 13, and 14
The Control of Prostitution in Florence

Although all three of these selections deal with Florence, in fact virtually all Renaissance and early modern cities, large and small, attempted to control prostitution in many of the same ways as did the Florentines. These three documents portray, first, the establishment of state-controlled brothels, second, the profits that were made, and third, the interaction of the court with two women accused of prostitution. Both had refused to wear the mandated garb of gloves on their hands, high heels, and a bell, prompting one of the charges against them.

Selection 12

THE ESTABLISHMENT OF COMMUNAL BROTHELS, 1415

Desiring to eliminate a worse evil by means of a lesser one, the lord priors . . . [and their colleges] have decreed that . . . the priors . . . [and their colleges] may authorize the establishment of two public brothels in the city of Florence, in addition to the one which already exists: one in the quarter of S. Spirito and the other in the quarter of S.

Source: Gene Brucker (ed.), *The Society of Renaissance Florence: A Documentary Study* (New York: Harper & Row, Inc., 1971), pp. 190–195.

Croce. [They are to be located] in suitable places or in places where the exercise of such scandalous activity can best be concealed, for the honor of the city and of those who live in the neighborhood in which these prostitutes must stay to hire their bodies for lucre, as other prostitutes stay in the other brothel. For establishing these places . . . in a proper manner and for their construction, furnishing, and improvement, they may spend up to 1,000 florins. . . .

Selection 13
PROFITS OF PROSTITUTION

[1427] . . . Rosso di Giovanni di Niccoló de' Medici . . . owns a house located at the entrance to the Chiasso Malacucina. . . . [It is rented by Biagio d'Antonio, a pork-butcher, for 12 florins per year.] . . . . There are six little shops beneath that house which are rented to prostitutes, who usually pay from 10 to 13 lire per month [for a room], and this rent is never higher. The innkeeper, Giuliano, keeps the keys and he puts whoever he wishes [into the rooms].

[1433] . . . Piero di Simone Brunelleschi and his mother Antonia . . . own two houses adjacent to each other in the Chiasso Malacucina, with furnishings required by prostitutes. . . . And there are several shops underneath those houses which are also inhabited by prostitutes. . . . They also report that they keep Giovanni di Marco of Venice in these houses . . . so that he, with some boys who stay with him, can collect the rents. They also state that they do not receive more than 4 florins per month from these houses and shops, on account of the depression. . . .

Selection 14
PROSTITUTES AND THE COURTS, 1398–1400

[Angela, wife of Nofri di Francesco, was convicted of plying the prostitute's trade without wearing the required garb, "gloves on her hands and a bell on her head." The following witnesses testified against her.]

Bartolo Gadini . . . stated that he was well informed about the contents of this process, namely that Angela had publicly sold her body for money in the parish of S. Maria a Verzaia, and that it is generally believed in the city of Florence . . . that she was and is a public prostitute. . . . Asked how he knew this, the witness said that he is Angela's neighbor, and that he saw many men openly coming to her house to copulate with her for money. . . . The witness further testified that during the previous November and December, on behalf of all of his neighbors and conforming to their will, he asked Angela to abandon her prostitute's career and live honestly. If she did so, he promised her, on behalf of the neighbors, to furnish her with a basket of bread each week for her sustenance. But Angela replied that she did not wish to give up prostitution unless her

neighbors first gave her 2 florins. Otherwise she intended to pursue the whore's life since she earned much more money than the amount which her neighbors wished to give her. . . .

Antonio di Zanobi . . . testified that he had information concerning this case. . . [He stated that] he had copulated with Angela and that for that act, she demanded 19 quattrini. Following the witness, a cloth worker from the parish of S. Frediano, Spina di Alimento, copulated with her and on that occasion he paid her a certain sum of money. . . .

Lorenzo di Riccomano . . . was and is a neighbor of Angela . . . and on several days and nights, he saw and heard men going to have carnal relations with her for money. On several occasions during this time, he reproached Angela for her dishonest and libidinous life. And he saw and heard her . . . say: "I am and I wish to remain a public whore, and I will sell my body to you for money."

This is the inquisition carried out by the excellent and honorable doctor of law, Messer Giovanni of Montepulciano, the appellate judge . . . of the city of Florence . . . against Salvaza, wife of Seze, parish of S. Lucia Ogni Santi. . . . It has come to the attention of the abovementioned judge and his court . . . that this Salvaza, wife of Seze . . . has publicly committed adultery with several persons and has sold her body for money. . . . With respect to all of these charges the judge intends to discover the truth; and if she is found guilty of walking without gloves and bells on her head or with high-heeled slippers, to punish her according to the Communal statutes; and if innocent to absolve her from this accusation.

This inquisition was begun by the judge against Salvaza on November 16, 1400. Sitting in tribunal in the accustomed seat of his office, the judge ordered . . . Bartolo di Bartolo, a public messenger of the Commune of Florence, to go to the home of Salvaza and order her to appear before the judge to clear herself of this accusation and to defend herself. . . .

November 16. The messenger has informed the judge and myself, the notary, that he went to the house of Salvaza and finding her there, informed her of everything herein inscribed and personally left a copy of this inquisition. . . .

November 19, 1400. Salvaza appeared personally at the residence of the judge, and since according to the statutes, no woman is allowed to enter there, the judge . . . ordered me, Jacopo de Silis, his notary, to descend to her near the entrance door . . . to hear and receive her reply, defense, and excuse. Before me, the notary, Salvaza replied to this accusation by stating that it was not true. . . . [She was then informed that she had eight days in which to furnish evidence of her innocence.]

November 24, 1400. Bartolo di Bartolo informed me, Jacopo de Silis, that he had personally informed the witnesses, identified below, from the parish of S. Lucia Ogni Santi, to appear on that same day before him at his accustomed residence to swear to tell the truth . . . concerning the statements in this accusation. . . .

The following witnesses against Salvaza were sworn in and examined by the judge and myself, the notary, on November 24, 1400.

Antonio di Ugo, parish of S. Lucia Ogni Santi . . . stated that everything in the accusation was true. When asked how he knew this, the witness replied that on numerous occasions, he had seen Salvaza enter the houses of many men— both natives and foreigners—by day and night. They played and danced with her, and did many illicit and indecent things with her, touching her and fondling her with their hands, as is done by public prostitutes. Asked whom he had seen touching and fondling her, and in whose houses, he replied that Salvaza went to the house of a certain Mancino, a Florentine citizen, and stayed with him for several days; also a certain pimp named Nanni, Niccolò, a tiler, and many others whose names he did not know. Asked about Salvaza's reputation, he replied that she is commonly regarded as a whore. When asked who voices this opinion, and where he heard it, he replied that it was the general opinion of nearly everyone in the parish. Asked about Salvaza's physical appearance and age, he replied that she is a big woman, about forty-five, quite attractive, with a dark complexion.

Vanni Migliore, parish of S. Lucia, . . . stated that he knew Salvaza, wife of Seze, very well; she lives in the street called the Prato Ogni Santi. He said that the contents of this accusation are true. When asked how he knew, he replied that he had seen many men, both citizens and foreigners, enter her house both day and night, and that she committed adultery with them. He had seen her engaged in indecent acts with them. Asked whom he had seen entering this house and participating in these indecencies, he identified a certain Martino of the parish of S. Paolo, Niccolò, a tiler, and many others whom he did not know. He stated that one night his door was closed and he was told that Niccolò had closed it. Thereupon, the witness encountered Niccolò and quarreled with him and told him that he was doing wrong. And Niccolò replied: "And I will fornicate wherever I please," and he held a key in his hands, and Salvaza was mouthing obscenities at him. Asked about Salvaza's reputation, he replied that among all of the residents of the parish, she had a bad reputation as a prostitute. Asked about her physical appearance and age, he replied that she was a large, dark woman of about forty years of age. . . .

Monna Leonarda, widow of Damello, parish of S. Lucia, . . . said that the contents of this accusation were true. Asked how she knew, she replied that she had seen many men entering Salvaza's house . . . both day and night when her husband was absent, and that men were said to have committed adultery with Salvaza. Asked whom she had seen entering the house, she replied that she had seen a certain Mancino and many others. Asked about Salvaza's reputation, she replied that she had a bad reputation and was considered a whore by nearly everyone in the parish.

Paula, wife of Lorenzo of the parish of S. Lucia, asserted that the contents of the inquisition were true. Asked how she knew this, the witness replied that she was Salvaza's neighbor and that she had often seen men enter her house, and had often heard her playing and joking with them. She also stated that on one occasion, a foreigner wished to go to Salvaza and the witness was standing on her doorstep. Feeling ashamed, the foreigner said to her: "You should go inside to your house," and then the witness went inside and the foreigner entered Salvaza's house. . . .

Margherita, widow of Ugo . . . stated that the contents of the accusation were true. When asked how she knew this, she replied that she is a near neighbor of Salvaza, and that she had often seen men enter her house. . . . The witness said that she had frequently looked through a window of Salvaza's house and had seen her nude in bed with men, engaging in those indecent acts which are practiced by prostitutes. [Salvaza was declared to be a public prostitute, and was required to wear gloves, bells, and high-heeled slippers.]

SIX

The Artist

One feature of the modern world that immediately leaps to mind as a product of the Renaissance is its artistic culture. To this day, we in the West think of the visual arts, in both content and style, as having been shaped for the past five hundred years by the masters who lived between the mid-1300s and the mid-1600s (the period that is the focus of this book). Even the painters, sculptors, and architects of the twentieth century, for all their attempts to break free from the past, have still been struggling with the heritage of the Renaissance. And yet there was certainly great art created long before 1300. What was it that made the years that followed so deeply influential? The answer lies both in the kind of art that was produced and—above all—in the transformation of the status of the artist.

NEW FORMS OF ART

That a revolutionary new style should have emerged first in Florence is not too surprising. As the Pope and the Emperor lost political influence over Italy in the 1300s, the major cities were able to act independently and enter into aggressive rivalries with one another. One of the marks of prestige in these rivalries was a city's literary and artistic fame, and in both areas, Florence had a unique advantage, as the birthplace of the most famous writer and the most famous painter of the age: Dante and Giotto, who died in 1321 and 1337, respectively. During the century that followed, the Florentines developed a cultural program that swept all Italy.

The creators of this program were Francesco Petrarca (Petrarch) and his followers, who came to be known as "Humanists." Dismayed by the intellectual, spiritual, and moral leadership of their own times, particularly in the Church, they looked instead for guidance to the ancient world of Greece and Rome. The ancients, they believed, possessed true virtue. If we want to be good, they argued, we should imitate them. The Humanists promoted this message mainly in literature and philosophy, but it was soon applied in the arts as well.

Petrarch's family was from Florence, and the movement he helped create found ready disciples among the Florentines. Before long, the impact of Humanism was visible in the flourishing community of artists and artisans who, as internationally sought designers of luxury goods, were (together with bankers) a major reason Florence was such a rich city. The prosperity of this great center of commerce and finance enabled its citizens to patronize craftsmanship in gold, silver, silk, and textiles that reached standards admired throughout Europe. Significantly, many of the leading artists of the next two hundred years were to start their careers as apprentices to goldsmiths. In these workshops, they mastered creative techniques as well as aesthetic principles that were to stand them in good stead when they turned to painting, sculpture, or architecture.

The revolution in these three disciplines was started by three friends, who were united by a determination to apply the Humanists' lessons to art. They wanted to break with the styles of the immediate past and create paintings, statues, and buildings that would not merely imitate the glories of Rome but would actually bring them back to life, in a rebirth, or Renaissance. All three went to Rome in the 1420s, hoping by direct observation and study of ancient masterpieces to recreate their qualities and thus fulfill the Humanists' goal of reviving the spirit of classical times. The Romans regarded the three as rather strange, for they went around measuring, taking notes, and calculating sizes and proportions. The lessons they learned, however, enabled them to transform the styles and purposes of art.

The painter among the three, Masaccio, used the inspiration of the ancients to put a new emphasis on nature, on three-dimensional human bodies, and on perspective. In depicting Adam and Eve, not only did he paint the first nudes since antiquity, but he showed them coming through a rounded arch that was the mark of Roman architecture, as opposed to the pointed arch of the Middle Ages (Figure 34). The chapel he decorated in a Florentine church, the Carmine, between 1425 and 1428, was for centuries a pilgrimage site for painters, who came to regard it as the first place where the values of ancient art—especially its emphasis on the individual human figure—were reborn.

Masaccio's friend Donatello was primarily a sculptor, and the figures he created in three dimensions had the same qualities as Masaccio's had in two. Once again, the focus was on the beauty of the body itself, because that had been a notable and distinctive concern of the ancients. The interest in the nude, accurately displayed, transformed the very purpose of art, for it led to an idealized representation of the human form that had not been seen in centuries. Donatello's depiction of the biblical hero David, completed around 1430, shows him in triumph over Goliath (Figure 35). In addition to creating a sensuous image, Donatello also was celebrating symbolically the victory of the newly independent and vigorous Florence over one of its larger rivals, in this case Milan. Not unexpectedly, the Florentines made David a favorite subject.

The most spectacular of these three pioneers, however, was the architect Brunelleschi. For decades, his fellow citizens had been building a new cathedral, which, as a sign of their artistic superiority, was going to be the largest in Italy. Seen from above, it was shaped—as was traditional—like a cross. The basic structure was complete, but the space where the horizontal and vertical met, the crossing, had not yet been covered. Amid the discussion of the most appropriate way to complete the building, Brunelleschi came forward and, using what he had learned in Rome,

Figure 34. Masaccio, *The Expulsion of Adam and Eve*, Santa Maria del Carmine, Florence. Masaccio shows Adam and Eve expelled from paradise through a rounded archway that recalls ancient architecture. Also indicative of the influence of Roman art is the attempt to create what we would consider realistic (rather than stylized) human beings and to portray them nude, displaying powerful, recognizable emotions. This was one of the paintings that made the Brancacci Chapel an inspiration to generations of artists.

proposed covering the crossing with the largest dome built in Europe since antiquity. Although the first reaction was that it was impossible, he got the commission in 1420. In an extraordinary feat of engineering, which required that he build the dome in rings, without using scaffolding, he erected a structure which (though still unfinished when he died in 1446) became not only a fitting climax to the cathedral but also the hallmark of Renaissance Florence and an inspiration for all

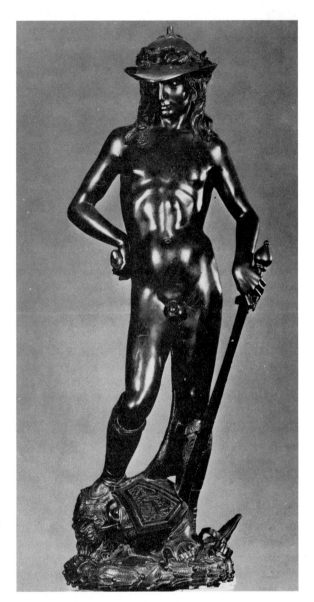

Figure 35. Donatello, *David* (bronze). Like Masaccio, Donatello imitated the Romans by creating idealized nude bodies. His *David* has just killed and decapitated Goliath, whose head lies at his feet. Goliath's helmet recalls those worn by Florence's enemies, which makes this sculpture a work of patriotism as well as art. It happens also to have been the first lifesize bronze figure cast since antiquity.

architects (Figure 36). And the symmetrical simplicity of his other building projects shaped a new aesthetic of harmony and balance that matched what Masaccio and Donatello accomplished in painting and sculpture. In the work of all three, the imitation of ancient Rome inspired subjects and styles that broke decisively with their immediate, medieval past.

During the remaining years of the 1400s, a succession of artists, not just in Florence, but increasingly in other parts of Italy as well, built on the achievements of the pioneer generation. They experimented with perspective and the modeling

Figure 36. *Florence Cathedral* (dome by Filippo Brunelleschi). Brunelleschi's famous dome—the first built in Italy since the fall of the Roman Empire—embodied the revival of classical forms in architecture that Masaccio and Donatello brought to painting and sculpture. The contrast with the bell tower designed a century earlier by Giotto, with its suggestion of pointed Gothic arches, is unmistakable. The dome dominates the skyline of Florence as decisively today as it did during the Renaissance.

of bodies and drapery so as to recapture the ancients' mastery of depth, and they made close observations of nature. The sculptors created monumental figures, some on horseback, in imitation of Roman models. And the architects perfected the use of the rounded arches and symmetrical forms they saw in antique buildings. Subject matter also changed, as artists produced increasing numbers of portraits of their contemporaries and depicted stories out of Roman and Greek myths as well as traditional religious scenes. By the end of the 1400s, the leading Florentine painter of the day, Botticelli, was presenting ancient subjects such as the birth of Venus, goddess of love, in exactly the way a Roman might have fashioned them (Figure 37).

The artists at work in the early years of the 1500s are often referred to as the generation of the "High Renaissance." Four in particular—Leonardo, Raphael, Michelangelo, and Titian—are thought of as bringing the new movement that had begun a hundred years before to a climax. Only two, Leonardo and Michelangelo, were born Florentines, and they all spent most of their lives elsewhere, but they can still be regarded as the culmination of the movement that began in Florence the previous century.

Figure 37. Sandro Botticelli, *The Birth of Venus*. The wistful, ethereal look on Venus's face has been seen as an indication of the growing influence in Florence of Plato, who emphasized otherworldliness and believed there were analogies among all ideas. Botticelli is imitating classical models, depicting an ancient myth as ancient painters would have shown it, yet he also may have been suggesting that Venus resembled the Virgin Mary as a source of divine love. Above all, however, this is a scene of idealized beauty, which helped to create an aesthetic standard that has been admired ever since.

The oldest, Leonardo, was the epitome of the experimental tradition. An extraordinarily inventive figure in many fields, from anatomy to fortifications, he was unable to resist the challenge of solving practical problems, even in his paintings. They are marvels of technical virtuosity, which make difficult angles, tricks of perspective, and bizarre geologic formations look easy. His portrait of the *Mona Lisa* (1504), for example, is famous not only for her mysterious smile but also for the incredible rocky landscape in the background (Figure 38). Unfortunately, he also experimented with methods of painting, and as a result, one of his masterpieces, the *Last Supper* (1498), has almost completely disintegrated.

Raphael, by contrast, used the mastery of perspective and ancient styles that had been achieved in the 1400s to produce works of perfect harmony, beauty, and serenity. His paintings, notably his tranquil Madonnas, give an impression of utter relaxation, of an artist in complete command of his materials and therefore able to

Figure 38. Leonardo da Vinci, *Mona Lisa.* This is probably the most celebrated image in Renaissance art. The famous hint of a smile and the calm and solid pose are so familiar that we all too easily forget how striking it seemed at the time and how often it inspired later portraits. As in his *Last Supper*, however, Leonardo was experimenting with his materials, and the picture has therefore faded over the years.

create, at ease, sunny scenes that are balanced and at peace. His tribute to the ancient world, *The School of Athens* (Figure 39), places in a classical architectural setting the great philosophers of Greece, many of whom are portraits of the artists of the day—Plato, for instance, pointing to heaven, has Leonardo's face. If the philosophers were the chief glory of Athens, Raphael seems to be saying, then the artists are the crowning glory of the Renaissance.

Michelangelo, who was equally at home in poetry, architecture, painting, and sculpture (his favorite art), often seems the ultimate embodiment of the achievements of his age. Yet there is little of Raphael's relaxed qualities in his work. He once said that no two of the thousands of figures he depicted were the same, and one might add that just about every one of them conveys the sense of latent strength, of striving, that was Michelangelo's signature. Although Adam, shown at the moment of his creation, has not yet received the gift of life from God, he already displays the vigor that Michelangelo gave to every human body (Figure 40). The same is true of his version of David, seemingly tranquil but showing his potential power in his

Figure 39. Raphael, *The School of Athens*, Vatican Palace. Painted in 1510 and 1511, this fresco celebrates the glories of Greek philosophy. That the classical setting and theme could have been accepted as appropriate for a wall of the Vatican suggests how completely Humanism had captured intellectual life. A number of the figures are portraits of artists whom Raphael knew—the notoriously moody Michelangelo broods, with his head on his arm, at the front.

massive, oversized hand (Figure 41). The sculptor relishes his ability to show the human being in full majesty as an independent and potent individual.

In Venice, the developments in art took a slightly different form. This was also a rich trading city, sophisticated, with broad international connections, but here Humanism was not so central, and the art—as befitted a materialistic, down-to-earth place—was more sensuous, more tactile. The most famous Venetian painter,

Figure 40. Michelangelo, *The Creation of Adam,* Sistine Chapel. Michelangelo worked on the ceiling of the Sistine Chapel in the Vatican from 1508 to 1512 and painted hundreds of figures. None has come to symbolize both the rebirth associated with the Renaissance and the power of creative genius so forcefully as the portrayal of God extending a finger to bring the vigorous body of Adam to life. Tucked under God's other arm is the figure of Eve, ready to join Adam in giving birth to mankind.

Titian, a contemporary of Michelangelo, depicted rich velvets, lush nudes, stormy skies, and dogs with wagging tails with a directness and immediacy that enable the viewer almost to feel them (Figure 42). His friend Aretino said of one of his pictures: "I can say nothing of the crimson of the garment nor of its lynx lining, for in comparison real crimson and real lynx seem painted, and these seem real." Looking out his window at a sunset, he compared even Nature's effects with Titian's and cried out, "Oh, Titian, where are you?"

Titian lived into his nineties, and by the time he died, in 1576, the qualities of Renaissance art—stability, balanced proportions, and imitation of the ancients—had evolved into a new style known as "Mannerism." The aim now was to disturb, to unsettle. Having gained the ability to show nature, artists used their skills to create an uneasy psychological mood. Canvases became so crowded that figures could not fit within the frame; there were odd, awkward, gestures; bodies were distorted; and the meaning of scenes was puzzling (Figure 43). In part, these purposes were the consequence of a tormented century of religious wars; in part, though, they also represented a reaction against the calm and perfection of much of Renaissance art. Once the great revolution in style had taken place, there was no way to stop further change, as artists looked for new ways to depict the world.

To this point, in the late 1500s, the revolution had been led by Italians. Yet there had been major advances in northern Europe, too. Indeed, oil painting—on wood

Figure 41. Michelangelo, *David*. Like Donatello before him, Michelangelo produced a sculpture of David that became a symbol of Florence. Indeed, this marble figure was commissioned by the city itself and placed in front of its main government building. It was recognized immediately as a remarkable depiction of a man radiating latent power as he awaits the approach of the giant Goliath. The combination of the active and the contemplative embodies a Renaissance ideal, and the artistry led a contemporary to say that people needed to see no other sculpture once they had seen this one.

Figure 42. Titian, *Bacchanal*. The earthy realism of Venice contrasted sharply with the idealization common in Florentine art. The setting and even the sky seem more tangible, and Titian's lush nude in the foreground (who was to be much copied) is the essence of sensuality. It has been suggested that the painting represents the different stages of life, from the incontinent child through the vigorous youths and adults to the old man who has collapsed in the back.

or canvas—was invented in the Netherlands, and its first great exponent, Van Eyck, a contemporary of Donatello, revealed both the similarities and the differences between North and South. Van Eyck was less interested in idealization than the Florentines and more fascinated with the details of the physical world. One sees almost every thread in a carpet. His 1434 portrait (Figure 44) of an Italian couple, the Arnolfinis, however, is shot through with religious symbolism as well as a sly sense of humor about sex and marriage. The dog is a sign of fidelity, and the carving

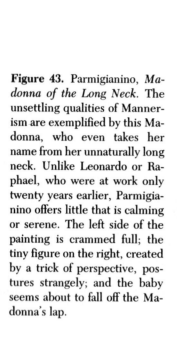

Figure 43. Parmigianino, *Madonna of the Long Neck*. The unsettling qualities of Mannerism are exemplified by this Madonna, who even takes her name from her unnaturally long neck. Unlike Leonardo or Raphael, who were at work only twenty years earlier, Parmigianino offers little that is calming or serene. The left side of the painting is crammed full; the tiny figure on the right, created by a trick of perspective, postures strangely; and the baby seems about to fall off the Madonna's lap.

on the bedpost is of St. Margaret, the patron saint of childbirth; but the single candle is what newlyweds are supposed to keep burning on their wedding night, and the grinning grotesque figures on the chair behind their clasped hands are a wry comment on their marriage. The picture displays a combination of earthiness and piety that places it in a tradition unlike any that one finds in Italy.

The leading northern artist of the period of the High Renaissance was a German, Dürer, who deliberately sought to blend southern and northern styles. He made two trips to Venice, in 1494 and 1505, and the results were clear in a self-portrait that shows him as a fine gentlemen, painted in the Italian style (Figure 45). Yet he continued, especially in the engravings that made him famous, to emphasize the detailed depiction of nature and the religious purposes that were characteristic of northern art (Figure 51).

Figure 44. Jan van Eyck, *Portrait of Giovanni Arnolfini and his Wife*. The symbolism that permeates this depiction of a husband and wife has led to the suggestion that it is a wedding picture. The shoes have been removed, as the Bible requires, before a holy place; the bed and seeming pregnancy are symbols of marriage; and the husband blesses his wife as he bestows the sacrament of marriage (for which the Church had not yet required a priest). On the back wall, the mirror reflects the witnesses attending the wedding.

Figure 45. Albrecht Dürer, *Self-Portrait*, 1498. (See Figure 46.)

In the following generation, a Flemish painter, Pieter Brueghel the Elder, combined the crowded canvases of the Mannerists with the interest in ordinary life characteristic of the North in a series of paintings that were unlike any that had come before. He took as his subject the common people of his native land, showing them not only going about their daily lives in almost documentary fashion—as in a huge painting (Figure 47) entitled *Children's Games* (1560)—but also in portrayals of

Figure 46. Albrecht Dürer, *Self-Portrait*, 1500. These self-portraits, painted two years apart, reflect the influence of Italian as well as German traditions on Dürer. The first, completed when he returned from a visit to Italy, shows him in the fashionable clothes and aristocratic setting that were favored in the South. The second, more austere, gives a Christ-like impression that recalls the powerful religious traditions of the North. Both, however, emphasize the importance of creativity, which can raise an artist to high social rank or, alternatively, enable him to serve as evidence of divine inspiration.

Figure 47. Pieter Brueghel the Elder, *Children's Games*. Although it is crowded with scores of figures, this painting still gives a sense of the street life of a town in 1560. Despite the Mannerist features of an unbalanced composition, a scene filled to overflowing, and a picture that makes the viewer work, the setting is solid and realistic. Brueghel's purpose in depicting dozens of adults playing children's games, however, remains enigmatic.

biblical stories, such as *Census at Bethlehem*. Many of his paintings had allegorical purposes. Why, for instance, were all the games played by adults? To suggest that what they did all day was no more serious than a game? It was a new way of using art—characteristic of the Mannerists—to raise questions among those who saw it.

Around 1600 these developments took another major turn, the final one of the period we are considering. A new style emerged—the "Baroque"—which emphasized dramatic effects, powerful emotions, and soaring grandeur. Although Dutch art, more subdued, remained an exception and continued to emphasize scenes of ordinary life, the Baroque swept most of Europe, and the contrasts between North and South largely disappeared. Indeed, its leading figures were Flemish painters like Rubens, Italians such as the painter Caravaggio and the sculptor and architect Bernini, and Spaniards, most notably the painter Velazquez.

The style was first noticeable in the 1590s, when Caravaggio and a few other Italians began to try to create more vivid and direct emotions than anything the

Figure 48. Caravaggio, *Supper at Emmaus.* Contemporaries were shocked when Caravaggio used ordinary people whom he had seen on the streets of Rome as models for holy figures in biblical scenes. Once the shock subsided, however, his audience came to appreciate Caravaggio's powerful sense of drama, exemplified by the highly emotional moments (in this case, the disciples' sudden recognition of the resurrected Christ) that he brought to life with startling gestures and sharp contrasts of light and dark. This theatricality was to shape a new style in art.

Mannerists had sought. They no longer wanted to disturb; they wanted to move. Using sharp contrasts of dark and light, they depicted highly dramatic moments that seemed almost to leap out of their canvases. The instant when the disciples recognized the resurrected Christ, whom they thought dead, while having supper in the village of Emmaus inspired Caravaggio in 1600 to depict an almost theatrical scene (Figure 48). The figures are of ordinary people, but the power of the miracle seems to burst out of the painting and overwhelm those who see it.

    The same impulse drove Rubens, who died in 1640, to produce huge canvases on resounding themes: exalted portraits of heroic generals, agonized evocations of such terrible events as the descent of Christ from the cross, and swirling portrayals of crowds in rapid motion. His concern was to arouse intense emotions, and he did so in some of the most powerful and sensuous pictures ever painted (Figure 18).

Figure 49. Diego Velazquez, *Las Meninas*. In addition to being an extraordinary evocation of a huge room in the palace at Madrid, this scene of Velazquez painting the five-year-old Spanish princess amidst her attendants symbolized the new importance of the artist. As is apparent in the mirror on the back wall, King Philip IV and his queen have come to visit the painter—a remarkable gesture of respect in itself. Moreover, Velazquez is wearing on his chest the order of knighthood that had elevated him into the ranks of the aristocracy.

Although Rubens' younger Spanish contemporary Velazquez was less openly dramatic, he too conveyed the majesty of his subjects in huge canvases, often with strong contrasts of light and shade. He froze the action, for example, at the instant when King Philip IV and his queen entered his studio to see how his painting of their daughter was progressing (Figure 49). The result, *Las Meninas* (1656), is a breathtaking image of a place that bursts into life and draws the spectator into a

Figure 50. Gian Lorenzo Bernini, *The Ecstasy of St. Teresa*, Santa Maria della Vittoria, Rome. Bernini's subjects were as dramatic in sculpture as Caravaggio's had been in painting. The moment that St. Teresa described in her autobiography when she attained mystic ecstasy, as an angel repeatedly pierced her heart with a dart, became in Bernini's hands the centerpiece of a theatrical tableau. On two walls of the chapel that houses this altarpiece he placed the patrons who had commissioned the work, sitting in what seem to be boxes and looking at the stage on which the drama unfolds.

room that has long since disappeared. Velazquez finds his drama by capturing a second of time that we almost experience as we stand before the painting.

Bernini made this purpose unmistakable. Commissioned to decorate a chapel centered on an altarpiece honoring St. Teresa, he picked the most striking moment in her life, when she said she had gone into ecstasy as an angel repeatedly drove darts into her body (Figure 50). The movement and passion Bernini carved into the marble turn the episode into a dazzling display. He left no doubt as to its dramatic intent, however, because on the wall alongside the altar he depicted the patrons who had paid for the sculpture, sitting in box seats as if watching St. Teresa in theatrical performance. The whole scene took seven years to complete, from 1645 to 1652, and his most massive undertaking, the transformation of the square in front of the Vatican into a vast colonnaded showplace—the largest such open space in Europe—required eleven years, from 1656 to 1667. In St. Peter's itself he set the altar under an ornate canopy with a sunburst as backdrop that made each service a spectacle. Bernini's work made the Baroque's fondness for exuberant action, strong feeling, and grandiose effects as notable in sculpture and architecture as in painting.

These successive artistic movements shaped the aesthetic principles of Western art down to our own times. Although the modern movement has tried to break with this heritage by avoiding representations of reality and direct appeals to the emotions, the very qualities it opposes keep bursting through afresh. The great figures of the Renaissance and Baroque defined what we still consider beautiful, and they achieved levels of creativity that we continue to think of as the standard against which we judge artistic excellence. Perhaps most important, however, they transformed the role they occupied in society. They attained a new status that has remained one of the distinguishing features of our culture, evidenced by the extraordinary prices paintings can command. How did this second revolution come about?

STATUS AND PERCEPTION

To the generation of Masaccio, a painter was merely one of the many craftsmen in a city, not inherently more admired than a skilled leather finisher or a mason. Like them, he was a member of a guild; he had to pass a carefully regulated apprenticeship; and he was subject to the rules that controlled his trade. Both Donatello and Brunelleschi were trained as goldsmiths, and the latter was even briefly imprisoned by his guild for not paying his dues while he was working—as an independent person, so he thought, and thus outside the guild structure—on the cathedral dome.

Given the Florentines' interest in gaining fame by beautifying their city, it was not surprising that the work of these artists should have attracted considerable attention. Yet it rarely occurred to anyone in the early 1400s—as Brunelleschi discovered from his guild—that artists might deserve special respect or be considered anything more elevated than middle-class tradesmen. It was true that some of them were becoming famous throughout Italy, but would that lead to a change in their social status?

The answer is that it did, and again, the impetus came from the Humanist movement. Three consequences of the revival of antiquity in particular began a reevaluation of the position of the artist. First was the recognition that the most vivid and convincing recreations of the achievements of the ancient world were being produced in the visual arts. No letter written like Cicero's or poem that imitated Vergil could compare with a painting, a statue, or a building as a means of bringing Rome back to life for all to see—as an open and public display of the virtues of classical times.

A second influence was the Humanists' new interest in personal fame. This had been an acceptable aspiration in antiquity, but during the Middle Ages, spiritual concerns encouraged a disdain for worldly matters, and so it was a problem for Petrarch to admit that, like the ancients he admired, he wanted to be famous. He wrote a long dialogue in the early 1340s, called his "Secret," in which he struggled to justify his ambition, but he could never shake free of the guilt it aroused in him. For later Humanists, the doubts receded, and the princes who valued their ideas eagerly accepted the notion that they should devote their lives to attaining fame. This was what they had won as warriors, but now there was a more reliable way of ensuring that one's name lived forever.

The route to immortality was provided by the third of the Humanists' lessons: The truly moral person had to combine the contemplative with the active life. A prince, therefore, ought to cultivate the fine as well as the martial arts. No aristocratic court could be complete without its poets and painters, who sang their patron's praises while fashioning the masterpieces that not only brought prestige but also endured far longer than a brief human life. As a result, if a duke or a count wanted to be remembered, it was no longer enough to be a famous warrior; increasingly, it became essential to build a splendid new palace or have his portrait done by a famous painter. To be most like the virtuous heroes of Rome who were the society's ideal, he had to be a patron of culture as well as a vigorous leader. And this outlook was not confined to the males who now tried to unite artistic and military glory. Noble women, whose chief role had long been to offer an idealized object of chivalric devotion, also provided patronage that could be crucial in fashioning a princely image. Without Isabella d'Este, for example, the court in Mantua that she graced from 1490 to 1539 would not have achieved all the fame it won as a center of painting, architecture, and music. That her portrait was done both by Leonardo and by Titian was a reflection not of her husband's importance but of her own, independent contribution to the arts. Her rooms, surrounding a lovely garden, remain one of the wonders of the palace at Mantua and a worthy testimony to the fame she achieved as a patroness.

The result of this new attitude was a transformation in the standing of artists. They became highly sought after at the courts of aristocrats, who saw them as extraordinarily effective image makers. Perhaps the most famous princely family in Italy, the Medici of Florence, was envied throughout Europe mainly because, for generations, its leaders seemed always to have as their protegés the finest painters, sculptors, and architects of the age. Two members of the Medici family became popes, and they brought Raphael and Michelangelo to Rome, just as their ancestors had patronized Brunelleschi, Donatello, and Botticelli in Florence.

In the mid-1500s, a leading protegé of the Medici, an architect and painter named Giorgio Vasari, decided to try to figure out how and why it was that artists like him were being showered with privileges. He himself had been given the responsibility to design, build, and decorate a large new building in the center of the city for the government's offices—or, in Italian, *Uffizi* (now the main museum of Renaissance art in Florence). He had been knighted for his services and was a significant figure at the Medici court. To understand his own good fortune, he looked to the past and published in 1550 *The Lives of the Painters*, the first major work of what became, in his hands, a new field of study: the history of art.

Vasari was not an unbiased observer. At the outset, for example, he explained that the rebirth of art was, quite naturally, the work of Tuscany, the province in which his home city of Florence was located:

> The benign ruler of heaven saw that in the practice of painting, sculpture, and architecture, the Tuscan genius has always been pre-eminent, for the Tuscans have devoted to all the various branches of art more labor and study than all the other Italian peoples.

It was Vasari who put forward the idea that certain artists were filled with a special spirit, what he called "genius," that set them apart from—and above—other people. Most of us have accepted this idea ever since, and it has been the root of the reverence we have shown toward great creative figures.

Vasari even identified the people who—as most historians still agree—began to transform both art and the status of the artist during the preceding century:

> The appearance of a man of outstanding creative talent is very often accompanied by that of another great artist at the same time and in the same part of the world so that the two can inspire one another. The truth of this can be seen in the fact that during the same period Florence produced Brunelleschi, Donatello, and Masaccio. Each was an outstanding artist, and through them the crude style which had existed up to that time was finally discarded.

Vasari went on to praise Botticelli, Raphael, Leonardo, and above all Michelangelo. God, he wrote, "chose to have Michelangelo born a Florentine, so that one of her own citizens might bring to absolute perfection the achievements for which Florence was already justly famous."

The status artists had achieved was, in Vasari's account, richly deserved. They were appropriate courtiers, and even minor aristocrats, because of their genius and their fame. He wrote of them as if it were impossible to remember that just a century before they been considered mere craftsmen. Titian, for example, lived like a member of one of the finest families in Venice. He had a splendid house and was welcomed at the grandest occasions. Although he was in huge demand throughout Europe, he chose not to leave his native city. He might visit a king or an emperor, but he did not need to be attached to their court—as Botticelli was, for instance, to the Medici—in order to maintain his noble standing. It was said that while he was painting the Emperor Charles V he dropped his brush, and the Emperor himself bent to pick it up for him—just as Alexander the Great had done for a portraitist in ancient times, to acknowledge the superiority of the artist.

In the 1600s, the leading figures who succeeded Titian—Rubens, Velazquez, and Bernini—behaved openly like aristocrats. Rubens amassed his own art collection, just like a nobleman, and served as a diplomat for Habsburg governments. Velazquez was a major presence at the Spanish court. He painted the king and queen visiting him so that he could emphasize how important he was, and he showed himself in the picture wearing his order of knighthood. Bernini, meanwhile, moved in the highest social circles in Rome, often indistinguishable from the princes with whom he associated.

The transformation of a tradesman into an aristocrat delighted Vasari; what he did not perhaps realize was that the rise of artists to their new status was as significant in the shaping of Western culture as the changes in style he described. Nor was he aware that this profound shift did not advance at the same speed in all places. In Germany, for example, Dürer refused to break completely with the craft origins of his vocation. He knew, from his visits to Venice, that Italian painters could live like lords, and he was invited by the Emperor Charles V to join his court. Dürer preferred to remain in his home city of Nuremberg, however, earning his living more through the sale of his prints than from the stipends he was offered by patrons. Indeed, he became a highly successful entrepreneur, creating different kinds of prints for different markets—the elite liked elegant and expensive copper engravings, while others preferred cruder but cheaper woodcuts—and producing a bestseller in a book that illustrated the Apocalypse (Figure 51). Working with his wife, who was a highly effective seller of his prints, he seemed as much engaged in

Figure 51. Albrecht Dürer, *The Four Horsemen of the Apocalypse* (woodcut). The best-seller Dürer published in 1498 has the text of the biblical account of the Apocalypse on one side and full-page woodcuts on the other. The four horsemen who will wreak vengeance on the damned during the final Day of Judgment are Conquest holding a bow, War holding a sword, Famine or Justice holding scales, and Death or Plague riding a pale horse.

business as in art. By the next century, such distinctions had vanished. The great figures, both in the North (Rubens) and in the South (Bernini), had left craft and trade far behind. They were rich, respected, and welcome members of the international aristocracy, thoroughly at home in princely circles.

NEW IMAGES AND ROLES

As artists grew more prominent in society, they became the subject of endless discussion. Previously, as mere craftsmen, they had not aroused a great deal of interest. Now, possessed of mysterious power and insight, they inspired much speculation. The central question, of course, was the nature of their creativity. Where did it come from, and how could one recognize it? Did their inspiration come solely from God, as Vasari suggested, or did it flourish only in certain kinds of human beings? Was genius, then, a quality of special individuals, and if so, what was it that made them unique? As they pondered these issues, the writers and commentators of the Renaissance focused on a number of characteristics that have remained essential to the image of the artist to this day. Three in particular, though familiar to us, had already attracted notice in the 1500s and 1600s.

First was eccentricity. As soon as artists became famous, it was noticeable that they did not behave like other people and had no interest in conforming. Donatello and Brunelleschi ignored the curious Romans who could not understand why they were scraping away at ruins and measuring their dimensions, nor were they prepared to explain themselves. Vasari described one of his own contemporaries, the painter Pontormo, as avoiding all crowds and "solitary beyond belief;" to preserve his privacy, Pontormo worked on a high platform and pulled the ladder up behind him so that nobody would bother him.

What we think of today as a Bohemian lifestyle was noticed as early as the 1500s. One group of young artists in Florence had habits that shocked contemporaries, as a commentator noted:

> They lived like swine and brute beasts. They never washed their hands, nor their faces or hair or beards; they did not sweep their houses and never made their beds save once every two months; they laid their tables with the drawings for their pictures, and they drank only from the bottle or the jug. This miserable existence—living, as the saying goes, from hand to mouth—was held by them to be the finest life in the world.
>
> [Quoted in Wittkower, *Born Under Saturn* (p. 71). See page 231.]

From artists, such behavior was accepted, however grudgingly, because one assumed that it somehow went along with the creative spirit. They did not behave like ordinary people because they were not ordinary people. If they were sullen or antisocial or lived like pigs, so be it. It was worth it for the beauty they produced.

Michelangelo, in fact, was notorious for his moods. He had a terrible temper, he was grumpy, and everyone from the popes on down found him difficult to deal with. It was true that his patrons were hardly accommodating, but even Vasari, who revered Michelangelo, noted the contrast with Raphael, whose sweet disposition had made him widely beloved. "Nature," he wrote, "created Michelangelo to excel in art, but Raphael to excel in art and in manners also." He added, ruefully, that "most artists display a folly which renders them eccentric."

The extreme may have been reached by Caravaggio. Unlike his elegant colleagues, such as Titian or Rubens, who enjoyed aristocratic society, he liked to mix with beggars and criminals. He could fit in at noble households, especially if they were slightly decadent, and he was not reluctant to take on a number of large religious commissions. But the people of the streets were the main models for his pictures, and it was clear that he felt at home in their company. Violence was never far away, and after he had murdered a man in one encounter, he had to flee from Rome as an outlaw. Caravaggio's case was unusual, but in some ways it exemplified the aura of glamour, even danger, that now surrounded artists and made eccentricity (or worse) almost essential to their identity.

The second characteristic was related to the first: their independence. Of course they owed their rise in society to their patrons, and for the most part they remained duly obedient and grateful. Van Eyck and Botticelli, for example, were delighted to be subsidized (if not always on time) by the noble families that bought their work. And Dürer always remained respectful toward the nobility, as well as attuned to the markets in which he sold his many prints. The latter gave him some independence, but his fellow artists were beginning to assert their autonomy more dramatically. Eventually, geniuses have to go their own way, and by the 1500s it was apparent that they would not always knuckle under, even to the princes and popes who had long been accustomed to subservience.

Michelangelo, irascible and surly, led the way, but he was soon joined by his younger contemporary Pontormo. According to Vasari,

> What most annoyed other men about Pontormo was that he would not work save when and for whom he pleased, and after his own fancy. Often, as a result, when he was sought out by noblemen who desired a work by his hand—and once in particular by the excellent Ottaviano de' Medici—he would refuse to serve them. And then he would go and do anything in the world for some low and common fellow at a miserable price.

The two qualities of eccentricity and independence went hand in hand, but both seemed peculiarly innate to the artistic temperament. And both, for this reason, had to be tolerated.

A third characteristic was the capacity for insight. That, after all, was what genius meant: It enabled the creative mind to perceive what others could not. When Aretino said that an actual cloak seemed less real than a cloak in a picture by Titian, he was acknowledging the painter's ability to penetrate to an essence not visible to anyone else. People spoke of works of art as revelations precisely because they enabled their viewers to see what previously had been hidden.

One reason that patrons were so eager to have distinguished artists in their service was this ability to reveal and, hence, to convince. For the Medici, paintings, sculptures, and buildings were a powerful means of propaganda. They dotted Florence with their coat of arms, as a kind of reminder that the beautiful things they had paid for displayed the glory not just of the city but also of their family. From generations of artists they commissioned tributes and flattering portrayals that were expected to be persuasive—and often were—for the very reason that they were the product of uniquely creative and hence perceptive minds. And the Medici were only one dynasty in a long line of princes and rulers who enlisted art in the service of official propaganda.

Once this role opened up, however, its antithesis also became possible: the artist as critic of government and society. If painters, for example, were to be admired not only because they made beautiful things but also because they could comment especially profoundly on the world around them, then *all* their views had to be taken seriously. At first, living as they did under authoritarian regimes, artists were reluctant to take up dissenting roles. Yet in this area, too, the Renaissance witnessed the first pioneering steps: attacks on religious authorities, on the brutality of war, on oppression of the poor, and on the subservience of women.

The most remarkable of the critics was the Flemish painter Pieter Brueghel the Elder. He seems to have used the biblical story of the massacre of the innocents, for example, to show the Spanish troops who occupied his native land slaughtering local women and children. And his scenes of ordinary life often emphasized the shortcomings of humanity at large. Terribly crippled beggars reveal the effects of war but also of indifference—an unconcern that Christ himself experiences as he carries his cross, amid a huge crowd of people preoccupied with their own business, on his way to Calvary. So biting were some of Brueghel's critiques that on his death bed, fearing for his wife's safety, he made her promise to burn his remaining paintings.

Equally disturbing, though hardly recognized as such in her time, was the work of a woman born in 1593 into a family of painters and much influenced by Caravaggio: Artemisia Gentileschi. As a young adult, Gentileschi was raped by a family friend, and it has long been apparent that this traumatic event was crucial to her art. It is notable, for example, that in the 1600s male portrayals of Judith, the biblical heroine who beheaded Holofernes, were increasingly depicting her as a vacuous mannequin or even an evil temptress. For Gentileschi, by contrast, she was a strong, competent woman. And although some see the scene as an expression of revenge against her rapist, it has more recently been understood as an assertion of self-liberation. Whatever the interpretation, however, the painting clearly bestows on women, in personal terms, a power that Gentileschi's society was not yet ready to allow.

It would be a long time before provocative artists like Brueghel or Gentileschi would be accepted as the consciences, rather than the eccentrics, of society. Their rise in status, however, and the growing admiration for their creative achievements ensured that they would take on new roles and find new significance for their work. If, thereafter, they would always be regarded as somehow different from their fellow citizens—privileged and yet on the outside—this gave them a vantage point and possibilities for insight that had already become in the Renaissance, and remain to this day, essential means of understanding ourselves.

Original Sources

The painters, architects, and sculptors of the Renaissance brought the classical forms of Greece and Rome to a new, appreciative audience and in the process transformed artistic culture decisively. The characterization of artists as unique individuals became prevalent, and for the first time they were renowned as much or more as the works of art they produced. Through their vision, we can see and touch Renaissance images and life.

I. KINDS OF ART

The kinds of art that were produced and the transformation of the status of the artist both contributed to the extraordinary creative ferment of the Renaissance. The first group of readings points up the appearance and recognition of different conceptions of art in general and new forms of art in particular. This new art owed much, it was increasingly realized, to the genius of the individual artist. As a result, the discussion of specific works of art was often bound up with praise for the greatness of the artists' visions and styles.

Selection 1
"The Lure of Rome"

Francesco Petrarca

Petrarca writes in March of 1337 to his friend, the Cardinal Giovanni Colonna, of his wonder at the grandeur of Rome. He heralds a new attitude toward the past and its uses for the present age, his own.

. . . At present I can hardly even begin to write, I am too overwhelmed by the miracle of so much grandeur and so many surprises. One thing, however, I want to say: the contrary of what you expected has happened. As I recall it, you were against my visiting Rome, warning me that the sight of the ruined city would contrast too sadly with all that I had heard and read about her, so that my fervent enthusiasm would dwindle. And I myself was not disinclined to postpone my visit in spite of my great longing, because I feared that the sight before my eyes would belittle the image formed in my mind. Reality is always the foe of famous names. But this time, o wonder, reality has diminished nothing but exceeded everything. Truly, Rome was grander than I had thought, grander too are her ruins! I am no longer astonished that this town has conquered the world. I am only surprised at its happening so late.

Source: Rudolf and Margot Wittkower, *Born Under Saturn: The Character and Conduct of Artists: A Documented History from Antiquity to the French Revolution* (New York: Random House, Inc., 1963), pp. 47–48.

Selection 2
Niccolo Niccoli and Lorenzo de Medici as Patrons

The prominent humanist scholar Poggio Bracciolini (1380–1459) here describes, in a letter and in his book *On Nobility*, the mania for collecting and also the goals of two famous patrons, Niccolo Niccoli (d. 1437) and Lorenzo de Medici (d. 1440). Lorenzo explains that sculptors and painters become ennobled themselves through their creation of great art.

Letter to Niccolo Niccoli in Florence, from Rome, September 23 (probably 1430):

I gave some commissions to Master Francesco of Pistoia when he left us, among which the main one was that he should acquire some marble images, even broken ones, or some good head, that he might bring back with him to me. I said there were plenty of them in those parts where he was going. He was quite diligent in executing my orders, for yesterday I got letters written to me by him from Chios, in which he tells me that he has in my name three marble heads, by Polycleitos and Praxiteles, of Juno, Minerva, and Bacchus, which he greatly praises, and he says he will bring them with him to Gaeta. I don't know about the names of the sculptors, Greeks as you know are talkative, and perhaps he faked the names to sell them higher. I would hope that is not so. He also writes that he got these heads from a certain Calorino who recently found about a hundred compete marble statues in a cave, beautiful and of marvelous workmanship. He writes no more, excusing himself because of illness. . . . I at once answered Master Francesco and also Andreolo, who I hear from our Rinuccio is quite well informed, to inquire whether they could get one of these statues, for either a price or a prayer, and be on their toes, and let me know quickly. I wanted you to take part in this discovery. I think his statues are of gods, because of these heads, and were hidden in some sanctuary. He writes that the head of Minerva has a laurel crown, and Bacchus two horns. When they come I will put them in my little study room. Minerva cannot do badly among us, I will place her among my books. Bacchus should feel right, for if he deserved a dwelling anywhere, he can rightly be in my country, in which he is especially honored. We will also give Juno a place. Since she was once the wife of an adulterer, now she will be a mistress. I have something here as well, which will be brought home. Donatello saw it, and praised it very highly. I don't want this letter to include any chatter other than the sculpture, so goodbye, and love me.

* * *

Some time ago, when I had retired from Rome to my own country for a change of air, there came to see me, both on my single request, my very learned friends Niccolò Niccoli and Lorenzo de Medici,* whom I had wheedled to come there especially by the display of some statues that I had brought from Rome. When they were in the garden, which, with my few curious marbles, I was longing to make famous by the show of some small household stuff, Lorenzo remarked, laughing, as he turned his eyes around: "Our host here has read that it was an old custom among those excellent men of early times to adorn their houses, villas, gardens, courtyards, and study rooms with various images and paintings of their ancestors, indeed with statues, for the fame and ennobling of their lineage, and since images of his progenitors were lacking, he sought to make this place, and himself too, noble with these trifles and bits of marbles, so that because of the novelty of the thing some of his glory might, through these, survive to posterity."

"If he is hungry for that," Niccolò said, "the foundation of nobility is found elsewhere, not in images and fragments of marbles, broken and not to be yearned for in the least by a wise man, but in the mind, that is, we must wrest it from wisdom

Source: Creighton E. Gilbert, *Italian Art 1400–1500: Sources and Documents* (Evanston, Ill.: Northwestern University Press, 1992), pp. 168–169.

* Brother of Cosimo, granduncle of his famous namesake, il Magnifico.

and virtue, which alone raise men to the praise of nobility."

"That is so," Lorenzo said. "I would regard it as the most suitable for bestowing nobility on men, virtue indeed is considered a divine thing to be yearned for by everyone. Yet we do see nobility being furnished with the aid of paintings and various images, with elegance, riches, and an abundance of property, with public offices above all, and we see virtue in those who are not famous for any other embellishment. And it is hungered and sought after by outstanding talents, for it is well known that the most learned men have devoted much labor and study to buying statues and paintings. . . ."

But Niccolò said: "If those who have statues and paintings in their house obtain nobility, then sculptors and painters would far surpass others in the tokens of nobility, pawnbrokers also. . . ." And Lorenzo: "We rightly do call noble, if you examine the word closely, the sculptors and painters whom their art makes famous and distinguished, and rich too, from things they have continually accomplished in one way or another, and widely known for their great achievements. Therefore, it is right to call noble both him who is outstanding in literary studies and him who is a famous thief, the latter on account of his outstanding punishment. . . . The ancients called noble a person known and notorious for any remarkable thing, and outstanding in any action or skill and famous in the talk of men."

Selection 3
Preface, *Lives of the Artists*
Giorgio Vasari

Vasari attempts to place the art of Greece and Rome in historical perspective, as well as suggesting that the development of art over time approaches perfection and comes closer to God as a result. Finally, he concludes that an artist's real fame is, ultimately, in the masterpieces he has produced.

. . . The works made by the Greeks, the Ethiopians, and the Chaldeans are all of equally uncertain antiquity, just as much as, or more than, ours are, and so all our judgements contain a large element of uncertainty. However, our conjectures are not so fanciful as to be completely wide of the mark, and I do not think that I myself have strayed from the truth. I am sure that anyone who considers the question carefully will come to the same conclusions as I have reached above: namely, that the origin of the arts we are discussing was nature itself, and that the first image or model was the beautiful fabric of the world, and that the master who taught us was that divine light infused in us by special grace, which has made us not only superior to the animal creation but even, if one may say so,

like God Himself. Now, in our own time (as I hope to show a little farther on by a number of examples) simple children, brought up roughly in primitive surroundings, have started to draw instinctively, using as their only models the trees around them, the lovely paintings and sculptures of nature, and guided only by their own lively intelligence. But the first men were more perfect and endowed with more intelligence, seeing that they lived nearer the time of the Creation; and they had nature for their guide, the purest intellects for their teachers, and the world as their beautiful model. So is there not every reason for believing that they originated these noble arts and that from modest beginnings, improving them little by little, they finally perfected them?

It goes without saying that the arts must have been discovered by some one person; and I realize that someone made a beginning at some time. And of course it is possible for one man to have helped

Source: Giorgio Vasari, *Lives of the Artists*, Vol. 1, trans. by George Bull (New York: Viking Penguin, Inc., 1987), pp. 30–31.

another, and to have taught and opened the way to design, colour, and relief; for I know that our art consists first and foremost in the imitation of nature but then, since it cannot reach such heights unaided, in the imitation of the most accomplished artists. Still, I think it is very dangerous to insist that the origin of the arts can be traced to this or that person, and in any case this is hardly something we need to worry about. We have, after all, already seen what is the true origin and basis of art. An artist lives and acquires fame through his works; but with the passing of time, which consumes everything, these works—the first, then the second, then the third—fade away. When there were no writers there was no way of leaving for posterity any record of works of art, and so the artists themselves also sank into obscurity. Then, when writers started to commemorate what had been done before their time, they could only take note of artists of whom some knowledge had come down to them; and so the first artists of whom any record was made are those whose memory was the most recent. . . .

Selection 4
Life of Filippo Brunelleschi (1377–1446)
Antonio Manetti

Brunelleschi's life reveals several personal and professional characteristics that gave him confidence in his own gifts and made him extraordinarily respected. This account of his life notes that he "longed for distinction in whatever he undertook." Brunelleschi—both artist and architect—was thereby encouraged to devote great care to every detail. The fact that he craved recognition did not make him an unpleasant person, however. In addition to listing some of Brunelleschi's many accomplishments, this life of the artist describes many admirable personal qualities, some of which were not shared by his contemporaries.

. . . Filippo was one of the Priors together with Lapo Niccolini as gonfaloniers or administrators of justice in May and June of 1425. Filippo represented the San Giovanni Quarter and Lapo represented the Santa Croce Quarter. He is recorded in the register of Priors as Filippo, the son of Ser Brunellesco Lippi, called Lippo after Ser Brunellesco's father. He also held other judiciary posts required in that period. Neither he nor his brother Tommaso had children.

The tomb of his forebears is in San Marco between the front portal of the church and the first railing, more or less under the pulpit where they preach.

Their coat of arms is divided diagonally into two parts. There are two green fig leaves in a field of gold in the upper half and green waves, also on a field of gold, in the lower half. Some say that

Source: Antonio Manetti, Vita di Brunelleschi—The Life of Brunelleschi, trans. by Catherine Enggass (University Park, Pa: Pennsylvania State University Press, 1970), pp. 38–42.

originally they came from Figherolo, a fortified town in the Ferrarese on the Po River, and that the two fig leaves and the waves of the river on the coat of arms derive from that. You ask for the most detailed and complete information that I am able to provide, and I will tell you all I know; however, you must have patience if I then appear too long-winded in some parts.

Following the general custom of men of standing in Florence, Filippo learned to read and write at an early age and to use the abacus. He also learned some Latin; perhaps because his father, who was a notary, thought of having him follow the same profession, since very few men in that period took up Latin—or were made to take it up—unless they expected to become a doctor, notary, or priest. He was very obedient, manageable, and fearful of disgrace. That fear was more effective than threats or any other device. He longed for distinction in whatever he undertook. From childhood he had a natural interest in drawing and painting and his work was very charming. For that reason he elected to become a goldsmith when his father, as was the custom, apprenticed him to a trade. Noting his aptitude, his father, who was a wise man, gave his consent.

Because of his foundation in drawing he quickly became very proficient in that profession in which he soon displayed himself most wonderfully. Within a brief period he became a complete master in niello, enamel, and ornamental architectural reliefs, as well as in cutting, mounting, and polishing all kinds of precious stones. It was in general the same in everything he dedicated himself to. In that art and what pertained to it he succeeded more marvelously than seemed possible at his age. That is the reason why he was commissioned in his youth to make certain large silver figures to be added to the very rich altar in San Jacopo in Pistoia. They were made by him, as he was a master although very young. He carved and painted a very beautiful life-size—or little less than life-size—wooden statue in the round of St. Mary Magdalen which was destroyed when the church of Santo Spirito burned in 1471. He carved in wood and painted a life-size crucifix in the round. It is attached to the pillar between the two side chapels on the side of the transept toward the old piazza in Santa Maria Novella. In the opinion of connoisseurs it is unsurpassed for excellence in sculpture, especially that of crucifixes. According to reports of his contemporaries he created other very beautiful works in bronze and other materials. However, all those I have mentioned I have seen.

Since, as we said, he revealed a marvelous genius, his advice about buildings was in great demand. His kinsman Apollonio Lapi employed him a great deal when he was building the house by the Canto de'Ricci toward the Mercato Vecchio, which now belongs to his son Bartolomeo. There is much that is good, comfortable, and pleasing to be seen on the inside; however, during that period the method of building was very crude as may be observed in contemporary and earlier buildings.

It is reported that when the construction of Villa Petraia was undertaken Filippo's advice was requested by the proprietor of the holding and that the tower was built in accordance with his advice. Although people have praised the tower to me, I have only seen it from a distance. The construction was interrupted because of a change of fortune [in the family].

When he was a young man it was necessary to construct the office and residence for the officials of the Monte as well as the room for their assistants in that part of the Signoria where there used to be mainly columned loggias. The loggias had been built for the beauty and splendor of the palace; they were much admired in their time and are still to be seen there. Filippo was asked to act as architect, designer, and director of construction in this undertaking and he did so. That he did not like the architectural details used in those days and did not use them can still be noted. He did it in a different way, but the manner which he later acquired after he had seen the ancient buildings of the Romans was not yet his.

During the same period he propounded and realized what painters today call perspective, since it forms part of that science which, in effect, consists of setting down properly and rationally the reductions and enlargements of near and distant objects as perceived by the eye of man: buildings, plains, mountains, places of every sort and location, with figures and objects in correct proportion to the distance in which they are shown. He originated the rule that is essential to whatever has been accomplished since his time in that area. We do not know whether centuries ago the ancient painters—who in that period of fine sculptors are believed to have been good masters—knew about perspective or employed it rationally. If indeed they employed it by rule (I did not previously call it a science without reason) as he did later, whoever could have imparted it to him had been dead for centuries and no written records about it have been discovered, or if they have been, have not been comprehended. Through industry and intelligence he either rediscovered or invented it.

Although he was preëminent over many others in many things and consequently refined his own and the following century, he was never known to boast or praise himself or vaunt or laud himself by a single word. Instead he proved himself by his deeds with the opportunities that came along. Unless greatly provoked by insulting or disrespectful acts, he never became angry and was amiable to his friends. It gave him pleasure to commend those who merited it. He willingly instructed those he thought wished to be instructed and who were capable of instruction. He was very skillful and discerning in that as he was in other things. . . .

Selection 5
Lives of the Artists
Giorgio Vasari

Here Vasari highlights Leonardo da Vinci's technical brilliance, as seen through the creation of Leonardo's masterpiece, the *Mona Lisa*. It is not incidental that Vasari characterizes Mona Lisa's smile as "divine rather than human," for that was a theme of Renaissance identification with the immortal.

. . . For Francesco del Giocondo Leonardo undertook to execute the portrait of his wife, Mona Lisa. He worked on this painting for four years, and then left it still unfinished; and today it is in the possession of King Francis of France, at Fontainebleau. If one wanted to see how faithfully art can imitate nature, one could readily perceive it from this head; for here Leonardo subtly reproduced every living detail. The eyes had their natural lustre and moistness, and around them were the lashes and all those rosy and pearly tints that demand the greatest delicacy of execution. The eyebrows were completely natural, growing thickly in one place and lightly in another and following the pores of the skin. The nose was finely painted, with rosy and delicate nostrils as in life. The mouth, jointed to the flesh-tints of the face by the red of the lips, appeared to be living flesh rather than paint. On looking closely at the pit of her throat one could swear that the pulses were beating. Altogether this picture was painted in a manner to make the most confident artist—no matter who—despair and lose heart. Leonardo also made use of this device: while he was painting Mona Lisa, who was a very beautiful woman, he employed singers and musicians or jesters to keep her full of merriment and so chase away the melancholy that painters usually give to portraits. As a result, in this painting of Leonardo's there was a smile so pleasing that it seemed divine rather than human; and those who saw it were amazed to find that it was as alive as the original. . . .

Source: Giorgio Vasari, *Lives of the Artists*, vol. 1, trans. by George Bull (New York: Penguin Classics, 1987), pp. 266–267.

II. STATUS AND PERCEPTION

Varying sources demonstrate in different ways the new and growing awareness artists came to have of themselves as more than craftsmen during the Renaissance. They were aided in this realization by the growing competition for their services among individual patrons as well as public officials who regarded works of art as reflections of civic pride. These selections show the development of such changes over a period of time.

Selection 6
Letter of Complaint to a Patron, March 25, 1470
Francesco del Cossa

In the early Renaissance, the artist Francesco del Cossa wrote his patron, the Duke of Ferrara, to complain of the Duke's practice of paying all artists the same—by the square foot! The Duke, it appears, was not persuaded. As a result, Cossa left his employ and instead worked in Bologna. Clearly, a good artist already had some flexibility with regard to such professional choices.

Most illustrious Prince and Excellent Lord my most particular Lord: I recently petitioned your lordship along with the other painters about the payment for the room at Schifanoia, to which your lordship answered that the account was persistent. Illustrious prince, I do not wish to be the one to annoy Pellegrino de Prisciano and others, and so I have made up my mind to turn to your lordship alone, because you may feel, or it may have been said to you, that there are some who can be happy or are overpaid with a wage of ten pennies. And to recall my petition to you, I am Francesco del Cossa, who have made by myself the three wall sections toward the anteroom. And so, illustrious lord, if your lordship wished to give me no more than ten pennies per foot, and even though I would lose forty to fifty ducats, since I have to live by my hands all the time, I would be happy and well set, but since there are other circumstances, it makes me feel pain and grief within me. Especially considering that I, when after all I have begun to have a little of a name, should be treated and judged and compared to the sorriest assistant in Ferrara. And that my having studied, and I

study all the time, should not at this point have a little more reward, and especially from your lordship, than a person gets who had avoided such study. Surely, illustrious lord, it could not be that I would not feel grief and pain. And because my work proves what I have done, and I have used gold and good colors, if they were of the same value as those who have gone ahead without such labors it would seem strange to me, and I say this, lord, because I have done almost the whole work in fresco, which is a complex and good type of work, and this is known to all the masters of the art. All the same, illustrious lord, I put myself at your lordship's feet, and I pray you, if your objection should be to say: I don't want to do it for thee because I would have to do it for the others, my lord, your lordship could always say that the appraisals were this way. And if your lordship doesn't want to follow the appraisals, I pray your lordship may wish to give me, if not all that I perhaps would be entitled to, then whatever part you may feel in your grace and kindness, and I will accept it as a gracious gift, and will so proclaim it. My compliments to your illustrious lordship. Ferrara, March 25, 1470.

[Annotated by the Duke:] Let him be content with the fee that was set, for it was set for those chosen for the individual fields.

Source: Robert Klein and Henri Zerner, *Italian Art 1500–1600: Sources and Documents* (Evanston, Ill.: Northwestern University Press, 1989), pp. 9–10.

Selection 7
A Patron's Generosity
Philip the Good, Duke of Burgundy

Another patron, far from Italy—Philip the Good, Duke of Burgundy (1396–1467)—fully recognized the power that a renowned artist, in this case Jan van Eyck, might have to change masters. The Duke specifically instructed his account keepers to continue the artist's income so that van Eyck would not leave his service. Two differences may have operated to give van Eyck more leverage than del Cossa had. First, the Duke of Burgundy was known far and wide as a truly generous patron of the arts, and second, van Eyck's fame was greater, at that time as well as today.

LETTERS OF AN OFFICIAL AND THE DUKE HIMSELF

Jan van Eyck, former painter and equerry of the late Lord John, Duke of Bavaria, was known for his ability and craftsmanship by my said lord who had heard thereof from several of his people and which he knew to be true, being acquainted personally with the said Jan van Eyck. Confident of his loyalty and probity, my lord has retained said Jan as his painter and equerry, with the customary honors, prerogatives, franchises, liberties, rights, profits and usual emoluments pertaining to this position. And to the end that he shall be held to work for him in painting whenever it pleases him, my lord has ordered him to have and to take on his general receipt from Flanders, the sum of 100 parisis in Flemish money in two settlements yearly, half at Christmas and the other half at Saint John's, of which he wishes the first payment to be at Christmas 1425 and the other at Saint John's, and so from year to year and payment to payment, as long as it shall please him. Ordering to the masters of his household and his other officers that all his present honors, rights, prerogatives, profits and emoluments above mentioned they shall make and allow the said Jan to enjoy peaceably without prevention or disturbance; in addition, ordering to his said receiver general of Flanders, present and future,

Source: Elizabeth Gilmore Holt (ed.), *A Documentary History of Art,* vol. 1 (Princeton, N.J.: Princeton University Press 1957), pp. 303–305.

that he shall pay, give and deliver every year the said sum of 100 Parisian pounds per year on the above declared terms to the said Jan, his painter and equerry, so all that is said on these matters may appear more plainly in the letters patent of my beforementioned lord, given in his city of Bruges, the 19th day of May in the year 1425. By virtue of that attestation is briefly given here to make payment for the term of Christmas 1425, and that which will follow to make a payment of 50 pounds on his quittance.

For the terms of St. John and Christmas 1426 together is made payment of 100 pounds on his quittance.

To our beloved and faithful keepers of our accounts at Lille.

In the name of the Lord, amen. In the year of our Lord 1495, in the thirteenth Indiction, at the time of the most Holy Father in Christ, Pope Alexander VI, ruling by Divine Providence, the eighth day of March. Drawn up in Perugia in the monastery of St. Peter in the presence of the following witnesses: Eusebio di Jacopo of Porta Santa Susanna of Perugia, Gianfrancisco Ciambello of Porta Sole of Perugia. The most Reverend Father in Christ, D. Lucianus of Florence, Abbot of the monastery of St. Peter of the Benedictine Order and of the congregation of Santa Giustina at Perugia, and D. Benedetto of Siena, and D. Daniele of Perugia, as the syndics of the order and procurators of the named monastery, with the permission, consent and desire of the above-mentioned Abbot, who is present and consenting, . . . have ordered and commissioned the most honorable man, master Pietro Cristoforo of Castel della Pieve, a most accomplished painter, who is present and has accepted the commission, to paint and ornament the picture for the main altar of the church of St. Peter. The picture must be painted in the following way:

In the rectangular panel, the Ascension of our Lord, Jesus Christ, with the figure of the glorious Virgin Mary, the Twelve Apostles and some angels and other ornaments, as may seem suitable to the painter.

In the semicircle above, supported by two angels, should be painted the figure of God the Almighty Father.

The predella below is to be painted and adorned with stories according to the desire of the present Abbot. The columns, however, and the mouldings and all other ornamentation of the panel should be embellished with fine gold and other fine colors, as will be most fitting, so that the panel will be beautifully and diligently painted, embellished and gilded from top to bottom as stated above and as it befits a good, experienced, honorable, and accomplished master. It will be

Selection 8
Contract of Pietro Perugino with the Benedictine Monks of S. Pietro at Perugia (1495)

The form of this contract is wholly typical of others of the time and demonstrates not only the widespread use of contracts and legal documents during the Renaissance but the increasingly professional response to artists and works of art. Artists could now sue in order to receive payment for their work, while patrons could, in turn, force recalcitrant artists to complete a work of art or provide financial compensation.

In the name of the Lord, amen. In the year of our Lord 1495, in the thirteenth Indiction, at the time of the most Holy Father in Christ, Pope Alexander VI, ruling by Divine Providence, the eighth day of March. Drawn up in Perugia in the monastery of St. Peter in the presence of the following witnesses: Eusebio di Jacopo of Porta Santa Susanna of Perugia, Gianfrancisco Ciambello of Porta Sole of Perugia. The most Reverend Father in Christ, D. Lucianus of Florence, Abbot of the monastery of St. Peter of the Benedictine Order and of the congregation of Santa Giustina at Perugia, and D. Benedetto of Siena, and D. Daniele of Perugia, as the syndics of the order and procurators of the

Source: Elizabeth Gilmore Holt (ed.), *A Documentary History of Art*, vol. 1 (Princeton, N.J.: Princeton University Press, 1957), pp. 268–270.

named monastery, with the permission, consent and desire of the above-mentioned Abbot, who is present and consenting, . . . have ordered and commissioned the most honorable man, master Pietro Cristoforo of Castel della Pieve, a most accomplished painter, who is present and has accepted the commission, to paint and ornament the picture for the main altar of the church of St. Peter. The picture must be painted in the following way:

In the rectangular panel, the Ascension of our Lord, Jesus Christ, with the figure of the glorious Virgin Mary, the Twelve Apostles and some angels and other ornaments, as may seem suitable to the painter.

In the semicircle above, supported by two angels, should be painted the figure of God the Almighty Father.

The predella below is to be painted and adorned with stories according to the desire of the present Abbot. The columns, however, and the mouldings and all other ornamentation of the panel should be embellished with fine gold and other fine colors, as will be most fitting, so that the panel will be beautifully and diligently painted, embellished and gilded from top to bottom as stated above and as it befits a good, experienced, honorable, and accomplished master. It will be executed within the space of the coming two and a half years, all at the cost and expense of the said master Pietro himself. The said master Pietro has promised the Reverend Abbot . . . to carry out this agreement in general and in particular under the penalties herein specified. The painter pledges all his goods, real and movable property, present and future.

This the said master Pietro consented to because the Reverend Father, the Abbot, has promised and agreed with him on the pledge of the monastery and his possessions to the said master Pietro, who is present and is executing this contract: namely, to give to him or to his heirs and actually to pay him for his painting, for paints, gold and other things necessary and suitable for the execution of the said painting, as well as for the ornaments of the said panel, 500 gold ducats, payable within four years, counting from the day on which the painting shall be begun, at the rate of one quarter of the sum each year.

In said account, however, the frame which surrounds the panel is not to be included, nor the ornaments placed at the top of said frame, but only the panel itself with its ornaments. . . .

Selection 9
The *Cronica*, Florence (1472)

In this selection we see a Florentine chronicler cataloging his city's accomplishments with pride. The boastful emphasis here is on the number of workshops of master craftsmen, with the splendor of their artistic creations highlighted throughout.

. . . Florence the fair has 270 shops of the wool guild within the city between Via Maggio and in San Martino and the Vigna and the via del Palagio and at the Peliciai and at S. Procolo and the Porta Rossa and at the Guild of Druggists and at the Ferravecchi and in the Fondaccio and at S. Felicita in the Piazza and in Borgo San Jacopo, who make cloths for Rome, for Florence, for Sicily, for the Marches, for Naples, for Turkey, for Constantinople, for Pera, for Adrianople, for Bursa, for Chios in 1471, as is well known to the Genoese and Ragusans, and other merchants. Florence the fair has 83 lordly shops of the Silk Guild [similar details] . . . and 33 banks [likewise] . . . and 84 shops of woodworkers, in inlay and carving, and 54

shops for stone, dressed and rough, and masters of carving and relief and half relief and foliage, inside and outside the city, in all perfection, and 70 shops of butchers in the city, and 8 poulterers [similar details]. Florence the fair has 39 shops of goldbeaters and silver filigree, and expert masters of wax images the equal of the world, and if you make a comparison in these two arts, and take Venice and take Genoa and take Milan and take Lucca, for these four cities make silver filigree, and in wax images I would have you take Bruges and London and Germany and France and Spain and Hungary and Italy, any city at all or that ever was in the world, you won't find and can't find masters of wax images equal to these, who are in the city of Florence today, and the Nunziata [church known for wax images] shows it to everyone. Florence the fair has 44 shops of goldsmiths and silversmiths. . . .

Source: Creighton E. Gilbert, *Italian Art 1400–1500: Sources and Documents* (Evanston, Ill.: Northwestern University Press, 1992), p. 184.

Selection 10
Life of Donatello

Giorgio Vasari

Artists could not help but be influenced by praise and were often anything but self-effacing in their view of their own work. Although Donatello said that he was always anxious to return to Florence whenever he was absent, because there he would be "constantly criticized and so would have an incentive for studying and winning even greater glory," he could respond vociferously when he considered that his creations were insufficiently valued, as this following passage shows.

. . . It is said that a Genoese merchant ordered from Donatello a life-size head of bronze, a beautiful piece of work which was made very light, since it had to be carried a long distance, and that Donatello obtained the commission through Cosimo's recommendation. Now when the head was finished and the merchant wanted to pay for it, he objected that Donatello was asking too much. So the dispute was referred to Cosimo, who had the head carried to the upper court of the palace and placed between the battlements overlooking the street, where it could be better seen. Then, when Cosimo tried to settle the matter, he found what the merchant was offering a long way from what

Donatello was asking, and so he remarked that in his opinion the offer was too small. And at this the merchant, who thought it was too much, complained that, since he had finished the work in a month or a little over, Donatello would be making over half a florin a day. Donatello considered himself grossly insulted by this remark, turned on the merchant in a rage, and told him that he was the kind of man who could ruin the fruits of a year's toil in a split second; and with that he suddenly shoved the head down on to the street where it shattered into pieces and added that the merchant had shown he was more used to bargaining for beans than for bronzes. The merchant at once regretted what he had done and promised to pay twice as much if Donatello would do the head again; but neither his promises, nor the entreaties of Cosimo, could persuade Donatello to do so. . . .

Source: Giorgio Vasari, *Lives of the Artists*, vol. 1, trans. by George Bull (New York: Penguin Classics, 1987), pp. 180–181.

III. NEW IMAGES AND ROLES

During the Renaissance—for the first time since antiquity—artists wrote of their own work and artistic goals. Such efforts were meant for their own pleasure and the prescriptive edification of others. The initial selection from *The Craftsman's Handbook* of Cennino d'Andrea Cennini, for example, combines practical advice on mixing paints, identifying colors, and preparing paper with more philosophical interpretations of the nature and value of art.

Selection 11
The Craftsman's Handbook
Cennino d'Andrea Cennini

The title of the second chapter in this selection, "How You Should Regulate Your life in the Interests of Decorum and the Condition of Your Hand; and in What Company; and What Method You Should Adopt for Copying a Figure From High Up," specifies the artist's need for moderation in food and drink and equates art with more lofty pursuits such as philosophy and theology.

CHAPTER XXVIII

How, beyond masters, you should constantly copy from nature with steady practice

Mind you, the most perfect steersman that you can have, and the best helm, lie in the triumphal gateway of copying from nature. And this outdoes all other models; and always rely on this with a stout heart, especially as you begin to gain some judgment in draftsmanship. Do not fail, as you go on, to draw something every day, for no matter how little it is it will be well worth while, and will do you a world of good.

CHAPTER XXIX

How you should regulate your life in the interests of decorum and the condition of your hand; and in what company; and what method you should first adopt for copying a figure from high up

Source: Cennino d'Andrea Cennini, *The Craftsman's Handbook*, trans. by Daniel V. Thompson, Jr. (New York: Dover Publications, Inc., 1960), pp. 15–16.

Your life should always be arranged just as if you were studying theology, or philosophy, or other theories, that is to say, eating and drinking moderately, at least twice a day, electing digestible and wholesome dishes, and light wines; saving and sparing your hand, preserving it from such strains as heaving stones, crowbar, and many other things which are bad for your hand, from giving them a chance to weary it. There is another cause which, if you indulge it, can make your hand so unsteady that it will waver more, and flutter far more, than leaves do in the wind, and this is indulging too much in the company of woman. Let us get back to our subject. Have a sort of pouch made of pasteboard, or just thin wood, made large enough in every dimension for you to put in a royal folio, that is, a half; and this is good for you to keep your drawings in, and likewise to hold the paper on for drawing. Then always go out alone, or in such company as will be inclined to do as you do, and not apt to disturb you. And the more understanding this company displays, the better it is for you. When you are in churches or chapels, and beginning to draw, consider, in the first place, from what section you think you wish to copy a scene or figure; and notice where its darks and half tones and high lights come; and this means that you have to apply your shadow with washes of ink; to leave the natural ground in the half tones; and to apply the high lights with white lead.

Selection 12
Advice to Painters
Leonardo da Vinci

To Leonardo, the arts represented a totality, for the depiction of beauty called forth an effort from all senses. In his famed *Notebooks*, Leonardo wrote of the artist's life, ranging from a discussion of how and under what working conditions painters can be most productive and creative to conclusions about the supremacy of painting as an art above all others and the universality of great artists.

THE PRECEPTS OF THE PAINTER

Painting

The mind of the painter should be like a mirror which always takes the colour of the thing that it reflects and which is filled by as many images as there are things placed before it. Knowing therefore that you cannot be a good master unless you have a universal power of representing by your art all the varieties of the forms which nature produces,—which indeed you will not know how to do unless you see them and retain them in your mind,—look to it, O Painter, that when you go into the fields you give your attention to the various objects and look carefully in turn first at one thing and then at another, making a bundle of different things selected and chosen from among those of less value. And do not after the manner of some painters who when tired by imaginative work, lay aside their task and take exercise by walking in order to find relaxation, keeping, however, such weariness of mind as prevents them either seeing or being conscious of different objects; so that often when meeting friends or relatives, and being saluted by them, although they may see and hear them they know them no more than if they had met only so much air.

How from age to age the art of painting continually declines and deteriorates when painters have no other standard than work already done

The painter will produce pictures of little merit if he takes the works of others as his standard; but if he will apply himself to learn from the objects of nature he will produce good results. This we see was the case with the painters who came after the time of the Romans, for they continually imitated each other, and from age to age their art steadily declined.

After these came Giotto the Florentine, and he,—reared in mountain solitudes, inhabited only by goats and such like beasts—turning straight from nature to his art, began to draw on the rocks the movements of the goats which he was tending, and so began to draw the figures of all the animals which were to be found in the country, in such a way that after much study he not only surpassed the masters of his own time but all those of many preceding centuries. After him art again declined, because all were imitating paintings already done; and so for centuries it continued to decline until

Source: Edward MacCurdy, *The Notebooks of Leonardo da Vinci* (New York: Charles Scribner's Sons, 1906), pp. 163–185.

such time as Tommaso the Florentine, nicknamed Masaccio, showed by the perfection of his work how those who took as their standard anything other than nature, the supreme guide of all the masters, were wearying themselves in vain. Similarly I would say as to these mathematical subjects, that those who study only the authorities and not the works of nature are in art the grandsons and not the sons of nature, which is the supreme guide of the good authorities.

Mark the supreme folly of those who censure such as learn from nature, leaving uncensored the authorities who were the disciples of this same nature!

The life of the painter in the country

The painter requires such knowledge of mathematics as belongs to painting, and severance from companions who are not in sympathy with his studies, and his brain should have the power of adapting itself to the tenor of the objects which present themselves before it, and he should be freed from all other cares.

And if while considering and examining one subject a second should intervene, as happens when an object occupies the mind, he ought to decide which of these subjects presents greater difficulties in investigation, and follow that until it becomes entirely clear, and afterwards pursue the investigation of the other. And above all he should keep his mind as clear as the surface of a mirror, which becomes changed to as many different colours as are those of the objects within it, and his companions should resemble him in a taste for these studies, and if he fail to find any such he should accustom himself to be alone in his investigations, for in the end he will find no more profitable companionship.

Of the life of the painter in his studio

The painter or draughtsman ought to be solitary in order that the well-being of the body may not sap the vigour of the mind, and more especially when he is occupied with the consideration and investigation of things which by being continually present before his eyes furnish food to be treasured up in the memory.

If you are alone you belong entirely to yourself; if you are accompanied even by one companion you belong only half to yourself, or even less in proportion to the thoughtlessness of his conduct; and if you have more than one companion you will fall more deeply into the same plight.

If you should say, 'I will take my own course; I will retire apart, so that I may be the better able to investigate the forms of natural objects,' then I say this must needs turn out badly, for you will not be able to prevent yourself from often lending an ear to their chatter; and not being able to serve two masters, you will discharge badly the duty of companionship and even worse that of endeavouring to realise your conceptions in art.

But suppose you say, 'I will withdraw so far apart that their words shall not reach me nor in any way disturb me,' I reply that in this case you will be looked upon as mad, and bear in mind that in so doing you will then be solitary.

If you must have companionship choose it from your studio; it may then help you to obtain the advantages which result from different methods of study. All other companionship may prove extremely harmful.

How the painter is not worthy of praise unless he is universal

We may frankly admit that certain people deceive themselves who apply the title 'a good master' to a painter who can only do the head or the figure well. Surely it is no great achievement if by studying one thing only during his whole lifetime he attain to some degree of excellence therein! But since, as we know, painting embraces and contains within itself all the things which nature produces or which result from the fortuitous actions of men, and in short whatever can be comprehended by the eyes, it would seem to me that he is but a poor master who only makes a single figure well. For do you not see how many and how varied are the actions which are performed by men alone? Do you not see how many different kinds of animals there are, and also of trees and plants and flowers?

What variety of hilly and level places, of springs, rivers, cities, public and private buildings; of instruments fitted for man's use; of divers costumes, ornaments, and arts?—Things which should be rendered with equal facility and grace by whoever you wish to call a good painter.

How the mirror is the master of painters

When you wish to see whether the general effect of your picture corresponds with that of the object represented after nature, take a mirror and set it so that it reflects the actual thing, and then compare the reflection with your picture, and consider carefully whether the subject of the two images is in conformity with both, studying especially the mirror. The mirror ought to be taken as a guide,— that is the flat mirror—for within its surface substances have many points of resemblance to a picture; namely that you see the picture made upon one plane showing things which appear in relief, and the mirror upon one plane does the same. The picture is one single surface, and the mirror is the same. The picture in intangible, inasmuch as what appears round and detached cannot be enclosed within the hands, and the mirror is the same. The mirror and the picture present the images of things surrounded by shadow and light, and each alike seems to project considerably from the plane of its surface. And since you know that the mirror presents detached things to you by means of outlines and shadows and lights, and since you have moreover amongst your colours more powerful shadows and lights than those of the mirror, it is certain that if you but know well how to compose your picture it will also seem a natural thing seen in a great mirror.

*   *   *

Painters oftentimes deceive themselves by representing water in which they render visible what is seen by man; whereas the water sees the object from one side and the man sees it from the other; and it frequently happens that the painter will see a thing from above and the water sees it from beneath, and so the same body is seen in front and behind, and above and below, for the water reflects the image of the object in one way and the eye sees it in another.

Of judging your own picture

We know well that mistakes are more easily detected in the works of others than in one's own, and that oftentimes while censuring the small faults of others you will overlook your own great faults. In order to avoid such ignorance make yourself first of all a master of perspective, then gain a complete knowledge of the proportions of man and other animals, and also make yourself a good architect, that is in so far as concerns the form of the buildings and of the other things which are upon the earth, which are infinite in form; and the more knowledge you have of these the more will your work be worthy of praise; and for those things in which you have no practice do not disdain to draw from nature. But to return to what has been promised above, I say that when you are painting you should take a flat mirror and often look at your work within it, and it will then be seen in reverse, and will appear to be by the hand of some other master, and you will be better able to judge of its faults than in any other way. It is also a good plan every now and then to go away and have a little relaxation; for then when you come back to the work your judgment will be surer, since to remain constantly at work will cause you to lose the power of judgment. It is also advisable to go some distance away, because then the work appears smaller, and more of it is taken in at a glance, and a lack of harmony or proportion in the various parts and in the colours of the objects is more readily seen.

Of variety in figures

The painter ought to strive at being universal, for there is a great lack of dignity in doing one thing well and another badly, like many who study only the measurements and proportions of the nude figure and do not seek after its variety; for a man may be properly proportioned and yet be fat and short or long and thin, or medium. And whoever does not take count of these varieties will always make his figures in one mould so that they will all appear sisters, and this practice deserves severe censure.

Of the order of acquiring this universality

It is an easy matter for whoever knows how to represent man to afterwards acquire this universality, for all the animals which live upon the earth resemble each other in their limbs, that is in muscles, sinews, and bones, and they do not vary at all, except in length or thickness as will be shown in the Anatomy. There are also the aquatic animals, of which there are many different kinds; and with regard to these I do not advise the painter to make a fixed standard, for they are of almost infinite variety; and the same is also true of the insect world.

How the painter ought to be desirous of hearing every man's opinion as to the progress of his work

Surely when a man is painting a picture he ought not to refuse to hear any man's opinion, for we know very well that though a man may not be a painter, he has true conception of the form of another man and will judge aright whether he is hump-backed or has one shoulder high or low, or whether he has a large mouth or nose or other defects.

Since then we recognise that men are able to form a true judgment as to the works of nature, how much the more does it behove us to admit that they are able to judge our faults. For you know how much a man is deceived in his own works, and if you do not recognise this in your own case observe it in others and then you will profit by their mistakes. Therefore you should be desirous of hearing patiently the opinions of others, and consider and reflect carefully whether or no he who censures you has reason for his censure; and correct your work if you find that he is right, but if not, then let it seem that you have not understood him, or—in case he is a man whom you esteem— show him by argument why it is that he is mistaken.

How in works of importance a man should not trust so entirely to his memory as to disdain to draw from nature

Any master who let it be understood that he could himself recall all the forms and effects of nature would certainly appear to me to be endowed with great ignorance, considering that these effects are infinite and that our memory is not of so great capacity as to suffice thereto. Do you therefore, O Painter, take care lest the greed for gain prove a stronger incentive than renown in art, for to gain this renown is a far greater thing than is the renown of riches. For these, then, and other reasons which might be given, you should apply yourself first of all to drawing in order to present to the eye in visible form the purpose and invention created originally in your imagination; then proceed to take from or add to it until you satisfy yourself; then have men arranged as models draped or nude in the way in which you have disposed them in your work; and make the proportion and size in accordance with perspective, so that no part of the work remains that is not so counselled by reason and by the effects in nature. And this will be the way to make yourself renowned in your art.

Of studying as soon as you are awake or before you go to sleep in bed in the dark

I have proved in my own case that it is of no small benefit on finding oneself in bed in the dark to go over again in the imagination the main outlines of the forms previously studied, or of other noteworthy things conceived by ingenious speculation; and this exercise is entirely to be commended, and it is useful in fixing things in the memory.

A way to stimulate and arouse the mind to various inventions

I will not refrain from setting among these precepts a new device for consideration which, although it may appear trivial and almost ludicrous, is nevertheless of great utility in arousing the mind to various inventions. And this is that if you look at any walls spotted with various stains or with a mixture of different kinds of stones, if you are about to invent some scene you will be able to see in it a resemblance to various different landscapes adorned with mountains, rivers, rocks, trees, plains, wide valleys, and various groups of hills. You will also be able to see divers combats and figures in quick movement, and strange expressions of faces, and outlandish costumes, and an infinite number of things which you can then reduce into separate and well conceived forms. With such walls and blends of different stones it comes about as it does with the sound of bells, in whose clanging you may discover every name and word that you can imagine.

Of the games in which draughtsmen should indulge

When you draughtsmen wish to find some profitable recreation in games you should always practise things which may be of use in your profession, that is by giving your eye accuracy of judgment so that it may know how to estimate the truth as to the length and breadth of objects. So in order to accustom the mind to such things let one of you draw a straight line anywhere on a wall, and then let each of you take a light rush or straw in his hand, and let each cut his own to the length which the first line appears to him when he is distant from it a space of ten braccia, and then let each go up to the copy in order to measure it against the length which he has judged it to be, and he whose measure comes nearest to the length of the copy has done best and is the winner, and he should receive from all the prize which was previously agreed upon by you. Furthermore you should take measurements foreshortened, that is, you should take a spear or some other stick and look before you to a certain point of distance, and then let each set himself to reckon how many times this measure is contained in the said distance. Another thing is to see who can draw the best line one braccio in length, and this may be tested by tightly drawn thread. Diversions such as these enable the eye to acquire accuracy of judgment, and this is the primary essential of painting.

* * *

Painters have a good opportunity of observing actions in players, especially at ball or tennis or with the mallet when they are contending together, better indeed than in any other place or exercise.

Of the proper time for studying the selection of subjects

The winter evenings should be spent by youthful students in study of the things prepared during the summer; that is, all the drawings from the nude which you have made in the summer should be brought together, and you should make a choice from among them of the best limbs and bodies and practise at these and learn them by heart.

Of attitudes

Afterwards in the ensuing summer you should make choice of some one who has a good presence, and has not been brought up to wear doublets, and whose figure consequently has not lost its natural bearing, and make him go through various graceful and elegant movements. If he fails to show the muscles very clearly within the outlines of the limbs, this is of no consequence. It is enough for you merely to obtain good attitudes from the figure, and you can correct the limbs by those which you have studied during the winter.

An indication whether a youth has an aptitude for painting

There are many men who have a desire and love for drawing but no aptitude for it, and this can be discerned in children if they are not diligent and never finish their copies with shading.

The painter is not worthy of praise who only does one thing well, as the nude, or a head, or draperies, or animal life, or landscapes, or such other special subject, for there is no one so dull of understanding that after devoting himself to one subject only and continually practising at this, he will fail to do it well.

Painting

Men and words are actual, and you, painter, if you do not know how to execute your figures, will be like an orator who does not know how to use his words.

*   *   *

The painter who draws by practice and judgment of the eye without the use of reason, is like the mirror which reproduces within itself all the objects which are set opposite to it without knowledge of the same.

This rule ought to be given to children who paint

We know clearly that the sight is one of the swiftest actions that can exist, for in the same instant it surveys an infinite number of forms; nevertheless it can only comprehend one thing at a time. To take an instance, you, O Reader, might at a glance look at the whole of this written page and you would instantly decide that it is full of various letters, but you will not recognise in this space of time either what letters they are or what they purport to say, and therefore it is necessary for you if you wish to gain a knowledge of these letters to take them word by word and line by line. Again, if you wish to go up to the summit of a building it will be necessary for you to ascend step by step, otherwise it will be impossible to reach the top. So I say to you whom nature inclines to this art, if you would have a true knowledge of the forms of different objects you should commence with their details and not pass on to the second until the first is well in your memory and you have practised it. If you do otherwise you will be throwing away time, and to a certainty you will greatly prolong the period of study. And remember to acquire diligence rather than facility.

How one ought first to learn diligence rather than rapid execution

If as draughtsmen you wish to study well and profitably, accustom yourself when you are draw-

ing to work slowly, and to determine between the various lights which possess the highest degree of brightness and in what measure, and similarly as to the shadows which are those that are darker than the rest, and in what manner they mingle together, and to compare their dimensions one with another; and so with the contours to observe which way they are tending, and as to the lines what part of each is curved in one way or another, and where they are more or less conspicuous and consequently thick or fine; and lastly to see that your shadows and lights may blend without strokes or lines in the manner of smoke. And when you shall have trained your hand and judgment with this degree of care, it will speedily come to pass that you will have no need to take thought thereto.

Of the order to be observed in study

I say that one ought first to learn about the limbs and how they are worked, and after having completed this knowledge one ought to study their actions in the different conditions in which men are placed, and thirdly to devise figure compositions, the studies for these being taken from natural actions made on occasion as opportunities offered, and one should be on the watch in the streets and squares and fields, and there make sketches with rapid strokes to represent features, that is for a head one may make an *o*, and for an arm a straight or curved line, and so in like manner for the legs and trunk, afterwards when back at home working up these notes in a completed form.

My opponent says that in order to gain experience and to learn how to work readily, it is better that the first period of study should be spent in copying various compositions made by different masters either on sheets of paper or on walls, since, from these one acquires rapidity in execution and a good method. But to this it may be replied that the ensuing method would be good if it was founded upon works that were excellent in composition and by diligent masters; and since such masters are so rare that few are to be found, it is safer to go direct to the works of nature than to those which have been imitated from her originals with great deterioration and thereby to acquire a bad method, for he who has access to the fountain does not go to the water-pot.

The order of learning to draw

First of all copy drawings by a good master made by his art from nature and not as exercises; then from a relief, keeping by you a drawing done from the same relief; then from a good model, and of this you ought to make a practice.

Of the way to fix in your mind the form of a face

If you desire to acquire facility in keeping in your mind the expression of a face, first learn by heart the various different kinds of heads, eyes, noses, mouths, chins, throats, and also necks and shoulders. To take as an instance noses. They are of ten types: straight, bulbous, deep-set, prominent either above or below the centre, aquiline, regular, ape-like, round, and pointed. These divisions hold good as regards profile. Seen from in front noses are of twelve types: thick in the middle, thin in the middle, with the tip broad and narrow at the base, or narrow at the tip and broad at the base, with nostrils broad or narrow, or high or low, and with the openings either distended or hidden by the tip. And similarly you will find variety in the other features; of which things you ought to make studies from nature and to fix them in your mind. Or when you have to draw a face from memory, carry with you a small note-book in which you have noted down such features, and then when you have cast a glance at the face of the person whom you wish to draw, you can then look privately and see which nose or mouth has a resemblance to it, and make a tiny mark against it in order to recognise it again at home. Of monstrous faces I here say nothing, for they are kept in mind without difficulty.

Of the parts of the face

If nature had only one fixed standard for the proportions of the various parts, then the faces of all men would resemble each other to such a degree that it would be impossible to distinguish one from another; but she has varied the five parts of the face in such a way that although she has made an almost universal standard as to their size she has not observed it in the various conditions to such a degree as to prevent one from being clearly distinguished from another.

Of the grace of the limbs

The limbs should fit the body gracefully in harmony with the effect you wish the figure to produce; and if you desire to create a figure which shall possess a charm of its own, you should make it with limbs graceful and extended, without showing too many of the muscles, and the few which your purpose requires you to show indicate briefly, that is without giving them prominence and with the shadows not sharply defined, and the limbs, and especially the arms, should be easy, that is that no limb should be in a straight line with the part that adjoins it. And if the hips, which form as it were the poles of the man, are by his position placed so that the right is higher than the left, you should make the top shoulder joint so that a line drawn from it perpendicularly falls on the most prominent part of the hip, and let this right shoulder be lower than the left. And let the hollow of the throat always be exactly over the middle of the joint of the foot which is resting on the ground. The leg which does not support the weight should have its knee below the other and near to the other leg.

The positions of the head and arms are numberless, and therefore I will not attempt to give any rule; it will suffice that they should be natural and pleasing and should bend and turn in various ways, with the joints moving freely so that they may not seem like pieces of wood.

Painting

O painter skilled in anatomy, beware lest the undue prominence of the bones, sinews, and muscles cause you to become a wooden painter from the desire to make your nude figures reveal all their emotions. And if you wish to remedy this you should consider in what way the muscles of old or lean persons cover or clothe the bones, and furthermore note the principle on which these same muscles fill up the spaces of the surface which come between them, and which are the muscles that never lose their prominence in any degree of fatness whatsoever, and which those whereof the tendons become indistinguishable at the least suggestion of it. And there are many cases when several muscles grow to look one from the increase of fat, and many in which when any one becomes lean or old a single muscle divides into several; and in this treatise all their peculiarities shall be set forth each in its place, and especially with regard to the spaces that come between the joints of each limb. Further you should not fail to observe the variations of the aforesaid muscles round the joints of the limbs of any animal, due to the diversity of the movements of each limb; for on any side of these joints the indication of these muscles becomes completely lost by reason either of the increase or diminution of the flesh of which these muscles are composed.

Of painting

It is a necessary thing for the painter in order to be able to fashion the limbs correctly in the positions and actions which they can represent in the nude, to know the anatomy of the sinews, bones, muscles and tendons in order to know in the various different movements and impulses which sinew or muscle is the cause of each movement, and to make only these prominent and thickened, and not the others all over the limb, as do many who in order to appear great draughtsmen make their nudes wooden and without grace, so that it seems rather as if you were looking at a sack of nuts than a human form or at a bundle of radishes rather than the muscles of nudes.

How it is necessary for the painter to know the inner structure of man

The painter who has acquired a knowledge of the nature of the sinews, muscles, and tendons will know exactly in the movement of any limb how many, and which of the sinews are the cause of it, and which muscle by its swelling is the cause of this sinew contracting, and which sinews having been changed into most delicate cartilage surround and contain the said muscle. So he will be able in divers ways and universally to indicate the various muscles by means of the different attitudes of his figures; and he will not do like many who in different actions always make the same things appear in the arm, the back, the breast, and the legs; for such things as these ought not to rank in the category of minor faults.

Of the nature of the folds of draperies

That part of the fold which is furthest from the ends where it is confined will return most closely to its original form. Everything naturally desires to remain in its own state. Drapery being of uniform density and thickness on the reverse and on the right side, desires to lie flat; consequently, whenever any folds or pleats force it to quit this condition of flatness, it obeys the law of this force in that part of itself where it is most constrained, and the part furthest away from such constraint you will find return most nearly to its original state, that is to say, lying extended and full.

Selection 13
Professional Standards
Artemisia Gentileschi

Artemisia Gentileschi's life has emerged from obscurity only within the past few years. She has been termed the most successful woman painter prior to the modern era; she was certainly one of the first to be self-supporting. The obstacles Artemisia overcame were monumental. They included an artist father who subjugated and exploited her, rape at the age of 17 by one of her father's colleagues, followed by a grueling public trial and a forced marriage at the age of 20 to hide her "shame." The power of her personality and of her work gained favor among aristocratic patrons and is increasingly recognized today. In this letter to an important patron she plays the role of the prideful artist as well as anyone, but she also displays a rueful recognition of the fact that, as a woman, she has to prove herself in ways that were not required of men.

My Most Illustrious Sir,

I would prefer not to discuss our business in this letter, in case that gentleman [the bearer] should read it. However, I say to Your Most Illustrious Lordship, with regard to your request that I reduce the price of the paintings that I had quoted, [I can do] a little, but [the price] must be no less than four hundred ducats, and you must send me a deposit as all the other gentlemen do. But I can tell you for certain that the higher the price, the harder I will strive to make a painting that will please Your Most Illustrious Lordship, and that will conform to my taste and yours. Concerning the painting that I have already finished for Your Most Illustrious Lordship, I cannot give it to you for less than I asked, as I have already overextended myself to give the lowest price. I swear, as your servant, that I would not have given it even to my father for the price that I gave you. Signor Don Antonio, my Lord, I beg you for God's sake not to reduce [the price] I stated, because I am sure that when you see it, you will say that I was not presumptuous. Your nephew the Duke thinks that I must hold great affection for Your Most Illustrious Lordship to charge you such a price. I only wish to remind you that there are eight [figures], two dogs, and landscape and water. Your Most Illustrious Lordship will understand that the expense for models is staggering.

I will say no more, except what I have on my mind, that I think Your Most Illustrious Lordship will not suffer any loss with me, and that you will find the spirit of Caesar in this soul of a woman.

And with this, I pay you most humble reverence.

From Naples, the 13th of November, 1649.

The most humble servant of Your Most Illustrious Lordship,

Artemisia Gentileschi

Source: Mary D. Garrard, *Artemisia Gentileschi: The Image of the Female Hero in Italian Baroque Art* (Princeton, N.J.: Princeton University Press, 1989), pp. 396–399.

SEVEN

The Scientist

Of all the transformations we are considering here, none has had a more profound influence on the modern world than the Scientific Revolution. A distinguished historian has written that "it outshines everything since the rise of Christianity." And indeed, the fundamental reshaping of the way we understand the physical world that was achieved by the scientists of the Renaissance and early modern times proved to be a unique moment not only in European history but also in all history. No other culture has ever been able to shake off so thoroughly the intuitive, supernatural, and superstitious assumptions about nature that had dominated human thinking from its earliest days. How this breakthrough happened, and how it gave new status to those who brought it about, is one of the most remarkable stories of the age.

THE PRECURSORS OF SCIENCE: THREE TRADITIONS AND PARACELSUS

From the beginnings of recorded time, people have observed the forces that surround them and have speculated about their meaning. Since many phenomena (such as the weather) seem uncontrollable, wonderful and mysterious stories have been invented to account for what one sees. Thus the ancient Greeks believed that the Sun crossed the sky each day because the god Apollo drove it across heaven in his chariot. The grand regularities of nature influenced not only how people made a livelihood, especially in agriculture, but other forms of behavior as well. At Stonehenge, for example, early Britons created a stone structure whose purpose, though not explained to this day, was clearly designed to make use of the position of the Sun at dawn on midsummer's day each year.

To some degree, any attempt to describe or understand nature implies the hope that the resultant knowledge will enable one to control its power. To men and women who could be ruined by a storm or a fire or enriched by a timely rainfall, it

253

was vital to learn as much as possible about the processes that dominated their lives. If one did not know when to plant or how high a river could rise, one courted disaster. For some, the information may merely have satisfied curiosity; for most, though, it was essential to survival—and at this basic level every society has studied nature. Equally inevitable has been the attempt to go beyond day-to-day discoveries and to create systematic, comprehensive explanations of physical events. These might be sought for their practical applications or because knowledge was considered worthwhile for its own sake, but above all they seem to have satisfied a deep human need for an overall structure that makes sense of our existence and of the world around us.

In the Middle Ages, religion provided the basic answers to questions about the purpose of life and the relation of human beings to God and nature. Religion offered little, however, in the way of day-to-day practical advice for solving material problems or much guidance in explaining how the physical world was structured, beyond the belief that God was responsible for all of creation. For more concrete information or ideas, Europeans relied on three major traditions that sought, by various means, to come to terms with nature. Each was associated with a different social setting, but each was to make a crucial contribution to the emergence of the new way of thinking we call "science."

The first tradition was the one that occupied artisans and engineers. From the village blacksmith to the designer of fortifications, these were the solvers of practical problems. They saw it as their task to devise not only tools that could make life easier but also workable defences against the dangers nature (or other human beings) posed. They invented windmills and ploughs; they erected dams and walls; they molded metal into nails, horseshoes, and swords; and they built the roads, ships, and towns that sustained European society. They had attained a down-to-earth understanding, and even control, of some of nature's operations, but they had little interest in its larger structures or in explaining how it worked. This was to come from other sources, but one cannot minimize the importance to later developments of the practical commitment to the arts of measurement, calculation, and direct observation that were at the heart of the artisanal/engineering tradition.

The second tradition also had its representatives both among ordinary people and among the educated. Identified with figures as different as the "wise" men and women of Europe's villages and the learned alchemists and astrologers of cities and courts, this was the tradition of magical speculation. It suggested that there was indeed a vast and mysterious system that bound all nature together. How one explored, understood, or controlled that system varied enormously, depending on the particular outlook one embraced. The local "wise" woman might rely on omens, talismans, herbs, and spells to explain how nature worked and to mitigate its effects. The alchemist, experimenting in a fantastic workshop filled with strange liquids, metals, powders, and animal parts, felt it was possible to unlock the secret of matter through mixtures and formulas that would transform one element into another or would cure wounds and ailments (Figure 52). The astrologer believed that the stars determined all human fate. What linked all the magicians, however, were two assumptions that had considerable influence on later scientists: that nature was organized in regular, uniform structures and that the discovery of those underlying structures would have practical consequences.

Figure 52. After Pieter Brueghel the Elder, *The Alchemist* (engraving). The combination of theoretical speculation and experimentation that characterized the alchemist is captured in this unflattering portrayal by Brueghel. The alchemist gestures from his book, while his disreputable female assistants (who resemble witches) work on various materials at their feet.

The third tradition was centered in Europe's universities. Here the achievements of the distant past were studied, elaborated, and taught. From Aristotle, professors learned what they regarded as the basics of physics and of the study of nature in general; from Ptolemy, the elements of astronomy; and from Galen, the principles of anatomy. These ancient Greek writers—whose discoveries were a uniquely European legacy—had dominated their respective fields for over a thousand years, and most of the teaching and research about the natural world at universities revolved around them, although there was also important new work in such areas as optics and the study of motion. In the main, however, the ancient writings were thought to hold the truth, and the task of later generations of "natural philosophers"—as these professors were called—was primarily to explain and elaborate the texts they had inherited.

Until the 1400s and 1500s, these three traditions operated largely independently of one another. Each concentrated on its own set of problems—the artisan improving the techniques of daily work, the magician seeking shattering revelations such as the aptly named "philosopher's stone," which was supposed to change lead into gold, and the professor of natural philosophy finding examples that showed how the views of famous ancestors explained natural events. What was now to transform these traditions and make possible the emergence of the very different outlook we associate with science was the gradual crumbling of the barriers that divided them. By taking their inspiration from all three of these enterprises, a remarkable group of pioneers created an entirely new way of investigating the physical world.

One figure of the early 1500s in particular indicated the unprecedented directions such studies might take. His name was Aureolus Theophrastus Bombast von Hohenheim, and his career was as colorful as his name. Known as Paracelsus, and born in 1493, he was the greatest alchemist of his day (Figure 53). Yet he was no mere magician. He was above all an experimenter, someone who felt that by observing and manipulating herbs, metals, and other physical materials he could uncover the basic secrets of nature. Human intervention was essential, he felt, because

> . . . nature does not produce anything that is perfect in itself. Man must bring everything to perfection. This work of bringing things to their perfection is called alchemy. And he is an alchemist who carries what nature creates for the use of man to its destined end.

Yet the purpose was not just to discover the hidden principles that governed matter; it was to serve human needs. Much of Paracelsus's work was intended for medical applications, and he may have discovered the first cure for a new disease that was sweeping Europe, syphilis. Fascinated by metals, rather than the traditional herbal remedies, he learned that by very careful application, small doses of mercury could cure syphilis—if they did not kill the patient first.

Students were enthralled by Paracelsus, especially when he told them that they should ignore the old authorities. He burned the works of Galen, a favorite of natural philosophers, in a public square in Basel, and he was in constant trouble with university and other officials. But he was undeterred. His credo was "Give heed to those who each day seek for something new and each day find something new." Taking his own advice, he looked to the speculations of magic, combined with the practical knowledge of ordinary people (but not natural philosophers), to find ways of understanding nature. As he put it:

> Magic has a power to experience and fathom things which are inaccessible to human reason. For magic is a great secret wisdom. The universities do not teach things, so a doctor must seek out old wives, gypsies, sorcerers, wandering tribes, old robbers, and such outlaws, and take lessons from them. A doctor must be a traveller.

Some of the elements of what was to become science were beginning to take shape: the boundless curiosity, the determination to reject old assumptions and methods, the willingness to try anything new, the faith in observation and experiment, and the belief that there were underlying regularities that bound the physical world together. Yet Paracelsus was still too enamored of mystic speculation for its own sake to move on to the scientific outlook as we know it. This was to emerge as a result of other kinds of investigation, primarily in astronomy, mathematics, and physics.

Figure 53. Follower of Quentin Massys, *Paracelsus (?)—Portrait of a Man Before a Landscape*. Although he was a controversial figure, who seemed to enjoy his battles with medical and academic authorities, Paracelsus did not object to having himself portrayed as a respectable learned man in an elegant painting that describes him as the "famous doctor."

THE NEW SCIENCE: FROM COPERNICUS TO NEWTON

The scientific revolution was the creation of an extraordinary succession of geniuses who worked in many fields from the early 1500s to the late 1600s. If we have space here to focus on but a few, they nevertheless can be taken to exemplify the major developments of the period. And it is important to emphasize that most of them had connections to more than one of the three traditions that nurtured science: to practical engineering, to speculative magic, or to university learning.

The barriers between the first and the last were among the hardest to cross, because they marked a major social as well as intellectual divide. Nowhere was the distinction more apparent than in the teaching of anatomy. At the classes, a professor on a platform would read from a book—usually Galen—or from notes, while below him a barber-surgeon would cut up a cadaver and display the anatomic parts described in the reading. It was inconceivable that the lecturer, the noble exponent of matters of the mind, would have anything to do with the dissection, the lowly manual labor that was the province of the artisan. It was a perfect representation of the independence of the two traditions.

At the university of Padua in northern Italy, however, this crucial boundary line began to be crossed, possibly because of the more pragmatic interests for which Venice, which ruled Padua, was famous. Whatever the reason, anatomists began to perform dissections themselves; as a result, it became common for direct observation to affect learned theory. This cross-fertilization made Padua a major center of research into nature during the Renaissance and an important breeding ground for the new outlook of science.

An extraordinary roster of the famous figures of the scientific revolution studied or taught at Padua, notably in the field of anatomy. Both Andreas Vesalius, from Flanders, and the Englishman William Harvey, for example, were associated with Padua, and they transformed our understanding of the workings of the human body, first through Vesalius's observations of anatomy (Figure 54), published in 1543, and then, even more notably, when Harvey explained the function of the heart and demonstrated the circulation of the blood in 1628. Probably the most famous Paduans, however, were two astronomers—the young Polish cleric, Nicholas Copernicus, who came to the university in 1501, and the Italian Galileo Galilei, who followed him nearly a century later.

Copernicus was no experimenter, and not much of an observer, for he regarded himself primarily as a mathematician. But practical problems did concern him. What was especially troubling was that the classical picture of the heavens, inherited from Ptolemy, was encountering growing problems. In the Ptolemaic theory, the universe was like a huge set of concentric crystalline—glasslike—spheres, with the Earth at its center. The stars, the Sun, the Moon, and the planets were stuck to these spheres, which revolved at different speeds around the earth, and this was why they passed by overhead at regular intervals. The trouble was that observations revealed some planets apparently moving backwards. To account for these anomalies—in fact caused by the Earth's and the planets' elliptical orbits—it had been suggested that they moved in epicycles, that is, around smaller spheres which themselves were stuck to the main spheres. As complications grew, observers had added semiepicycles and even semi-demiepicycles to the system.

Copernicus believed that the complexity of Ptolemaic astronomy was outrunning its usefulness, and he had another practical reason for seeking an improvement.

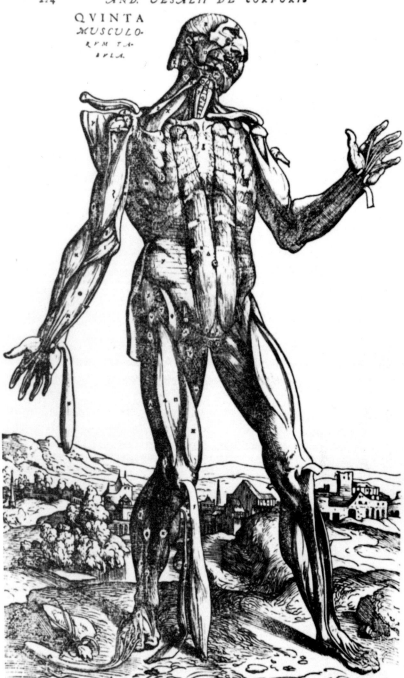

QVINTA
MUSCULO-
RVM TA-
BVLA.

Figure 54. Andreas Vesalius, *De Humani Corporis Fabrica* (1543)—musculature (engraving). The magnificent illustrations of Vesalius's great work on anatomy were prepared in Titian's studio. The muscles are displayed on a gesturing figure, and the landscape in the background shows the countryside near Padua, where Vesalius taught.

Figure 55. *The Copernican Planetary System* (engraving). Although the Sun has been moved to the center of the universe in this depiction of the Copernican system, and we see the satellites of Jupiter that Galileo revealed, there is no sign of Kepler's earlier discovery that the orbits of the planets are elliptical, not circular.

Europe's calendar, inherited from ancient Rome and named the "Julian" calendar after Julius Caesar, was based on a slight miscalculation. Its inventors, believing the year to be slightly longer than it is, added a day every fourth, or leap, year (we now count only every fourth century year as a leap year). As a result, the date of Easter, which depends on the day each spring when day and night are both exactly 12 hours long, was falling later and later in the year. Eventually, so churchmen like Copernicus feared, it might have to be celebrated at Christmas time!

To solve these problems, Copernicus proposed a radical solution: Make the Sun, not the Earth, the center of the system. To justify such boldness, he assured his readers (correctly) that the theory was not new but had been held by an ancient Greek astronomer. And just as geocentric (earth-centered) theorists took philosophic support from the belief that human beings should be the center and measure of all things, so Copernicus argued for the heliocentric (Sun-centered) view (Figure 55) by asking whether there was "any better place to set [the Sun] in this cosmic

Figure 56. *Tycho Brahe's Observatory* (engraving). It was from this specially constructed chair that Brahe made his remarkably accurate observations of the movements of the heavens.

temple than in the center, where it can shed its light equally on all?" However, his theory was little less complex than Ptolemy's, and he never challenged the notion of crystalline spheres.

For all his conservatism, however, Copernicus began a huge upheaval in astronomy. He was a widely respected mathematician; his recalculations had to be taken seriously; and indeed, the reform that eventually created the modern calendar (enacted in 1582 by Pope Gregory XIII and therefore known as the "Gregorian" calendar) was in large part stimulated by Copernicus's work, published in 1543, which was dedicated to a pope. For nearly a century, astronomers struggled to decide, in the absence of convincing proof either way, whether the new theory was better than Ptolemy's. In the course of this struggle, they created the mode of thought and analysis we call "science."

The generation following Copernicus had no way of testing the validity of his theory. The greatest astronomer of the time, the Dane Tycho Brahe, came up with a complicated interpretation that could be regarded as *both* geocentric *and* heliocentric. More important, he compiled, night after night for some twenty years, the most remarkable set of observations of the movement of the heavens before the invention of the telescope (Figure 56). His data, passed on when he died in 1601 to his protegé, the German astronomer Johannes Kepler, at last provided the evidence from which the next step could be taken.

Kepler, like Brahe, did not do his work at a university. He held various public positions, most notably as court astrologer and mathematician, from 1601 to 1612, to the Emperor Rudolf II, Europe's leading patron of magic and the occult. As befitted

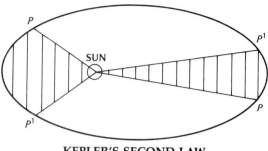

Figure 57. Diagram of Kepler's Second Law of Planetary Motion. If P and P^1 are any two points on the orbit between which a planet passes in equal time, then the area described by Sun − P − P^1 is always equal.

KEPLER'S SECOND LAW

the holder of this position, Kepler was much attracted by magical ideas, and his discoveries can be seen as a remarkable amalgam of vast speculations about the underlying structure of nature, observation, and the traditions of natural philosophy. What held them all together was mathematics, the language in which the new science was to be written, and of which Kepler was a master.

Using Brahe's observations, Kepler uncovered three basic laws of planetary motion that undermined every aspect of the Ptolemaic system. Published in 1609 and 1619, the laws stated that planetary orbits were elliptical, not circular, with the Sun as one focus of the ellipse; that the speed of the orbit increased as the planet came closer to the Sun in such a way that if a line were drawn from the planet to the Sun, it would sweep equal areas in equal time (Figure 57); and that there was a relationship, uniting all the planets, that linked their distance from the Sun and the time of their complete orbits. The crystalline spheres, the epicycles, the geocentric theory, and the belief in the perfection of circular motion were all gone. By removing the boundaries, Kepler had created the basis for an infinite universe, though he himself still rejected the idea.

Yet the study of orbits was only one of Kepler's many endeavors. He also made important contributions in optics, physics, and mathematics. At the same time, his magical inclinations led him to suggest mysterious relationships among the proportions of solids (such as cubes and spheres) and between the intervals that separate musical notes and those which separate the planets. The latter led him to revive an ancient notion that the planets gave off sounds as they orbited the Sun, a basic harmony of nature that he called the "music of the spheres."

Kepler's more mystical investigations gave him an eccentric air, and for more than half a century even Copernican astronomers—including so acute a coworker as Galileo—refused to accept Kepler's three planetary laws. Kepler often got into trouble. His religious beliefs were questioned by both Catholics and Protestants, and a book in which he imagined (quite brilliantly) what it would be like if his mother flew to the Moon on a broomstick helped get her accused of witchcraft. Far more convincingly than Paracelsus, however, Kepler demonstrated that regardless of the occasional eccentricity of the impulse, the search for a comprehensive new way of understanding nature was beginning not only to uncover new knowledge but also to forge a new form of intellectual inquiry.

The person who was to crystallize this advance was Kepler's contemporary, the Italian Galileo Galilei, born in 1564. Galileo was a mathematician who came straight out of the university natural philosophy tradition. Indeed, it was his dependence on his academic job that made him cautious, even in his thirties, about openly admitting he was a Copernican. He knew his colleagues would not want to rewrite their lectures and would suspect a newcomer who espoused an unproven theory. "I would dare to publish my thoughts," he wrote to Kepler in 1597, "if there were many like you; but since there are not, I shall forbear." Predictably, Kepler, the younger of the two, rejected such caution:

> I could only have wished that you, who have so profound an insight, would choose another way. You advise us to retreat before the general ignorance and not oppose the violent attacks of the mob of scholars. But after a tremendous task has been begun in our time, first by Copernicus, and then by many learned mathematicians, and when the assertion that the Earth moves can no longer be considered something new, would it not be much better to pull the wagon to its goal by our joint efforts, and gradually to shout down the common herd?
>
> Be of good cheer, Galileo, and come out publicly. If I judge correctly, only a few of the distinguished mathematicians of Europe would part company with us, so great is the power of truth.

But Galileo waited. He was making a fine reputation and had won a post at Padua a few years before the correspondence with Kepler. A series of experiments in physics, in which he applied geometry to problems of motion, was convincing him that Artistotle's ancient assumption that all motion was unnatural and that only rest was natural might be wrong. Admired for his research, he was asked by the rulers of nearby Venice to serve as a consultant at the Arsenal—the huge armaments and shipbuilding complex that was essential to the city's naval strength—in order to advise the workers about moving great weights like cannon. Tireless experimenter that he was, Galileo probably learned as much about leverage and falling objects by watching the crews at the Arsenal as he ever taught them.

The very fact that artisans sought practical advice from a university professor indicates that the barriers between natural philosophy and engineering, between theory and experiment, were breaking down. And it was his ability to combine both worlds that finally induced Galileo to go public, in one of the most sensational books of the seventeenth century, a book that was to make him, and science, famous. Published in 1610, it was called *The Starry Messenger,* and that is literally what it was: a messenger bringing new information from the stars.

Some time earlier, Galileo had heard that a Dutch glazier had found a way of making distant objects seem closer by moving two lenses back and forth in a tube. Creating his own "telescope"—as the instrument was to be called—Galileo first showed it to Venetian leaders as a way of seeing further on land, enabling them to spot returning ships hours before they were visible to the naked eye. But then, in a decisive gesture, Galileo turned it to the heavens. What he saw, and what he was able to interpret with his theoretical and mathematical training, transformed astronomy forever.

The most startling of the discoveries reported in *The Starry Messenger* were the fact that the Moon has mountains, which cast shadows that lengthen as the sun sets, just like those on Earth (Figure 58), and the existence of three moons around Jupiter, which circle that planet in the same way as our Moon circles the Earth. Galileo became the sensation of Italy, in demand at the most fashionable social gatherings of the day, from Venice to Rome, where people could look through his

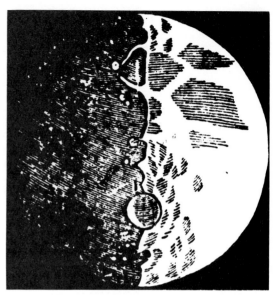

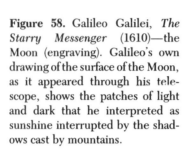

Figure 58. Galileo Galilei, *The Starry Messenger* (1610)—the Moon (engraving). Galileo's own drawing of the surface of the Moon, as it appeared through his telescope, shows the patches of light and dark that he interpreted as sunshine interrupted by the shadows cast by mountains.

telescope for themselves. By 1613, Cosimo de Medici, the ruler of his native city, Florence, had appointed him court mathematician, and he could leave the uncertainties of academic life forever.

But other problems now began to appear. Conservative professors remained convinced—and not without reason—that the truth of Copernicanism still had not been proved, and a number of theologians began to emphasize that the theory posed major problems, especially in the way Galileo was expounding it. Not only did the Bible assert that the Earth stood still—for example, in the 93rd Psalm—but traditional cosmology regarded the heavens, where the angels lived, as perfect and unchanging, in contrast to the corrupt earth, where decay and change were proof of the materials world's imperfections. If the Moon and Jupiter were now subject to the same changes, how could one draw an essential difference between heaven and earth?

Galileo responded sharply to such questions and in so doing laid out the basic credo of the scientist:

> Nothing physical which sense-experience sets before our eyes, or which necessary demonstrations prove to us, ought to be called in question on the testimony of biblical passages. I do not believe that that same God who has endowed us with senses, reason, and intellect has intended us to forgo their use. He would not require us to deny sense and reason in physical matters which are set before our eyes. Truly demonstrated physical conclusions need not be subordinated to biblical passages. If in order to banish the opinion in question it were sufficient to stop the mouth of a single man, that would be easily done. But it would be necessary to forbid men to look at the heavens.

The wit and sarcasm that he now directed at his critics, as his confidence in his achievements and reputation grew, made him dangerous enemies. They had him called before the Roman Inquisition of the Church in 1616 and ordered not to teach Copernicanism as more than a hypothesis. When a long-time admirer of his became

Pope in 1623, however, he began to put together his major work on astronomy, the *Dialogue on the Two Chief Systems of the World* which was finally published in 1632 (Figure 59).

The two systems were the Ptolemaic and the Copernican, and there could be no question which one the author thought was true. Although he made some mistakes—he thought tides were caused by the motion of the Earth—he produced powerful arguments for believing in the daily rotation of the Earth and its orbiting of the Sun. He noted, for example, that

> . . . a most true maxim of Aristotle teaches us that "that is done in vain by many means which may be done by fewer." This renders it more probable that the daily motion belongs to the Earth alone than to the whole Universe, excepting only the Earth.

In this way, he used even ancient authorities to bolster his case. Moreover, his elegant and often funny book was written in Italian, which anyone could read, not the usual Latin of learned scholarship. Once again, therefore, Galileo caused a sensation, but this time it had dire consequences. In 1632 the aged, nearly blind astronomer was again hauled before the Inquisition.

His friend the Pope could not help him because Galileo was accused of having disobeyed the earlier order of the Inquisition not to teach Copernicanism. He claimed it was only a theory in the *Dialogue* (not a very convincing argument), but now he was told that he had been forbidden to teach it at all—an assertion backed up by a supposed document of 1616 which many scholars believe to have been a forgery. Seeing no way out, and fearing excommunication, Galileo recanted and rejected Copernicanism. Condemned to house arrest, he returned for the last nine years of his life to Florence, where he completed, and had printed in Protestant Holland in 1638, his masterpiece on physics, the *Dialogue on Two New Sciences*, a revolutionary mathematical analysis of such topics as motion—he showed that it was no more unnatural than rest—acceleration, and kinetics.

The discoveries Galileo made about motion and astronomy were united in a single system that also embraced Kepler's laws by the last of the great figures of the scientific revolution, Isaac Newton (Figure 60). An Englishman born in 1642, the year Galileo died, Newton was again a university mathematician, this time at Cambridge. His chief work, *The Mathematical Principles of Natural Philosophy,* was published in 1687, and it was seen as resolving all the issues of physics and astronomy that had arisen since Copernicus began working in the early 1500s.

Newton's three laws of motion posited that action and reaction are equal and opposite; that a body will continue in motion, following a straight line, until acted on, when "the change of motion is proportional to the motive force impressed, and is made in the direction of the line in which that force is impressed;" and that universal gravitation links all particles in the universe in a system of mutual attraction that is governed by the so-called inverse square law, in which distance determines the force of the attraction. With these fundamental principles, Newton was able to solve problems as different as the elliptical shape of planetary orbits, the causes of tides, and the reason a pendulum with a one-second swing is shorter at the Equator than in Europe. It was a staggering achievement, which, together with other works, established Newton as the supreme student of physics, optics, mathematics, and astronomy of the age—the true climax of the scientific revolution.

Figure 59. Galileo Galilei, *Dialogue on the Two Chief Systems of the World* (1632), frontispiece (engraving by Stefano della Bella). On the title page of Galileo's *Dialogo*, dedicated to the Grand Duke of Tuscany, three astronomers conduct the discussion that makes up the content of the book. On the left is the questioner, the middle one is labeled the Ptolemaic, and the one on the right is labeled the Copernican.

Figure 60. *Portrait of Isaac Newton,* artist unknown. The intense gaze in this portrait of Newton suggests the power of scientific insight that contemporaries thought he embodied.

What Newton completed, too, was the rise of the scientist to an unprecedented status in European society. This was the new expert, the solver of problems, and the touchstone for all intellectual endeavor. Although Newton himself dabbled in alchemy, numerology, and mystical biblical speculations, these were always quite separate interests and did not detract from his reputation as the embodiment of human reason. It was because he seemed to have raised genius to new levels that he—and the enterprise he was engaged in—came to be revered. He was the first man of learning ever knighted in England, and his funeral in 1727 was described as fit for a king. Yet there was much besides their problem-solving capabilities that explains the position science and the scientist attained in the late 1600s.

SCIENCE AND SOCIETY

Even before the major breakthroughs had taken place or gained wide admiration, proponents of the new ways of studying nature were arguing for the special importance of their ideas. Galileo himself had insisted that his "truly demonstrated physical conclusions" had independent value and could not be challenged by any method but his own. And his English contemporary, Francis Bacon, made the point even more strongly.

Bacon came to science with a deep suspicion of grand systems. Unlike the magicians, he was uneasy about vast, unifying theories; as a result, he was able to reject both the notion that all planets had to move in circular orbits and Copernicanism. Both ideas, he felt, rested on assumptions that had not been proved. As he wrote in 1620 (Figure 61):

> The human understanding is of its own nature prone to suppose the existence of more order and regularity in the world than it finds. Though there be many things in nature which are singular, it devises for them parallels which do not exist. The understanding must not therefore be supplied with wings, but rather hung with weights, to keep it from leaping and flying. Now this has never yet been done; when it is done, we may entertain better hopes of the sciences.

What he proposed was a heavy reliance on observation; conclusions, he said, should be reached only by induction—reasoning from the particular to the general. As information was gathered, the experimental findings could be linked together in more general statements, but the process had to be slow, built up block by block. Bacon wanted to apply this technique to many new areas of research, such as heat, and he was delighted by the new instruments, such as the telescope, that unlocked hidden information. Yet it was his vision of how the results would improve human society that most influenced his age.

Since research was so laborious, Bacon wanted it to be a cooperative enterprise. In his description of an ideal country, *The New Atlantis* (1627), everybody had some role in the advance of science, from the humblest preparer of materials for an experiment to the highest generalizers. And their purpose was to use science to improve the quality of life—"for the relief of man's estate," as he put it. This cooperative, pragmatic goal became the inspiration of the scientific societies that began to be founded throughout Europe in the mid-1600s. Patronized by aristocrats and royalty, they put the final seal on the rise of the scientist.

The admiration for science, however, was not merely the result of its ability to solve particular problems. What was crucial was that this quality struck a chord, filled a powerful need, in the larger society, because it happened that the late sixteenth and early seventeenth centuries were a time of deepening self-doubt. The terrible wars of religion between Protestants and Catholics and the undermining of traditional assumptions by the discovery of new lands and people overseas, by rapid population growth and economic change, and by the rise of more powerful governments had caused profound anxieties. Among the philosophers of the time, for example, the doubts had created a crisis in epistemology—the system for investigating the nature of human knowledge and determining what is true.

The bitter conflicts over truth, especially in religion, raised worries as to whether certainty could ever be achieved again. Many thinkers adopted sceptical positions,

Figure 61. Francis Bacon, *New Organon* (1620), frontispiece. The title page of Bacon's principal work advocating scientific research shows a ship returning from a voyage above the inscription, "Many shall venture forth and knowledge shall be increased."

arguing that real knowledge was simply unattainable. The most famous of them, the Frenchman Michel de Montaigne, suggested that one could go no further than identifying what was possible. His motto, "What do I know?" implied that he could not even assert "I know nothing"—he had to raise the issue in the form of a question.

It was into this situation that science came, suggesting that answers and certainty were indeed possible. Its theorists, like Bacon, agreed that one had to move carefully, but in the end, some level of assurance would be achieved. And Bacon's younger contemporary, the Frenchman René Descartes (Figure 62), who made important contributions in mathematics, physics, astronomy, and optics, responded directly to Montaigne. He admitted in his *Discourse on Method,* published in 1637, that one had to be cautious: ". . . like a man who walks alone in darkness, I resolved to go so slowly that, if I did not get ahead very rapidly, at least I was safe from falling." But Montaigne's total doubt was not necessary. The mind *was* capable of discovering truth. For a start, one could prove one's own existence from the fact that one was thinking: "I think, therefore I am." Any idea that was clearly perceived, Descartes said, had to be true.

At the same time, Descartes suggested that science offered a means of understanding all of nature. According to the mechanical philosophy Descartes proposed, which had enormous influence, everything in the world could be compared by analogy to a machine. In the body, the arm was like a lever, the elbow like a hinge.

Figure 62. Frans Hals, *Portrait of René Descartes*. When Descartes settled in Amsterdam, he sat for the Dutch portrait painter Hals, who created a rich sense of the Frenchman's intellectual powers even while showing him as an austere figure, dressed in black and white.

For every effect, he said, there had to be a cause. By applying this principle, all physical phenomena could eventually be explained.

It was because the scientists' discoveries in the 1600s appeared to promise epistemologic certainty that they seemed such an effective remedy for the doubts of Montaigne's generation in the late 1500s. It was, above all, the recognition that truth could again be found that won such wide admiration for scientific achievements. By the 1650s, science seemed to be offering a model for all knowledge. It had become a fashionable pursuit for aristocrats, who often had no idea what it entailed but thought they were applying it if they described the changing shapes of the dunes on a beach or started herbariums in their gardens. Public dissections were attracting large crowds of paying customers, and every discipline, from the design of fortifications and gardens to political theory and the invention of social statistics, was taking scientific method as its standard.

A few doubts were expressed about the sudden triumph of the scientist. In the 1650s, a brilliant French mathematical prodigy, Blaise Pascal, who had helped create the laws of probability and had discovered barometric pressure, raised troubling questions about the reverence for science. Concerned that other forms of insight, notably religion, were being shunted aside, he complained that the limitations of the new discoveries were being forgotten—that profound truths remained beyond their reach. In a memorable phrase that was appreciated more by later generations—when doubts about science reappeared—than by his own time, he identified the problem unmistakably: "The heart has its reasons that reason cannot know."

Pascal's was a lonely voice. Newton's discoveries seemed only to confirm what everyone already believed: that scientists displayed human capabilities at their best. They epitomized the workings of reason and provided an ideal against which all thought could be measured. The magician was no longer needed, since this new expert raised the hope that nature would at last be mastered. Amid such assurance, Pascal's warning that excessive confidence might create new problems fell on deaf ears. Relieved that its worst anxieties had been overcome, European society was ready to embrace even the most arcane of university studies in order to celebrate the new hero who had emerged out of the intellectual struggles of the Renaissance: the scientist.

Original Sources

The Renaissance gave rise to new methods of understanding, interpreting, and even reshaping the physical world. The changes that occurred in investigations of nature during this period were so extensive that the results have come to be known as the "Scientific Revolution."

It is important to remember, however, that at the same time that these new theories and activities were unfolding, earlier traditions continued to hold sway. It was not until *after* the Scientific Revolution, for example, that those who followed the older Aristotelian tradition were finally silenced.

There were also a number of mavericks who rejected the scientific establishment in some of the same ways as the courageous Galileo. Perhaps the most famous of these was the alchemist Paracelsus, but sorcerers, witches, and magicians, as well as some of Paracelsus's more dubious followers, all shared the European arena with the early scientists and were themselves very much a part of the study of nature.

I. BEFORE THE SCIENTIFIC REVOLUTION

Investigations of nature during the Middle Ages were dominated by the followers of the ancient Greek philosopher Aristotle. In retrospect, Aristotle and his followers laid the foundations for those who came later, although at the time of the Scientific Revolution itself, scientists turned decisively against Aristotelian thought. Medieval thinkers developed new ideas about induction and about mathematics, which foreshadow the kind of questioning that made the Scientific Revolution possible.

Along with these medieval thinkers who were respectable members of society, some who preceded the coming of the Scientific Revolution were reviled and persecuted as magicians or sorcerers. At times, they were considered superstitious fools. During the Middle Ages, the line between respectability and transgression was thin, and the boundaries were frequently unclear. However, adherence to Aristotle's theories and fundamental principles was considered essential.

Selection 1
"On Magic and the World of Nature"

St. Thomas Aquinas

Thomas Aquinas (1225–1274) was the foremost philosophical adherent of Aristotle during the Middle Ages and an important scholar in his own right. In this excerpt from the *Summa Contra Gentiles*, Aquinas considers investigation into the "World of Nature" as one step removed from *maleficium*, that is, "black magic," which is associated with witches and demons.

That the works of magicians result not only from the influence of heavenly bodies. Some there were

Source: Thomas Aquinas, "Summa Contra Gentiles," in Alan C. Kors and Edward Peters, eds., *Witchcraft in Europe 1100–1700* (Philadelphia: University of Pennsylvania Press, 1972), pp. 53–62.

who averred that such works as seem wonderful to us, being wrought by the magic art, are done, not by certain spiritual substances, but by the power of the heavenly bodies. This would seem to be indicated by the fact that those who practise works of this kind, observe the position of the stars: and are assisted by the employment of certain herbs and other corporeal things, for the purpose, as it were, of preparing matter of lower degree to receive the influence of the celestial power.

But this is in contradiction with the apparitions (in the works of magicians). For as it is impossible that an intellect be formed from corporeal principles, as we proved above, it is impossible for effects that are caused exclusively by the intellectual nature, to be produced by the power of a heavenly body. Now in these works of magicians, things appear that are exclusively the work of a rational nature; for instance, answers are given about stolen goods, and the like, and this could not be done except by an intelligence. Therefore it is not true that all such effects are caused by the mere power of a heavenly body.

Further. Speech is an act proper to the rational nature. Now in these works people appear to men and speak to them on various matters. Therefore such things cannot be done by the mere power of heavenly bodies. If, however, someone say that these apparitions are present, not to the sensorial organ, but only to the imagination:—this is, in the first place, apparently untrue. For imaginary forms do not seem real to anyone, unless his external senses be suspended: since it is not possible for a person to look on a likeness as a reality, except the natural judgements of the senses be tied. Now these conversations and apparitions are addressed to those who have free use of their external senses. Therefore these apparitions and speeches cannot be imaginary.

Besides, no imaginary forms can lead a person to intellectual knowledge beyond the natural or acquired faculty of his intellect: this is evident in dreams; since even if they contain some indication of the future, it is not every dreamer that understands the meaning of his dreams. Now, in these apparitions and speeches that occur in the works of magicians, it frequently happens that a person obtains knowledge of things surpassing the faculty of his intelligence, such as the discovery of hidden treasure, the manifestation of the future, and sometimes even true answers are given in matters of science. Either, therefore, these apparitions or speeches are not purely imaginary; or at least it is the work of some higher intelligence, and not only

of a heavenly body, that a person obtain the aforesaid knowledge through these imaginings.

Again. That which is done by the power of heavenly bodies, is a natural effect: since they are natural forms that are caused in this lower world by the powers of heavenly bodies. Hence that which cannot be natural to anything, cannot be caused by the power of the heavenly bodies. And yet some such things are stated to be caused by the aforesaid works: for instance, it is averred that at the mere presence of a certain person all doors are unlocked, that a certain man becomes invisible, and many like occurrences are related. Therefore this cannot be done by the power of heavenly bodies.

Further. The reception, through the power of heavenly bodies, of that which follows, implies the reception of what precedes. Now movement of its very nature, is the result of having a soul: since it is proper to animate things to move themselves. Therefore it is impossible for an inanimate being to be moved by itself, through the power of a heavenly body. Yet it is stated that by the magic art an image is made to move of itself, or to speak. Therefore it is not possible for the effects of the magic art to be caused by a celestial power.

And if it be said that the image in question is endowed with some vital principle by the power of the heavenly bodies; this is impossible. For the principle of life in all living things is the substantial form, because, as the Philosopher says (2 *De Anima*, iv.) *in living things to be is to live*. Now, it is impossible for anything to receive anew a substantial form, unless it lose the form which it had previously, since *the generation of one thing is the corruption of another* (3 *Phys.* viii.). But in the making of an image no substantial form is discarded, and there is only a change of shape which is an accident: since the form of copper or something of the kind remains. Therefore the image in question cannot possibly be endowed with the vital principle.

Further. If anything is moved by a principle of life it necessarily has sensation, for the principle of movement is sensation or understanding. But understanding is not found without sensation in things that come to be and pass away. Now there cannot be sensation where there is not the sense of touch; nor the sense of touch without an organ of mean temperature. Such a temperature, however, is not found in the stone or wax or metal out of which the statue is made. It is not possible, therefore, that statues of this sort should be moved by a principle of life.

Besides. Perfect living things are generated not only by a celestial power, but also from seed: for *man and the sun generate man* (2 *Phys.* ii.): and such as are generated by a celestial power alone without seed, are animals formed by putrefaction, and such belong to a lower grade than the others. Accordingly if these images be endowed with the vital principle by a celestial power alone, so as to move themselves, it follows that they belong to the lowest grade of animals. And yet this would be false if they worked by an intrinsic principle of life: since among their operations some are of a high degree, for they give answers about hidden things. Therefore it is not possible that their operations and movements proceed from a principle of life.

Again. We find sometimes a natural effect produced by the power of heavenly bodies without the operation of art: thus, although one may produce frogs, or something of the kind by means of some artifice, frogs do happen to be produced without any artifice. Consequently if these images that are made by necromancy, are endowed with the vital principle by the power of heavenly bodies, it will be possible for them to be formed without the operation of art. But this is not the case. Therefore it is evident that such images have not the principle of life, nor are they moved by the power of heavenly bodies.

Hereby we refute the opinion of Hermes who, according to Augustine (8 *De Civ. Dei* xxiii.) expressed himself thus: *As God is the cause of the heavenly gods, so man fashions the gods that reside in temples, being satisfied to live near men. I refer to those animal images, endowed with sense and spirit, that do great and wonderful things, images gifted with knowledge of the future, and who foretell by dreams and many other things; who afflict men with ailments and heal them, who bring sorrow and joy to them according to their merits.*

This opinion is also refuted by divine authority. For it is said in the Psalm (cxxxiv. 15 *seqq.*): *The idols of the Gentiles are silver and gold, the works of men's hands. They have a mouth but they speak not . . . neither is there any breath in their mouths.*

Yet seemingly we must not absolutely deny the possibility of some kind of efficacy being in these things through the power of the heavenly bodies: but only for such effects as certain lower bodies are able to cause by the power of the heavenly bodies.

Whence the works of magicians derive their efficacy

It remains for us to inquire whence the magic arts derive their efficacy: a question that will present no difficulty if we consider their mode of operation.

For in the practice of their art they make use of certain significative words in order to produce certain definite effects. Now, words, in so far as they signify something, have no power except as derived from some intellect; either of the speaker, or of the person to whom they are spoken. From the intellect of the speaker, as when an intellect is of such great power that it can cause things by its mere thought, the voice serving to convey, as it were, this thought to the things that are to be produced. From the intellect of the person to whom the words are addressed, as when the hearer is induced to do some particular thing, through his intellect receiving the signification of those words. Now, it cannot be said that these significative words uttered by magicians derive efficacy from the intellect of the speaker. For since power follows essence, diversity of power indicates diversity of essential principles. Moreover, man's intellect is invariably of such a disposition that its knowledge is caused by things, rather than that it is able by its mere thought to cause things. Consequently if there be any men that are able of their own power to transform things by words expressive of their thoughts, they will belong to another species, and it would be an equivocation to call them men.

Further. By learning we acquire, not the power to do a thing, but the knowledge of how to do it. Yet some, by learning, are rendered able to perform these magic works. Therefore they must have not only knowledge but also the power to produce these effects.

If someone say that these men, by the influence of the stars, are born with the aforesaid power, while others are excluded from it; so that however much the others, who are born without this power, may be instructed, they cannot succeed in performing these works; we reply, first that, as shown above, heavenly bodies cannot make an impression on the intellect. Therefore a man's intellect cannot, through the influence of the stars, receive a power whereby the vocal expression of its thoughts is productive of something.

And if it be said that the imagination produces an effect in the utterance of significative words, and that heavenly bodies can work on the imagination, since its operation is performed by a bodily organ:—this does not apply to all the results produced by this art. For we have shown (ch. civ.) that these effects cannot all be produced by the power of the stars. Neither, therefore, can anyone by the power of the stars, receive the power to produce those effects. Consequently it follows that these effects are accomplished by an intellect to whom the discourse of the person uttering these words is addressed. We have an indication of this in the fact that the significative words employed by the magician are *invocations*, *supplications*, *adjurations*, or even *commands* as though he were addressing another.

Again. Certain characters and definite figures are employed in the observances of this art. Now a figure cannot be the principle of either action or passion; else, mathematical bodies would be active and passive. Therefore matter cannot, by definite figures, be disposed to receive a certain natural effect. Therefore magicians do not employ figures as dispositions. It remains, then, that they employ them only as signs, for there is no third solution. But we make signs only to other intelligent beings. Therefore the magic arts derive their efficacy from another intelligent being, to whom the magician's words are addressed.

And if someone say that certain figures are appropriate to certain heavenly bodies; and so the lower bodies are determined by certain figures to receive the impressions of certain heavenly bod-

ies:—seemingly this is an unreasonable statement. For the patient is not directed to receive the impression of the agent, except through being in potentiality. Hence those things alone determine it to receive a particular impression, that cause it to be somehow in potentiality. Now figures do not cause matter to be in potentiality to any particular form, because a figure, as such, abstracts from all matter and sensible forms, since it is something mathematical. Therefore a body is not determined by figures or characters to receive the influence of a heavenly body.

Besides. Certain figures are appropriate to heavenly bodies as the effects thereof; for the figures of the lower bodies are caused by heavenly bodies. Now, the aforesaid arts do not use characters or figures as produced by heavenly bodies, in fact they are produced by man in the practice of the art. Therefore, the appropriateness of figures to certain heavenly bodies has nothing to do with the question.

Further. As we have shown, matter is nowise disposed to form by means of figures. Hence the bodies on which these figures are impressed, are as capable of receiving the influence of heavenly bodies, as other bodies of the same species. Now, that a thing act on one rather than another of several equally disposed, by reason of something appropriate to be found in it, is a mark of its operating not by natural necessity, but by choice. Hence it is clear that these arts which employ figures in order to produce certain effects, derive their efficacy, not from something that acts by nature, but from some intellectual substance that acts by intelligence. This is also proved by the very name of *character* which they apply to these figures: for a character is a sign. Whereby we are given to understand that they employ these figures merely as signs shown to some intellectual nature.

Since, however, in the products of art figures are like specific forms, someone might say that there is no reason why, through the influence of a heavenly body, some power should not shape the figure that gives an image its species, not indeed as a figure, but as specifying the product of art, which acquires this power from the stars. But as to the letters that form an inscription on an image, and other characters, nothing else can be said of them, but that they are signs: wherefore they are directed to an intelligence only—This is also proved by the sacrifices, prostrations and other similar practices, which can be nothing else than signs of reverence shown to an intellectual nature.

That the intellectual substance which gives efficacy to the practices of magic is not good according to virtue

We must furthermore inquire what is this intellectual nature by whose power these words are done.

And in the first place it is plain that it is not good and praiseworthy: for it is the mark of an ill-disposed mind to countenance things contrary to virtue. Now this is done in these arts: for they are often employed in order to further adultery, theft, murder and like malefices, wherefore those who practise these arts are called *malefics*. Therefore the intellectual nature on whose assistance these arts depend is not well disposed according to virtue.

Again. It is not the mark of a mind well disposed according to virtue, to befriend and assist men of evil life, rather than every upright man. Now those who practise these arts are often of evil life. Therefore the intellectual nature from whose assistance these arts derive their efficacy is not well disposed according to virtue.

Further. It is the mark of a well disposed mind to guide men towards those goods that are proper to man, namely the goods of reason. Consequently to lead men away from these, and to draw men to goods of the least worth, shows a mind of evil disposition. Now by these arts men progress, not in the goods of reason, which are science and virtue, but in goods of least account, such as the discovery of stolen goods, the capture of thieves, and so forth. Therefore the intellectual substances whose assistance these arts employ, are not well disposed according to virtue.

Moreover. There is certain deception and unreasonableness in the works of these arts: for they require a man indifferent to lustful pleasure, whereas they are frequently employed to further lustful intercourse. But there is nothing unreasonable or contradictory in the work of a well-disposed mind. Therefore these arts do not employ the assistance of an intellect that is well disposed as to virtue.

Besides. It is an ill-disposed mind that is incited by the commission of crime to lend his assistance to another. But this is done in these arts: for we read of innocent children being slain by those who practise them. Therefore the persons by whose assistance such things are done have an evil mind.

Again. The proper good of the intellect is truth. Since therefore it belongs to good to lead others to good, it belongs to any well-disposed intellect to lead others to truth. In the works of the magicians, however, many things are done by which men are mocked and deceived. The intellect whose help they use, therefore, is not morally well disposed.

Further. A well-disposed intellect is allured by truth in which it takes delight, but not by lies. The magicians, however, in their invocations make use of various lies, whereby they allure those whose help they employ; for they threaten certain impossible things, as for instance that, unless the one who is called upon gives help, he who invokes him will shatter the heavens or displace the stars, as Porphyry narrates in his *Letter to Anebontes*. Those intellectual substances, therefore, with whose help the works of the magicians are performed do not seem to be intellectually well disposed.

Moreover. That a superior should be subject as an inferior to one that commands him; or that an inferior should allow himself to be invoked as a superior, would seem to indicate a person of an ill-disposed mind. Now, magicians call upon those whose assistance they employ, as though these were their superiors: and as soon as they appear they command them as inferiors. In no way therefore are they seemingly of a well-disposed mind. Hereby we refute the error of pagans who ascribed these works to the gods.

Selection 2
"The Famous Alchemist Bragadini"

The desire to turn dross—or waste matter—into gold is not only a twentieth-century preoccupation. In sixteenth-century Italy this alchemist attained wide renown for his supposed accomplishments, detailed in these letters from a German merchant of the time.

From Venice, the 1st day of November 1589

Your Grace will no doubt have learnt from the weekly reports of one Marco Antonio Bragadini, called Mamugnano. He is the bastard son of a nobleman here and was born in Cyprus. He is reported to be able to turn base metal into gold. Our government has had him conveyed hither under safe escort because the Inquisition has put him under ban. He is forty years old and was formerly possessed of no mean fortune, but spent it in riotous living. Then for a time he was mint-master to the Grand Duke Francis. From thence he came to the late Pope Gregory, who held him in great esteem. He thus obtained several thousand ducats. But when these too had been spent, he became a Capuchin and had taken his second vows. But since he could not subject himself to the strict rule of the order, he absconded without dispensation (hence the excommunication ban by the Holy Office) and betook himself to France. There he served several princes incognito. Latterly he has returned again to Bergamo in Italy and has exhibited his art in Valcamonica and in a short time increased his fortune to over and above two hundred thousand crowns. He has expounded his craft to several persons and it had got so far that he was prevailed upon to come here of his free will. Such a host of princes and lords beleaguered him that he was scarcely safe, although he had a bodyguard of fifty archers. This man is now here in this city, holds banquet daily for five hundred people and lives in princely style in the Palazzo Dandolo on the Giudecca. He literally throws gold about in shovelfuls. This is his recipe: he takes ten ounces

Source: Victor von Klarvill (ed.), *The Fugger Newsletters: Being a selection of unpublished letters from the Correspondents of the House of Fugger during the Years 1568–1605,* trans. by Pauline de Chary (New York: Putnam's Sons, 1924), pp. 140–142.

of quicksilver, puts it into the fire and mixes it with a drop of liquid, which he carries in an ampulla. Thus it promptly turns into good gold. He has no other wish but to be of good use to his country, the Republic. The day before yesterday he presented to the Secret Council of Ten two ampullas with this liquid, which have been tested in his absence. The first test was found to be successful and it is said to have resulted in six million ducats. I doubt not but that this will appear mighty strange to Your Grace. It verily sounds like a fairy tale, but Your Grace will surely believe us, for everything is so obvious that it cannot be doubted. The confectioning of this liquid is, however, his secret, for in his letter of safe conduct he made express demand that he be not forced to divulge this. He also craves nothing more from this our Government but that it may exercise good watch over his life and his person. In return he will provide them with gold in sufficiency according to their demands. He has already made known that he is greatly amazed at the ignorance of the world, in not discovering this art before, considering that little is requisite for this achievement. This is truly marvellous and quite novel to all of us. The alchemists have taken heart of grace again and are working night and day. One hears of nothing but of this excellent man who, as already stated, has no other wish but to serve his country.

From Venice, the 8th day of December 1589

You have learnt latterly that the craft of the alchemist Marco Bragadini after being tested has been approved of. The tests have shown this sufficiently. The most noble personages here address him by the title "Illustrissimo" and feast with him daily. The Duke speaks to him in the second person. By day noblemen attend upon him, by night he is guarded by armed barges. Whereas so many strange people have arrived here, the Government holds in readiness three fully equipped galleys.

From Venice, the 16th day of December 1589

The alchemist is said to be at work now in making five thousand sequins per month at the request of our rulers. Thereafter he will make fifteen or sixteen millions more which he has promised to hand over to it. Day by day he shows himself in great pomp. He makes his friends presents of twenty thousand and more ducats at a time. Monday last he gave a banquet in honour of the Duc de Luxembourg, the French Catholic Ambassador in Rome, which, without counting all kinds of special confectionery, cost near upon six hundred crowns.

From Rome, the 16th day of December 1589

The Venetian Ambassador has solemnly besought the Pope that Mamugnano, the alchemist, who now resides in Venice, may remain there without molestation by the Holy Office, on account of his being a former Capuchin. Thereupon the Pope made answer that he was not a little surprised at the afore-mentioned Rulers putting so much faith in that man. Though his art might be found to be successful, yet it only could accrue unto him by the help of Satan.

From Venice, the 4th day of January 1590

It is said of our Mamugnano that his craft for transforming quicksilver into gold does suffice for small quantities, but fails to produce larger ones. It is reported that the night before last he made two ingots in the presence of some of our patrician aldermen, each one of the weight of one pound. There no longer exists any doubt in the matter. Discussion, however, is rife amongst some of this city's philosophers as to whether Mamugnano can renew the material wherewith he has made his gold, once it is used up. Some say yes, and others say no, so that it is doubtful what they really think about it.

Selection 3
The Theories of Paracelsus

The doctor, professor of medicine, and alchemist Paracelsus (1493–1541) took his name to show that he was superior to one of the great ancient writers on medicine, Celsus. He wandered over much of Europe, often hounded out of cities by authorities who were angered by his attacks on traditional writings. However, his experiments in medicine and alchemy (the art of changing one substance into another) made him not only the most remarkable magician of his age but also a prophet of science in his insistence on the observation of nature at first hand.

. . . What sense would it make or what would it benefit a physician if he discovered the origin of the diseases but could not cure or alleviate them? And since the fit manner of preparation is not to be found in pharmaceutics, we must explore further; that is to say, we must learn from alchemy. In it we find the true cause and everything that is needed. Although alchemy has now fallen into contempt and is even considered a thing of the past, the physician should not be influenced by such judgments. For many arts, such as astronomy, philosophy, and others are also in disrepute. I am directing you, physicians, to alchemy for the preparation of the *magnalia*, for the production of the *mysteria*, for the preparation of the *arcana*, for the separation of the pure from the impure, to the end that you may obtain a flawless, pure remedy, God-given, perfect, and of certain efficacy, achieving the highest degree of virtue and power. For it is not God's design that the remedies should exist for

Source: J. Jacobi (ed.) and N. Guterman (trans.), *Paracelsus: Selected Writings* (Princeton, N.J.: Princeton University Press, 1958), pp. 84–87, 120–123, 144–145.

us readymade, boiled, and salted, but that we should boil them ourselves, and it pleases Him that we boil them and learn in the process, that we train ourselves in this art and are not idle on earth, but labour in daily toil. For it is we who must pray for our daily bread, and if He grants it to us, it is only through our labour, our skill and preparation.

The first and highest book of medicine is called *Sapientia*. Without this book no one will achieve anything fruitful. . . . For this book is God himself. In Him who has created all things lies also wisdom, and only He knows the primal cause of all things. . . . Without Him everything is mere foolishness. . . . For what is wisdom but the ability to recognize and know our talents and our calling? But we cannot do this by ourselves, no more than we have power over day and night, summer and winter. . . . Although the remedy is given by nature. . . .it must be revealed to us by the all-highest book, so that we may learn what is in it, how it is made, how it is obtained from the earth, and how and to what patients it should be administered. . . . The remedy must flow from the spirit that dwells in man . . . therefore the first teaching is—and every inquiry must begin with it—that we should above all seek the kingdom of God. There lies the treasure, the school that leads to the primal causes of wisdom within each man's sphere of action. . . . For what is there more noble than that we should pray and implore God's grace? . . . No one, then, should be surprised if I say that God is the first book; and who can recognize a work better than he who has accomplished it? He alone can state and show its virtues. And who else has created the remedy but God? It flows from Him as warmth flows from the sun, which also makes the flowers grow. No differently could our wisdom flow from God. What has ever been discovered in the wide world that has not come to us from God? He holds everything in His hand, and we should accept it from Him.

The second book of medicine-of this too you must take note—is the firmament. But this book must be studied after the first. . . . For it is possible to write down all medicine in the letters of one book, to the end that everyone may learn it by reading the book, and the firmament is such a book containing all the virtues and propositions . . . and he who has not penetrated into this book cannot be a physician or be called a physician. Just as a man reads a book on paper, so the physician is compelled to spell out the stars of the firmament in order to know his conclusions. For just as every word has special virtues but does not embody the whole sentence, and acquires its complete meaning only when it is supplemented by other words and the sentence is rounded into a whole, so the stars in heaven must be taken together in order that we may read the sentence in the firmament. . . . It is like a letter which has been sent to us from a hundred miles off, and in which the writer's mind speaks to us; as though in such a letter, the firmament speaks to us. . . . This is the way to study medicine, this is the book of the highest school of medicine.

The book of medicine is nature itself. And just as you see yourself in a mirror, so you must rediscover all your sciences in nature, with exactly the same certainty and with as little illusion as when you see yourself in a mirror.

Marvellous virtues are inherent in the remedies. One would hardly believe that nature contained such virtues. . . . For only a great artist is able to discover them, not one who is only versed in books, but only one who has acquired his ability and skill through the experience of his hands. . . . It is an important art, and therefore it cannot be clearly described, but can only be learned by experience. . . . These remedies must not be known merely as physics, they must be termed arcana, occult healing substances. They have such noble and lofty advantages and operate in so marvellous a manner that only with difficulty can our minds conceive and know from what properties and virtues their efficacy is derived.

Why is the world made in such a way that one herb is female and another male? The reason for this is that the diseases too are different. If they were all identical, why should nature have divided the remedies into these two species? But because there exist two worlds, the world of woman and the world of man, there are also two kinds of remedies. And just as man and woman are different in their infirmities, so their remedies differ.

Just as flowers grow from the earth, so the remedy grows in the hands of the physician. If he is a good physician, the remedy is like a root which grows a stem, which in turn unfolds into a flower, and which in the end becomes a fruit. For the physician's art is like the earth, which also conceals such potentialities in itself. . . . In the winter, no herb nor any flower grows in your garden; everything remains hidden in the earth, and you do not see and do not know what lies in it. Nevertheless you are sure that herbs, flowers, and all kinds of plants lie in it, although you cannot see them. It is no different with the remedy you hold in your hands. At first you do not see what it contains, but you know with certainty that something is in it, like a seed that is different from the fruit that grows out of it. The earth makes the seed ripen into a fruit. And if the seed did not bear fruit, it would be worthless. Similarly, the remedy is nothing but a seed which you must develop into that which it is destined to be. . . .

Everything that is within can be known by what is without

It is not God's will that all He has created for the benefit of man and has given him as his own should remain hidden. . . . And even if He did conceal some things, He left nothing unmarked, but provided all things with outward, visible marks, with special traits—just as a man who has buried a treasure marks the spot in order that he may find it again.

We men discover everything that lies hidden in the mountains by external signs and correspondences, and thus also do we find all the properties of herbs and everything that is in the stones. There is nothing in the depths of the seas, nothing on the heights of the firmament, that man is unable to discover. No mountain, no cliff, is so vast as to hide or conceal what is in it from the eyes of man; it is revealed to him by corresponding signs. . . . For each fruit is a sign, and through it we discover what is contained in that from which it stems. Similarly there is nothing in man that is not marked in his exterior, so that by the exterior one may discover what is in the individual who bears the

sign. . . . There are four ways by which the nature of man and of all living things can be discovered. . . . First, chiromancy; it concerns the extreme parts of man's limbs, namely the hands and feet. . . . Second, physiognomics; it concerns the face and the whole head. . . . Third, the *substantina*, which refers to the whole shape of the body. . . . And fourth, the customs and usages, that is to say, manners and gestures in which man appears and shows himself. . . . These four belong together; they provide us with a complete knowledge of the hidden, inward man, and of all things that grow in nature. . . . Nature is the sculptor: she endows everything with the form which is also the essence, and thus the form reveals the essence.

There is nothing that nature has not signed in such a way that man may discover its essence. . . . The stars have their orbits by which they are known. The same is true of man. As you can see, each herb is given the form that befits its nature; similarly, man is endowed with a form corresponding to his inner nature. And just as the form shows what a given herb is, so the human shape is a sign which indicates what a given man is. This does not refer to the name, sex, or similar characteristics, but to the qualities inherent in the man. The art of signs teaches us to give each man his true name in accordance with his innate nature. A wolf must not be called a sheep, a dove must not be called a fox; each being should be given the name that belongs to its essence. . . . Since nothing is so secret or hidden that it cannot be revealed, everything depends on the discovery of those things which manifest the hidden. . . . The nature of each man's soul accords with the design of his lineaments and arteries. The same is true of the face, which is shaped and formed according to the content of his mind and soul, and the same is again true of the proportions of the human body. For the sculptor of Nature is so artful that he does not mould the soul to fit the form, but the form to fit the soul; in other words, the shape of a man is formed in accordance with the manner of his heart. . . . Artists who make sculptors proceed no differently. . . . And the more accomplished an artist would be, the more necessary it is that he master the arts of signs. . . . No artist can paint or carve, no one can produce an accomplished work, without such knowledge. . . . Only he who has some knowledge of this can be a finished artist.

Behold the *Satyrion* root, is it not formed like the male privy parts? No one can deny this. Accordingly magic discovered it and revealed that it can restore a man's virility and passion. And then we have the thistle; do not its leaves prickle like needles? Thanks to this sign, the art of magic discovered that there is no better herb against internal prickling. The *Siegwurz* root is wrapped in an envelope like armour; and this is a magic sign showing that like armour it gives protection against weapons. And the *Syderica* bears the image and form of a snake on each of its leaves, and thus, according to magic, it gives protection against any kind of poisoning. The chicory stands under a special influence of the sun; this is seen in its leaves, which always bend toward the sun as though they wanted to show it gratitude. Hence it is most effective while the sun is shining, while the sun is in the sky. As soon as the sun sets, the power of chicory dwindles. Why, do you think, does its root assume the shape of a bird after seven years? What has the art of magic to say about this? If you know the answer, keep silent and say nothing the scoffers; if you do not know it, try to find out; investigate, and do not be ashamed to ask questions.

When a carpenter builds a house, it first lives in him as an idea; and the house is built according to this idea. Therefore, from the form of the house, one can make inferences about the carpenter's ideas and images. What nature has in mind . . . no one can know until it has acquired form and shape. . . . Now note well that virtue forms the shape of a man, just as the carpenter's ideas become visible in his house; and a man's body takes shape in accordance with the nature of his soul. . . . Nature acts no differently. She gives man an outward appearance that is in keeping with his inner constitution. . . . And each man's soul can be recognized, just as the carpenter can be known by his house. . . .

The great virtues that lie hidden in nature would never have been revealed if alchemy had not uncovered them and made them visible. Take a tree, for example; a man sees it in the winter, but he does not know what it is, he does not know what it conceals within itself, until summer comes and discloses the buds, the flowers, the fruit. . . . Similarly the virtues in things remain concealed to man, unless the alchemists disclose them, as the summer reveals the nature of the tree.—And if the alchemist brings to light that which lies hidden in nature, one must know that those hidden powers are different in each thing—they are different in locusts, different in leaves, different in flowers, and different in ripe and unripe fruits. For all this is so marvellous that in form and qualities the last fruit of a tree is completely unlike the first one. . . . And each thing has not only one virtue but many, just as a flower has more than one colour, and each colour has in itself the most diverse hues; and yet they constitute a unity, one thing.

Alchemy is a necessary, indispensable art. . . . It is an art, and Vulcan is its artist. He who is a Vulcan has mastered this art; he who is not a Vulcan can make no headway in it. But to understand this art, one must above all know that God has created all things; and that He has created something out of nothing. This something is a seed, in which the purpose of its use and function is inherent from the beginning. And since all things have been created in an unfinished state, nothing is finished, but Vulcan must bring all things to their completion. Things are created and given into our hands, but not in the ultimate form that is proper to them. For example, wood grows of itself, but does not transform itself into boards or charcoal. Similarly, clay does not of itself become a pot. This is true of everything that grows in nature. . . .

II. THE NEW SCIENCE AND ITS PURSUIT IN A VARIETY OF SCIENTIFIC DISCIPLINES

The "new science" as it pertains to astronomy has its origins in the work of Nicholas Copernicus, whose *De Revolutionibus* was published at the end of his life in 1543. It was intended for the mathematically competent specialist, and Copernicus became widely known only through the work and writings of Galileo.

Selections 4 and 5
The Starry Messenger
Galileo Galilei

The Starry Messenger was the first important work of Galileo Galilei. Two excerpts are included here. The first is the title page and the dedication of the work, to Cosimo de Medici, Grand Duke of Tuscany. As was the case with artists and writers, scientists needed patrons who would support their work. In the dedication, Galileo justifies his work, realizing full well that Cosimo might be a powerful supporter on whom he could rely. The second excerpt is from the text itself. Note that here Galileo unequivocally states that the "earth is a wandering body" and thus not the stationary center of the universe, as traditionally had been believed.

Selection 4

TITLE PAGE:
THE STARRY MESSENGER

Revealing great, unusual, and remarkable spectacles, opening these
to the consideration of every man,
and especially of philosophers and
astronomers;
AS OBSERVED BY GALILEO GALILEI
Gentleman of Florence
Professor of Mathematics in the
University of Padua,
WITH THE AID OF A
SPYGLASS
lately invented by him,
In the surface of the Moon, in innumerable
Fixed Stars, in Nebulae, and above all
in FOUR PLANETS
swiftly revolving about Jupiter at
differing distances and periods,
and known to no one before the

Author recently perceived them
and decided that they should
be named
THE MEDICEAN STARS

Venice
1610

DEDICATION:
TO THE MOST SERENE
COSIMO II DE MEDICI
FOURTH GRAND DUKE OF TUSCANY

Surely a distinguished public service has been rendered by those who have protected from envy the noble achievements of men who have excelled in virtue, and have thus preserved from oblivion and neglect those names which deserve immortality. In this way images sculptured in marble or cast in bronze have been handed down to posterity; to this we owe our statues, both pedestrian and equestrian; thus have we those columns and pyramids whose expense (as the poet says) reaches to the stars; finally, thus cities have been built to bear the names of men deemed worthy by posterity of commendation to all the ages. For the nature of

Source: Stillman Drake (trans. and ed.), *Discoveries and Opinions of Galileo* (Garden City, N.Y.: Doubleday & Co., 1957), pp. 21–26, 40–46.

the human mind is such that unless it is stimulated by images of things acting upon it from without, all remembrance of them passes easily away.

Looking to things even more stable and enduring, others have entrusted the immortal fame of illustrious men not to marble and metal but to the custody of the Muses and to imperishable literary monuments. But why dwell upon these things as though human wit were satisfied with earthly regions and had not dared advance beyond? For, seeking further, and well understanding that all human monuments ultimately perish through the violence of the elements or by old age, ingenuity has in fact found still more incorruptible monuments over which voracious time and envious age have been unable to assert any rights. Thus turning to the sky, man's wit has inscribed on the familiar and everlasting orbs of most bright stars the names of those whose eminent and godlike deeds have caused them to be accounted worthy of eternity in the company of the stars. And so the fame of Jupiter, of Mars, of Mercury, Hercules, and other heroes by whose names the stars are called, will not fade before the extinction of the stars themselves.

Yet this invention of human ingenuity, noble and admirable as it is, has for many centuries been out of style. Primeval heroes are in possession of those bright abodes, and hold them in their own right. In vain did the piety of Augustus attempt to elect Julius Caesar into their number, for when he tried to give the name of "Julian" to a star which appeared in his time (one of those bodies which the Greeks call "comets" and which the Romans likewise named for their hairy appearance), it vanished in a brief time and mocked his too ambitious wish. But we are able, most serene Prince, to read Your Highness in the heavens far more accurately and auspiciously. For scarce have the immortal graces of your spirit begun to shine on earth when in the heavens bright stars appear as tongues to tell and celebrate your exceeding virtues to all time. Behold, then, four stars reserved to bear your famous name; bodies which belong not to the inconspicuous multitude of fixed stars, but to the bright ranks of the planets. Variously moving about most noble Jupiter as children of his own,

they complete their orbits with marvelous velocity—at the same time executing with one harmonious accord mighty revolutions every dozen years about the center of the universe; that is, the sun.

Indeed, the Maker of the stars himself has seemed by clear indications to direct that I assign to these new planets Your Highness's famous name in preference to all others. For just as these stars, like children worthy of their sire, never leave the side of Jupiter by any appreciable distance, so (as indeed who does not know?) clemency, kindness of heart, gentleness of manner, splendor of royal blood, nobility in public affairs, and excellency of authority and rule have all fixed their abode and habitation in Your Highness. And who, I ask once more, does not know that all these virtues emanate from the benign star of Jupiter, next after God as the source of all things good? Jupiter; Jupiter, I say, at the instant of Your Highness's birth, having already emerged from the turbid mists of the horizon and occupied the midst of the heavens, illuminating the eastern sky from his own royal house, looked out from that exalted throne upon your auspicious birth and poured fourth all his splendor and majesty in order that your tender body and your mind (already adorned by God with the most noble ornaments) might imbibe with their first breath that universal influence and power.

But why should I employ mere plausible arguments, when I may prove my conclusion absolutely? It pleased Almighty God that I should instruct Your Highness in mathematics, which I did four years ago at that time of year when it is customary to rest from the most exacting studies. And since clearly it was mine by divine will to serve Your Highness and thus to receive from near at hand the rays of your surpassing clemency and beneficence, what wonder is it that my heart is so inflamed as to think both day and night of little else than how I, who am indeed your subject not only by choice but by birth and lineage, may become

---

* This is the first published intimation by Galileo that he accepted the Copernican system. It was not until 1613, however, that Galileo unequivocally supported Copernicus in print.

known to you as most grateful and most anxious for your glory? And so, most serene Cosimo, having discovered under your patronage these stars unknown to every astronomer before me, I have with good right decided to designate them by the august name of your family. And if I am first to have investigated them, who can justly blame me if I likewise name them, calling them the Medicean Stars, in the hope that this name will bring as much honor to them as the names of other heroes have bestowed on other stars? For, to say nothing of Your Highness's most serene ancestors, whose everlasting glory is testified by the monuments of all history, your virtue alone, most worthy Sire, can confer upon these stars an immortal name. No one can doubt that you will fulfill those expectations, high though they are, which you have aroused by the suspicious beginning of your reign, and will not only meet but far surpass them. Thus when you have conquered your equals you may still vie with yourself, and you and your greatness will become greater every day.

Accept then, most clement Prince, this gentle glory reserved by the stars for you. May you long enjoy those blessings which are sent to you not so much from the stars as from God, their Maker and their Governor.

Your Highness's most devoted servant,

Galileo Galilei
Padua, March 12, 1610

Selection 5 (see Figure 58)

. . . The eyesight from F reaches the moon in the central region, at A for example, through a lesser thickness of the vapors DA, while toward the extreme edges a deeper stratum of vapors, EB, limits and shuts out our sight. One indication of this is that the illuminated portion of the moon appears to be larger in circumference than the rest of the orb, which lies in shadow. And perhaps this same cause will appeal to some as reasonably explaining why the larger spots on the moon are nowhere seen to reach the very edge, probable though it is that some should occur there. Possibly

they are invisible by being hidden under a thicker and more luminous mass of vapors.

That the lighter surface of the moon is everywhere dotted with protuberances and gaps has, I think, been made sufficiently clear from the appearances already explained. It remains for me to speak of their dimensions, and to show that the earth's irregularities are far less than those of the moon. I mean that they are absolutely less, and not merely in relation to the sizes of the respective globes. This is plainly demonstrated as follows.

I had often observed, in various situations of the moon with respect to the sun, that some summits within the shadowy portion appeared lighted, though lying some distance from the boundary of the light. By comparing this separation to the whole diameter of the moon, I found that it sometimes exceeded one-twentieth of the diameter.

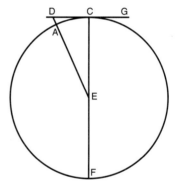

Accordingly, let CAF be a great circle of the lunar body, E its center, and CF a diameter, which is to the diameter of the earth as two is to seven.

Since according to very precise observations the diameter of the earth is seven thousand miles, CF will be two thousand, CE one thousand, and one-twentieth of CF will be one hundred miles. Now let CF be the diameter of the great circle which divides the light part of the moon from the dark part (for because of the very great distance of the sun from the moon, this does not differ appreciably from a great circle), and let A be distant from C by one-twentieth of this. Draw the radius EA, which, when produced, cuts the tangent line GCD (representing the illuminating ray) in the point D. Then the arc CA, or rather the straight line CD, will consist of one hundred units whereof CE contains one thousand, and the sum of the squares of DC and CE will be 1,010,000. This is equal to the square of DE; hence ED will exceed 1,004, and AD will be more than four of those units of which CE contains one thousand. Therefore the altitude AD on the moon, which represents a summit reaching up to the solar ray GCD and standing at the distance CD from C, exceeds four miles. But on the earth we have no mountains which reach to a perpendicular height of even one mile. Hence it is quite clear that the prominences on the moon are loftier than those on the earth.

Here I wish to assign the cause of another lunar phenomenon well worthy of notice. I observed this not just recently, but many years ago, and pointed it out to some of my friends and pupils, explaining it to them and giving its true cause. Yet since it is rendered more evident and easier to observe with the aid of the telescope. I think it not unsuitable for introduction in this place, especially as it shows more clearly the connection between the moon and the earth.

When the moon is not far from the sun, just before or after new moon, its globe offers itself to view not only on the side where it is adorned with shining horns, but a certain faint light is also seen to mark out the periphery of the dark part which faces away from the sun, separating this from the darker background of the aether. Now if we examine the matter more closely, we shall see that not only does the extreme limb of the shaded side glow with this uncertain light, but the entire face of the moon (including the side which does not receive the glare of the sun) is whitened by a not inconsiderable gleam. At first glance only a thin luminous circumference appears, contrasting with the darker sky coterminous with it; the rest of the surface appears darker from its contact with the shining horns which distract our vision. But if we place ourselves so as to interpose a roof or chimney or some other object at a considerable distance from the eye, the shining horns may be hidden while the rest of the lunar globe remains exposed to view. It is then found that this region of the moon, though deprived of sunlight, also shines not a little. The effect is heightened if the gloom of night

has already deepened through departure of the sun, for in a darker field a given light appears brighter.

Moreover, it is found that this secondary light of the moon (so to speak) is greater according as the moon is closer to the sun. It diminishes more and more as the moon recedes from that body until, after the first quarter and before the last, it is seen very weakly and uncertainly even when observed in the darkest sky. But when the moon is within sixty degrees of the sun it shines remarkably, even in twilight; so brightly indeed that with the aid of a good telescope one may distinguish the large spots. This remarkable gleam has afforded no small perplexity to philosophers, and in order to assign a cause for it some have offered one idea and some another. Some would say it is an inherent and natural light of the moon's own; others, that it is imparted by Venus; others yet, by all the stars together; and still others derive it from the sun, whose rays they would have permeate the thick solidity of the moon. But statements of this sort are refuted and their falsity evinced with little difficulty. For if this kind of light were the moon's own, or were contributed by the stars, the moon would retain it and would display it particularly during eclipses, when it is left in an unusually dark sky. This is contradicted by experience, for the brightness which is seen on the moon during eclipses is much fainter and is ruddy, almost copper-colored, while this is brighter and whitish. Moreover the other light is variable and movable, for it covers the face of the moon in such a way that the place near the edge of the earth's shadow is always seen to be brighter than the rest of the moon; this undoubtedly results from contact of the tangent solar rays with some denser zone which girds the moon about. By this contact a sort of twilight is diffused over the neighboring regions of the moon, just as on earth a sort of crepuscular light is spread both morning and evening; but with this I shall deal more fully in my book on the system of the world.

To assert that the moon's secondary light is imparted by Venus is so childish as to deserve no reply. Who is so ignorant as not to understand that from new moon to a separation of sixty degrees between moon and sun, no part of the moon which is averted from the sun can possibly be seen from Venus? And it is likewise unthinkable that this light should depend upon the sun's rays penetrating the thick solid mass of the moon, for then this light would never dwindle, inasmuch as one hemisphere of the moon is always illuminated except during lunar eclipses. And the light does diminish as the moon approaches first quarter, becoming completely obscured after that is passed.

Now since the secondary light does not inherently belong to the moon, and is not received from any star or from the sun, and since in the whole universe there is no other body left but the earth, what must we conclude? What is to be proposed? Surely we must assert that the lunar body (or any other dark and sunless orb) is illuminated by the earth. Yet what is there so remarkable about this? The earth, in fair and grateful exchange, pays back to the moon an illumination similar to that which it receives from her throughout nearly all the darkest gloom of night.

Let us explain this matter more fully. At conjunction the moon occupies a position between the sun and the earth; it is then illuminated by the sun's rays on the side which is turned away from the earth. The other hemisphere, which faces the earth, is covered with darkness; hence the moon does not illuminate the surface of the earth at all. Next, departing gradually from the sun, the moon comes to be lighted partly upon the side it turns toward us, and its whitish horns, still very thin, illuminate the earth with a faint light. The sun's illumination of the moon increasing now as the moon approaches first quarter, a reflection of that light to the earth also increases. Soon the splendor on the moon extends into a semicircle, and our nights grow brighter; at length the entire visible face of the moon is irradiated by the sun's resplendent rays, and at full moon the whole surface of the earth shines in a flood of moonlight. Now the moon, waning, sends us her beams more weakly, and the earth is less strongly lighted; at length the moon returns to conjunction with the sun, and black night covers the earth.

In this monthly period, then, the moonlight gives us alternations of brighter and fainter illumination; and the benefit is repaid by the earth in

equal measure. For while the moon is between us and the sun (at new moon), there lies before it the entire surface of that hemisphere of the earth which is exposed to the sun and illuminated by vivid rays. The moon receives the light which this reflects, and thus the nearer hemisphere of the moon—that is, the one deprived of sunlight—appears by virtue of this illumination to be not a little luminous. When the moon is ninety degrees away from the sun it sees but half the earth illuminated (the western half), for the other (the eastern half) is enveloped in night. Hence the moon itself is illuminated less brightly from the earth, and as a result its secondary light appears fainter to us. When the moon is in opposition to the sun, it faces a hemisphere of the earth that is steeped in the gloom of night, and if this position occurs in the plane of the ecliptic the moon will receive no light at all, being deprived of both the solar and the terrestrial rays. In its various other positions with respect to the earth and sun, the moon receives more or less light according as it faces a greater or smaller portion of the illuminated hemisphere of the earth. And between these two globes a relation is maintained such that whenever the earth is most brightly lighted by the moon, the moon is least lighted by the earth, and vice versa.

Let these few remarks suffice us here concerning this matter, which will be more fully treated in our *System of the world*. In that book, by a multitude of arguments and experiences, the solar reflection from the earth will be shown to be quite real—against those who argue that the earth must be excluded from the dancing whirl of stars for the specific reason that it is devoid of motion and of light. We shall prove the earth to be a wandering body surpassing the moon in splendor, and not the sink of all dull refuse of the universe; this we shall support by an infinitude of arguments drawn from nature.

Thus far we have spoken of our observations concerning the body of the moon. Let us now set forth briefly what has thus far been observed regrading the fixed stars. And first of all, the following fact deserves consideration: The stars, whether fixed or wandering, appear not to be enlarged by the telescope in the same proportion as that in which it magnifies other objects, and even the moon itself. In the stars this enlargement seems to be so much less that a telescope which is sufficiently powerful to magnify other objects a hundredfold is scarcely able to enlarge the stars four or five times. The reason for this is as follows.

When stars are viewed by means of unaided natural vision, they present themselves to us not as of their simple (and, so to speak, their physical) size, but as irradiated by a certain fulgor and as fringed with sparkling rays, especially when the night is far advanced. From this they appear larger than they would if stripped of those adventitious hairs of light, for the angle at the eye is determined not by the primary body of the star but by the brightness which extends so widely about it. This appears quite clearly from the fact that when stars first emerge from twilight at sunset they look very small, even if they are of the first magnitude; Venus itself, when visible in broad daylight, is so small as scarcely to appear equal to a star of the

sixth magnitude. Things fall out differently with other objects, and even with the moon itself; these, whether seen in daylight or the deepest night, appear always of the same bulk. Therefore the stars are seen crowned among shadows, while daylight is able to remove their headgear; and not daylight alone, but any thin cloud that interposes itself between a star and the eye of the observer. The same effect is produced by black veils or colored glasses, through the interposition of which obstacles the stars are abandoned by their surrounding brilliance. A telescope similarly accomplishes the same result. It removes from the stars their adventitious and accidental rays, and then it enlarges their simple globes (if indeed the stars are naturally globular) so that they seem to be magnified in a lesser ratio than other objects. In fact a star of the fifth or sixth magnitude when seen through a telescope presents itself as one of the first magnitude.

Selection 6
Microscopy
Henry Power

Renaissance discoveries in anatomy and physiology, notably William Harvey's demonstration of the function of the heart and the circulation of the blood in 1628, were to be as earthshaking as the astronomical discoveries of Copernicus and Galileo. Many of these breakthroughs depended on a new reliance on observation and on the invention of new instruments that made possible experiments never before imagined. Henry Power's work, *Experimental Philosophy*, was published in London in 1664. Here he uses the microscope to observe the "ant, . . . or pismire," and "little white eels or snigs."

OBSERVATIONS ON LITTLE ANIMALS

Observation XXII
The Ant, Emmet, or Pismire

This little Animal is that great Pattern of Industry and Frugality: To this Schoolmaster did Solomon send his sluggard, who those virtues not only excells all Insects, but most men. Other excellent Observables there are in so small a fabric: As the Herculean strength of its body, that it is able to

carry its triple weight and bulk; the agility of its limbs, that it runs so swiftly; the equality of its motion, that it trips so nimbly away without any saliency or leaping, without any fits or starts in its progression. Her head is large and globular, with a prominent snout: her eye is of a very fair black colour, round, globular, and prominent, of the bigness of a pea, foraminulous and latticed like that of other Insects: her mouth (in which you may see something to move) is armed with a pair of pincers, which move laterally, and are indented on the inside like a saw, by which she bites, and better holds her prey; and you may often see them

Source: Henry Power, *Experimental Philosophy* (London, 1664), pp. 25, 32–36.

carry their white oblong eggs in them for better security.

Observation XXX
Of the Little White Eels or Snigs, in Vinegar

They appear like small Silver-Eels, or little Snigs, and some of them as long as my little finger, constantly wriggling and swimming to and fro with a quick, smart, and restless motion. In which smallest of Animals these things are most remarkable.

First, they are not to be found in all sorts of Vinegar or Alegar, but only in such, probably, as has arrived to some peculiar temper or putrefaction, of which I can give you no characteristical signs; for, I have found them in all sorts of vinegar, both in the keenest and smartest, as well as in the weakest and most waterish vinegar; and in all these sorts, you shall sometimes find none at all; and I have both found them, and also vainly sought them, in the former liquors, at all seasons and times of the year also.

Secondly, the manner and best way of observing them is, upon a plain piece of white glass, whereon two or three drops of the said liquors are laid; and so laying that glass on the object-plate, and fitting your Microscope to it, you may distinctly see them to play and swim in those little ponds of vinegar (for so big every drop almost seems) to the very brink and banks of their fluid element.

Thirdly, nay you may see them (especially in old Alegar) with the bare eye, if you put a little of it into a clear Venice-glass, especially into those pure thin white bubbles, they call essence-glasses; you may then see an infinite company of them swimming at the edges of the liquor, nay and in the body of it too, like so many shreds of the purest Dutch thread, as if the whole liquor was nothing else but a great shoal or mass of quick eels or hair worms.

I have another advantageous way of discoverance of them to the bare eye also, which is by putting a little of those liquors into a little cylinder of white glass, of a small bore and length, either sealed or closed up with cork and wax at one end: therein, if you invert this glass cylinder and often turn it topsy turvy, no liquor will fall out, only a little bubble of air will always pass and repass through the inverted liquor, and one pretty thing I have herein observed, that when this bubble has stood in the superior end of the glass (and sometimes it would do so for a pretty while together before it broke) I have seen some of those small snigs or animals on the top of it, crawling over the smooth convexity of the bubble (like so many eels over a looking glass) without breaking through the tender cuticle and film of so brittle and thin a substance.

Fourthly, that as the liquor (dropped upon your object plate) spends and dries up, so you shall see those little Quicks to draw nearer and nearer together, and grow feebler in their motion; and when all the vinegar or alegar is dried away, they lie all dead, twisted and complicated all together, like a knot of eels, and after a little time dry away to nothing.

Fifthly, their heads and tails are smaller than the rest of their bodies; which is best observed by the microscope, when the liquor wherein they swim is almost spent and dried up, so that their motion thereby is rendered more feeble and weak, or when they lie absolutely dead.

Sixthly, another remarkable thing is, their exceeding exiguity; for certainly of all animals they are least that can be seen by the bare eye, which is helped and advantaged also by the rarefaction of the water wherein they swim.

Seventhly, if you take a spoonful of the aforesaid vinegar and heat it over a few coals, it presently destroys all the quicks in it, so that you may see them all stretched out as their full length, like a pencil chopped small, or little bits of hairs swimming up and down the liquor, which in a short time will precipitate and all sink down to the bottom of the glass.

Nay these poor vermin are not only slain by actual heat, but by a potential one also: for putting but a few drops of the oil of vitriol into an essence-glass full of that vinegar, it also shortly destroyed them in the same manner as the fire had done before.

Eighthly, now though heat hath that killing property, yet it seems that cold hath not: for I have taken a jar-glass full of the said vinegar, and by applying snow and salt to it, I have artificially frozen all the said liquor into a mass of ice (wherein all those animals it seemed lay incrystalled) though I could discover none of them in it (though I have taken the icy mass out on purpose to look at it) so that now I gave them [up] for gone for ever: yet when I came again (about two or three hours after,) to uncongeal the liquor, by keeping the glass in my warm hand, when the vinegar was again returned to its former liquidity, all my little animals made their reappearance, and danced and frisked about as lively as ever. Nay I have exposed a jar-glass full of this vinegar all night to a keen frost, and in the morning have thawed the ice again, and these little vermin have appeared again and endured again that strong and long conglaciation without any manifest injury done to them; which is both a pretty and a strange experiment.

Ninthly, I have filled an essence-glass half with the said vinegar, and half with oil, (which floated on the vinegar) in a distinct region by itself, and I have observed that in frosty weather when the vinegar has been congealed, that all the little eels have run up into the superincumbent oil to preserve themselves there, and would not return till some warmth was applied to the vinegar again, and then they would always presently return down into their native liquor again.

Tenthly, their motion is very remarkable, which is restless and constant, with perpetual undulations and wavings, like eels or snakes; so that it seems, that animals that come nearest the class of plants, have the most restless motions.

Eleventhly, the innumerable number and complicated motion of these minute animals in vinegar, may very neatly illustrate the doctrine of the incomparable Descartes, touching fluidity: (viz.) That the particles of all fluids are in a continual and restless motion, and therein consists the true nature of fluidity: for by this ocular example, we see there may be an intestine restless motion in a liquor, notwithstanding that the unassisted eye can discover no such matter.

III. SCIENCE AND SOCIETY

The impact of the Scientific Revolution permeated every level of society. As this chapter observes, scientific certainties were important to a society in desperate need of answers to deeply held self-doubts. The popularization of science, further, reached both the inquiring intellectual and the dabbling dilettante. Scientific societies' lectures were heard and pamphlets and treatises were read by literate women and men throughout Europe.

Selection 7
An Example of Popular Anti-Copernicanism

This selection, "The Fourth Day," is from the English translation of a French text on "The Week, or the Creation of the World." While the French version, by Guillaume du Bartas, was published in 1578, this text appeared in 1605 and demonstrated the continuing strength of anti-Copernicanism.

THE FOURTH DAY OF THE FIRST WEEKE

. . . My Muse may sing in sacred Eloquence,
To vertues Friends, their vertuous Excellence:

Source: Guillaume de Saluste du Bartas, *His Deuine Weekes and Workes,* trans. by Joshua Sylvester (London, 1605), pp. 115–122.

And with the Load-stone of my conquering verse,
Above the Poles attract the most perverse. . . .
   God's none of these faint idle Artizens
Who, at the best abandon their designes,
Working by halfes, as rather a great deale,
To doo too much quickly, then to doo it well:
But rather, as a workeman never wearie,
And all-sufficient, he his works doth carrie

To happie end; and to perfection,
With sober-speed brings what he hath begun.
  Having therefore, the Worlds wide Curten
    spread
About the circuit of the fruitfull Bed,
Where, to fill all with her un-numbred Kin,
Kinde Natures selfe each moment lyeth-in:
To make the same for ever admirable,
More stately pleasant, and more profitable; . . .
For, God selecting lightest of that Light,
Garnisht Heav'ns feeling with those torches bright.
Or else devided it, and pressing close
The parts, did make the Sunne and Starres of those.
  But, if thy wits thirst, rather seeke these things,
In *Greekish* cesternes then in *Hebrew* springs;
Then I conclude, that as of moist-full matter
God made the people that frequent the Water,
And of an Earthie stuffe the stubborne droues
That haunt the Hills & Dales and Downs and
    Groves: So, did he make by his Almightie might
The Heav'ns and Starres of one selfe substance
    bright.
To th' end these Lampes dispersed in the Skies,
Might with their Orbe, it with them Sympathize.
And as with us under the Oaken barke
The knurrie knot with branching vaines, we marke
To be of substance all one with the Tree,
Although farre thicker and more tough it bee:
So those guilt studs in th' upper storie driven,
Are nothing but the thickest part of Heaven.
  When I obserue their Light and Heat blent,
(Meere accidents of th' upper Element)
I thinke them Fire: but not such Fire as lastes
No longer then the fuell that it wastes:
For then I thinke all th' Elements too-little
To furnish them onely with one daies victuall.
  As th' Ague-sicke upon his shiv'ring pallet,
Delayes his health oft to delight his palate;
When wilfully his taste-les Taste delights

In things unsauorie to sound Appetites:
Even so some Brain-sicks live thear now-adaies,
That lose themselves still in contrarie waies;
Preposterous Wits that cannot row at ease,
On the smooth Channell of our common Seas.
And such are those (in my conceit at least)
Those Clarkes that thinke (thinke how absurd a jest)
That neither Heav'ns, nor Starres doo turne at all,
Nor dance about this great round Earthly Ball;
  But th' Earth itselfe, this massie Globe of ours
Turnes round-about once everie twice-twelve how-
    ers:
And we resemble Land-bred novices
New brought abroad to venture on the Seas,
Who, at first launching from the shoare, suppose
The ship stands still, and that the ground it goes. . . .
  Arm'd with these reasons, 't were superfluous
T'assaile the reasons of *Copernicus*,
Who, to solue better, of the Stars th' apparance,
Unto the Earth a three-fold motion warrants:
Making the Sun the Center of this All,
Moone, Earth, and Water, but one onely Ball.
But since heere, nor time nor place doth sute,
His *Paradox* at length to prosecute:
I will proceed, grounding my next discourse
On the Heav'ns motions, and their constant
    course. . . .
  He that to number all the Starres would seeke,
Had need invent som new Arithmeticke;
And who, to cast that reck'ning Takes in hand
Had need for Counters take the Oceans sand:
Yet have our wise and learned Elders found
Foure dozen Figures in the Heavenly Round,
For aide of memorie; and to our eyes
In certaine *Howses* to devide the Skyes:
Of these, are Twelve in that rich Guirdle graft
Which God gave Nature for her New-yeares-
    guift. . . .

Selection 8
"The New Organon"

Francis Bacon

Although the preceding selection provides an example of the ways in which the new ideas were satirized, other writers who were famous advocates of science received wide attention as well. In this selection, Francis Bacon (1561–1626) speaks as a prophet of the innovative approach to nature. Bacon developed a view of scientific progress based on observation, and argued for it by showing the shortcomings of received opinion. He attacks Aristotelian thought and scholastic philosophy with vigor and decisiveness.

Aphorisms concerning the interpretation of nature and the kingdom of man

I

Man, being the servant and interpreter of Nature, can do and understand so much and so much only as he has observed in fact or in thought of the course of nature: beyond this he neither knows anything nor can do anything.

II

Neither the naked hand nor the understanding left to itself can effect much. It is by instruments and helps that the work is done, which are as much wanted for the understanding as for the hand. And as the instruments of the hand either give motion or guide it, so the instruments of the mind supply either suggestions for the understanding or cautions.

III

Human knowledge and human power meet in one; for where the cause is not known the effect cannot be produced. Nature to be commanded must be obeyed; and that which in contemplation is as the cause is in operation as the rule.

IV

Towards the effecting of works, all that man can do is to put together or put asunder natural bodies. The rest is done by nature working within.

Source: James Spedding (ed.), *The Works of Francis Bacon* (Cambridge: Riverside Press, 1863), pp. 67–99.

V

The study of nature with a view to works is engaged in by the mechanic, the mathematician, the physician, the alchemist, and the magician; but by all (as things now are) with slight endeavor and scanty success.

VI

It would be an unsound fancy and self-contradictory to expect that things which have never yet been done can be done except by means which have never yet been tried.

VII

The productions of the mind and hand seem very numerous in books and manufactures. But all this variety lies in an exquisite subtlety and derivations from a few things already known; not in the number of axioms.

VIII

Moreover the works already known are due to chance and experiment rather than to sciences; for the sciences we now possess are merely systems for the nice ordering and setting forth of things already invented; not methods of invention or directions for new works.

IX

The cause and root of nearly all evils in the sciences is this—that while we falsely admire and extol the powers of the human mind we neglect to seek for its true helps.

X

The subtlety of nature is greater many times over than the subtlety of the senses and understanding; so that all those specious meditations, speculations, and glosses in which men indulge are quite from the purpose, only there is no one by to observe it.

XI

As the sciences which we now have do not help us in finding out new works, so neither does the logic which we now have help us in finding out new sciences.

XII

The logic now in use serves rather to fix and give stability to the errors which have their foundation in commonly received notions then to help the search after truth. So it does more harm than good.

. . .

XXIX

In sciences founded on opinions and dogmas, the use of anticipations and logic is good; for in them the object is to command assent to the proposition, not to master the thing.

XXX

Though all the wits of all the ages should meet together and combine and transmit their labours, yet will no great progress ever be made in science by means of anticipations; because radical errors in the first concoction of the mind are not to be cured by the excellence of functions and remedies subsequent.

XXXI

It is idle to expect any great advancement in science from the superinducing and engrafting of new things upon old. We must begin anew from the very foundations, unless we would revolve for ever in a circle with mean and contemptible progress.

XXXII

The honour of the ancient authors, and indeed of all, remains untouched; since the comparison I challenge is not of wits or faculties, but of ways and methods, and the part I take upon myself is not that of a judge, but of a guide.

XXXIII

This must be plainly avowed: no judgment can be rightly formed either of my method or of the discoveries to which it leads, by means of anticipations (that is to say, of the reasoning which is now in use); since I cannot be called on to abide by the sentence of a tribunal which is itself on its trial.

XXXIV

Even to deliver and explain what I bring forward is no easy matter; for things in themselves new will yet be apprehended with reference to what is old.

XXXV

It was said by Borgia of the expedition of the French into Italy, that they came with chalk in their hands to mark out their lodgings, not with arms to force their way in. I in like manner would have my doctrine enter quietly into the minds that are fit and capable of receiving it; for confutations cannot be employed, when the difference is upon first principles and very notions and even upon forms of demonstration.

XXXVI

One method of delivery alone remains to us; which is simply this: we must lead men to the particulars themselves, and their series and order; while men on their side must force themselves for awhile to lay their notions by and begin to familiarise themselves with facts.

XXXVII

The doctrine of those who have denied that certainty could be attained at all, has some agreement with my way of proceeding at the first setting out; but they end in being infinitely separated and opposed. For the holders of that doctrine assert simply that nothing can be known; I also assert that not much can be known in nature by the way which is now in use. But then they go on to destroy the authority of the senses and understanding; whereas I proceed to devise and supply helps for the same.

XXXVIII

The idols and false notions which are now in possession of the human understanding, and have taken deep root therein, not only so beset men's minds that truth can hardly find entrance, but even after entrance obtained, they will again in the very instauration of the sciences meet and trouble us, unless men being forewarned of the danger fortify themselves as far as may be against their assaults.

XXXIX

There are four classes of Idols which beset men's minds. To these for distinction's sake I have assigned names,—calling the first class *Idols of the Tribe;* the second, *Idols of the Cave;* the third, *Idols of the Marketplace;* the fourth, *Idols of the Theatre.*

XL

The formation of ideas and axioms by true induction is no doubt the proper remedy to be applied for the keeping off and clearing away of idols. To point them out, however, is of great use; for the doctrine of Idols is to the Interpretation of Nature what the doctrine of the refutation of Sophisnes is to common Logic.

XLI

The Idols of the Tribe have their foundation in human nature itself, and in the tribe or race of men. For it is a false assertion that the sense of man is the measure of things. On the contrary, all perceptions as well of the sense as of the mind are according to the measure of the individual and not according to the measure of the universe. And the human understanding is like a false mirror, which, receiving rays irregularly, distorts and discolours the nature of things by mingling its own nature with it.

XLII

The Idols of the Cave are the idols of the individual man. For every one (besides the errors common to human nature in general) has a cave or den of his own, which refracts and discolours the light of nature; owing either to his own proper and peculiar nature; or to his education and conversation with others; or to the reading of books, and the authority of those whom he esteems and admires; or to the differences of impressions, accordingly as they take place in a mind preoccupied and predisposed or in a mind indifferent and settled; or the like. So that the spirit of man (according as it is meted out to different individuals) is in fact a thing variable and full of perturbation, and governed as it were by chance. Whence it was well observed by Heraclitus that men look for sciences in their own lesser worlds, and not in the greater or common world.

XLIII

There are also Idols formed by the intercourse and association of men with each other, which I call Idols of the Market-place, on account of the commerce and consort of men there. For it is by discourse that men associate; and words are imposed according to the apprehension of the vulgar. And therefore the ill and unfit choice of words wonderfully obstructs the understanding. Nor do the definitions or explanations wherewith in some things learned men are wont to guard and defend themselves, by any means set the matter right. But words plainly force and overrule the understanding, and throw all into confusion, and lead men away into numberless empty controversies and idle fancies.

XLIV

Lastly, there are Idols which have immigrated into men's minds from the various dogmas of philosophies, and also from wrong laws of demonstration. These I call Idols of the Theatre; because in my judgment all the received systems are but so many stage-plays, representing worlds of their own creation after an unreal and scenic fashion. Nor is it only of the systems now in vogue, or only of the ancient sects and philosophies, that I speak; for many more plays of the same kind may yet be composed and in like artificial manner set forth; seeing that errors the most widely different have nevertheless causes for the most part alike. Neither again do I mean this only of entire systems, but also of many principles and axioms in science, which by tradition, credulity, and negligence have come to be received.

But of these several kinds of Idols I must speak more largely and exactly, that the understanding may be duly cautioned.

XLV

The human understanding is of its own nature prone to suppose the existence of more order and regularity in the world than it finds. And though there be many things in nature which are singular and unmatched, yet it devises for them parallels and conjugates and relatives which do not exist. Hence the fiction that all celestial bodies move in perfect circles; spirals and dragons being (except in name) utterly rejected. Hence too the element of Fire with its orb is brought in, to make up the square with the other three which the sense perceives. Hence also the ratio of density of the so-called elements is arbitrarily fixed at ten to one. And so on of other dreams. And these fancies affect not dogmas only, but simple notions also.

XLVI

The human understanding when it has once adopted an opinion (either as being the received opinion or as being agreeable to itself) draws all things else to support and agree with it. And though there be a greater number and weight of instances to be found on the other side, yet these it either neglects and despises, or else by some distinction set aside and rejects; in order that by this great and pernicious predetermination the authority of its former conclusions may remain inviolate. And therefore it was a good answer that was made by one who when they showed him hanging in a temple a picture of those who had paid their vows as having escaped shipwreck, and would have him say whether he did not now acknowledge the power of the gods,—"Aye," asked he again, "but where are they painted that were drowned after their vows?" And such is the way of all superstition, whether in astrology, dreams, omens, divine judgments, or the like; wherein men, having a delight in such vanities, mark the events where they are fulfilled, but where they fail, though this happen much oftener, neglect and pass them by. But with far more subtlety does this mischief insinuate itself into philosophy and the sciences; in which the first conclusion colours and brings into conformity with itself all that come after, though far sounder and better. Besides, independently of that delight and vanity which I have described, it is the peculiar and perpetual error of the human intellect to be more moved and excited by affirmatives than by negatives; whereas it ought properly to hold itself indifferently disposed towards both alike. Indeed in the establishment of any true axiom, the negative instance is the more forcible of the two.

XLVII

The human understanding is moved by those things most which strike and enter the mind simultaneously and suddenly, and so fill the imagination; and then it feigns and supposes all other things to be somehow, though it cannot see how, similar to those few things by which it is surrounded. But for that going to and fro to remote and heterogeneous instances, by which axioms are tried as in the fire, the intellect is altogether slow and unfit, unless it be forced thereto by severe laws and overruling authority.

XLVIII

The human understanding is unquiet; it cannot stop or rest, and still presses onward, but in vain. Therefore it is that we cannot conceive of any end or limit to the world; but always as of necessity it occurs to us that there is something beyond. Neither again can it be conceived how eternity has flowed down to the present day; for that distinction which is commonly received of infinity in time past and in time to come can by no means hold; for it would thence follow that one infinity is greater than another, and that infinity is wasting away and tending to become finite. The like subtlety arises touching the infinite divisibility of lines, from the same inability of thought to stop. But this inability interferes more mischievously in the discovery of causes: for although the most general principles in nature ought to be held merely positive, as they are discovered, and cannot with truth be referred to a cause; nevertheless the human understanding being unable to rest still seeks something prior in the order of nature. And then it is that in struggling towards that which is further off it falls back upon that which is more nigh at hand; namely, on final causes: which have relation clearly to the nature of man rather than to the nature of the universe; and from this source have strangely defiled philosophy. But he is no less an unskilled and shallow philosopher who seeks causes of that which is most general, than he who in things subordinate and subaltern omits to do so.

XLIX

The human understanding is no dry light, but receives an infusion from the will and affections; whence proceed sciences which may be called "sciences as one would." For what a man had rather were true he more readily believes. Therefore he rejects difficult things from impatience of research; sober things, because they narrow hope; the deeper things of nature, from superstition; the light of experience, from arrogance and pride, lest his mind should seem to be occupied with things mean and transitory; things not commonly believed, out of deference to the opinion of the

vulgar. Numberless in short are the ways, and sometimes imperceptible, in which the affections colour and infect the understanding.

L

But by far the greatest hindrance and aberration of the human understanding proceeds from the dulness, incompetency, and deceptions of the senses; in that things which strike the sense outweigh things which do not immediately strike it, though they be more important. Hence it is that speculation commonly ceases where sight ceases; insomuch that of things invisible there is little or no observation. Hence all the working of the spirits inclosed in tangible bodies lies hid and unobserved of men. So also all the more subtle changes of form in the parts of coarser substances (which they commonly call alteration, though it is in truth local motion through exceedingly small spaces) is in like manner unobserved. And yet unless these two things just mentioned be searched out and brought to light, nothing great can be achieved in nature, as far as the production of works is concerned. So again the essential nature of our common air, and of all bodies less dense than air (which are very many), is almost unknown. For the sense by itself is a thing infirm and erring; neither can instruments for enlarging or sharpening the senses do much; but all the truer kind of interpretation of nature is effected by instances and experiments fit and apposite; wherein the sense decides touching the experiment only, and the experiment touching the point in nature and the thing itself.

LI

The human understanding is of its own nature prone to abstractions and gives a substance and reality to things which are fleeting. But to resolve nature into abstractions is less to our purpose than to dissect her into parts; as did the school of Democritus, which went further into nature than the rest. Matter rather than forms should be the object of our attention, its configurations and changes of configuration, and simple action, and law of action or motion; for forms are figments of the human mind, unless you will call those laws of action forms.

LII

Such then are the idols which I call *Idols of the Tribe;* and which take their rise either from the homogeneity of the substance of the human spirit, or from its preoccupation, or from its narrowness, or from its restless motion, or from an infusion of the affections, or from the incompetency of the senses, or from the mode of impression.

LIII

The *Idols of the Cave* take their rise in the peculiar constitution, mental or bodily, of each individual; and also in education, habit, and accident. Of this kind there is a great number and variety; but I will instance those the pointing out of which contains the most important caution, and which have most effect in disturbing the clearness of the understanding.

LIV

Men become attached to certain particular sciences and speculations, either because they fancy themselves the authors and inventors thereof, or because they have bestowed the greatest pains upon them and become most habituated to them. But men of this kind, if they betake themselves to philosophy and contemplations of a general char· acter, distort and colour them in obedience to their former fancies; a thing especially to be noticed in Aristotle, who made his natural philosophy a mere bond-servant to his logic, thereby rendering it contentious and well nigh useless. The race of chemists again out of a few experiments of the furnace have built up a fantastic philosophy, framed with reference to a few things; and Gilbert also, after he had employed himself most laboriously in the study and observation of the loadstone, proceeded at once to construct an entire system in accordance with his favourite subject.

LV

There is one principal and as it were radical distinction between different minds, in respect of philosophy and the sciences; which is this: that some minds are stronger and apter to mark the differences of things, others to mark their resemblances. The steady and acute mind can fix its contemplations and dwell and fasten on the subtlest distinctions: the lofty and discursive mind recognises and puts together the finest and most general resemblances. Both kinds however easily err in excess, by catching the one at gradations the other at shadows.

LVI

There are found some minds given to an extreme admiration of antiquity, others to an extreme love and appetite for novelty; but few so duly tempered that they can hold the mean, neither carping at what has been well laid down by the ancients, nor despising what is well introduced by the moderns. This however turns to the great injury of the sciences and philosophy; since these affectations of antiquity and novelty are the humours of partisans rather than judgments; and truth is to be sought for not in the felicity of any age, which is an unstable thing, but in the light of nature and experience, which is eternal. These factions therefore must be abjured, and care must be taken that the intellect be not hurried by them into assent.

LVII

Contemplations of nature and of bodies in their simple form break up and distract the understanding, while contemplations of nature and bodies in their composition and configuration overpower and dissolve the understanding: a distinction well seen in the school of Leucippus and Democritus as compared with the other philosophies. For that school is so busied with the particles that it hardly attends to the structure; while the others are so lost in admiration of the structure that they do not penetrate to the simplicity of nature. These kinds of contemplation should therefore be alternated and taken by turns; that so the understanding may be rendered at once penetrating and comprehensive, and the inconveniences above mentioned, with the idols which proceed from them, may be avoided.

LVIII

Let such then be our provision and contemplative prudence for keeping off and dislodging the *Idols of the Cave,* which grow for the most part either out of the predominance of a favourite subject, or out of an excessive tendency to compare or to distinguish, or out of partiality for particular ages, or out of the largeness or minuteness of the objects contemplated. And generally let every student of nature take this as a rule,—that whatever his mind seizes and dwells upon with peculiar satisfaction is to be held in suspicion, and that so much the more care is to be taken in dealing with such questions to keep the understanding even and clear.

LIX

But the *Idols of the Marketplace* are the most troublesome of all; idols which have crept into the understanding through the alliances of words and names. For men believe that their reason governs words; but it is also true that words react on the understanding; and this it is that has rendered philosophy and the sciences sophistical and inactive. Now words, being commonly framed and applied according to the capacity of the vulgar, follow those lines of division which are most obvious to the vulgar understanding. And whenever an understanding of greater acuteness or a more diligent observation would alter those lines to suit the true divisions of nature, words stand in the way and resist the change. Whence it comes to pass that the high and formal discussions of learned men and oftentimes in disputes about words and names; with which (according to the use and wisdom of the mathematicians) it would be more prudent to begin, and so by means of definitions reduced them to order. Yet even definitions cannot cure this evil in dealing with natural and material things; since the definitions themselves consist of words, and those words beget others: so that it is necessary to recur to individual instances, and those in due series and order; as I shall say

presently when I come to the method and scheme for the formation of notions and axioms.

. . .

LXI

But the *Idols of the Theatre* are not innate, nor do they steal into the understanding secretly, but are plainly impressed and received into the mind from the play-books of philosophical systems and the perverted rules of demonstration. To attempt refutations in this case would be merely inconsistent with what I have already said: for since we agree neither upon principles nor upon demonstrations there is no place for argument. And this is so far well, inasmuch as it leaves the honour of the ancients untouched. For they are no wise disparaged—the question between them and me being only as to the way. For as the saying is, the lame man who keeps the right road outstrips the runner who takes a wrong one. Nay it is obvious that when a man runs the wrong way, the more active and swift he is the further he will go astray.

But the course I propose for the discovery of sciences is such as leaves but little to the acuteness and strength of wits, but places all wits and understandings nearly on a level. For as in the drawing of a straight line or a perfect circle, much depends on the steadiness and practice of the hand, if it be done by aim of hand only, but if with the aid of rule or compass, little or nothing; so is it exactly with my plan. But though particular confutations would be of no avail, yet touching the sects and general divisions of such systems I must say something; something also touching the external signs which show that they are unsound; and finally something touching the causes of such great infelicity and of such lasting and general agreement in error; that so the access to truth may be made less difficult, and the human understanding may the more willingly submit to its purgation and dismiss its idols.

LXII

Idols of the Theatre, or of Systems, are many, and there can be and perhaps will be yet many more. For were it not that now for many ages men's minds have been busied with religion and theology; and were it not that civil government, especially monarchies, have been averse to such novelties, even in matters speculative; so that men labour therein to the peril and harming of their fortunes,—not only unrewarded, but exposed also to contempt and envy; doubtless there would have arisen many other philosophical sects like to those which in great variety flourished once among the Greeks. For as on the phenomena of the heavens many hypotheses may be constructed, so likewise (and more also) many various dogmas may be set up and established on the phenomena of philosophy. And in the plays of this philosophical theatre you may observe the same thing which is found in the theatre of the poets, that stories invented for the stage are more compact and elegant, and more as one would wish them to be, than true stories out of history.

In general however there is taken for the material of philosophy either a great deal out of a few things, or a very little out of many things; so that on both sides philosophy is based on too narrow a foundation of experiment and natural history, and decides on the authority of too few cases. For the Rational School of philosophers snatches from experience a variety of common instances, neither duly ascertained nor diligently examined and weighed, and leaves all the rest to meditation and agitation of wit.

There is also another class of philosophers, who having bestowed much diligent and careful labour on a few experiments, have thence made bold to educe and construct systems; wresting all other facts in a strange fashion to conformity therewith.

And there is yet a third class, consisting of those who out of faith and veneration mix their philosophy with theology and traditions; among whom the vanity of some has gone so far aside as to seek the origin of sciences among spirits and genii. So that this parent stock of errors—this false philosophy—is of three kinds; the Sophistical, the Empirical, and the Superstitious.

LXIII

The most conspicuous example of the first class was Aristotle, who corrupted natural philosophy by his logic: fashioning the world out of categories;

assigning to the human soul, the noblest of substances, a genus from words of the second intention; doing the business of density and rarity (which is to make bodies of greater or less dimensions, that is, occupy greater or less spaces), by the frigid distinction of act and power; asserting that single bodies have each a single and proper motion, and that if they participate in any other, then this results from an external cause; and imposing countless other arbitrary restrictions on the nature of things; being always more solicitous to provide an answer to the question and affirm something positive in words, than about the inner truth of things; a failing best shown when his philosophy is compared with other systems of note among the Greeks. For the Homoeomera of Anaxagoras; the Atoms of Leucippus and Democritus; the Heaven and Earth of Parmenides; the Strife and Friendship of Empedocles; Heraclitus's doctrine how bodies are resolved into the indifferent nature of fire, and remoulded into solids; have all of them some taste of the natural philosopher,—some savour of the nature of things, and experience, and bodies; whereas in the physics of Aristotle you hear hardly anything but the words of logic; which in his metaphysics also, under a more imposing name, and more forsooth as a realist than a nominalist, he has handled over again. Nor let any weight be given to the fact, that in his books on animals and his problems, and other of his treatises, there is frequent dealing with experiments. For he had come to his conclusion before; he did not consult experience, as he should have done, in order to the framing of his decisions and axioms; but having first determined the question according to his will, he then resorts to experience, and bending her into conformity with his placets leads her about like a captive in a procession; so that even on this count he is more guilty than his modern followers, the schoolmen, who have abandoned experience altogether.

LXIV

But the Empirical school of philosophy gives birth to dogmas more deformed and monstrous than the Sophistical or Rational school. For it has its foundations not in the light of common notions, (which though it be a faint and superficial light, is yet in a manner universal, and has references to many things,) but in the narrowness and darkness of a few experiments. To those therefore who are daily busied with these experiments, and have infected their imagination with them such a philosophy seems probable and all but certain; to all men else incredible and vain. Of this there is a notable instance in the alchemists and their dogmas; though it is hardly to be found elsewhere in these times, except perhaps in the philosophy of Gilbert. Nevertheless with regard to philosophies of this kind there is one caution not to be omitted; for I foresee that if ever men are roused by my admonitions to betake themselves seriously to experiment and bid farewell to sophistical doctrines, then indeed through the premature hurry of the understanding to leap or fly to universals and principles of things, great danger may be apprehended from philosophies of this kind; against which evil we ought even now to prepare.

LXV

But the corruption of philosophy by superstition and an admixture of theology is far more widely spread, and does the greatest harm, whether to entire systems or to their parts. For the human understanding is obnoxious to the influence of the imagination no less than to the influence of common notions. For the contentious and sophistical kind of philosophy ensnares the understanding; but this kind, being fanciful and tumid and half poetical, misleads it more by flattery. For there is in man an ambition of the understanding, no less than of the will, especially in high and lofty spirits.

Of this kind we have among the Greeks a striking example in Pythagoras, though he united with it a coarser and more cumbrous superstition; another in Plato and his school, more dangerous and subtle. It shows itself likewise in parts of other philosophies, in the introduction of abstract forms and final causes and first causes, with the omission in most cases of causes intermediate, and the like. Upon this point the greatest caution should be used. For nothing is so mischievous as the apotheosis of error; and it is a very plague of the understanding for vanity to become the object of veneration. Yet in this vanity some of the moderns have with extreme levity indulged so far as to attempt to found a system of natural philosophy on the first chapter of Genesis, on the book of Job, and other parts of the sacred writings; seeking for the dead among the living: which also makes the inhibition and repression of it the more important, because from this unwholesome mixture of things human and divine there arises not only a fantastic philosophy but also an heretical religion. Very meet it is therefore that we be sober-minded, and give to faith that only which is faith's.

LXVIII

So much concerning the several classes of Idols, and their equipage: all of which must be renounced and put away with a fixed and solemn determination, and the understanding thoroughly freed and cleansed; the entrance into the kingdom of man, founded on the sciences, being not much other than the entrance into the kingdom of heaven, whereinto none may enter except as a little child.

Selection 9
"Proposals for the Académie Royale des Sciences"
Christiaan Huygens

As was the case with the Renaissance Humanists who formed a kind of international community, so, too, the proponents of the "new science" in various countries communicated with one another on an international as well as a national level. Here Christiaan Huygens outlines in a memorandum for the French Minister Colbert the work that the community as a whole ought to be doing, as advocated by Francis Bacon and already started by a group organized for this purpose, the Royal Society in England. It indicates how complex was the organization of these groups as the ideas of science began to become fashionable in European society.

Carry out experiments on the vacuum with the pump and by other means, and determine the weight of the air.

Examine the explosive force of small amounts of gunpowder enclosed in an iron or very thick copper box.

Examine in the same manner the force of water rarified by fire.

Examine the force and speed of the wind, and its uses in navigation and with machines.

Examine the force of percussion or the communication of motion during impact, a subject of which I believe I was the first to present the true laws.

For the Scientific Meeting

The main and most useful project of this group, in my opinion, is to work on a natural history, approximately to Verulamius' [Bacon's] plan. This history consists of experiments and observations and is the only means of gaining knowledge of the causes of all which one perceives in nature. To ascertain the properties of weight, heat, cold, magnetic attraction, light, colours, the particles that compose the atmosphere, water, fire, and all other bodies, the purpose of animal respiration, how metals, stones, and plants grow—of these things one knows little or nothing yet, even though there is nothing in the world of which knowledge is more desirable or useful.

It would be necessary, by pursuing different subjects, of which I have just named some, to establish the chapters of this history and to gather under these headings all the observations and experiments relating to each one specifically; and it is unnecessary to trouble oneself with reporting on obscure and difficult experiments instead of experiments which seem essential for the discovery of that which is being sought, even though these are very ordinary.

Such a carefully prepared history will be useful to all mankind and to all ages to come, because aside from various uses which may be derived from particular experiments, the collection of all these experiments is a solid foundation for the establishment of a natural philosophy in which it is essential to proceed from the knowledge of effects to the knowledge of causes.

Chemistry and the dissection of animals are certainly necessary for this plan; but it is essential that the research in these two areas should tend to add to this history in some important point directed toward the discovery of something proposed, without losing time on various observations of certain circumstances, about which knowledge is inconsequential. Thus the reproach which Seneca made to the ancient philosophers may not be incurred: "That they might perhaps have discovered useful things if they had not sought out superfluous ones."

It would be necessary to begin with the subjects judged most critical and most useful, assigning several at a time to various group members who will report on and read what has been sent in every week. Therefore the conduct of business will be very orderly and the results will undoubtedly be very great.

Huygens

Source: Joseph Bertrand, *L'Academie des Sciences et les Academiciens de 1666 á 1793* (Paris: J. Hetzel, 1869), pp. 8–10. Trans. by A. Borchert.

EIGHT

Conclusion

For most of us, Europe would hardly have seemed more familiar in 1700 than in 1350. Most people still lived in conditions that we would have viewed as unimaginably primitive. The smells of cities with open sewers we would have considered overpowering; travel and communication would have continued to seem agonizingly slow; we would have found literacy minimal and the omnipresence of religion, with Church bells ringing much of the time, extraordinary; and we would probably have been appalled, as before, by the enormous disparity between the way of life of the privileged and educated, on the one hand, and the vast majority of the populace, on the other. Above all, perhaps, we might have noticed how little change there had been in the relative size of the small elite that could enjoy the political and social freedom that we now regard as a major achievement of Western civilization. And yet, as we have seen in the past six chapters, much had in fact been transformed. In politics, warfare, religious diversity, economics, art, and science, new conditions had arisen that we would find familiar and which paved the way for the emergence of the modern world.

The questions that the people of the Renaissance grappled with, however, and the new ones they raised have by no means vanished from our horizons. In each of the areas considered in this book, we can look back to the years between the fourteenth and seventeenth centuries not only for the origin of concerns that remain important but also to appreciate the continuity of the attempts that have been made to come to terms with issues that have endured into our own times.

In politics, it is true, the profound process of democratization lay largely in the future. Not until the age of the French Revolution in the late 1700s and the subsequent revolutions that swept the world did the processes of government become more open to those outside the traditional elite. One may sometimes wonder, especially in a manipulative age when the choices among candidates for office may seem minimal, whether the boundaries of political action have been extended very far. There is no question, however, that the right to be heard is of a different order than it was in the 1600s, even during the most heady days of the English Revolution.

Nevertheless, the problems of winning acceptance for authority, of creating the right image for those who govern, and of devising acceptable mechanisms of protest and dissent have not essentially changed. Those who seek power, or wish to retain it, can still learn from a Machiavelli or a Queen Elizabeth I, and they often sound like these predecessors when they justify their actions. Revolutionaries, too, continue to echo idealists like the Levellers in arguing that society must be fundamentally reformed if it is to offer fairness and equality to all. There are few who discuss politics who do not rely, in important ways, on those who struggled with these matters in the Renaissance and early modern times, and it is no wonder that, to this day, ideas about government are often derived from the great theorists of that era.

Much the same is true when the subject is warfare. If it was the invention of gunpowder that first demonstrated how profoundly armed conflict can be transformed by technology and how far-ranging the consequences may be, this is not a set of problems that have become easier to solve with the passage of time. Just as the armored knight of old was forced, in the age of guns, to rethink the nature of honor, the social role of the aristocrat, and the acceptability of violence, so today we have had to reevaluate the feasibility of *any* all-out war in the wake of the atomic bomb. To the extent that we agonize over the disastrous effects of a blind adherence to ideology, we mirror those who were troubled by the fanatical struggles of Protestants and Catholics in the sixteenth century. When we doubt the usefulness of war and wonder if soldiers should be peacemakers rather than destroyers, we engage the very issues that affected sensitive observers such as Rubens during the Thirty Years' War. They set the questions, and we are still looking for the answers.

Where religion itself is concerned, many people pride themselves on the distance the West has moved from the fierce and brutal disputes of the Renaissance and Reformation, and they may assume, in consequence, that they have little to learn from that passionate and tormented age. By and large, they might argue, we have left behind the assumption that faith must determine all political, social, and intellectual relations and that violence is an appropriate means of stamping out heresy. Since the less "advanced" cultures, outside the West, are alone (aside from rare exceptions, such as Northern Ireland) in adopting such fundamentalist positions, it is for them, not for us, to take lessons from the era of religious wars.

If we shift our attention away from Renaissance and Reformation conflicts at their most intense, however, and focus instead on those elements in the period's dissenting tradition which brought the destruction to an end, we will discover that we still have a long way to go to learn what the Castellios and the Miltons tried to teach. The dissenters of early modern times not only broke the traditional Church's monopoly on truth, and in so doing caused death and devastation, but they also inspired the belief that, ultimately, it is self-defeating to try to spread truth by coercion. Few in the early generations of the Reformation—certainly not major figures like Luther—would have accepted that second conclusion; they were trying to replace one orthodoxy with another. Eventually, however, this corollary of dissent, the quest for toleration, became a vital aspiration for Western society. Politicians seeking order, theologians troubled by intemperate claims, and people of good will who were dismayed by conflicting assertions of right and wrong began to explore ways of persuading sworn enemies to live with one another in peace. They had a hard time gaining a hearing, let alone respect, for their views, and the effort has rarely been easy in the years since 1700. That it has had to continue, however, suggests that we are still in no position to put behind us one of the central issues that agitated the dissenters of early modern Europe.

Since the Industrial Revolution lay in the future in 1700 and the worldwide financial mechanisms and activities we take for granted today could not even have been imagined, it may be easy to assume that our economic system is so radically different that the issues of the Renaissance have lost all relevance. Yet the very recognition that economic change has the power to affect all society is itself a heritage from that time. The realization, among Spaniards, that their dominance of Europe was crumbling because of their failings in this area and the amazement inspired by the Dutch, whose rise to prominence, despite the tiny size of their country, rested entirely on their trading skills, were enough to give this aspect of society a centrality in the 1600s that was unprecedented and has only increased in the interim.

The result has been a series of attempts to explain in theory and implement in policy the conditions that promote prosperity. The first such broad attempt, known as "mercantilism," we owe to the 1600s; that it soon proved ineffective, though, did not stop economists and politicians from trying to reshape society, according to a succession of new theories, at regular intervals thereafter. Moreover, the ability of merchants in particular and of commercial interests in general to determine political and social developments was already becoming apparent in 1700. What this led to was an unease about the effects of the West's preoccupation with economics that has not only persisted but has gained strength until our own time. In the 1600s the anxiety was prompted by the decline of older notions of community, status, and faith; today, we focus on materialism and the destruction of the environment. Whatever the specific issues, however, the basic paradox—that we seek economic advance even as we worry about its effects—remains unresolved to this day.

In the worlds of art and science, the connections are more self-evident. After all, artists and scientists openly acknowledge their debt to their ancestors of this period. Even if painters often see themselves as reacting against, or superseding, Renaissance aesthetics and students of nature address problems and use methods that Newton would have found astounding, they derive many of their basic assumptions and purposes from the geniuses who gave shape to their fields between 1400 and 1700. Yet there are also areas that have to do not with the content of their work but with their status in society that demonstrate the continuities between past and present.

The crucial ambition that first appeared in the Renaissance and continues to animate both the artistic and the scientific communities is independence. When Brunelleschi broke with traditional constraints and when Kepler came into conflict with the powerful authorities of his time, they were, in effect, seeking to pursue their work free from outside restraint. It is this claim of autonomy that has continued to echo down the centuries. Both artists and scientists have always relied on support and approval from the larger society—whether in the form of private patronage, as was largely the case in the Renaissance, or from public funding, as is more common today. Whatever the system, however, they have had to depend on a general conviction that their work was in some ways both admirable and useful. The perennial dilemma they have faced is not only whether they need to compromise their own beliefs in order to win that wider approval but also whether the larger society is entitled to demand that they adapt themselves to its norms. If, today, we wonder if limits should be placed on "pornographic" art or on genetic research, we are merely expressing, in different terms, the quandary about independent action and intellectual freedom that bedeviled a Michelangelo and a Galileo.

That such fundamental issues have not been resolved in five hundred years should not surprise us. It may be that they will never be settled, because it seems unlikely that we will be able to define, permanently and acceptably, appropriate roles in society for government, war, dissent, economic activity, art, and science. What is remarkable is that in each of these areas, the central issues were joined, with the intensity and the configurations that prevail to this day, only during the centuries that have been our subject. It might seem that because they looked so anxiously to the past, attempting (in the words of Francis Bacon) only "by colour of Antiquity to introduce novelty," the people of this period were fundamentally different, for we do not stress our debts to history. If this book has been able to suggest anything, however, it is that these centuries shaped a set of concerns that remain essential to our continuing effort to understand and improve both ourselves and the society in which we live and that, therefore, we must recognize the origins of our own world in the ages we call Renaissance and early modern times.

Acknowledgments

FOUR CENTURIES: A BRIEF OVERVIEW

Selection 1 (p. 15)
Giorgio Vasari, *Lives of the Artists*, vol. 1, trans. by George Bull (London: Penguin Classics, 1987), pp. 46–47, copyright © George Bull, 1965.

Selection 2 (p. 16)
François Rabelais, *La Vie de Gargantua et de Pantagruel: Livre Second*, vol. 3 (Paris: Dalibon, 1823), pp. 259–261. Trans. by Angela Borchert.

Selection 3 (p. 16)
Jacob Burckhardt, *The Civilisation of the Renaissance in Italy*, trans. by S. G. C. Middlemore (New York: Macmillan & Co., 1890), pp. 134–135.

Selection 4 (p. 17)
Jacob Burckhardt, *The Civilisation of the Renaissance in Italy*, trans. by S. G. C. Middlemore (New York: Macmillan & Co., 1890), pp. 359–365.

THE PRINCE

Selection 1 (p. 42)
"The Coronation of Charles the Bald," from the "Ordo Coronationis Karoli II" in "Regno Hlotharii II Factae," *Capitularia Regum Francorum*, ed. by A. Boretius (Monumenta Germaniae Historica, Legum Sectio II, Vol. II, Hanover, 1890), pp. 456–458. Trans. by Anna Keaney.

Selection 2 (p. 44)
"Frederick Barbarosa's Constitution Concerning Fiefs," from "Constitutio de Iure Feudorum," *Constitutiones et Acta Publica imperatorum et regum*, ed. by L. Weiland, (Monumenta Germaniae Historica, Legum Sectio IV, Hanover 1893), pp. 247–249. Trans. by Anna Keaney.

Selection 3 (p. 46)
Vespasiano da Bisticci, *Vite di Uomini Illustri del Secolo XV*, ed. by Ludovico Frati (Bologna: Romagnoli-Dall'Acqua, 1893), pp. 302–304, 307–315, 317–320. Trans. by Anna Keaney.

Selection 4 (p. 49)
"Charles V affirms the Joyous Entry, 1515," from Jeanne Mennes, "De Staten van Brabant en de Blijde Inkomst van Kroonprins Filips in 1549," *Anciens Pays et Assemblées d'Etats/ Standen en Landen*, vol. 18 (Louvain: Edition E. Nauwelaerts, 1959), pp. 56–58, 64–68, 72–78, 156–164. Trans. by Sherrin Marshall.

Selection 5 (p. 50)
Lucy Aikin, *Memoirs of the Court of Queen Elizabeth*, vol. 1 (London: Longman, Hurst, Rees, Orme and Brown, 1819), pp. 94–95.

Selection 6 (p. 51)
Walter Scott (ed.), *A Collection of Scarce and Valuable Tracts, on the most interesting and entertaining Subjects: but chiefly such as relate to the History and Constitution of these Kingdoms*, vol. 1 (London: T. Cadell and W. Davies, 1809), pp. 429–430.

Selection 7 (p. 52)
G. W. Prothero (ed.), *Select Statutes and other Constitutional Documents Illustrative of the Reigns of Elizabeth and James I* (Oxford: Clarendon Press, 1913), pp. 293–294, 400–401.

Selection 8 (p. 53)
H. G. Judge, *Louis XIV* (London: Longman's, 1965), pp. 3–4, 6–12.

Selection 9 (p. 57)
Niccolo Machiavelli, *The Prince and the Discourses*, intro. by Max Lerner, trans. by Luigi Ricci, rev. by E. R. P. Vincent (New York: Random House, Inc., 1950), pp. 56–57, 63–66.

Selection 10 (p. 59)
Philippe Mornay and Hubert Languet, *Vindiciae contra tyrannos: A Defense of Liberty against Tyrants or the lawful power of the Prince over the People, and of the People over the Prince* (London: Richard Baldwin, 1689), pp. 57–73.

Selection 11 (p. 66)
Thomas Hobbes, *Leviathan Or the Matter, Forme and Power of A Commonwealth Ecclesiasticall and Civil* (London: Andrew Crooke, 1651), Book I, ch. 17.

THE WARRIOR

Selection 1 (p. 87)
Blaise de Monluc, *The Habsburg-Valois Wars and the French Wars of Religion*, ed. by Ian Roy, trans. by Charles Cotton (London: Longman's, 1971), pp. 104, 106–109, 113.

Selection 2 (p. 89)
H. J. C. von Grimmelshausen, *The Adventurous Simplicissimus* (London: William Heinemann, 1912), pp. 28–32.

Selection 3 (p. 91)
Journal of a Field Preacher of Prince Frederick Henry of Orange, *Schrick van Vlaenderen en Brabandt, Aenghedaen door sijn Hoogheydt Frederick Hendrick, Prince van Oraengien* (Middelburg, 1645), unpaged. Trans. by Craig Harline.

Selection 4 (p. 93)
Della Casa, "Galatea" from *The Portable Renaissance Reader*, ed. by James B. Ross and Mary Martin McGlaughlin, pp. 340–343, 345–347. Copyright 1953, © 1981 by Viking Penguin Inc. Used by permission of Viking Penguin, a division of Penguin Books USA Inc.

Selection 5 (p. 95)
Baldesarre Castiglione, *The Book of the Courtier*, Illus. Ed. by Edgar Mayhew, pp. 204–212. Copyright © 1959 by Charles S. Singleton and Edgar de N. Mayhew. Used by permission of Doubleday, a division of Bantam Doubleday Dell Publishing Group, Inc.

Selection 6 (p. 98)
Vespasiano da Bisticci, *Vite di Uomini Illustri del Secolo XV*, ed. by Ludovico Frati (Bologna: Romagnoli-Dall'Acqua, 1893), pp. 280–284. Trans. by Anna Keaney.

Selection 7 (p. 101)
Thomas More, *Utopia*, trans. by Bishop Burnet (London: Jones and Bumford, 1808), pp. 159–177.

Selection 8 (p. 106)
Correspondance de Guillaume le Taciturne, Prince d'Orange, vol. 6, ed. by Louis Prosper Gachard (Brussels: C. Muquardt, 1854), pp. 297–300. Trans. by Sherrin Marshall.

Selection 9 (p. 107)
Reprinted by permission of the publishers from *The Letters of Peter Paul Rubens*, trans. and ed. by Ruth Saunders Magurn (Cambridge, Mass.: Harvard University Press, 1955), pp. 408–409. Copyright © 1955 by the President and Fellows of Harvard College.

THE DISSENTER

Selection 1 (p. 127)
Franz Kobler (ed.), *Letters of Jews through the Ages: A Self-Portrait of the Jewish People*, vol. 1: *From Biblical Times to the Renaissance* (New York: Hebrew Publishing Co., 1952), pp. 272–275. Reprinted by permission of the Publishers, Hebrew Publishing Company, P.O. Box 157, Rockaway Beach, NY 11693. Copyright © 1952. All rights reserved.

Selection 2 (p. 129)
Matthew Spinka, *The Letters of John Hus* (Manchester, England: Manchester University Press, 1972), pp. 195–197.

Selection 3 (p. 130)
Reprinted from *Luther's Works: Career of the Reformer I*, vol. 31, ed. by Harold J. Grimm, pp. 343–350. Copyright © 1957 Fortress Press. Used by permission of Augsburg Fortress.

Selection 4 (p. 134)
Reprinted from *The Works of Martin Luther with an Introduction and Notes*, vol. 4, pp. 210–216. Copyright © 1931 Muhlenberg Press. Used by permission of Augsburg Fortress.

Selection 5 (p. 137)
Reprinted from *The Works of Martin Luther with an Introduction and Notes*, vol. 4, pp. 219–231. Copyright © 1931 Muhlenberg Press. Used by permission of Augsburg Fortress.

Selection 6 (p. 143)
Philip Marnix, Lord of St. Aldegonde, *The Beehive of the Romish Church*, trans. by George Gilpin the Elder (London: John Dawson, 1623), pp. 352–357.

Selection 7 (p. 146)
Thieleman von Bracht, *The Bloody Theater or Martyr's Mirror*, trans. by Daniel Rupp (Lancaster, Pa.: David Miller, 1837), pp. 895–898.

Selection 8 (p. 150)
Samuel Usque, *Consolation for the Tribulations of Israel*, trans. by Martin A. Cohen (Philadelphia: Jewish Publication Society, 1965), pp. 201–202.

Selection 9 (p. 151)
Victor von Klarvill (ed.), *The Fugger Newsletters: Being a selection of unpublished letters from the Correspondents of the House of Fugger during the years 1568–1605*, trans. by Pauline de Chary (New York: Putnam's Sons, 1924), pp. 30–34.

Selection 10 (p. 153)
Robert M. Kingdon (ed.), *Transition and Revolution: Problems and Issues of European Renaissance and Reformation History* (Minneapolis: Burgess Publishing Co., 1974), pp. 211–213; taken from *Zwo Newe Zeittung. Was man fur Hexen oder Unholden verbrendt hat, von dem siebenden Hornung an biss auff den zwentzigsten Howmonat diss MDLXXX. Jars, auch darbey angeseigt, an was ohrt und enden, auch was sie bekendt haben, etc.* (Hof, 1580). Trans. by Erik Midelfort.

Selection 11 (p. 156)
Robert M. Kingdon (ed.), *Transition and Revolution: Problems and Issues of European Renaissance and Reformation History* (Minneapolis: Burgess Publishing Co., 1974), pp. 220–226; taken from *Zwo Newe Zeittung. Was man fur Hexen oder Unholden verbrendt hat, von dem siebenden Hornung an biss auff den zwentzigsten Howmonat diss MDLXXX. Jars, auch darbey angeseigt, an was ohrt und enden, auch was sie bekendt haben, etc.* (Hof, 1580). Trans. by Erik Midelfort.

Selection 12 (p. 161)
Copyright © 1963 from *Montaigne's Essays and Selected Writings*, pp. 369–371, by Donald M. Frame (trans. and ed.). Reprinted with permission of St. Martin's Press, Inc.

THE MERCHANT

Selection 1 (p. 179)
Robert S. Lopez (ed.), *Medieval Trade in the Mediterranean World: Illustrative Documents* (New York: © Columbia University Press, 1990), pp. 71–74. Reprinted with the permission of the publisher.

Selection 2 (p. 181)
Eugenio Garin (ed.), *Prosatori Latini del Quattrocento* (Milan: Riccardo Ricciardi, n.d.), pp. 15–23. Trans. by Anna Keaney.

Selection 3 (p. 183)
Gene Brucker (ed.), *The Society of Renaissance Florence: A Documentary Study*, pp. 233–234. Copyright © 1971 by Gene Brucker. Reprinted by permission of HarperCollins Publisher.

Selection 4 (p. 184)
Gene Brucker (ed.), *The Society of Renaissance Florence: A Documentary Study*, pp. 14–15. Copyright © 1971 by Gene Brucker. Reprinted by permission of HarperCollins Publisher.

Selection 5 (p. 186)
Victor von Klarvill (ed.), *The Fugger Newsletters: Being a selection of unpublished letters from the Correspondents of the House of Fugger during the years 1568–1605*, trans. by

Pauline de Chary (New York: Putnam's Sons, 1924), pp. 13–14. © The Putnam Publishing Group.

Selection 6 (p. 187)
George T. Matthews (ed.), *The Fugger Newsletters* (New York: Capricorn Books, 1959), p. 232. © The Putnam Publishing Group.

Selection 7 (p. 188)
Hugo Grotius, *The Freedom of the Seas, or The Right which belongs to the Dutch to Take Part in the East India Trade*, ed. by James Brown Scott, trans. by Ralph Van Deman Magoffin (New York: Oxford University Press, 1916), pp. 7–10, 61–64, 72–76.

Selection 8 (p. 192)
E. B. O'Callaghan (ed.), *The Documentary History of the State of New York*, vol. 4 (Albany, N.Y.: Charles van Benthuysen, 1851), pp. 27–36.

Selection 9 (p. 197)
Alessandra Strozzi, *Lettere di una gentildonna fiorentina del secolo XV ai figliuoli esuli*, ed. by Cesare Guasti (Florence: Casa Editrice G. C. Sansoni, 1877), pp. 3–9. Trans. by Anna Keaney.

Selection 10 (p. 199)
Reprinted by permission of Greenwood Publishing Group, Inc., Westport, CT, from *The Dutch Gentry 1500–1650*, by Sherrin Marshall. Copyright by Sherrin Marshall and published in 1987 by Greenwood Press.

Selection 11 (p. 201)
"The City-Fathers of York (England) Regulate Trade (1626)," York City Archives, B. 35 (*City of York House Book 1625–1637*), fol. 24r; courtesy of Diane Willen.

Selections 12–14 (p. 201)
Gene Brucker (ed.), *The Society of Renaissance Florence: A Documentary Study*, pp. 190–195. Copyright © 1971 by Gene Brucker. Reprinted by permission of HarperCollins Publisher.

THE ARTIST

Selection 1 (p. 231)
Rudolf and Margot Wittkower, *Born Under Saturn: The Character and Conduct of Artists: A Documented History from Antiquity to the French Revolution*, pp. 47–48. Copyright © 1963 by Rudolf and Margot Wittkower. Copyright renewed 1991 by Margot Wittkower. Reprinted by permission of Random House, Inc.

Selection 2 (p. 232)
Creighton E. Gilbert, *Italian Art 1400–1500: Sources and Documents* (Evanston, Ill.: Northwestern University Press, 1992), pp. 168–169.

Selection 3 (p. 233)
Giorgio Vasari, *Lives of the Artists* vol. 1, trans. by George Bull (Penguin Classics, 1987), pp. 30–31. Copyright © George Bull, 1965.

Selection 4 (p. 234)
Antonio Manetti, *Vita di Brunelleschi—The Life of Brunelleschi*, trans. by Catherine Enggass (University Park, Pa.: The Pennsylvania State University Press, 1970), pp. 38–42.

Copyright 1970 by the Pennsylvania State University. Reproduced by permission of the publisher.

Selection 5 (p. 236)
Giorgio Vasari, *Lives of the Artists*, vol. 1, trans. by George Bull (Penguin Classics, 1987), pp. 266–267. Copyright © George Bull, 1965.

Selection 6 (p. 237)
Robert Klein and Henri Zerner, *Italian Art, 1500–1600: Sources and Documents* (Evanston, Ill.: Northwestern University Press, 1989), pp. 9–10.

Selection 7 (p. 238)
Elizabeth Gilmore Holt (ed.), *A Documentary History of Art*, pp. 303–305. Copyright © 1957 renewed by Princeton University Press. Reprinted by permission of Princeton University Press.

Selection 8 (p. 239)
Elizabeth Gilmore Holt (ed.), *A Documentary History of Art*, pp. 268–270. Copyright © 1957 renewed by Princeton University Press. Reprinted by permission of Princeton University Press.

Selection 9 (p. 240)
Creighton E. Gilbert, *Italian Art 1400–1500: Sources and Documents* (Evanston, Ill.: Northwestern University Press, 1992), p. 184.

Selection 10 (p. 241)
Giorgio Vasari, *Lives of the Artists*, vol. 1, trans. by George Bull (Penguin Classics, 1987), pp. 180–181. Copyright © George Bull, 1965.

Selection 11 (p. 242)
Cennino d'Andrea Cennini, *The Craftsman's Handbook*, trans. by Daniel V. Thompson, Jr. (New York: Dover Publications, Inc., 1960), pp. 15–16.

Selection 12 (p. 243)
Edward MacCurdy, *The Notebooks of Leonardo da Vinci* (New York: Charles Scribner's Sons, 1906), pp. 163–185.

Selection 13 (p. 251)
Mary D. Garrard, *Artemisia Gentileschi: The Image of the Female Hero in Italian Baroque Art*, pp. 396–399. Copyright © 1989 by Princeton University Press. Reprinted by permission of Princeton University Press.

THE SCIENTIST

Selection 1 (p. 272)
Thomas Aquinas, "Summa Contra Gentiles" in Alan C. Kors and Edward Peters, eds., *Witchcraft in Europe 1100–1700* (Philadelphia: University of Pennsylvania Press, 1972), pp. 53–62.

Selection 2 (p. 277)
Victor von Klarvill (ed.), *The Fugger Newsletters: Being a selection of unpublished letters from the Correspondents of the House of Fugger during the years 1568–1605*, trans. by Pauline de Chary (New York: copyright © Putnam's Sons, 1924), pp. 140–142.

Selection 3 (p. 278)
J. Jacobi (ed.) and N. Guterman (trans.), *Paracelsus: Selected Writings*. Copyright © 1958 renewed 1979 by Princeton University Press, pp. 84–87, 120–123, 144–145. Reprinted by permission of Princeton University Press.

Selections 4–5 (p. 282)
Stillman Drake (trans. and ed.), *Discoveries and Opinions of Galileo* (Garden City, N.Y.: Doubleday & Co., 1957), pp. 21–26, 40–46. Copyright © 1957 by Stillman Drake. Used by permission of Doubleday, a division of Bantam Doubleday Dell Publishing Group, Inc.

Selection 6 (p. 287)
Henry Power, *Experimental Philosophy* (London, 1664), pp. 25, 32–36.

Selection 7 (p. 289)
Guillaume de Saluste du Bartas, *His Devine Weekes and Workes*, trans. by Joshua Sylvester (London, 1605), pp. 115–122.

Selection 8 (p. 291)
James Spedding (ed.), *The Works of Francis Bacon* (Cambridge: Riverside Press, 1863), pp. 67–99.

Selection 9 (p. 300)
Joseph Bertrand, *L'Academie des Sciences et les Academiciens de 1666 á 1793* (Paris: J. Hetzel, 1869), pp. 8–10. Trans. by Angela Borchert.

Photo Credits

Figure 27.   Lorg P. Anders/Staatliche Museen, Preussische Kulturbesitz Gemäldegalerie, Berlin
Figure 28.   National Gallery of Art, Rosenwald Collection
Figure 29.   Culver Pictures
Figure 30.   The Granger Collection
Figure 31.   The Bettmann Archive
Figure 32.   National Gallery of Art, Washington, D.C.; Alisa Mellon Bruce Fund
Figure 33.   Metropolitan Museum of Art, Robert Lehman Collection, 1975
Figure 34.   Alinari/Scala/Art Resource
Figure 35.   Museo Nazionale del Bargello, Firenze/Alinari/Art Resource
Figure 36.   Mick Gold
Figure 37.   Anderson
Figure 38.   Louvre, Paris/Musées Nationaux
Figure 39.   Scala/Anderson
Figure 40.   Anderson
Figure 41.   From Lee A. Jacobus, *Humanities: The Evolution of Values*, McGraw-Hill, 1986
Figure 42.   Museo del Prado, Madrid/Art Resource
Figure 43.   Gallerie Pitti Firenze/Scala/Art Resource
Figure 44.   National Gallery, London
Figure 45.   Museo del Prado, Madrid
Figure 46.   Alte Pinakothek, Munich
Figure 47.   Bildarchiv Foto, Marburg/Art Resource
Figure 48.   National Gallery, London
Figure 49.   Museo del Prado, Madrid
Figure 50.   Alinari/Art Resource
Figure 51.   The Art Museum, Princeton University
Figure 52.   Photographie Giraudon
Figure 53.   Giraudon, Louvre, Paris/Art Resource
Figure 54.   The Bettmann Archive
Figure 55.   British Museum
Figure 56.   Deutsches Museum, Munich
Figure 57.   From Mortimer Chambers, Raymond Grew, David Herlihy, Theodore K. Rabb, and Isser Woloch, *The Western Experience*, 5th ed., McGraw-Hill, 1991.
Figure 58.   New York Public Library, Picture Collection
Figure 59.   The Pierpont Morgan Library, New York, PML 30841
Figure 60.   The Bettmann Archive
Figure 61.   The Bettmann Archive
Figure 62.   Hubert Joesse/ EPI, Inc.

INDEX

Note: Page numbers in *italics* refer to illustrations and maps.